Proceedings of the American Cat

Science, Reason, and Religion

Volume 85, 2011

Edited by:

R. E. Houser
Center for Thomistic Studies
University of Saint Thomas

Papers for the regular sessions were selected by the program committee:

Catherine Deavel
Alex Eodice
Glen Statile

Issued by the National Office of the American Catholic Philosophical Association
University of Saint Thomas
Houston, TX 77006

The *Proceedings of the American Catholic Philosophical Association* are published as an annual supplement to the *American Catholic Philosophical Quarterly* and distributed to members of the ACPA as a benefit of membership. The *Proceedings* are also available for purchase to libraries, departments, institutions, and individuals. For information regarding subscriptions and/or back issues, please contact:

Philosophy Documentation Center
P.O. Box 7147
Charlottesville, VA 22906-7147
Phone: 800-444-2419 (U.S. and Canada); 434-220-3300
Fax: 434-220-3301
E-mail: order@pdcnet.org
Web: www.pdcnet.org

The *Proceedings of the American Catholic Philosophical Association* are indexed in *Academic Search Premier, American Humanities Index, Catholic Periodical and Literature Index, Current Abstracts, Expanded Academic ASAP, Index Philosophicus, Index to Social Science & Humanities Proceedings, InfoTrac OneFile, International Bibliography of Periodical Literature (IBZ), International Philosophical Bibliography, ISI Alerting Services, Periodicals Index Online, Philosopher's Index, Reference and Research Book News,* and *Religious & Theological Abstracts.*
The *Proceedings of the American Catholic Philosophical Association* are also available in POIESIS: Philosophy Online Serials. The full text of the *Proceedings, American Catholic Philosophical Quarterly,* and *The New Scholasticism* are available online to libraries that subscribe both to the Proceedings and to POIESIS and to members of the American Catholic Philosophical Association. For more information, contact the Philosophy Documentation Center at order@pdcnet.org.

ISSN 0065-7638 (print)
ISSN 2153-7925 (online)
ISBN 978-1-889680-90-3
ISBN 1-889680-90-7

Published by the Philosophy Documentation Center, Charlottesville, Virginia.

Proceedings of the American Catholic Philosophical Association

Science, Reason, and Religion

Volume 85, 2011

TABLE OF CONTENTS

Galileo's Legacy: Finding an Epistemically Just Relationship In-Between Science and Religion

Dominic J. Balestra

Abstract. The paper explores the question of the relationship between science and religion today in light of its modern origin in the Galileo affair. After first presenting Ian Barbour's four standard models for the possible relationships between science and religion, it then draws on the work of Richard Blackwell and Ernan McMullin to consider the Augustinian principles at work in Galileo's understanding of science and religion. In light of this the paper proposes a fifth, hybrid model, "dialogical convergence," as a more adequate model of the relationship in-between science and religion because it is epistemically just in its coherence with the last fifty years of philosophy of science by which it affords more than the mere tolerance of an independence view which leaves no space for the possibility of a theological understanding of nature.

I. Introduction

The question of science and religion is an all important instance of the perennial question of faith and reason in our modern age of science and its technologies. The question is not new to those familiar with the Catholic or Anglican intellectual tradition; however, it is renewed and reformed especially when reason's findings undergo a major transformation as in the thirteenth-century's accommodation of Aristotle's natural philosophy or the seventeenth-century scientific revolution or the nineteenth-century Darwinian revolution or the twentieth-century revolutions in physics and mathematics. An important role of philosophy is to bring to light the changes in the fundamental presuppositions in such transformations and their significance for our understanding of reality, human knowing, and human values—moral, political and religious. Today, from the side of religion, at one extreme is a fundamentalist understanding of faith which simply rejects any science which conflicts with the assertions of a literal reading of faith's revelation. Recent creationist theories of the origins of life represent instances of such religious fundamentalism. At the other extreme is another kind of inverted "fundamentalism,"—scientism which simply holds that the only cognitively

© 2012, *Proceedings of the ACPA*, Vol. 85
DOI: 10.5840/acpaproc2011851

significant considerations are those of science. At the outset it closes the door to any kinds of knowing or understanding other than a scientific one. Accordingly, it rejects as irrational, even meaningless, any religious belief whatsoever and replaces it by an uncritical expansion of particular scientific theories as comprehensive worldviews, or metaphysics. It is a violation of what I elsewhere call "Epistemic Justice."[1] The Harvard sociobiologist E. O. Wilson's work *Consilience*[2] and the French biologist Jacque Monod's *Chance and Necessity*[3] are examples of scientism and Richard Dawkins's more recent book, *The God Delusion*[4] is a particularly virulent version. Today an intellectually responsible thinker who wants to sustain a tenable faith and reason relationship that she can take into the public square must find a standpoint between the two extremes of a dogmatic scientism and an anti-intellectual fundamentalism. In this paper I shall locate where such a standpoint in-between science and religion might be found in light of the Galileo affair and the last fifty years work in the philosophy of science. The remainder of this paper will do three things: first, present four standard models of the relationship between science and religion, more accurately said, between science and theology; second, follow the work of Richard Blackwell[5] and Ernan McMullin,[6] to explore the theological side of Galileo's confrontation with his Church; and third, in light of the results of the last fifty years in the philosophy of science consider the implication of the Galileo affair for our understanding of the relationship between science and theology for a Catholic and its significance for suggesting a more nuanced, fifth model.

II. Models of the Science and Religion Relationship

Is the Legacy of the Galileo affair with his Church that science, understood today as fallible, provisional knowledge, and theology as "eternal" revelation, can only meet at the end of history with nothing to exchange now? The Protestant theologian and physicist, Ian Barbour, offers a useful classification for developing a critically reflective answer to the question. In brief, Barbour partitions the possible relationships between science and theology into four models: Conflict, Independence, Dialogue, and Integration.[7]

In the first category, Jacque Monod's scientific reductionism and Edward Wilson's *Consilience*, despite its title, represent instances of a "scientism" which inevitably leads to a conflict with theology due to its aim to explain ethics and all religious belief via an uncritical expansion of science into a total metaphysics. By excluding any understanding other than science as valid, and adding the *a priori* lemma that there is no God (because the web of science can not recover any God), then there can be no rational room for any theology, revealed or natural. There can also be a conflict model from the side of religion, as we have seen in the case of "creationism," where naive literalist readings of Scripture invade the disciplinary integrity of the sciences, which we shall see partially manifest in Galileo's affair with his and, for many here, our Church. From different angles both the naive literalism of a fundamentalist theology and a naive realism and a methodological chauvinism in the sciences, set up an irreconcilable confrontation which generates more heat than light.

The second model views science and theology as independent of each other. Galileo's statement "the Bible instructs how to get to heaven not how the heavens go round" points toward a demarcation between the language of science and the language of theology, developed in his "Letter to the Grand Duchess Christina,"[8] is at moments an eloquent statement of an Independence type of relationship between science and theology. But as we shall see Galileo also acknowledges enough overlap so that conflicts can arise. The late paleontologist S. J. Gould's work, *Rock of Ages*[9] is a good popular statement of an independence view on science and religion, while Michael Ruse's work *Science and Spirituality*[10] offers a philosophically more sophisticated argument for an independence view.

In an interesting way the Conflict and Independence views share a naive realist perspective regarding reality and our knowledge of it. The Conflict model presupposes that the metaphysics of science or theology makes contact which presupposes a commensurable epistemic jurisdictional overlap of meaning/subject matter—enough to set up an eventually all-or-nothing promise of complete, final knowledge of reality or all inquiry is in vain. There is no *in-between*. And the Independence model agrees that there is no *in-between*, no possible highway to traffic some truth between science and religion. But the Independence model allows each to have its own epistemic jurisdiction, and thereby avoids scientism, so long as there is no significant communication across the divide. Arguably, Kant's critical epistemology signals an Independence view with its salutary declaration that "I have therefore found it necessary to deny *knowledge* in order to make room for *faith*."[11] Indeed, his transcendental idealism's apodictic grounding of the "new science" (Newton's physics), was of the latter as a strictly empirical science with no epistemic entitlement of an expansion into metaphysical claims about reality behind empirical appearances. To be sure Kant's first *Critique* argued that there can be no natural or rational theology grounded upon demonstrative proof. But he returns to his aim of "making room for *faith*" toward the end of his *Critique* in the "Transcendental Doctrine of Method" asserting "it is also apodictically certain that there will never be anyone who will be able to assert the *opposite* [a God does not exist] with the least show of proof, much less, dogmatically."[12]

But recent philosophy of science says, with virtual unanimity, that the boundaries of our sciences are permeable and its knowledge, by the nature of its logic or method, provisional and incomplete. Moreover, the history of science renders essentialist scientific realism untenable.[13] Accordingly, we find both the Conflict view and the Independence view—insofar as it permits a mutually exclusive metaphysics, to be unacceptable because of an attendant naïve, ahistorical realism that each presupposes. This conclusion may not be obvious in the case of the Independence view. For one might subscribe to disciplinary autonomy without claiming complete or permanent knowledge, conceding that our current science is provisional and incomplete. But what would this imply? A pluralism, one which is itself provisional and for which the possibility of convergence between science and theology, in the long run, can not be excluded. We will return to this in section IV below.

Many Christian traditions have always struggled to bring faith and reason together. In light of its doctrine of creation there is a presumption that human reason, the intellect as distinct from the will, is reliable. As a part of God's creation reason is adequate as an instrument to study nature. In our modern times, ever since Galileo met with Bellarmine in 1615, the struggle between faith and reason has unfolded as that between science and religion—more carefully stated, between science and theology. The religious thinker today, especially its theologians, can not rest with static understandings of the dogmatisms of yesterday whether they be those of the Conflict view or the momentary truce of the Independence view. Thus, for both philosophical reasons and for religious reasons, we reject the first two categories as acceptable accounts of the relation between science and theology today.

The last two models, Dialogue and Integration, represent positions more in line with the tension-filled perspective of St. Anselm's *fides quaerens intellectum*. Because of the provisional and incomplete nature of the findings of science, the Dialogue view cautiously restrains from any premature integration at either a substantive level or a methodological level. It recognizes a shared interest in the truth between the disciplines sufficient to warrant a dialogical relation between science and theology. In this relation it is usually theology reformulating its understanding of a basic doctrine, such as creation, in light of the best current knowledge from science. But it also recognizes disciplinary differences which require respecting the integrity of the distinct disciplines. In a qualified sense representatives of the Dialogue view are Wolfgang Pannenberg[14] among Protestant authors, and Ernin McMullin among Catholic authors. Whether quantum physicist and Anglican priest, John Polkinghorne, falls into this category or the Integration view is difficult to determine. But this may be due to an inadequacy in Barbour's taxonomy, for in his Yale Terry Lectures Professor Polkinghorne cautiously moves toward the possibility of a convergence for a dialogical theology of nature.[15]

The last model, Integration, holds that some sort of integration between the content of science and theology is possible. Barbour distinguishes three versions of Integration. One version is a "natural theology" which in Richard Swinburne's version claims that the existence of God can be inferred, as a "more probable than not" hypothesis from the evidence of design in nature which science discovers.[16] Like the eighteenth-century "physicotheology" which it resembles, this natural theology is subject to unexpected findings in science which might conflict with the basic theological claims.

The second version is a "theology of nature" which in appropriating scientific theories within its otherwise distinctly theological concepts may reformulate its understandings of basic theological doctrines, such as that of creation. The Jesuit paleontologist Teilhard de Chardin's controversial attempt to integrate science and theology into a process theology of nature , *The Phenomenon of Man*[17] readily comes to mind as an example of a theology of nature. More recently, the late theologian and biochemist, Arthur Peacocke,[18] worked a critical realist approach to develop a theology of nature. A major issue for the theology of nature is the nature of God's creative action: is it a continuous creation with God as remote but primary cause?

Or, is it a deistic like plan initiated and implemented into a proximate chain of secondary causality, the domain of scientific study? The third version of Integration, "systematic synthesis," is a comprehensive metaphysics which incorporates contributions from both science and theology into a coherent worldview. The process metaphysics of Alfred North Whitehead exemplifies this version of integration. It is interesting to note that each version of integration represents a standpoint which works the integration respectively from science to theology, from theology to science, and from both science and theology into an "overriding" metaphysics. In every case theology is affected by science, in the "natural theology" even the data of theology may be construed as derived from the findings of science. In the later two versions of Integration, theology's understandings of the data of theology may be affected by science. But are the concepts or theories of science ever reformed as a result of theological developments? Perhaps in a "theology of nature" but such a view risks an imprudent dismissal of "not-yet-proven" science as in the case of Galileo's confrontation with the theology of his Church. A better way may be through an indirect route, made possible by the subsumption of theology and science within a more comprehensive, integrative metaphysics. Aquinas's "integration" of Aristotelian *scientia naturalis* with Christian theology represents such a metaphysical achievement in its time. But unlike today, Aquinas did not need to contend with a hermeneutics of historical knowledge. Having briefly presented Barbour's models, let us now turn to Galileo's encounter with the question of science and religion.

III. The Galileo Affair

In 1543 Copernicus had published his *De Revolutionibus Orbium Caelestium* which inaugurated the upheaval in astronomy and, due to Galileo and Descartes,[19] in natural philosophy which we some years later call the Copernican Revolution. Yet more than seventy years passed before the Church's prohibition of Copernicanism as it was called during that time of radical challenges in theology from Luther and other reformers, in political theory, Renaissance humanism, and a changing economics during the Renaissance. So why so many years? One good reason, as Thomas Kuhn showed so well in his first book,[20] is that in the sixteenth-century astronomy was a mathematical science for "saving the appearances" and not a *scientia naturalis*.

> Though few aspects of Western thought were long unaffected by the consequences of Copernicus' work, that work itself was narrowly technical and professional. It was mathematical planetary astronomy, not cosmology or philosophy, that Copernicus found monstrous, and it was the reform of mathematical astronomy that alone compelled him to move the earth. (*CR*, 142)

Following a lucid presentation of the system of Ptolemy's *Almegest* and then that of Copernicus work, Kuhn concludes that "[J]udged on purely practical grounds, Copernicus' new planetary system was a failure; it was neither more accurate nor significantly simpler than its Ptolemaic predecessors. But historically it was a great success" (*CR*, 171). In as much as it had convinced a few, including Galileo, that a sun-centered astronomy held the key to solving the problem of the planets it was a qualified, albeit belated, success.

Moreover, Galileo also saw in its mathematics the key to a true, realist, knowledge of the physical world whether celestial or terrestrial. Accordingly, he pursued a defense of the Copernican theory as true, that is, as depicting the real motions of the planets which set him on a collision course with some Aristotelians in the universities of his Europe. As Galileo published his evidence in support of Copernicus in his *The Starry Messenger* 1611 (*DOG*, 21–58) and in the *Letters on Sunspots* 1613 (*DOG*, 87–144) his arguments became a threat to the Aristotelian establishment. Meanwhile, the Council of Trent at its fourth session in 1564 had already renewed and strengthened the Rules for the Interpretation of Scripture derived from St. Augustine's *De Genesi ad litteram* (*The Literal Meaning of Genesis*)[21] (see *GBB*, chap.1, "Trent and Beyond"). The Lutherans had already condemned the Copernican theory as conflicting with Holy Scripture. Indeed, in the Counter-Reformation concern to protect the Church from more doctrinal strife Pope Paul V in 1607 had ordered a moratorium on the twenty-year controversy between the Jesuits and the Dominicans over the question of Divine grace and human free will. To avoid any suspicion of non-compliance with the "solid and uniform doctrine" of the Church, the Superior General of the Society of Jesus, Claudio Aquaviva, S.J., in 1610 had ordered "the teaching of St. Thomas Aquinas in theology and of Aristotle in philosophy" in its schools and publications (*GBB*, 139). As Galileo's reputation grew as a defender of Copernicus and the debate over the theological acceptability of the Copernican ideas intensified in Rome, Galileo came under fire from both the pulpit of Casini and the Aristotelians. Concerned about the seeming conflict with Scripture he pursued a serious effort at an exegetical argument for permitting the Copernican theory in two letters: his *Letter to Castelli*, December 1613 (*GBB*, Appendix IV) and his *Letter to the Grand Duchess Christina*, 1615 (*DOG*, 172–216) which expands on the earlier letter to Castelli. Galileo knew that his Church did not hold to a literalist meaning of every word and sentence in Scripture. Indeed, early in the "Letter to the Grand Duchess . . .", Galileo states in no uncertain terms that "I hold the sun to be situated motionless in the center of the revolution of the celestial orbs while the earth rotates on its axis and revolves about the sun" (*DOG*, 177). This assertion explicitly connects Galileo's work on Copernican theory with the Church's Scriptural theology. Thus, he sets out to make two arguments: one, a theological argument on the nature of Biblical exegesis in his "Letter to the Grand Duchess . . ." which draws heavily from St. Augustine's *LMG*;[22] and the other in natural philosophy (science)—the needed demonstrative argument for the motion of the earth from the movement of the tides as due to the double motion required by the Copernican theory.[23]

It seems that Galileo believed that he had the argument at least for the earth's double motion, for he confidently drew upon two strong principles at the heart of Augustine's rules for reading Scripture in the Catholic conviction that faith and reason are compatible: principle of the *unity of truth* or the principle of *consistency*—

that because God is author of revelation and creator of the universe, truths found in either discourse can not conflict if properly understood (*GBB*, 76; *CG*, 92); and the *priority of demonstrated truths in science*—when there is a conflict between a proven truth about the physical world and a particular literal reading of Scripture, an alternative reading of the Scriptural passage *should* be sought. (*CG*, 93; *GBB*, 76) But if the demonstration does not succeed, then what?

Galileo provides his answer which acknowledges another exegetical principle that of the *priority of faith, de fide*, when undemonstrated or apparently demonstrated propositions of a science conflict with Scripture the former must be set aside (*CG*, 93).

> Yet even in those propositions which are not matters of faith, this authority [Scripture] ought to be preferred over that of all human writings which are supported only by bare assertions or probable arguments and not set forth in a demonstrative way. This I hold to be necessary and proper to the same extent that divine wisdom surpasses all human judgment and conjecture. (*DOG*, 183, and elsewhere in the "Letter," 194 and 197)

Insofar as he thought that he had demonstrated the earth's motion in his argument from the tides, Galileo believed that he had fulfilled the requirements of the above three principles of the reading of Scripture. But the argument from the tides falls short and Bellermine knew that.

The above makes clear that Galileo understood and accepted the priority of faith principle that when there is not a demonstrated truth of a relevant proposition in science, then one defers to Scripture. Since his argument from the tides only showed at best a probability of the earth's motion, it failed under the principles of the *demonstrated truths of science* and *priority of faith*. Accordingly, Bellermine could not endorse a reading of Scripture that had to cohere with the unproven Copernican propositions regarding the earth's motion. nor could he delay given the accelerated theological concerns pressed by Foscarini's letter to Bellermine[24] which presented a Scripture based theological argument for the earth's movement in its defense of Copernicus.

Galileo made another argument in the "Letter to the Grand Duchess . . . ." He distinguished three kinds of language at work in the apparent conflict of the Copernican theory and the religious doctrine of his own Catholic faith: the language of Scripture, ordinary language, and the language of natural philosophy or science (*DOG*, 201–202). Accordingly, he argued that since Scripture's principle purpose is salvation for all of us, it often needs to be written in the common or ordinary language of a people. Therefore, its ordinary language propositions, which are not intended to be assertions of science, can not conflict with the epistemic claims of science—even those yet to be demonstrated. On this point Galileo followed St. Augustine's recognition that "Sacred Scripture in its customary style of speaking within the limitations of human language in addressing men of limited understanding, while at the same time teaching a lesson to be understood by the reader who is able" (*LMG*, 5.6.19).[25] The distinction between kinds of language raises the question of who has the authority over the question of the kinds of meanings that are functioning in various Scripture passages. Galileo clearly defers to the Augustinian "principles" for interpreting Scripture. However, by the time Galileo had completed his "Letter to the Grand Duchess Christina," Cardinal Bellermine, in response to Foscarini, had added his own new rule for the interpretation of Scripture—a rule that is not in Augustine nor in the "updated" rules of Biblical exegisis proclaimed in the fourth session of the Council of Trent (*GBB*, Chapter 1 "Trent and Beyond"). Richard Blackwell calls Bellermine's new rule the *de dicto* rule which asserts:

> Nor can one reply that this is not a matter of faith, because even if it is not a matter of faith because of the subject matter [*ex parte objecti*], it is still a matter of faith because of the speaker [*ex parte dicentis*].[26]

Consequently, in any dispute with natural philosophy (science) the question of the meaning of any and all propositions in Scripture come under the jurisdiction of the authority of the Church by the mere fact that the proposition in dispute is found in Scripture. Since the truth of a proposition presupposes its properly understood meaning, Bellermine's new rule seems to trump St. Augustine's principle of accommodation and even his principle of the priority of demonstrated truths in science. Thus, the *de dicto* rule expands the Church's authority beyond matters of "faith and morals" as the highest court of appeal in all questions of the significance of *any* disputed proposition that is in Scripture. Bellermine's rule effectively rejects any "Independence" between the language of salvation and the language of natural philosophy. His *de dicto* rule in the science and theology relationship is a kind of inverted scientism—especially as seen from the side of science.

In spite of Galileo's good faith efforts to avoid the historic confrontation between science and religion, he did not succeed in holding off the Decree of the Holy Congregation of the Cardinals in charge of the Index issued on March 5, 1616, which statement concluded:

> Therefore, in order that this opinion [of a moving earth] may not creep any further to the prejudice of Catholic truth, the Congregation had decided that the books by Nicolaus Copernicus (*On the Revolutions of Spheres*) and Diego de Zuniga (*On Job*) be suspended until corrected; but that the book of the Carmelite Father Paulo Antonio Foscarini be completely prohibited and condemned. (*GA*, 148–148)

Although Galileo knew that some probable propositions of sense and reason may yet be proven, he did not avail himself of Augustine's prudent concern that "In matters [of natural philosophy] that are obscure and far beyond our vision, even in such as we may find treated in Holy Scripture, different interpretations are sometimes possible without prejudice to the faith we have received. In such a case we should not rush in headlong and so firmly take a stand on one side that, if further progress in the search for truth justly undermines this position, we too fall with it" (*LMG*, 1.18.37). Augustine's caution here is for two reasons: that Scripture is sometimes open to alternative meanings and progress in natural knowledge may eventually demonstrate a proposition which previously seemed not provable. In another passage Augustine counsels "We should always observe that restraint that is proper to a devout and serious person and on an obscure question entertain no rash belief. Otherwise, if the truth later appear, we are likely to despise it because of our attachment to our error, even though this explanation may not be in any way opposed to the sacred writings" (*LMG*, 2.18.38). Indeed, aware that science takes time to develop, the fifth-century St. Augustine counsels prudence in interpreting difficult passages in Scripture in cases of apparent conflict with not-yet demonstrated propositions in natural knowledge (science), and thereby makes "elbow room" for progress in our understanding of Holy Scripture along side new developments in scientific knowledge. Yet Galileo did not seize upon Augustine's principle of prudence to make "elbow room" for Copernicus, no doubt, because he believed he had the demonstration for the earth's motion from natural knowledge. But Bellermine's *de dicto* rule seemingly would have rendered Galileo's appeal to St. Augustine's principle of prudence ineffective, for by his rule Bellermine had made religion the high court of epistemic appeal by incorporating all hermeneutic questions under its jurisdiction. Bellermine's rule sets up a kind of inverted scientism, a theological fundamentalism—especially as seen from the side of science. What is more astounding is that this error is exacerbated by the Jesuit, Melchior Inchofer, who worked for the Congregation "behind the scenes" of the Galileo trial in 1633 and eight years after Bellermine's death. Since the words of "an immobile earth at the center" are not explicit in Scripture, Inchofer realized that Bellermine's *de dicto* rule might not be enough to show the full contradiction with Scripture in order to produce a theological justification of the trial's verdict of "vehement suspicion of heresy," seemingly in part *post facto*. . . . So he expanded the notion of "matters of faith and morals" to include "both explicitly revealed truths in the Scriptures and others that are inferred from the former in various ways"(*BSGT*, 62).[27] If Bellermine's *de dicto* rule did not insure that the Church was on a collision course with science, Inchofer's treatise defending the trial verdict, *Tractatus sylepticus* (1633)[28] most certainly did!

IV. Galileo's Legacy for His Church

As recently as 1950 in his encyclical *Humani generis* Pope Pius XII echoes two of Augustine's principles, the consistency/unity of truth and the priority of demonstration, in respect to the relationship between science and theological truth when he stated:

> In fact, not a few insistently demand that the Catholic religion take these [positive] sciences into account as much as possible. This certainly would be praiseworthy in the case of clearly proved facts; but caution must be used when there is rather question of hypotheses, having some sort of scientific foundation, in which the doctrine contained in Sacred Scripture or in Tradition is involved. If such conjectural opinions are directly or indirectly opposed to the doctrine revealed by God, then the demand that they be recognized can in no way be admitted.[29]

On the surface this seems a retreat from the "faith seeking understanding" of Augustine's developmental view of the understanding of revelation vis a vis the findings of natural knowledge/science. And I think it is.

It would seem that the Conflict view of science and religion was inevitable, and there is an echo of this in Pius XII's encyclical quoted above. If the best of our scientific knowledge is fallible, then what does this imply for the Augustinian Biblical hermeneutics? And what might this mean for the understanding of the possible relationships between science and religion?

Admittedly, there is a haunting hermeneutic question that shadows the above account. For like Augustine, Galileo was at the end of one age and the beginning of a new one. He had retained an Aristotelian conception of demonstrative proof in natural knowledge. Although his practice of science had the marks of a modern scientific method, Galileo did not develop a theory of the method of demonstration or justification for the newly emerging science, how could he? Yes there is a decisive difference between the Scholastic realist epistemology of the Thomistic synthesis of the Catholic faith in the thirteenth century and the current epistemology of modern science. The former countenanced demonstrative proof in natural philosophy, as did the first half of the twentieth century's dominant logical empiricists inductive confirmationists models of scientific rationality, Hume notwithstanding. Indeed, in 1950 when Pius XII published *Humani generis* the dominant epistemology of science underscored on the side of science the presumption that well founded science is based upon demonstration or proof. In an ironic way this tenet of logical empiricism inadvertently reinforced Pius XII's a-historical epistemology of science. However, the last fifty years work in the philosophy of science[30]—from Quine's "Two Dogmas," Popper's fallibalist model of "conjecture and refutation" for the hypothetical-deductive method of scientific "demonstration," through Kuhn's ironic revolutionary work, *The Structure of Scientific Revolutions*, Feyerabend's undoing, or is it outdoing of Popper, Lakatos's middle way between Kuhn and Popper, and others—has resulted in an unmistakable consensus that however well 'demonstrated' via a logic of confirmation or a logic of falsification, our best scientific theories are at best fallible, so provisional and therefore provide an incomplete knowledge of nature and where appropriate of ourselves as living, self-conscious organisms who ask scientific, philosophical and theological questions. In sum, philosophy of science has shown that our best scientific theories are historically-situated inferences to a best explanation at the time and, therefore, always subject to the critical scrutiny that seeks to find in what way our best but fallible theories fall short of inexhaustible reality. From the side of science might this be a path toward convergence with our developing understanding of nature's creator God? In Galileo's time there was a conflict between science and religion. For there to be a conflict some kind of contact must be made. But today when there is a conflict, or apparent conflict, between science and religion, the question of which court—science or religion—should rule on the nature of the truth, or more fundamentally, the presupposed meaning at issue, can not be decided in either the court of science or religion without begging the question. Only a philosophical stance that transcends both science and religion but remains open on the respective jurisdictions of science and religion and to exploring their relationships is entitled to make legitimate claims in the important matter of science and religion.

In June, 1988 Pope John Paul II wrote a letter to George Coyne, S.J. for the publication of the papers from a Vatican hosted conference on physics, philosophy and theology.[31] In his letter the Pope encouraged, even urged, an open pursuit of a "relational, dialogical unity" between science and theology. As relational the encouraged unity insists upon respecting the integrity of the distinct disciplines. Accordingly, he insisted that the unity is not that of an identity between science and theology, nor is it the unity of a reduction of one discipline to the other. Rather, it is the unity of a shared relationship upon which dialogue can proceed, a "Dialogical Unity." His letter manifested an awareness of recent themes in science and philosophy of science, some mentioned above. He holds up Aquinas's accomplishment in respect to Aristotle as the benchmark to be surpassed. But Aquinas could rely upon a *scientia naturalis* that transcended the particularities of time. The task for the theologian today is even more daunting, for history has entered into the bloodstream of science and its epistemology. John Paul's letter acknowledges implicitly this dimension of modern science in his observation that "physicists possess a detailed though incomplete and provisional knowledge of elementary particles." [M6] Perhaps more than most of his Catholic contemporaries Bernard Lonergan appreciated the challenge that historicity in science presents for a systematic theology as well as for the compatibility of faith and reason.

The Pope's perspective is a cautious one, recalling St. Augustine's principle of prudence, which seems to fall in the space *in-between* Barbour's categories of Dialogue and Integration—what I should like to call a fifth model of the space in-between science and theology, a *Dialogical Convergence*. This is close to what John Haught has classified as a space of Contact in-between science and religion wherein "dialogue, interaction, and "consonance" may take place.[32] There is a hint of a consonant convergence in Haught's classification. Though both Barbour and Haught offer useful models, I have indicated in this last section that recent philosophy of science makes it clear that scientific knowledge is provisional. Thus, it rules out any integration between science and religion *now*. Yet, as provisional the possibility of Convergence upon the truth, as a progress toward the truth, from the respective sides of science and religion can not be ruled out. Accordingly, the Catholic tradition's conviction of the compatibility of faith and reason, as stated in St. Augustine's unity of truth principle, would imply that only a Dialogue model of the relationship between science and theology, can serve as the ground of the hope of a progress toward a "Convergence" between science and religion. The adequacy of this Dialogical Convergence as a model between the content of scientific knowledge and theology will require a critical realism and an analogical notion of truth if it is to accommodate the historicity of science as well as theology—a historicity of the correlate *in-between* if it acknowledges our human desire to understand in the self-conscious knowledge of its limitations. For if one of theology's essential tasks is to overcome the prejudice within its own tradition's unfinished development of the theology of its lived faith tradition and culture, it must not close discovery of new, "additional meanings," i.e., new dimensions of its understandings of

God, humans and nature. For if it is not open to such new dimensions of meanings, it risk a dogmatic, closed stance in the domain of reason and, more importantly, in the domain of the compatibility of reason and revelation.

Seventeen centuries ago Augustine recognized the critical role of a prudential openness with patience for what yet might come forth from Creation including our knowledge of it. Four centuries ago in the apologetic mode of the Counter-Reformation Rome seemingly had forgotten Augustine's wisdom and made a significant error in prudence in its 1616 decree and in the 1633 trial of Galileo. John Paul II, and I suspect in the light of Vatican II, had opened the deeper memory of Augustine's gift to a Church that retains as essential to its tradition a faith seeking understanding. The truths of revealed theology may be eternal but our understandings of those revelations, as well as of science, hopefully are still improving as we travel on the road to Emmaus. And I wonder, wonder what St. Augustine might revise in his *The Literal Meaning of Genesis* in the light of the last fifty years work in the philosophy and history of science?

Fordham University

Notes

1. Dominic J. Balestra, "Epistemic Justice: A Response to Professor Goldberg," *Fordham Urban Law Journal* 30 (November 2002): 47–55.

2. E. O. Wilson, *Consilience: The Unity of Knowledge* (New York: Alfred A. Knopf, 1998). In particular, see the last two chapters, chap. 11 "Ethics and Religion," and chap. 12 "To What End?"

3. Jacque Monod, *Chance and Necessity: An Essay on the Natural Philosophy of Biology*, trans. Austryn Wainhouse (New York: Alfred A. Knopf, 1998).

4. Richard Dawkins, *The God Delusion* (New York: Houghton Mifflin Co., 2006). A very good short response which respects most of Dawkins work up to the latter's 2006 book is Alister McGrath's *The Dawkins Delusion? Atheist Fundamentalism and the Denial of the Divine* (London: Society for Promoting Christian Knowledge, 2007). See chap. 2 "Has Science Disproved God?" for McGrath's critique of Dawkins's scientism as violating, what I take to be an operative principle of epistemic justice, the recognition by many critically reflective scientists that "there are many questions that, by their very nature, must be recognized to lie beyond the legitimate scope of the scientific method, as this is normally understood" (17).

5. Richard J. Blackwell, *Galileo, Bellermine, and the Bible* (Notre Dame, Ind.: University of Notre Dame Press, 1991). Hereafter cited parenthetically in text as *GBB*. Richard J. Blackwell, *Behind the Scenes at Galileo's Trial*. (Notre Dame, Ind.: University of Notre Dame Press, 2006). Hereafter cited parenthetically in text as *BSGT*.

6. Ernan, McMullin, "Galileo's Theological Venture," in *The Church and Galileo*, ed. Ernan McMullin (Notre Dame, Ind.: University of Notre Dame Press, 2005), 88–116. Hereafter cited parenthetically in text as *CG*.

7. Ian G. Barbour, *Religion and Science: Historical and Contemporary Issues*, (San Francisco: Harper Collins Pub., 1997). Chapter 4 "Ways of Relating Science and Religion,"

77–105. This is a revised and expanded edition of his *Religion in an Age of Science: The Gifford Lectures, 1989–1991*, Volume I, 1990.

8. Galileo Galilei, "Letter to the Grand Duchess Christiana" in *Discoveries and Opinions of Galileo*, ed. and trans. Stillman Drake (New York: Doubleday, 1957), 173–216. Hereafter cited parenthetically in text as *DOG*.

9. Stephen Jay Gould, *Rocks of Ages: Science and Religion in the Fullness of Life* (New York: Ballantine Publishing Group, 1999).

10. Michael Ruse, *Science and Spirituality: Making Room for Faith in the Age of Science*, (Cambridge, U.K.: Cambridge University Press, 2010). In addition to a more sophisticated and comprehensive argument for an "Independence" view than Gould's, the argument keenly avoids any dogmatic scientism and is all the more persuasive inasmuch as Ruse is a self-proclaimed agnostic if not atheist.

11. Immanuel Kant, *Critique of Pure Reason*, trans. Norman Kemp Smith (New York: St. Martin's Press, 1965), "Preface to the Second Edition," Bxxx, 29.

12. Ibid., 595. An excellent, recent neo-Kantian critique of scientistic tendencies in philosophy, and in particular relatively recent attempts to revive "naturalism," including naturalizing epistemology, on the basis of a scientific philosophy is Tom Sorell. *Scientism: Philosophy and the Infatuation with Science* (London: Routledge, 1991).

13. See Karl Popper, *Conjectures and Refutations: The Growth of Scientific Knowledge* (New York: Harper Torchbooks, 1968), chap. 3, "Three Views Concerning Human Knowledge," 97–119.

14. For a good, short presentation of Pannenberg's synthetic view see John Polkinghorne, *Faith, Science and Understanding* (New Haven: Yale University Press, 2000), chap. 8.1 "Wolfhart Pannenberg's Engagement with the Natural Sciences," 156–173.

15. John Polkinghorne, *Belief in God In An Age of Science* (New Haven: Yale University Press, 1996). Chapter 2 presents a strong dialogical relation based on an historical analogy between how science arrived at quantum theory in its development of a theory of light, and how Christian theology arrived at a Trinitarian theory in its development of Christology. Chapter 4 introduces a "critical realism" as a way that science and theology respectively evaluate their encounter with their different subject matters. The parallel "critical realism" to my mind opens the possibility of a convergence, though Polkinghorne is not explicit on this point.

16. Richard Swinberne, *The Existence of God* (Oxford: Clarendon Press, 1979), 291.

17. Pierre Teilhard de Chardin, *The Phenonomenon of Man* (New York: Harper & Row, 1959). An English translation of the original French of 1955.

18. Arthur Peacocke, *Theology for a Scientific Age* (Minneapolis: Fortress Press, 1993).

19. I have argued for the importance of Descartes' providing a needed argument for a new, non-hermetic mathematical philosophy of nature in "At the Origins of Modern Science: Demythologizing Pythagoreanism," *The Modern Schoolman* 67 (January/March 1999): 195–210.

20. *The Copernican Revolution: Planetary Astronomy in the Development of Western Thought* (Cambridge, Mass.: Harvard University Press, 1957) 142–43. Hereafter cited parenthetically in text as *CR*. The above led to his explosive *The Structure of Scientific Revolutions* (Chicago: University of Chicago Press, 1962) which arguably generated a revolution in the philosophy of science. The second edition of 1970 adds a "Postscript-1969," 174–210, which is indispensable for any adequate understanding of Kuhn's thesis and its arguments.

21. St. Augustine, *The Literal Meaning of Genesis*, trans. John H. Taylor, S.J. (New York, N.Y.: Newman Press, 1982). Hereafter cited parenthetically in text as *LMG* by book, chapter and section.

22. Two excellent analyses which show the sophistication of Galileo's understanding of Augustine's Biblical hermeneutics are *GBB*, 75–66; and McMullin's "Galileo's Theological Venture" in *CG*, chap. 6, 88–116.

23. Galileo first wrote his argument called "Discourse on the Tides" in a 1616 letter to Cardinal Orsini. See *The Galileo Affair: A Documentary History*, ed. and trans. Maurice A. Finnacchiaro (Berkeley: University of California Press, 1989), 119–133.

24. Foscarini was a Carmelite priest and theologian.

25. Blackwell calls this Augustine's Principle of Scriptural Intention, (*GBB*, 76) and McMullin calls it the Principle of Accommodation (*CG*, 94). A very good summary of the Augustinian exegetical principles at work in Galileo's "Letter to the Grand Duchess . . . " is in *GBB*, 76.

26. Quoted in *GBB*, 105.

27. Short of reading Blackwell's book see my review of Richard J. Blackwell, *Behind the Scenes at the Galileo Trial* (University of Notre Dame Press, 2006) in *International Philosophical Quarterly* 49.1 (March, 2009): 116–19. Blackwell was one of a number of Galileo scholars who presented papers at Notre Dame's important conference on Galileo, organized by George Coyne, S.J. and Ernan McMullin in April, 2002. McMullin's *The Church and Galileo* contains the papers that emerged from the conference; but Blackwell's paper will not be found in that collection because it grew into Blackwell's 2006 *Behind the Scenes*. Together these two works present the best work to date on Galileo's affair with his Church and the infamous trial of 1633.

28. See in particular chapter 10, "Whether it is a Matter of Faith [*de fide*] That the Earth Is the Center of the Universe" and chapter 12 "Given that the earth at rest is a matter of faith [*de fide*] whether it is allowable to argue for the contrary" of Blackwell's translation of the *Tractatus*, "A Summary Treatise Concerning the Motion or Rest of the Earth and the Sun, in which it is briefly shown what is, and what is not, to be held as certain according to the teachings of the Sacred Scriptures and the Holy Fathers," Appendix One, *BSGT*, 105, 206.

29. Claudia Carlen, *The Papal Encyclicals, 1939–1958* (Wilmington, N.C.: McGrath, 1981) 181.

30. For a reliable, clear presentation of much of this philosophy of science see A. F. Chalmers, *What Is this Thing Called Science?*, third edition (Indianapolis: Hackett Publishing Company, 1999). Also see E. McMullin, "Two Faces of Science," *Review of Metaphysics* 27, 655–76, for a thoughtful exploration of the movement from an ahistorical conception of science to a dynamic, historical conception due to the work of Quine, Polanyi, Wittgenstein among others and Kuhn.

31. "Message of His Holliness Pope John Paul II" in Robert J. Russell, William R. Stoeger, S.J., and George V. Coyne, S.J., eds., *Physics, Philosophy and Theology*, (Vatican City State, 1988), 15 (M1–M14).

32.John Haught, *Science and Religion: From Conflict to Conversation*, (New York: Paulist Press, 1995). See Chapter 1"Is Religion Opposed to Science" for Haught's alternative set to Barbour's four models—Conflict, Contrast, Contact, and Confirmation.

Introduction of the Aquinas Medalist

Eleonore Stump

It is an honor and privilege for me to introduce to you tonight my friend Jorge Gracia, who is this year's recipient of the Aquinas Medal.

If we used the inference to the best explanation on Jorge's CV, we would certainly conclude that there are several different people who are designated by the name 'Jorge Gracia' and whose work is listed on that CV. At any rate, if we didn't know it to be true, we would certainly think it wildly implausible to suppose that any one person could accomplish as much as Jorge has. His productivity has been amazing, and it has been in several, highly disparate areas.

You would find his CV even more incredible if you knew the circumstances out of which Jorge came. He was raised in Cuba by a free-thinking father and an evangelical Protestant mother in the specially troubled world Cuba was then. In primary school, he himself became a Catholic; and, with the help of the local archbishop, he got a spot on the last ferry to leave Havana after the Bay of Pigs crisis. He arrived in West Palm Beach alone at the age of nineteen with $5 in his pocket and a diamond ring smuggled in his shoe. He had no English; but, by some miracle, he was accepted with a scholarship at Wheaton College. He learned English in one semester in order to survive there. And he was nothing if not spirited. With his accomplishment of learning English still so recent, he decided to double major in English literature and philosophy; and he received his undergraduate degree in those subjects at Wheaton in 1965.

Having mastered one language and its literature in such short order, Jorge decided to branch out and try others, to explore the world that language skill made possible for him. So he went to Chicago to study medieval philosophy, and then moved on to Toronto, where some of the best medieval philosophers in the world were teaching. Not content with conquering Latin and medieval paleography, for his dissertation he edited a fourteenth-century text in old Catalan.

SUNY Buffalo hired him as a medievalist, and he went on to do an immense amount of work in medieval philosophy. Among his many books and articles in medieval philosophy, there is his translation of two disputations by Suarez on the metaphysics of good and evil, his book on Suarez on individuation, his book on the problem of individuation in medieval philosophy. His articles in medieval philosophy

© 2012, *Proceedings of the ACPA*, Vol. 85
DOI: 10.5840/acpaproc2011852

are too numerous to count. They cover a broad range of medieval philosophy too, including discussions of work by Boethius, Thierry of Chartres, Aquinas, Raymond Lull, Duns Scotus, Domingo Banez, and many others. If you saw only this part of his record, you would think that by itself it merits the honor we are giving him tonight.

But while he was being so productive in medieval philosophy, Jorge was also developing one might almost say a second CV on Latin American philosophy. In this area, he has published many books and articles, too, in Spanish as well as English. His work in this and related areas has included books and articles on racial and ethnic identity as well as numerous studies of work in Latin American and Latino/Hispanic thought. This work, together with his concern for interpretation, inspired his Aquinas Lecture at Marquette on the nature of tradition and its role in communication, knowledge, and group identity. He has been at least as productive in these areas as he has been in his work on medieval philosophy.

At this point, I hope that you are suitably impressed, but you need to save room for more surprise, because this is not nearly the end of the story. Jorge ALSO has a flourishing research agenda in art and literature, and he has numerous books and articles in this field as well. Not content with writing and research in this area, he has also been active in curating and producing exhibits, including most recently an exhibit on art illustrating the literary work of Jorge Luis Borges.

Altogether Jorge's CV runs to fifty-five pages, and all those pages are needed to catalogue his achievements. Furthermore, this huge body of work has been very influential not only in our own Anglophone community, but around the world. Among other languages, Jorge's work has been translated into Spanish, Serbo-Croatian, and Chinese! He has also been the recipient of many honors, including most notably the Findlay prize, which he won for his book on individuation.

If I stopped here, I would have made it abundantly clear why he merits the ACPA's honoring of him, but I would still have left out something central to the man himself.

To show what else needs to be said, let me tell you how I first got to know Jorge, thirty years ago. We were both in Pavia for an international conference on Boethius. While we were there, I made friends with a tiny Italian child, who had been abandoned by her mother. Her impoverished old grandmother was trying to take care of her, but she and the child had nothing and needed everything. I got their address and the grandma's permission and went shopping. When I bumped into Jorge in Pavia around dinner time, I looked as if I'd gotten myself confused with Santa Claus, I had so many packages, including one huge dolly, which was almost too big for me to carry. And I was thoroughly lost. I should add that I wasn't a presentable person in any other way either. I was 7 months pregnant, about the size of a small barn, in dowdy maternity clothes. Jorge, by contrast, was dapper and elegant, and he was headed for a sophisticated night out on the town. When he saw me, lost and heavy laden in more than one way, he gave up his dinner and any hope of a night on the town. Although he barely knew me, he helped me figure out where I was supposed to be, and then he walked me there, carrying all my packages, including that ridiculously huge dolly. When we got to the grandma's house, Jorge stayed to be friendly and chat, but he also made sure that there was somebody to get me back to the hotel when my visit there was finished, so that I would not get lost on the walk back across the city in the dark. This was my first impression of Jorge, and all the years since then have only strengthened that first impression. I am here to testify that it is hard to imagine a more generous or a more caring human being than he is.

So Jorge Gracia is in every way a most worthy recipient of the Aquinas medal from the American Catholic Philosophical Association. Please join me in welcoming him.

Saint Louis University

Does Philosophy Have a Role to Play in Contemporary Society? The Challenges of Science and Culture

Jorge J. E. Gracia

I dedicate this Aquinas Medal Lecture to the memory of my three mentors at the Pontifical Institute of Mediaeval Studies in Toronto, also recipients of the Aquinas Medal: Joseph Owens, Armand Maurer, and Edward Synan. The first taught me to love metaphysics; from the second I learned the subtle techniques of textual analysis; and the third uncovered the wonders of history for me.

T he history of philosophy is full of examples where philosophy and its practitioners have had to face challenges, some so serious that involved even death and incarceration. We need only to remember Socrates and Averroes as examples. The first paid with his life for awakening the minds of young people in ancient Greece, and the latter languished in jail paying for what his accusers regarded as criticisms of the Islamic faith. Fortunately, today the challenges are not that drastic. Most philosophers are able to practice their craft in relative tranquility, at least in the West. But challenges are still present, although today they involve what some believe is the irrelevance of the discipline. Here I briefly explore two challenges that seem quite pernicious because they question the value of philosophy in the contemporary world and they are used to argue against a significant role for philosophy in contemporary society. Echoes of them can be found in the justifications used by college administrators to cut lines in philosophy and give them to other departments. The challenges I have in mind come from science and culture.

I. The Two Challenges

The success of science has been extraordinary in the twentieth century, and at the opening of the twenty-first, we expect even greater successes in every branch of scientific knowledge, ranging from the development of cures for diseases that up until recently have ravaged humanity, even to the discovery of fuels that will help us preserve the quality of our environment. Many regions of the world have made

© 2012, *Proceedings of the ACPA*, Vol. 85
DOI: 10.5840/acpaproc2011853

pp. 19–25

enormous strides in making the human lot better, as we can see in most countries. Science, and its offspring technology, have worked. They have safeguarded humanity and provided for its needs. Scientific claims can be verified empirically and openly made subject to public scrutiny. And science has the advantage of prediction. Science can tell us that a particular drug will cure us, or that a certain type of artifact will fly, whereas another type will not. Science can predict famine, the failure of crops, and it is even on the way to predicting phenomena that, until very recently, were completely unexpected, such as earthquakes. Indeed, we live immersed in a world dominated by science. From the moment we get up in the morning, there is practically nothing we do that does not rely heavily in some discovery due to science. We wake up through an alarm, the sheets we sleep on are the product of science, the clean water that comes out of the tap when we wash is a result of science, the electric toothbrush with which we brush our teeth is the product of science, and so on. So we may ask, given that the world we live in is dominated by science, is there a place in this world for philosophy? Does philosophy have a role to play in contemporary society?

Prima facie, philosophy appears irrelevant, a kind of armchair throw-back to the time when science was in its infancy. For what has philosophy done that can compare with the achievements of science? Has philosophy ever fed anyone? Has philosophy ever cured anyone? Has philosophy ever improved the lot of humanity in any significant and visible way? Then, why waste time and energy on it? Why pay philosophers to teach and talk about topics that appear useless? After all, did not Aristotle hold that the most important core of philosophy, namely metaphysics, is a discipline that has no practical value and responds merely to the natural curiosity of humans? Should we not, instead of philosophizing, engage in activities that lead to the betterment of humanity, of which science appears to be the most successful to date?

The second challenge faced by philosophy is posed by the relativity of culture. Humanity always has been divided along cultural lines, to be human is to have a culture. But culture varies from place to place and group to group, and the perception of this variety has become particularly acute in our time. The differences are vast and deep, concerning such aspects of human life as language, religion, music, food, and law, to mention just a few examples. With the growth of globalization and increasing connectivity, the evidence of the differences that separate human groups has become more obvious, and the evidence of cultural imperialism, whether intended or not, is more evident. This has prompted groups to close ranks and adopt a defensive mode with respect to their particular cultures. We want to preserve the idiosyncrasies of our languages, religions, laws, music, and what we consider to be our cultural achievements, because our culture is where we were born and nurtures us. Even more importantly, our culture and its practice make us feel worthwhile, it provides us with our social identities and gives us self-respect.

The emphasis on culture has directed our efforts toward the particular and away from the universal because the universal does exactly the opposite of what we long for, which is to feel safe and comfortable in who we are. The universal compares us with others and this has the potential to humiliate us when our social accomplishments do not appear to be as good as those of other cultures. We want to reject what seems alien to us, and dwell on what is familiar and we have achieved as a group. In this context, philosophy may be perceived as a particularly dangerous threat because it has always sought the universal. Philosophy seeks absolute truth, justice, and beauty to echo the words of ancient Greek philosophers, not the relative truth, justice, and beauty as seen from particular cultural perspectives. And for this reason, philosophy must be rejected unless it is itself understood as particular and culturally relative, and abandons any claim that smacks of universality. Indeed, as the argument frequently goes, there is no such universalism, there is only particularity passed on as universality. A frequently cited example of this attitude is Eurocentrism in philosophy, the belief that European philosophy is universal, whereas other philosophies, such as the Chinese or the Indian, are not.

The challenges of science and culture suggest that we would do well to abandon philosophy, or at least banish it to the realm of an esoteric curiosity for the exercise of a few, in order to concentrate our efforts on science because it is on science that the future well-being of humanity rests, and on culture because it helps to establish our social identity and self respect. But is this the right choice? I would like to argue that it is not because, regardless of what science and culture can do for us, philosophy still fills important gaps in our understanding of ourselves and the world left empty by science and culture.

II. The Shortcomings of Science and Culture

One of the major shortcomings of science is that it is not a single discipline, but rather a conglomerate of different disciplines such as physics, mathematics, linguistics, biology, archeology, history, geography, sociology, and psychology, among many others. It is misguided to talk about "science," for there is no such thing. There are only sciences that differ from each other significantly. Indeed, the perspectives adopted by each of these disciplines are, by themselves, too narrow for the appreciation of the depth and breadth of many of the issues they investigate. Each discipline looks at human experience from a certain angle, applies to it a certain methodology, and uses a specialized vocabulary. To be sure, both the angle and the methodology help to bring out aspects of the world that otherwise might not be noticed, but at the same time, they exclude something else: for the psychologist, there are phenomena that cannot effectively be translated into psychological categories; for the sociologist, there are facts that do not have an immediate expression in social reality; for the physicist, there are experiences that are not clearly part of the physical world; and so on.

The weakness of an exclusive disciplinary scientific approach has not been overlooked. Indeed, the call for interdisciplinary vantage points is frequently heard these days. We are told that we need to take into account observations from many different disciplines because phenomena have different and multi-faceted dimensions and affect more than one aspect of human experience. Indeed, David Mason has noted that, in the United States especially, there has been a concerted effort to use an interdisciplinary perspective when approaching certain issues of social pertinence.[1]

Combinations of two or more disciplines have been attempted, giving rise sometimes to entirely new sub-disciplines—e.g., social psychology—and sometimes to entirely new fields, such as American or cultural studies. All these new branches of learning have the same aim: to make up for the shortcomings of the insularity of particular disciplines. Nonetheless, these interdisciplinary approaches often end up being either disciplinary, un-rigorous, or both. In some cases, one of the disciplines that enters into the mix dominates those that are supposed to be its partners. In other cases, the result lacks proper unity and method, and yields no more than personal and subjective musings disguised as serious research. Indeed, many publications about certain topics, such as race and ethnicity, take the form of autobiographical testimonies and personal anecdotes. Obviously, these have an important function in the discourse on these topics, for they dramatize a situation that otherwise might appear abstract and removed. However, the theoretical contribution of these narratives is limited. More than this needs to be done. Recording abuses is one thing, understanding the causes of the abuses and providing a conceptual framework that could be used to mount preventive measures is another.

Clearly, a holistic approach is desirable, but this approach cannot be just a disorderly mixture of diverse approaches. And even if it were, there would still be important questions and problems, perhaps the most important ones, that would fall outside the disciplines that have been used most often. To recall a well-known statement of Wittgenstein: "We feel that even if *all possible* scientific questions be answered, the problems of life have still not been touched at all."[2] That science is not enough should be obvious insofar as it aims to describe rather than prescribe, and when it comes to many matters that concern human beings, we need more than mere description; we need guidance for our actions. As Max Weber put it: "[I]t can never be the task of an empirical science to provide binding norms and ideals from which directives for immediate practical activity can be derived."[3] Clearly, it is not enough to have descriptions, even if they are accurate about how the world works. Humans need more than this in order to live and to lead fruitful lives. We surely need to know how the world works, but we also need rules of action that will guide us in choosing what to do. We may know that a knife can kill, but we need to have a rule about whether to kill or not with it. We know that a murderer causes pain to the family of the person he murdered, but we need to have a rule that will guide us about what to do with the murderer. Should we keep him in prison until the end of his life? Should we put him to death? Or should we make him pay some monetary restitution? We know that poison can terminate our lives, but we also need to determine whether we should take it and in what circumstances. We also know how to terminate the life of a human fetus, but this gives us no guidance as to whether we should terminate its existence or not when the life of the mother is in danger. The sciences cannot provide an answer to any of these questions.

The two weaknesses of science I have pointed out—the diversity of the disciplines that compose it and the inability of the sciences to tell us what we should do—are reasons given by those who make a case for culture. As noted earlier, culture nurtures us and helps us to form and keep a certain identity that, in turn, helps us develop our social identities and our self respect. We are born in a culture, we are comfortable in it, and the culture provides unity to our lives and guidance for our actions. Culture tells us what to do and not to do in certain circumstances. Culture provides a place for each of us in our society, and we learn to behave according to its directives. I know that I can have only one wife in my culture and that if I were to have more than one, I would be punished. And I also know that I am expected to be on time when I am invited to dinner and, if I am not, I will not be invited again. Everyone in my culture is subject to the same set of rules, even if not exactly to the same rules.

But culture suffers from the same problems that science does, because there is no single culture for all humans, and different cultures have different rules of behavior that are often in conflict. Each science is the same for everyone, even though there are many sciences. In the case of culture, however, we do not have anything universal that corresponds to what we have in the sciences, for nothing about culture applies across the board. The most serious shortcoming of culture is its particularity—a culture does not apply to all humanity. My culture is of no help to you, if you belong to another culture, and many cultures differ so strongly that when those who are part of different cultures come into contact, serious clashes ensue. For some cultures, female circumcision is the norm, but for others it is anathema. Ultimately, there seems to be no way to resolve these clashes except through force, because when culture is regarded as absolute, there are no means to negotiate between different cultures.

Science and culture are not sufficient to fill our many intellectual and moral needs, and it is so because they are too narrow and particular, whereas what is needed is breadth and universality. The sciences claim to provide universal knowledge, but they are divided and give us many narrowly different perspectives that fail to come together into one coherent conception. The particularity of science consists in the diversity of scientific disciplines, each with its own special methodology and approach. The case of culture is similar in that it fails because there is no single culture for all humans.

III. The Case for Philosophy

The crux of my argument for the justification of a role for philosophy in our world rests on the claim that it is, in principle, the only discipline that can fill the gaps left by science and culture. Unlike scientific disciplines, which are narrow in scope and have developed specialized methodologies, philosophy aims to be comprehensive and lacks a single set of methodological norms. Philosophy tries to produce a comprehensive view that integrates all the knowledge we have, whereas the sciences are less inclusive insofar as they are circumscribed by their methodological boundaries and limited subject matter. A second reason we need philosophy in addition to the sciences is that philosophy raises certain questions that are outside the province of the sciences. A third reason is that philosophy functions as a watchdog of the sciences and of culture. And a fourth is that philosophy also functions as a broker between science and culture. All four differences give philosophy an advantage.

Philosophy is essentially interdisciplinary, insofar as its task consists in putting together as complete a picture of the world as possible based on the overall human experience of it, and it lacks a specific methodology. Although not all philosophers have thought so, philosophy's history vouches for its breadth. Philosophy is comprehensive in a way that no other discipline is. Psychology looks at the mind, sociology at social phenomena, mathematics at numbers, physics at the physical world, anatomy at the body, botany at plants, astronomy at the heavenly bodies, and so on. But philosophy tries to integrate the conclusions of all these into an overall conceptual framework that makes sense, is faithful to our experience, has support in sound arguments and evidence, and satisfies our diverse needs.

Moreover, some branches of philosophy—such as metaphysics, epistemology, logic, ethics, and politics—provide analyses not available anywhere else, including science or culture, even though these analyses are essential for developing human knowledge and carrying out human action. In metaphysics, philosophy is able to relate the categories studied in more specific sciences to the most general categories about which humans can think.[4] Epistemology establishes the conditions of knowledge and scrutinizes the adequacy of procedures to acquire it. Logic develops and monitors criteria of valid and adequate reasoning and is, therefore, at the heart of any disciplinary enterprise. And ethics and politics analyze the requirements of a sound individual and state morality and, therefore, supply the prescriptions for human action which cannot be derived from other humanities, science, or the arts.

Additionally, philosophy functions as a critic of science and culture. Each science, granted, criticizes itself. Indeed, sciences generally have very strict protocols of self-criticism. But not all sciences agree on methods and standards of criticism. There are schools within sciences that disagree about important procedures and the interpretation and validity of their outcomes. And even sciences in which all their practitioners share a uniform, or nearly uniform, view of their standards and procedures, benefit from having an external critic who does not share the presuppositions under which the science works. Of course, one science may function in this way with respect to another particular science, but there also needs to be criticism from outside of science. This criticism may originate in culture, but we have seen that culture is divided in ways that do not provide an overall approach, and it functions within certain parameters and under certain assumptions that make its criticism unacceptable to scientists and not credible outside the particular culture in question. This is why the task of criticism belongs to philosophy insofar as it is in the nature of philosophy to question all presuppositions, including the ones under which it itself works. Indeed, philosophy explicitly tries to insulate itself from presuppositions of all kinds, including cultural presuppositions, and if it does not succeed, at least it tries to make the presuppositions explicit.

Philosophy acts as a critic of culture, pointing out where cultural practices are unacceptable because of other views held within the culture or because of factual evidence to the contrary. An example of this is the defense of the American Indians that Bartolomé de Las Casas carried out.[5] He rejected the claims that Indians were barbarians, inferior people unable to govern themselves, and he based such defense on the evidence that he collected about their behavior.

Finally, perhaps even more importantly, philosophy functions as a broker between science and culture. These enterprises often conflict, which means that, in order to bring them together into a conceptually coherent overall point of view, the conclusions of some of them have to give way to the conclusions of the others. Moreover the criteria that philosophy uses as a broker is not taken from any of them. Philosophy imposes on these criteria, and on any synthesis of them, the requirement that they meet the most general criteria of understanding. This is a task resulting from both philosophy's comprehensive reach and certain areas of inquiry that are uniquely philosophical. By addressing issues that have to do with the overall require-ments of understanding and the very foundations of knowledge, philosophy stands guard over all sources of knowledge. And philosophy not only sits in judgment over them, but also relates their claims and methods, seeking to integrate all we know into a coherent conceptual framework. In short, philosophy is necessary because it is the only discipline that is able to put together science and culture, to work out their conflicts, and to build a general framework that is not subject to particularities or idiosyncrasies, but seeks to achieve universality. And this is the reason why the role of philosophy in contemporary society is fundamental. It is also the reason why I became a philosopher and have devoted my life to philosophy.

University at Buffalo

Notes

1. See David Mason, "The Continuing Significance of Race? Teaching Ethnic and Racial Studies in Sociology," in *Ethnic and Racial Studies Today*, ed. Martin Bulmer and John Solomos (London: Routledge, 1999), 13.

2. Ludwig Wittgenstein, *Tractatus Logico-philosophicus*, trans. D. F. Pears and B. F. McGuinness, § 6.52, 187 (London: Routledge and Kegan Paul, 1981).

3. Max Weber, *Methodological Essays* (New York: Free Press,1969), 52.

4. This view of metaphysics might seem idiosyncratic. I have defended it in Gracia, *Metaphysics and its Task: The Search for the Categorial Foundation of Knowledge* (Albany, N.Y.: State University of New York Press, 1999).

5. Bartolomé de Las Casas, *In Defense of the Indians*, trans. and ed. Stafford Poole (De Kalb, IL: Northern Illinois University Press, 1992).

Confronting the Cosmos:
Scientific Rationality and Human Understanding

John Cottingham

Abstract: A long tradition maintains that knowledge of God is naturally available to any human being, without the aid of special divine grace or revelation. St Paul declares that those who fail to recognize the divine authorship of the world are "without excuse." But the universe as scrutinized by an impartial and rational spectator can seem blank or inscrutable, and those who do not see it as the work of a divine creator do not seem guilty of any error of logic or observation. This paper suggests that in order to defend the idea of natural knowledge of God we need a different kind of religious epistemology—one that, rather than trying to make religious knowledge conform to a neutral, secular-style epistemic template, takes account of the special conditions under which God, if he exists, might be expected to manifest himself. The paper concludes by arguing that our responses to value, including our experience of natural beauty and of moral goodness, can be construed as manifestations of the divine. Such 'intimations of the transcendent,' do not qualify as scientific evidence on the one hand, nor on the other hand do they presuppose divine intervention or miraculous revelation; nevertheless they are a part of our human experience that, if we are open and attentive, we cannot in integrity ignore.

1. Natural Knowledge of God
and the Neutrality of the Cosmos

Anotable passage in Paul's letter to the Romans declares that "ever since the creation of the world, God's eternal power and divine nature, invisible though they are, have been understood and seen through the things he has made."[1] The idea seems to be that we can all infer God's existence from observable features of the natural world. And not just that we can do so, but that that we *ought* to—for Paul goes on to declare (in the same verse) that those who fail to recognize the divine authorship of the world and in consequence fail to give him thanks are "inexcusable."[2] Following this lead, there is a long tradition in Christian philosophical thought that maintains that natural inferential knowledge of God is readily available to humans. Aquinas's approach in the five ways provides

© 2012, *Proceedings of the ACPA*, Vol. 85
DOI: 10.5840/acpaproc2011854

a conspicuous example. And the First Vatican Council reaffirmed this tradition in 1870 when, explicitly invoking the passage from Paul, it laid it down that "God, the beginning and end of all things, can be known, from created things, by the light of natural human reason."[3]

It seems as unambiguous a position as anyone could wish. But actually, things are not quite as simple as may at first appear. The Pauline passage, though affirming our knowledge of God on the basis of his works, makes it clear that the divine attributes themselves, God's power and divine nature, are *not* known: they are beyond our ken, or as Paul puts it, *invisible*. This is in line with the frequent warnings in the New Testament, prefigured in the Hebrew Bible, that God is not to be seen by human eyes: he dwells (as the letter to Timothy expresses it) "in light inaccessible, whom no man hath seen or can see," or, as the book of Exodus puts it, rather more dramatically, "no man can see God and live."[4] Consistently with this, when we come to Aquinas, although the Five Ways patently aim to demonstrate God from his effects, the conception of God so arrived at is, in the words of one distinguished commentator, Brian Davies, a very "minimalist" one[5]: the proofs don't disclose the nature of the invisible God, but simply allow us to infer the existence of an original, uncaused, unmoved *something*, an ultimate X, to which, as Aquinas puts it, we apply the label "God."[6] And finally, to come to the passage from the First Vatican Council document, although a place for natural reason is clearly affirmed, this affirmation occurs in a concessive clause, which immediately leads on to an emphasis on the role, *not* of natural inference, but of special divine revelation and faith—the main subject of the document in question. So the sense of the relevant passage is somewhat as follows: although the mysterious and invisible God *can* certainly be inferred by the natural light via created things, nevertheless the truths on which our salvation depends are those revealed to the eyes of faith. The text goes on to say "this faith, which is the beginning of man's salvation, is a supernatural virtue, whereby . . . we believe that the things which he has revealed are true . . . *not* because of the intrinsic truth of the things, viewed by the natural light of reason." And it concludes by quoting the definition of faith in the letter to the Hebrews (1:11): faith is "the substance of things hoped for, the conviction of things *that appear not*."[7]

So despite Paul's thundering about those who fail to infer God being "inexcusable," and despite Vatican I's insistence that there can be natural knowledge of God, the emerging picture from a closer reading of these texts is that the natural light won't actually get us very far when it comes to knowing God. So even in what may be called mainstream Catholic Christianity, the results achievable by natural reason alone are somewhat limited, and I take it that the Protestant tradition is for the most part even more sceptical about what reason alone can tell us of God (think of Kierkegaard, for example; or, in the twentieth century, Karl Barth, who actually urged people to "turn their back on natural theology as a great temptation and source of error.")[8]

I don't, however, want to become embroiled in denominational controversies in this paper, but to try to get clear, from a philosophical perspective, on what it makes sense to say about natural knowledge of God—that is, the kind of knowledge that might be available to any human being without the aid of special divine grace or revelation. Let me start by saying outright that it's hard to accept Paul's stern insistence that those who fail to acknowledge God in this way are blameworthy or "without excuse," as he puts it. For it seems abundantly clear, at any rate, speaking in our own contemporary context, that there are many sincere atheists and agnostics: people who have honestly scrutinized the arguments and the evidence available from a purely rational perspective and have found them wanting. It's very hard to believe that such people have just omitted to draw obvious inferences or that they have culpably failed to notice something they ought to have noticed. On the contrary, it's much more plausible, I think, to regard the universe as contemplated from an impartial and open-minded perspective as *poker-faced*, to coin a phrase once used by the existentialist writer Colin Wilson: "the world," he said, "appears to have 'no grain,' to be poker-faced when interrogated about its relation to human aspirations and destiny."[9]

The processes giving rise to our planet and its biological systems can often appear to be at best *blank* or *neutral* with regard to us and our human concerns. The vision of the poet A. E. Housman of a "heartless, witless Nature" that "neither cares nor knows"[10] about us and our activities seems entirely consistent with a physical and biological system which allows entire species to be swept away and countless individuals to perish in the struggle to gain enough nutrition even to survive and reproduce. By "heartless," of course, Housman does not mean that nature is cruel or callous, merely that it is not the sort of thing to have emotional concerns or awareness of any kind—it just *is*. Or, as Tennyson so graphically put it in *In Memoriam*, imagining Nature speaking: "Thou makest thine appeal to *me*: I bring to life, I bring to death/The spirit does but mean the breath/ I know no more."[11] Yet on the other side, the following vision, recently articulated by England's Chief Rabbi Jonathan Sacks, is arguably also consistent with the observed facts:

> The story told by modern cosmology and Darwinian biology is wondrous almost beyond belief. It tells of a universe astonishingly precisely calibrated for the emergence, first of stars, then of second-, third- and fourth-generation stars, then of the formation of planets, one of which met exactly the conditions for the possibility of life. Then, in a way that still remains utterly mysterious, life emerged and evolved, through billions of years, yielding self-organizing systems of ever-increasing complexity, until finally one life form appears capable of standing outside its biological drives for long enough to become selfconscious . . . and sensing in all of this a vast intelligence that set it in motion and a caring presence that brought it into being in love.[12]

Which is more plausible—the view of Housman or the view of Sacks? Over half the world's population appears to believe that something like the second view is more plausible, but it is not my purpose to decide that question here. My point is that either view appears, in a certain light, to be quite tenable on rational grounds, and it does not seem remotely plausible to think that either side has made a simple inferential error or blame-worthily failed to advert to certain manifest observational facts. You may, of course, say that the second, religious picture, in speaking of a loving creator, wantonly fails to acknowledge the appalling facts of biological waste and individual suffering, or you may say that the first, purely naturalist picture, with its stress on a blind impersonal process, wantonly ignores the overwhelming improbability of complex conscious life emerging from a random series of contingencies. Both these adversarial strategies have been tried, but neither obviously succeeds, and it seems most reasonable to conclude that on present evidence, the honours are even. The universe, as scrutinized by an impartial and rational spectator, is indeed pokerfaced; and, *pace* Paul's strictures, those who do not see it as the work of a divine creator are, at the very least, not guilty of any obvious error of logic or observation.

2. The Epistemic Context for Human Awareness of God

One might conclude from the discussion so far that rational inquiry about God leads to a standoff, or an *impasse*, at least on the basis of evidence available to the natural light of rational inquiry. But before we rush to the Scottish verdict of "not proven," the idea of something's being obvious to the natural light may need further scrutiny. Our original Pauline text says that since the creation, God's invisible attributes, his eternal power and divinity, being grasped or understood (*noumena*) through his works, have been seen since the creation of the world. The King James translation, instead of just "seen," says "*clearly* seen," an emphasis followed in many subsequent English versions; but the original Greek verb *kathorao* lacks any such implication of obviousness—it simply means to see or observe or discern.[13] This prompts the thought that the divine authorship of the world might be something that is not supposed to be just clear or obvious to anyone who looks at it, but which might require a certain discernment or understanding to grasp.[14]

One analogy here might be that of scientific truths, such as some of the truths of modern nuclear physics: these may be clear enough, once the scientific work has been done to make the structure of the relevant phenomena intelligible, but they first require diligent and complex investigation to enable them to be uncovered and grasped. If knowledge of God is like this, then it could hardly be inexcusable not to attain to it, since many people might not be in a position to analyse the relevant evidence or to follow the complicated arguments needed to make the divine origins of our world discernible.

Of course there are a number of very distinguished philosophers of religion who do indeed think that knowledge of God is to be established on the basis of more or less complex probabilistic reasoning.[15] Although I greatly respect the high philosophical quality of much of this work, I do not happen to favour this approach myself, partly because (as already indicated) I am impressed by the "poker-faced" nature of the universe when it is impartially and dispassionately scrutinized, and partly because I think that we are not really in a position to speculate about what might have caused the cosmos, or what its observable features might reveal about its authorship, since when we are dealing with something *ex hypothesi* utterly unique, the mysterious singularity that is the existing universe, all normal probabilistic and inferential reasoning must break down. (So I agree here with the Dominican thinker Herbert McCabe, that invoking God does not have genuine explanatory power in anything like the scientific sense—it does not dissolve the mystery of existence.)[16] That, however, is a debate which I shan't pursue here, since I want in this paper to shift the focus to a *different kind of knowledge*, one that seems more relevant to Paul's wider purposes in his letter to the Romans, but more important—since my concern here is not with scriptural exegesis but with the epistemic status of religious belief—one that illuminates something crucial about how knowledge of God might reasonably be expected to become available to human beings.

When one reflects on traditional religious understandings of the nature and purposes of God, at any rate in the Judaeo-Christian tradition, I think it becomes clear that the scientific analogy for knowledge of God is curiously beside the point. To read the canonical texts of the great Abrahamic faiths is to realise that the principal focus of religious belief is not on explanatory hypotheses about the world or the workings of nature, but rather on the meaning of human existence and about how we should live our lives. The collective evidence of Scripture, which is a rich source for our grasp of what is involved in religious belief and allegiance, is pretty clear on this point: the divine call is chiefly heard as a moral and practical as opposed to a theoretical or purely cognitive one. God is, to be sure, often described as "the maker of heaven and earth," but his exalted role as creator is *always linked to what he requires of humans morally*. The reality which the patriarchs and prophets of the Hebrew Bible and the key protagonists of the New Testament are made aware of is one that calls them to change their lives, to follow a certain path of righteousness, to hear the cry of the oppressed, to love one another, to forgive those who have wronged them, and so on through a long catalogue of luminous moral insights that form the living core of the Judaeo-Christian tradition.[17]

The primary domain of religious thought and language, in short, is the *practical domain of meaning and morality, not the theoretical domain of science or explanatory theory.* Jonathan Sacks, from whom I quoted earlier, draws attention to the fact that three of the most seminal thinkers of our modern intellectual culture, Einstein, Freud and Wittgenstein, all concur on this point. "To know an answer to the question 'What is the meaning of life?' means to be religious," said Einstein; "the idea of life having a meaning stands or falls with the religious system," said Freud; "to believe in God means to see that life has a meaning," says Wittgenstein.[18] You may think that a triple *argumentum ad verecundiam*, appealing to three authorities in one sentence, is a bit much. But the agreement of the three intellectual giants in espousing a moral and hermeneutic rather than a theoretical and explanatory conception of God is nonetheless striking. Such a conception, moreover, has some interesting motivational implications. If the primary motivation for believing in God is that one finds the God hypothesis plausible, then a major factor in one's religious allegiance will be the thought that one is in possession of an intellectually satisfying explanatory theory. Should the God hypothesis lose its appeal in this respect, should one be able to say with Laplace *"je n'ai pas besoin de cette hypothèse,"* then the allegiance will be significantly undermined. By contrast, if the allegiance to God is based on my seeing that commitment to God gives my life meaning and value, then the stakes are rather different. My allegiance will be bound up with questions about salvation, transformation of life, the ability to live with affirmation and hope—the questions that have always been at the heart of the religious life as traditionally conceived. It is in this context, I am suggesting, that we can most fruitfully approach the question of how knowledge of God might be available to human beings.

Such a perspective points us towards a different kind of religious epistemology—one that, rather than trying to make religious knowledge conform to a neutral, secular-style epistemic template, takes account of the special conditions under which God, if he exists, might be expected to manifest himself. The primary focus will be on the moral and practical context in which awareness of God can be expected to be generated, rather than on the context of abstract speculative or theoretical belief. Now the God of the Judaeo-Christian tradition has often been conceived as Blaise Pascal underlined, as *Deus absconditus*, the hidden God: his purpose of entering into a free and loving relationship with his creatures would be thwarted were he to coerce their allegiance, so he can be expected (in Pascal's words) "to appear openly to those who seek him with all their heart, and hidden from those who shun him." It is entirely consistent with this that God should provide signs that offer, in Pascal's words, "enough light for those who desire to see, and enough darkness for those of a contrary disposition."[19] This crucially alters the epistemic rules that govern what we can expect by way of evidence in the case of God. Instead of evidence of the kind that is available to any objective and detached observer, one might expect the signs of God's existence to more closely related to God's salvific purposes.

This last point gives us a further reason for rejecting the idea that knowledge of God might be like technical or scientific knowledge, needing complicated and diligent investigational techniques in order to be disclosed. If the call to turn to God is primarily a moral and spiritual call, then given the basic premise of Abrahamic monotheism about a universally loving and compassionate God, one would *prima facie* expect the call to be able to be heard without special training or expertise or intellectual prowess. To put it in the Christian terms famously rehearsed by René Descartes in Part One of his *Discourse on the Method*, the kingdom of heaven must be "no less open to the most ignorant than to the most learned."[20] So one might conclude from this that knowledge of God cannot in principle be something complicated for humans to attain: rather, it seems one ought to expect that, like the divine mercy of which Portia spoke, it must drop "as the gentle rain from heaven upon the place beneath."[21]

However, though not requiring complex inferential processes or learned scientific investigations, such knowledge need not be supposed to be quite as universal and freely available as the drops of rain which fall on all alike whether they like it or not. The Pascalian phrase just mentioned ("enough light for those who desire to see, and enough darkness for those of a contrary disposition") suggests that, instead of an unavoidable rain shower, a rather more apt simile for how awareness of God comes about might be the fleeting appearance of morning dew—certainly not something that needs complicated techniques to experience, but something that requires you to be interested enough to get up early in the morning and go out into the fields. A somewhat similar point has recently been put by Stephen Evans, who argues that we ought to expect knowledge of God to be both "widely accessible" (given the deity's benign purposes), but also "easily resistible" (as it ought to be if human freedom is to be respected).[22] What kind of knowledge might fit these conditions?

3. "Kardiatheology" and Personal Transformation

One answer to this question has been proposed by Paul Moser, in his two recent books *The Elusive God* and *The Evidence for God*, both of which display a marked scepticism about the value and appropriateness of traditional arguments for God offered by natural theology.[23] Moser rails against the demand made by "skeptics and philosophers" that God should provide us with what he calls "spectator evidence" of divine reality—the kind of evidence that can be gathered and evaluated by a detached impartial observer. Such a demand, argues Moser, misses what would be the main redemptive aim of the Jewish and Christian God, by allowing the topic of divine reality to become a matter for "casual speculative discussion," and thereby in a certain sense trivializing it.[24] Moser offers instead a quite different model of theology, a *kardiatheology*, as he calls it, which is aimed "primarily at one's motivational heart, including one's will."[25] And this connects crucially with the question of evidence. Moser maintains that on any plausible understanding of the nature of a God worthy of worship, "divine self-revelation and its corresponding evidence . . . would seek to transform humans *motivationally*, and not just intellectually, towards perfect love and its required volitional cooperation with God." It follows from this, Moser argues, that the traditional methods and arguments of natural theology suffer from a "debilitating flaw": they offer "no evidence whatever" of a living personal God who is worthy of worship and seeks fellowship with humans.[26]

But what does "kardiatheology" yield in the way of evidence? Moser's answer is that the evidence will take the form of *individual experience of divine transformative power*. That might suggest a very personal and subjective approach, bordering on fideism—an appeal to the need to trust oneself to the salvific power of God either without rational support, or even in the face of reason. But Moser is adamant that faith needs the support of reason—it needs to be "cognitively commendable," and this in turn requires that there be a rational basis for commendation. Such a rational basis, according to Moser, can be found in the radical change *I myself* find myself undergoing as I open myself to the transforming Spirit of God. We are now a million miles from neutral, secular epistemology, both because the evidence invoked makes irreducible reference to the transforming Spirit of God, and also because it involves not some impersonally accessible body of data, but something that becomes, as Moser puts it, "salient to me, as I, myself, am increasingly willing to become such evidence—that is, evidence of God's reality."[27]

The epistemology implied here raises some interesting philosophical questions. Moser himself calls it a "grace-based" epistemology,[28] and this may lead some secular critics to dismiss the whole idea as question-begging, nothing more than an appeal to the unsubstantiated theistic claims of a cosy club of insiders. Certainly, such humanly experienced acquaintance with God's call will hardly be accepted by all as a coercive argument for God's existence, but it is not meant to be: Moser's case, and it seems hard to gainsay, is that it can still validly function as evidence for a given person of God's existence. Admittedly we are dealing here with what might be called "insider information"—reports in favour of a certain outlook coming from individuals caught up in a process that already implies being committed to that outlook, or at least being deeply receptive to the possibility of its truth. But so far from this being an unusual situation in human life, there are many parallels. Sigmund Freud, in citing the evidence supporting his psychoanalytic outlook, readily acknowledged that his evidence was not of a kind to satisfy normal scientific rules of procedure. The processes involved, he admitted, are not susceptible of public investigation under normal observer conditions, since the psychotherapeutic process takes place in a "private consulting room" and "only under the conditions of a special affective relationship to the physician."[29] His underlying point is that the kinds of insight gained in therapy are not achieved via objective and detached scrutiny; on the contrary, the patient who maintains a sceptical and detached stance is already in a condition that tends to block the healing effects of the process, or even prevent it getting off the ground in the first place. Only by allowing oneself to be vulnerable and open to the images dredged up from the depths of the unconscious—a process which itself requires a certain openness to the terms of the "affective relationship" with the therapist—will the work of healing be able to make itself felt. The affective dimension, including the painfulness and the vulnerability, is quite simply part of the process, and the subject's entering into such a state is a precondition for the confirmatory evidence to be manifested.

Some sceptics may be inclined to respond: "so much the worse for the epistemic status of the claims of psychoanalysis." But whatever one feels about this particular example, it seems hard to deny that there are phenomena which are not such as to be apprehended under the standard scientific conditions for what counts as objective evidence, but which require receptivity by the subject, and possibly even internal transformation, in order to make themselves manifest. If one does not like the psychoanalytic example, there are other more familiar instances. People speak of the transformative power of love, or of great music or poetry, yet the relevant evidence for such power is available only to *insiders*, those who find themselves undergoing radical change as the result of what they allow themselves to be exposed to.

There are, to be sure, some caveats here to be entered here, before we give a blank cheque to the claims of this kind of "insider evidence." In the first place, we need to be clear what the evidence is supposed to be evidence *for*. Roger Scruton, describing the experience of a great work of music, speaks of "sacred" moment, moments "outside time, in which the deep loneliness and anxiety of the human condition is overcome," and "the human world is suddenly irradiated from a point beyond it."[30] Evidently one might accept his claim about the power of great music to produce the changes he describes without conceding that this is evidence for a transcendent source of change—something that irradiates the world "from a point beyond it." So, similarly, the personal and moral changes undergone by someone who believes they are opening themselves to God do not automatically guarantee that the source of those changes is the external transcendent source that the believer takes it to be. In the second place, evidence need not be *conclusive* evidence: there may be "defeaters." So if I take certain spiritual transformations I myself undergo to be evidence for God ("personifying evidence," as Moser puts it), this does not remove the need to consider possible counter-evidence for God's existence (for instance, evidence arising from the problem of evil). Nevertheless, and notwithstanding these caveats, it seems reasonable to conclude from this part of our argument that there are certain areas or dimensions of reality, where the relevant evidence is available only to insiders in the form of the personal transformation they themselves experience.

4. Natural Intimations of the Transcendent

How do our conclusions so far bear on the traditional theological claims concerning natural knowledge of God? Here I want to broaden the discussion beyond the specifics of Moser's arguments by considering the more general approach to religious epistemology that they exemplify—what might be called the "Pascalian" approach. By this I mean an approach which emphasises evidence for God that arises not in the context of theoretical theological argument, but in the context of interior change and personal transformation—evidence, in short, of the kind that is by its very nature available only to insiders, in the sense of those who have undergone the relevant interior changes.

How, then, does this "Pascalian" epistemology bear on the question of natural knowledge of God? The Vatican Council document of 1870, quoted at the start of this paper, follows a long-standing distinction between on the one hand the "natural light" of human reason, and on the other supernatural revelation (for example the revelations reported in Scripture, or handed down via apostolic authority), which must be believed on faith. But if we start to think in terms of Pascalian epistemology, it seems clear that the kinds of phenomena it invokes don't fit very well into the traditional dichotomy between faith and reason.

The stark dichotomy between "two sources of illumination," as René Descartes put it (following a long Christian philosophical tradition)—the *lumen naturale*, or light of reason, and the lumen *supernaturale*, or light of faith,[31] suffers from the following problem: it suggests that *either* evidence has to be such as to be accessible by purely natural human secular reason, *or else* it has to be revelatory and/or perceptible only to the eyes of faith. Aquinas's idea of faith "making up" for the deficiencies of the ordinary natural senses encapsulates this idea.[32] However, there is surely a *tertium quid*. Let us suppose, for example, that someone is not satisfied with the logic of the five ways; or let us suppose they find contemporary arguments for the "fine-tuning" of the universe insufficient to licence the inference of a cosmic intelligence at work, and suppose they have similar dissatisfactions with the other weapons of standard natural and/or science-based theology. Does it follow that to come to knowledge of God they are now dependent on the supernatural light, on faith and revelation?

The answer, I suggest, is no, and I want to close by drawing attention to some crucial aspects of our human experience that function, if you will, as a kind of bridge between what we can access through our natural human endowments, and what seems to depend on the gracious bestowal of something more extraordinary and special. Consider the "transcendent" moments that very many people will from time to time have experienced, the times when the drab, mundane pattern of our ordinary routines gives way to something vivid and radiant, and we seem to glimpse something of the beauty and significance of the world we inhabit. Wordsworth expressed it as follows, in a famous passage in *The Prelude*:

> There are in our existence spots of time,
>
> That with distinct pre-eminence retain
>
> A renovating virtue, whence—depressed
>
> By false opinion and contentious thought,
>
> Or aught of heavier or more deadly weight,
>
> In trivial occupations, and the round
>
> Of ordinary intercourse—our minds
>
> Are nourished and invisibly repaired;
>
> A virtue, by which pleasure is enhanced,
>
> That penetrates, enables us to mount,
>
> When high, more high, and lifts us up when fallen.[33]

What "lifts us up" is the sense that our lives are not just a disorganized concatenation of contingent episodes, but that they are capable of fitting into a pattern of meaning, where responses of joy and thankfulness and compassion and love for our fellow creatures are intertwined, and where they make sense because they reflect a splendour and a richness that is not of our own making. Notice that this kind of "transfiguration" is not a "religious experience," if that latter term is understood in the rather narrow way that has become common in our culture, when philosophers speak, for example, of the "argument from religious experience." What is often meant under this latter heading is some kind of revelation which is taken to be evidence for, or to validate, the supposed truths of some particular creed or cult—a vision of the Virgin Mary, for example, or the sense (reported by one of William James's correspondents) of "the close presence of a sort of mighty person."[34] This kind of notion is I think uppermost in many people's minds when they insist that they have never had a "religious experience." By contrast, the kinds of "transcendent" experience described by Wordsworth and many other writers involve not so much a revelation of supernatural entities, but rather a heightening, an intensification, that transforms the way in which we experience the world. The term "transcendent" seems appropriate not in the sense that there is necessarily an explicit invocation of metaphysical objects that transcend ordinary experience, but rather because the categories of our mundane life undergo a radical shift: there is a sudden irradiation that discloses a beauty and goodness, a meaning, that was before occluded.

Other examples could be drawn from the world of music, for instance as described in the work of Roger Scruton which I mentioned earlier. Yet another example presents itself in the exercise of our human moral faculties. The Danish philosopher Knud Løgstrup speaks of the "ethical demand" in terms of the trust and self-surrender that are a basic part of human life.[35] His particular focus is the openness and responsiveness to another person which is morally required in any human encounter or relationship. But a phenomenologically somewhat similar process occurs, it seems to me, in our responsiveness to central moral values. What philosophers have come to call "normativity" is one way of referring to a remarkable feature of moral values like the wrongness of cruelty, for example, or the goodness of compassion: such values exert a demand upon us, they call forth our allegiance, irrespective of our inclinations and desires. When we contemplate such proper-ties, with the required combination of attentiveness yet receptivity, we transcend ourselves, as Pascal might have put it (I am thinking of his dictum *l'homme passe l'homme*—humanity transcends itself):[36] we are taken beyond our own inclinations or endogenous attitudes to something higher and more authoritative. No matter what you or I may feel about cruelty—even if we develop a taste for it—it remains wrong, wrong in all possible worlds. And no matter how disinclined you or I may be to show compassion, the goodness of compassion retains its authority over us and demands our admiration and our compliance, whether we like it or not.

Now all these cases I have mentioned, our vivid awareness of natural beauty, our responses to the mysterious power of music, and our sense of awe before the authoritative demands of morality—all these may described by the believer as revela-tions of the sacred, as intimations of the divine reality that is the source of all truth, beauty and goodness. But it is also striking that they do not necessarily present as supernatural or miraculous irruptions in to the natural world; they are in a way perfectly "natural." They are not, to be sure, everyday or routine occurrences, since they characteristically raise us up to something higher than our mundane habits and inclinations, but the relevant experiences depend on faculties and sensibilities that are an integral part of our human heritage. Except in tragic cases where these sensibilities have been irretrievably damaged by trauma or abuse or serious illness, such heightenings, or intensifications, transforming the way in which we experience the world, can come to all of us, from time to time, and if we honestly interrogate ourselves, we are hard pressed to deny it.

I want to suggest that these experiences fall, simply and uncomplicatedly, into the category of awareness of God by means of the natural light. They are, if you like, natural intimations of the transcendent, glimpses of the sacred dimension that forms the ever present horizon of our natural human existence. I am, to be sure, here somewhat widening the traditional extension of the phrase "natural light," since that is normally taken to be the natural light of *reason*: the terms *lumen naturale* and *lux rationis* are virtually interchangeable in many Christian writers.[37] But *that* I think is simply an instance of an intellectualist bias that is prevalent among many philosophers and theologians. If something can't be turned into an argument or a logical intuition, then it is supposed to be not worth its salt—or else it is allowed because it is construed as something supernatural that, as Descartes put it, "whisks us up at a stroke to infallible faith."[38] But the kinds of experience I have been speaking of are, on the one hand, not supernatural short cuts; yet, on the other hand, they are not exercises of our rational or inferential faculties, but something much more spontaneous and direct and intuitive. They are natural glimpses of the divine.

But even if they are not themselves arguments or intuitions of the intellect, can these glimpses at least be the *basis* for intellectual inference to God? Well, in a sense perhaps they can, in the following sense: since it is a rational requirement, a requirement of intellectual integrity, to take proper account of all aspects of our experience, any worldview that wantonly ignores, or fails properly to accommodate, these aspects of our experience is to that extent intellectually weakened in comparison with its theistic competitors. Yet, in another sense, I am inclined to say that construing such experiences as grist for an inferential mill would be a distortion. For if we take on board the lessons of Pascalian epistemology, we should see that there is not here a body of evidence from which there is a logical or probabilistic conclusion to be drawn by anyone who responsibly attends to the data. In the first place, no one can be compelled to have, or to acknowledge, such experiences: they require a certain kind of focused attention, a certain motivational stance which might best be described as a listening or attunement.[39] And in the second place, they are not "data" presented for our speculative assessment and inference. Rather, we ourselves are part of the evidence, as we open ourselves to something that is resistible, something that does not compel our assent, but which, if we are responsive, has the power to transform us, not in such a way as to enhance our store of knowledge or to allow us to make better inferences, but so as to irradiate our lives with meaning and value that we cannot create for ourselves.

In this sense, to come full circle back to the Pauline dictum with which we began, God's power and divine nature are indeed manifest in what he has created—in the beauty and wonder of creation, in the glory of the works of music and art that celebrate that creation, and in the majesty of the moral law that inspires the human race, made in his image, with awe and longing. Nothing in logic or ordinary observation compels us to see things in such a transfigured light, so when such manifestations fail to occur, or for various reasons pass people by, or are interpreted in a sceptical or deflationary way, there is no point in issuing condemnations about their having "no excuse."

And the context, in any case, is quite unlike that of ordinary human reasoning, scientific investigation, or speculative inquiry. In the very special character of our distinctive human responses to the transcendent, there is always an implied call, a call to change and to bring our weak and wasteful lives into closer harmony with the enduring source of being and value. The standard Christian view is that we cannot do that unaided, and that our salvation requires faith and a voluntary act of openness to divine grace. But the special theology of faith and grace builds on the ordinary natural responses that are already at work in our experience of the natural and human world. So there is a link between the natural and the supernatural light, a bridge between the workings of nature and of grace, which together have the power to guide us home to our ultimate source and end. Or, if you will forgive me for allowing the last word to Wordsworth, this time from a different but equally famous poem, the Intimations Ode:

> Hence in a season of calm weather
>
> Though inland far we be,
>
> Our Souls have sight of that immortal sea
>
> Which brought us hither.[40]

The "sight" that Wordsworth refers to is not "objective evidence," but neither is it "insider knowledge," restricted to the club of believers or the saved. It arises out of a pattern of response that is part of our ordinary natural human heritage: we only need to find the time to attune ourselves to it and allow ourselves to glimpse its true meaning.

Heythrop College, University of London, and University of Reading

Notes

1. τὰ γὰρ ἀόρατα αὐτους ἀπὸ κτίσεως κόσμου τοῖς ποιήμασιν νοούμενα καθορᾶται, ἥ τε ἀίδιος αὐτοῦ δύναμις καὶ θειότης. Romans 1:20. The thought is a recapitulation of earlier ideas, found, for example, in The Wisdom of Solomon 13:1 "Surely vain are all men by nature who are ignorant of God, and could not out of the good things that are seen know him that is; neither by considering the works did they acknowledge the workmaster."

2. *Anapologêtos.* Romans 1:20. Compare Wisdom 18:8: "Neither are they to be pardoned."

3. Sancta mater Ecclesia tenet et docet, Deum, rerum omnium principium et finem, naturali humanae rationis lumine e rebus creatis certo cognosci posse: "invisibilia enim ipsius a creatura mundi, per ea quae facta sunt, intellecta, conspiciuntur" [Rom 1. 20]. First Vatican Council, *Dogmatic Constitution on the Catholic Faith (Dei Filius)* [1870], chap. 2.

4. God dwells in "light inaccessible, whom no man hath seen nor can see" (φῶς οἰκῶν ἀπρόσιτον, ὃν εἶδεν οὐδεὶς ἀνθρώπων οὐδὲ ἰδεῖν δύναται), I Timothy 6:16. Cf. Colossians 1:15: Christ, who has "delivered us from the power of darkness" is the "image of the invisible God" (εἰκὼν τοῦ θειοῦ ἀοράτου). See also I John 4:12 ("No man hath seen God at any time"). For the Hebrew Bible, see Exodus 33:17, 20 (Moses) and I Kings 19:13 (Elijah): no human can see God and live.

5. B. Davies, *Aquinas* (London: Continuum, 2002), 27.

6. See Thomas Aquinas, *Summa theologiae* [1266–1273], Part I, question 2, article 3 ("and this we call God," or some such phrase, is found at the end of each of the Five Ways).

7. *Dei Filius*, chap. 3. The Greek word here translated as "substance" is *hypostasis*. But this rendering (found for example in the King James Version) makes things sound, to my ear, far too settled and solid. *Hypostasis*, rather, is a prop or support. I have argued elsewhere that a willed act of trust can be epistemically facilitating—it opens us to seeing what, if all goes well, will confirm the appropriateness of the trust—and also psychologically and morally facilitating (it supports or reinforces the hopeful pursuit of something that is not yet in our grasp.) It's worth adding that in the second half of the phrase, "the certainty of things unseen," the Greek term is *elenchus*. But elenchus in Greek is a demanding, open-ended process—like the *elenchus* Socrates made famous—a probing inquiry, a reaching forward, which might lead to impasse or aporia. So, to transfer this to the religious context, faith is a reaching forward—not, to be sure in the Socratic spirit of critical inquiry, but still as a kind of risk, a test, like thrusting a piece of iron into the fire that will test it, and either destroy it or temper and refine it so as to make it stronger.

8. Karl Barth, *Nein!* [1934] trans. in Emil Brunner and Karl Barth, *Natural Theology* (Eugene, Ore.: Wipf and Stock, 2002) 75; cited in B. Davies, "Is God Beyond Reason?" *Philosophical Investigations* 32.4 (October 2009): 342.

9. Colin Wilson, *Beyond the Outsider* (London: Houghton Mifflin, 1965), 27.

10. "For Nature, heartless, witless nature,/Will neither care nor know/What stranger's feet may find the meadow/And trespass there, and go/Nor ask, amid the dews of morning/If they be mine or no." Final stanza of "Tell Me Not Here, It Needs Not Saying," A. E. Housman, *Last Poems* [1922], XL, repr. in *Collected Poems* (Harmondsworth: Penguin, 1956), 152–153.

11. Alfred Lord Tennyson, *In Memoriam* [1850], lvi.

12. J. Sacks, *The Great Partnership: God, Science and the Search for Meaning* (London: Hodder & Stoughton, 2011), 232.

13. Luther's German version has simply *ersehen*.

14. This would be consistent with Paul's typically intense way of expressing himself: the phrase τὰ ἀόρατα . . .καθορᾶται (things invisible are seen) is evidently a kind of paradox or oxymoron deliberately used for rhetorical effect.

15. Most notably and most impressively by Richard Swinburne, in a series of distinguished studies; see especially *The Existence of God* (Oxford: Clarendon, 2nd ed., 2005).

16. Compare Herbert McCabe, *Faith Within Reason* (London: Continuum, 2007).

17. Similar calls, for compassion and self-purification, for example, are found in the Islamic scriptures. For an expansion of the point developed in this paragraph, see J. Cottingham, "Conversion, Self-discovery and Moral Change," in *Conversion*, ed. I. Dalferth, Claremont Studies in the Philosophy of Religion (Tübingen: Mohr Siebeck, forthcoming).

18. Albert Einstein, *Ideas and Opinions* (New York: Dell, 1954), 11; Sigmund Freud *Civilization and its Discontents* [*Das Unbehagen in der Kultur*,1929], chap. 2 (PFL, Vol. 12, 263); Ludwig Wittgenstein, *Notebooks 1914–1916*, 2nd ed, trans G. E. M. Anscombe (Chicago: University of Chicago Press, 1979), 74e, 8.7.16. All cited in Sacks, *Great Partnership*, 204 and 318.

19. "Il y a assez de lumière pour ceux qui ne désirent que de voir, et assez d'obscurité pour ceux qui ont une disposition contraire." Pascal, *Pensées* [c. 1660], ed. L. Lafuma (Paris: Seuil, 1962), no. 149.

20. "Le chemin [au ciel] n'en est pas moins ouvert au plus ignorants qu'aux plus doctes." René Descartes, *Discours de la Méthode* [1637], part i.

21. "The quality of mercy is not strained. /It droppeth, as the gentle rain from heaven,/ upon the place beneath." William Shakespeare, *The Merchant of Venice* [c. 1597] Act IV, scene 1.

22. "One thing we might expect, given God's intentions for humans, is that the knowledge of God would be widely available, not difficult to gain. If we assume God cares about all humans, and that all of them are intended by God to enjoy a relationship with God, then it seems reasonable to believe that God would make it possible at least for very many humans to come to know his existence. . . . I shall call this the 'Wide Accessibility Principle'." C. Stephen Evans, *Natural Signs and Knowledge of God* (Oxford: Oxford University Press, 2010). 13. "According to [the "Easy Resistibility Principle"] . . . knowledge of God is not forced on humans. Those who would not wish to love and serve God if they were aware of God's reality [should] find it relatively easy to reject the idea that there is a God. To allow such people this option, it is necessary for God to make the evidence he provides for himself to be less than fully compelling. It might for instance, be the kind of evidence that requires interpretation, and include enough ambiguity that it can be interpreted in more than one way." Ibid., 15.

23. Paul Moser, *The Elusive God* (Cambridge: Cambridge University Press, 2008), and *The Evidence for God* (Cambridge: Cambridge University Press, 2010).

24. "For purposes of cognitively rational belief that God exists, skeptics and philosophers generally demand that God provide us with *spectator evidence* of divine reality. In doing so, they miss what would be the main redemptive . . . aim of the Jewish and Christian God. . . . Spectator evidence from God would allow God to be . . . domesticated and taken for granted by us in our selfish ways, because it would lack corrective judgement toward us and our selfishness. Given spectator evidence, the topic of divine reality would readily become a matter for casual, speculative discussion, and would thereby be trivialized. . . . Opposing selfish human pride, authoritative divine evidence would work by *cognitive grace*, a free, unmerited gift from God, rather than by any human earning that supposedly obligated God to redeem a person or to give divine self-revelation to a person. . . . The God of perfectly authoritative evidence would therefore not fit well with the docile gods of the philosophers and natural theologians." Moser, *Elusive God*, pp. 47–49; cf. p. 10.

25. Moser, *Evidence for God*, 26; cf. 253.

26. Ibid., 158.

27. Ibid., 172.

28. Ibid., 172.

29. Sigmund Freud, *A General Introduction to Psychoanalysis* [1920], Lecture I, trans. J. Riviere (New York: Washington Square Press, 1952), 22–24.

30. Compare Roger Scruton, who, describing the experience of a great work of music, speaks of "sacred" moment, moments "outside time, in which the deep loneliness and anxiety of the human condition is overcome," and "the human world is suddenly irradiated from a point beyond it." Roger Scruton "The Sacred and the Human" [2010] http://www.st-andrews.ac.uk/gifford/2010/the-sacred-and-the-human/ accessed 30 March 2010.

31. "The clarity or transparency which can induce our will to give its assent is *of two kinds (duplex)*: the first comes from the natural light (*lumen naturale*), while the second

comes from divine grace. . . . Those who read my books will not be able to suppose that I did not recognize this supernatural light (*lumen supernaturale*), since I expressly stated in the Fourth Meditation that it produces in our inmost thought a disposition to will, without lessening our freedom." René Descartes, *Meditations* [1641], Second Replies (AT VIII 148: CSM II 105–106). 'AT' refers to C. Adam and P. Tannery, *Œuvres de Descartes*, 12 vols., revised ed. (Paris: Vrin/CNRS, 19641976); 'CSM' refers to J. Cottingham, R. Stoothoff, and D. Murdoch, *The Philosophical Writings of Descartes*, vols. I and II (Cambridge: Cambridge University Press, 1985).

32. From the hymn *Pange lingua* [1260]. Aquinas's position on the relation between faith and reason is not what is sometimes called a "fideist" one, that faith *substitutes* for reason; the two, rather, are complementary. Thomas elsewhere describes an "ascent" via natural reason, coupled with a "descent" from God via revealed truth: *Summa contra Gentiles* [1259–1265], trans. A. C. Pegis (Notre Dame, Ill.: Notre Dame University Press, 1975), Bk IV, Ch. 1, and see Introduction to Vol. I, p. 39.

33. William Wordsworth, *The Prelude* 12, 208–218 [1805 edition].

34. William James, *Varieties of Religious Experience* [1902] (London: Fontana, 1960), chap. 3, p. 75.

35. Knud E. Løgstrup, *The Ethical Demand* [*Den Etiske Fordring*, 1956] ed. H. Fink and A. MacIntyre (Notre Dame, Ill.: University of Notre Dame Press, 1997).

36. Pascal, *Pensées*, ed. Lafuma, no 131.

37. The notion of *lux rationis* or "the light of reason," found in the *Regulae* [c. 1628] (AT X 368: CSM I 14), becomes, in the *Meditations*, *lumen naturale*, "the natural light" (e.g., AT VII 40: CSM II 28).

38. René Descartes, Preface to the 1647 French translation of the *Principles of Philosophy*, AT IXB 4: CSM II 181.

39. Compare Heidegger's term *Stimmung* (cf. *Being and Time* [*Sein und Zeit*, 1927], trans. J. Macquarrie and E. Robinson {New York: Harper and Row, 1962}, H 137), as interpreted by George Steiner: "Metaphysical techniques of argument and systematization prevent us from 'thinking the question of being,' from putting our thoughts into the vital register of interrogation (I use "register" to recall the notion of Stimmung, of tuning and accord between question and being). . . . [This] underlies Heidegger's 'counter-logic,' the peculiar design to replace the aggressive inquisitorial discourse of Aristotelian, Baconian and positivist investigation with an unresolved, even circuitous, nevertheless dynamic dialectic. In Aristotelian analysis, nature is made to bear witness; Bacon tells of putting natural phenomena on the rack so as to make them yield objective truths. In French 'la question' signifies judicial torture. In Heidegger's 'questioning of being,' an activity so central that it defines, or should define, the human status of man, there is neither enforcement nor a programmatic thrust from inquisition to reply. . . . To question truly is to enter into harmonic concordance with that which is being questioned. Far from being initiator and sole master of the encounter, as Socrates, Descartes and the modern scientist-technologist so invariably are, the Heideggerian asker lays himself open that that which is being questioned and becomes the vulnerable locus, the permeable space of its disclosure." Georg Steiner, *Heidegger* (London: Fontana, 2nd ed., 1992), 55.

40. William Wordsworth, "Ode: Intimations of Immortality, From Recollections of Early Childhood," from *Collected Poems* [1815].

Making Room For Faith in an Age of Science: The Science-Religion Relationship Revisited

Michael Ruse

Abstract: Are science and religion necessarily in conflict? This essay, by stressing the importance of metaphor in scientific understanding, argues that this is not so. There are certain important questions about existence, ethics, sentience and ultimate meaning and purpose that not only does science not answer but that science does not even attempt to answer. One does not necessarily have to turn to religion—one could remain agnostic or skeptical—but nothing in science precludes religion from offering answers. One may criticize the answers of religion, but so long as religion is not attempting surreptitiously to offer scientific answers, the criticisms must be theological or philosophical or of like nature, and cannot simply be purely scientific.

The relationship between science and religion has often been tense and never more so than today.[1] On the one side, we have the so-called New Atheists, who praise science and who denigrate religion, all religions, and who argue that the two are incompatible and that science has pushed religion entirely to one side. On the other side, we have various forms of religious fundamentalists—usually Christian, but increasingly Jewish and (even more so) Muslim—people who reject science as and when it comes into conflict with their deeply held faith commitments. There are those in the middle—somewhat sneeringly known as "accommodationists"—who who argue that, at least in some wise, it is possible to hold both to the importance and truth of science and to the essential claims of one or more of the great world religions. But although members of this group set about their work with vigor, one senses often that there is no underlying framework. They offer a number of alternatives—usually either arguing for the different aims and natures of science and religion (independence) or for the co-habiting and working of science and religion (dialog or even integration)—but give no theory as to why one should adopt one position rather than another.

I am an accommodationist. Raised a Quaker, it has been long since I held any religious beliefs at all, although I think I am more accurately described as an agnostic

© 2012, *Proceedings of the ACPA*, Vol. 85
DOI: 10.5840/acpaproc2011855

or skeptic than an atheist. However, I respect religion and do not conclude automatically that those with religious beliefs are cowardly or unintelligent or uninformed. Both politically and intellectually, I believe that we need a proper understanding of the science-religion relationship and, although in this paper I cannot offer an answer to every pressing question, my immodest aim is to offer an underlying framework on which we can build. To do this, I shall turn to both the history and the philosophy of science. I cannot pretend that everyone in those two fields would accept everything that I say. But I do want to emphasize that the material on which my position is based is not eccentric or otherwise idiosyncratic. I do not want to make my case by relying on foundations that few if any would find plausible. That would rather defeat the purpose of what I am trying to do.

For ease of exposition, I am going to focus on western science. If needed, I would justify this decision by saying that it is in the West that the science-religion tensions have arisen. I think and certainly hope that what I shall have to say applies to all religions, at least to all of the major world religions. But, if only for tactical reasons, just as I shall focus on western science, I am going to focus exclusively on Christianity and on that part of Christianity to be found in the West. By Christianity I mean the central beliefs, about God as creator, about our special place in His Heart, about the coming of Jesus and his death on the cross for our sins, and the subsequent resurrection and the possibility of eternal salvation. I do not want to spend a long time arguing the details of every sect to be found under this umbrella. In particular, I do not want to spend time on the nineteenth-century-emanating beliefs of American evangelical Protestants who think that the only true reading of the Bible is one that takes Genesis absolutely literally. I take it that, at least since the time of Saint Augustine, traditional Christians have recognized the need to treat the scriptures with care and understanding, seeing their real message and not just staying with the surface text (Ruse 2005).

Root Metaphors: From Organism to Machine

Let me start with the history of science, although this means that at once I must start to talk about the nature of science, that is I must plunge into the philosophy of science. Along with I suspect the majority—and if not the majority then a very large number—of today's historians and philosophers, I argue that science is deeply metaphorical (Hesse 1966; Kuhn 1977). It is not, to use a metaphor (!), just a matter of giving a police photographer's view of reality. Just the facts, ma'am, just the facts. We view and make sense of reality through metaphors. Geneticists, for instance, do not just think that there is a line of sub-molecules along the back of the larger DNA molecule. There is a line with information. And to get at that information, there is a "code" that had to be "cracked." Anatomists do not just think that there is a muscle that is moving within our chests, or that liquid just goes in and out. There is a heart that is "pumping" blood around our bodies. Physicists do not just think that two pieces of metal join up together. There is a magnet and one piece of iron "attracts" another. And so it goes.

I am not concerned now as to whether metaphors are essential in the sense that we could never get rid of them. Some think they are essential; others doubt it. The fact is that science uses metaphors, all of the time. And even if they are theoretically dispensable, in fact one wants to get rid of them on a daily basis. Apart from anything else, metaphors have incredibly important heuristic functions. By thinking of the DNA sequence as a code or the heart as a pump, you can go on to ask a host of new questions and throw light on areas hitherto in the dark, if indeed one knew that the areas existed at all.

Some metaphors are obviously more important than others—in a way, they cover or include others (Lakoff and Johnson 1980). Suppose we think of the world of organisms as a world of design. Even if you think there was a literal designer, namely God, you are still using a metaphor of human design. The organic world is as if someone or some team had designed it. Then beneath the overall metaphor of design, you have specific metaphors applying to particular parts of the organic world. Hearts as pumps, eyes as telescopes, fins as stabilizers, that sort of thing. The really big, all embracing metaphors are often called "root" metaphors, a metaphor itself that is fairly easy to understand. Simply, I argue that the history of western science is the story of the change of one root metaphor for another. We start back with the Greeks (let's keep simplifying the story and forget the Babylonians and others) who believed that the world in some sense is a great big organism. Plato argued this directly in the *Timaeus* and although Aristotle did not think that there is one organism in play, he certainly saw the world through organic glasses, as one might say. Specifically, he argued that we must ask not only about proximate causes but also about final causes. For instance, "it is both by nature and form that the swallow makes its nest and the spider its web, and plants grow leaves for the sake of the fruit and send their roots down (not up) for the sake of nourishment." Thus, "it is plain that this kind of cause is operative in the things which come to be and are by nature" (Physics 199a26–30, in Barnes 1984, 340).

Not everyone held to this view of the world. The atomists are an obvious exception. But for most of us it seems silly to put everything down to pure randomness. For most people, the organicist view of the world seemed sensible and fruitful. And that is why it endured for two thousand years. But then, during the Scientific Revolution of the sixteenth and seventeenth centuries, things changed. In the words of one of the greatest historians of the times, there was a "mechanization of the world picture" (Dijksterhuis 1961). A new root metaphor came in, namely that of a machine. From now on, the world was to be seen in these terms only. And final causes were to be expelled. Vestal virgins, as they were called by Francis Bacon. Decorative but sterile. Even bodies can be thought of in this sort of way. In the *Discourse on Method*, Descartes discussed Harvey's work showing that the heart is a pump (a machine) and the similar mechanistic functioning of other bodily parts.

> This will hardly seem strange to those who know how many motions can be produced in automata or machines which can be made by human industry, although these automata employ very few wheels and

other parts in comparison with the large number of bones, muscles, nerves, arteries, veins, and all the other component parts of each animal. (Descartes 1964, 41)

Robert Boyle, chemist and philosopher, spelt things out in detail. Making specific reference to a device built in the late sixteenth century, he argued that the world is

> like a rare clock, such as may be that at Strasbourg, where all things are so skillfully contrived that the engine being once set a-moving, all things proceed according to the artificer's first design, and the motions of the little statues that as such hours perform these or those motions do not require (like those of puppets) the peculiar interposing of the artificer or any intelligent agent employed by him, but perform their functions on particular occasions by virtue of the general and primitive contrivance of the whole engine. (Boyle 1996, 12–13)

Organisms—Including Humans

In other words, the way we are supposed to look at the world is purely in terms of blind law driving things endlessly, without purpose. Without purpose? Surely the point is that machines do have purposes. The clock is for time telling, for example. If nothing else, is not the world God's machine and His ends or purposes are all important? True, but it was not long before people started to feel that as far as their science was concerned, God should stay out of it. This does not mean that people became atheists or even agnostics (as we today might call them). But rather that within science these sorts of questions lead nowhere. So they might as well be dropped. In the words of the historian just mentioned, God became a "retired engineer." Unfortunately, there was a major fly in the ointment, organisms themselves. You may not need final-cause talk when dealing with mountains or moons, but it does seem needed in the case of organisms. After the Scientific Revolution, one may no longer have asked what the moon is for? One could still ask what the nose is for? And wings and leaves and much much more. This led Immanuel Kant to conclude that at some level, because of the need of final-cause talk, you will never extend the machine metaphor fully to biology. There will always be a gap.

> We can boldly say that it would be absurd for humans even to make such an attempt or to hope that there may yet arise a Newton who could make comprehensible even the generation of a blade of grass according to natural laws that no intention has ordered; rather, we must absolutely deny this insight to human beings." (Kant 1790, 270)

The world may be a machine, but there are aspects of it that will forever elude our understanding.

It was Charles Darwin's genius to speak to this problem. In his *On the Origin of Species* (1859), he argued not only that all organisms are the end products of a long, slow, natural process of development—evolution—but that this comes through the mechanism of natural selection. More organisms are born than can survive and reproduce; only some get through and these are the ancestors of all to come; and because of natural variation, some will have features that help in this process and so there will be a natural process of differentiation. Darwin called this "natural selection" and the argument is that, given enough time, this will lead to full-blown evolutionary change. What is important is that selection does not just lead to change. It leads to change of a particular kind: adaptation. Through a natural process, organisms have the features—eyes, teeth, feathers, leaves—that seem to call for final cause understanding (Ruse 2003). The machine metaphor triumphs in the world of organisms.

The final bastion to be conquered is humankind, specifically human thought and action. And ultimately this means the brain. In the past half century, major advances have been made in this direction by so-called "cognitive science." The basic approach is to treat the brain as a sophisticated calculating machine, otherwise known as a computer.

> The computer scientist, Marvin Minsky once described the human brain as a meat machine—no more, no less. It is, to be sure, an ugly phrase. But it is also a striking image, a compact expression of both the genuine scientific excitement and the rather gung-ho materialism that has tended to characterize the early years of cognitive science research. Mindware—our thoughts, feelings, hopes, fears, beliefs, and intellect—is cast as nothing but the operation of the biological brain, the meat machine in our head. (Clark 2000, 7)

Thus runs the course of Western science in the two and a half thousand years or so of its history. Understand that I am not saying that I personally find every aspect totally compelling. I myself am entirely happy with the physics part of the machine metaphor viewpoint and I would extend that to the organic world also, although I am much aware that there are those (those genuinely within the realm of science) who are less than convinced that Darwinism holds every answer. About cognitive science I am much less certain, although these are still early days and undoubtedly there has been a huge amount of really important and revealing science done in this direction. But it is enough for this discussion here and now to accept that the machine metaphor has and still does hold sway. And this is surely true even in the face of the truly astonishing ideas coming from the physical sciences in the past century. Whatever the ultimate status of quantum mechanics, it is after all still mechanics and that is enough for us here and now. That it requires us to think about machines in ways that would have astonished Descartes and Boyle is surely what one might have expected. They had no knowledge of the Newcomen Engine, and yet it has been the fundamental metaphor of geology since the Vulcanist days of the Scot James Hutton to the sweeping success of the still-recent paradigm of plate tectonics powering continental drift.

Unasked Questions—Answers not Given

Take the science as given and move on now to the second part of my argument. As Thomas Kuhn pointed out, metaphors (things incidentally that he identified with paradigms) are two-edged things. As pointed out already, with the right metaphor in the right hands, they are fantastical heuristic tools. They throw up questions that never occurred to people before and point researchers in the directions of right answers. Science gets done through and because of metaphors. You look at the stegosaurus in the light of design, and you start asking questions about the purpose or function of the funny looking plates all down its back. And eventually you come up with a satisfactory answer, in this case that they serve the end of heat regulation. They let the brute heat up in the morning and cool off in the middle of the day (Farlow et al 1976). The other side of metaphors is that they function so well by cutting off or making inappropriate whole ranges of questions. They are a little bit like the blinkers you put on a race horse. They focus the horse on the track and not on the stands and the spectators. Metaphors cut out a whole range of discourse. So for instance, I say that "my love is a red, red rose." You know she is beautiful, fresh, probably high colored and more. If I am joking a bit, you might understand that I am saying she can be a bit prickly. What I am not doing is telling you about her mathematical abilities or her religious convictions. It is not that I am giving you the wrong answers. It is just that these are not the sorts of things I am talking about.

My claim simply is that the root metaphor of modern science, specifically the root metaphor of the machine, is tremendously fruitful. But it does so in part by making certain questions off limits—or at least irrelevant—in its domain of discourse. These are somewhat empirical matters and embedded in history. So I am not able to give you a list of off-limit questions, now and forever decided. Apart from anything else, as I have pointed out that our understanding of machines—their nature and their scope—changes. So, understanding the tentative level at which I am talking, let me offer four areas or questions that I don't think the machine metaphor speaks to. Note that I am saying all of this irrespective of anything to do with religion. We will get to that, but not yet.

First, there is what has been called the "fundamental question" (Heidegger 1959). Why is there something rather than nothing? Some philosophers (Wittgenstein) think that this is a bogus question. I beg to differ. It makes perfectly good sense to me to ask why there is something rather than nothing. It is a bit like Paley's watch although it is not, I stress, the argument from design. I see an old jalopy in a field. It makes good sense to ask why it is there rather than not. I do not at all see why I cannot extend that question to everything. Why is there something rather than nothing? I just don't see that science under the machine metaphor touches this question. Science is a bit like the cookbook. First take your hare. Of course, science can go back a long way, at least to the Big Bang. I am quite open to its going back before that event. But still there is the question of why is there something rather than nothing? The machine metaphor shows why this question is unanswered. In talking of machines, ultimately you take the components as given. The sheet metal to make the body, the rubber to make the tires, the plastic to make the dash. Go back to the iron ore or the rubber tree or the crude oil. At some point you stop and say, enough. Here are the components. Now tell me how you make a Chevrolet or a Ford and how they work. That is what the machine metaphor leads you to ask and that is what the machine metaphor is very good at directing your questions. Not about ultimate sources and beginnings.

Second, morality or ethics. I am a follower of David Hume (1739–1740). I do not think you can get "ought" conclusions out of "is" premises. Machines are. Morality is an add on. Machines can be used for good. Machines can be used for bad. That is another matter. Of course, some machines basically only have one purpose and you might or might not like that purpose. I do not much care for the gallows. But that is an opinion that I have about the machine, and not the machine itself. As is only too obvious, particularly in the part of the world in which I live, a good many people think the gallows is a very good thing. You have Adolf Hitler all trussed up and ready to drop. Would you pull the lever? Would you not pull the lever? So here is a second area that in principle I just do not think science under the machine metaphor can touch. Later I am going to suggest that there is more to the question than this, but it will do for the moment. And I do not think the fact that you might—as indeed I do think you can—show how moral thoughts come about as part of our human nature touches the point I am making. Science cannot justify morality.

Third, and here I recognize that many philosophers and brain scientists will not go with me, I do not think that machines can or probably ever will explain consciousness. Where by "consciousness" I mean "sentience" in some wise. Note that I am not denying that brains cause consciousness and that if you are a materialist that is all there is to it. I am saying that consciousness is not explained, and this fact follows from the related fact that machines do not think. As Leibniz says, basically machines just do things.

> One is obliged to admit that *perception* and what depends upon it is *inexplicable on mechanical principles*, that is, by figures and motions. In imagining that there is a machine whose construction would enable it to think, to sense, and to have perception, one could conceive it enlarged while retaining the same proportions, so that one could enter into it, just like into a windmill. Supposing this, one should, when visiting within it, find only parts pushing one another, and never anything by which to explain a perception. Thus it is in the simple substance, and not in the composite or in the machine, that one must look for perception. (Leibniz 1714, section 17)

I realize that this leaves too many questions in the air. What about Hal in 2001? Could he think? And wasn't he a machine? Perhaps it is better to say that so long as one focuses on the machine-nature of machines one is not going to get an explanation of sentience. You can't get a silk purse out of a sow's ear and you can't get an understanding of sentience, something radically different, from cogs and gears, even the electronic variety.

You might think that I am wrong on this or at least too pessimistic (Churchland 1995). Two hundred years ago, I would probably have said the same thing about life itself, and now I think that it can be explained fully in terms of molecules. This is true. There are some philosophers who think that you can give an argument that sentience cannot be and will never be explained by machines (McGinn 2000). I am not sure I want to go there. Rather I would refer back to the point made above about the historical nature of my argument. I don't think it has been done. More importantly, I don't myself see that any real steps have been made to getting it done. It is not like say the origin of life, so far unexplained but with lots of good work done and clues on where to go next. I think we are still at square one. But I could be wrong on this and I accept this as a possibility.

Finally, fourth, there is the matter of what it all means. As we have seen, the post scientific revolution machine metaphor leaves God out of the equation. It just don't do God talk, as someone once said in British politics (comparing themselves rather smugly to the Americans). So the point is that modern science simply doesn't ask about ultimate meanings. Note that this is not the same as saying there are no ultimate meanings or that questions about ultimate meanings are wrong. It is just that it doesn't ask about them and cannot do so within the terms of its reference. Hence when someone like Steven Weinberg (1977) says that the more he does science the less he sees any meaning to anything, I am not surprised. I am only surprised that he would think that anyone would be surprised.

This is my list of four. There may be other questions. Some probably even now would include life itself. Machines just don't speak to that. I have indicated that I don't agree. Others perhaps would put the free will question in here. Machines tell you nothing about free will. I am a compatibilist, thinking you can have deter-minism—the determinism of machines—and a real notion of free will also. But I don't want to stop and argue these points here and now, nor do I want to trawl for other possible questions that machine-talk might not answer. We have enough for my purposes.

I also here do not want to get into the question of whether the machine meta-phor is going to be the only root metaphor for science for evermore. Even supposing there are humans around twenty thousand years from now, I am not about to say that they still will look back to 1543, the date of the publication of Copernicus's great work, or 1859, the date of the publication of Darwin's great work, and say that from those days on everything was fixed from the perspective of metaphor. What I will say is that even if there are new metaphors, they too will have unanswered questions and I will leave it at that. Although I will add as a kind of codicil that there are even today those who would go back in time and have us take up the organic metaphor again. I am thinking of various kinds of holists and emergentists and (naturally) organicists. Again rather stating than proving, I would suggest that making such a move does not take one from unanswered questions—it couldn't if we are still with metaphor—and ultimately I am not sure that the unanswered questions don't basically come down to those of the mechanist. Does organicism tell you why things started or what the purpose of it all is? I think not. You might say that the purpose is to keep things flourishing, but then I say, why should we keep things flourishing? The fact that things are alive does not in itself give you the ultimate answers. So let us leave it at that, recognizing that probably more discussion is needed at this point.

The Four Questions

I move now to the next stage of my argument. Science does not even set out to answer certain questions. Are the questions genuine? Already I have given my opinion on the fundamental question—why is there something rather than nothing? Morality needs no argument? Why should we be good? You tell me! (Actually, leave it a moment, and I will tell you.) What is sentience? Even the most reductive of philosophers does not deny that this is a genuine question. The question is how we answer if indeed we have not already answered it. What is the meaning of it all? You may think this a silly question. What you cannot do is say that because science does not answer it, it is unanswerable or silly. At least, you cannot without another argument saying that any question not answered by science is silly or unanswerable. And that is a very different matter. Consider: "Are there genuine questions not answered by science?" Is this question a scientific question? If not, then don't ask it or pretend to answer it!

Are the questions important? Again, don't get caught in the trap of saying that because science cannot answer them then necessarily they are not important. Apart from the self-reflective sorts of questions just asked in the last paragraph, what about: Do you love me? Is Fidelio a total failure or the greatest opera ever written? Is this essay convincing? (Okay, I agree that that is pushing the envelope!) Obviously some of my four questions are important by any measure. In fact, they all are. Why is anything around at all? What should I do and why should I do what I should do? Why do we think and what is it? Wouldn't we all be much happier if we were robots? C-3P0 or R2-D2? (Actually, do they think?) And why bother? Is it all a fraud or just a waste of time? If these questions are not important, then is any question important? (And if you say no, then I want an argument for this very non-intuitive response.)

The questions are genuine. The questions are important. The questions are not asked or answered by science. Where do we go from here? One answer, my answer, is that we go nowhere. We cannot answer the questions, so leave it at that. I am a skeptic about all answers to these questions. I think them genuine questions. I do not think I or anyone else can answer them. I should say that this does not really surprise me. We are mid-sized mammals with adaptations for getting out of the woods and up on our hind legs and making a living on the plains. I do not see why we should necessarily have the abilities needed to answer every question, particularly those of the ilk that I am discussing now. The proto-human who went around asking why there is something rather than nothing rather than where the next big chunk of protein (aka dead animal) is to be found was liable to stay proto rather than advance to actual.

However, because science cannot answer the questions and because I will not answer the questions, this is not to preclude others trying their hand. I and others can criticize the tentative solutions, but that is another matter. The only restriction is that the answers provided must not be quasi-scientific. You cannot try to slip in science-type questions. You must answer the questions in another way in their own right. And of course what I am really suggesting is that it is perfectly legitimate for the religious person to offer solutions to the questions. I can criticize the answers, but I cannot criticize the answers because the answers are not scientific—that is the very point—nor can I say that because science cannot answer the questions no one else can even try—that too is part of the point.

Religious Answers

What I find interesting and surely significant in some sort of way is that, having arrived at my questions quite independently of religion, I find that religion (remember I am talking about western Christianity now) offers answers to precisely the questions I have highlighted. I am encouraged by this because, without now digging into history, such a coincidence strikes me that truly it is no coincidence. Perhaps it doesn't mean very much. Perhaps once upon a time religion tried to answer everything, and the only things now that it can try to answer are those things not yet answered by science. But whatever the reason, it does mean that we are not talking past each other.

Why is there something rather than nothing? Because a Good God freely decided to create the universe, including humans, out of love. I don't think you can just leave things there. On the one side you are going to have some philosophical questions. On the other side, you are going to have some scientific ones. (It is for this reason that, although in an important sense I am proposing a science-religion position that is essentially one of independence, two Magisteria in the well-known language of the late Stephen Jay Gould (1999), I am arguing for rather more. I think there will be interaction between the two fields as you try to make sure that there are no conflicts.) With respect to this question, philosophically (call it theology if you will, I am not that bothered) you have got to deal with such issues as the nature of God's existence. In science, there is always the possibility of one causal step back. What caused everything? The Big Bang! What caused the Big Bang? Likewise, what caused God? You have got to cut off this line of questioning and, as Christian thinkers have shown in some detail, this means that you have got to ascribe to God some form of necessary existence—whether this be logically necessary existence (as I think you get with Anselm) or some other kind, "aseity" (as you get with Aquinas). I am not going to go into this here, but I simply point out that at some stage you must go into it.

With respect to this question, scientifically you have got to turn to the scientists and ask how the creation might proceed. It seems that God did not do this all at one fell swoop but sequentially through evolution. Is this acceptable theologically or philosophically? Augustine suggests strongly that it is. But what about today's scientific mechanism of change, natural selection? This is tricky, especially when it comes to humans (Ruse 2001). I do not think on the Christian scenario that we can be contingent. We had to exist—perhaps with green skin and twelve fingers, but thinking, moral beings are not an optional extra. Yet natural selection is contingent, with no guarantees of the evolutionary emergence of anything. Selection is not a tautology but what succeeds is what succeeds. And the variations of change, mutations, are random in the sense of not appearing to need or direction. A number of solutions have been offered. Although hardly a friend of Christianity, Richard Dawkins (1986) argues that humans (or human-like beings) were very likely to appear because of evolutionary arms races. Lines of organisms compete against each other developing better methods of attack and defense—the prey gets faster and so the predator gets faster, the shell gets thicker and so the beak gets stronger—and that eventually, as with real arms races, on-board computers get evolved and ever stronger (that is, bigger and better brains). It is no chance that humans appeared. Simon Conway-Morris (2003) argues (in a way similar to earlier thinking of Stephen Jay Gould [1985]) that ecological niches exist, that organisms evolve through selection to occupy them, and that obviously a cultural niche existed and if we had not found our way in then someone else at some time would have done so. I myself have argued that neither of these approaches guarantees human-like beings. I prefer to invoke multiverses—many universes—and to suggest that, with enough universes and enough time, since humans did evolve they would have evolved at some point.[2] God, being outside time and space, does not care how many failed attempts there were. Again though, here I am not endorsing any of these positions. Simply showing that you have got to take science seriously, that you cannot cheat by invoking non-science like Intelligent Design Theory (that has God directing the path of evolution), and that some work is needed to get science and religion into harmony. That's why I am not arguing for a simple independence position.

Why are we moral? Because God laid down certain rules for us to follow. I do not see how or why the Christian would avoid the divine command theory in some sense. (This prejudice may reflect my Quaker upbringing. When asked why we were pacifists, we answered simply: Because that is the Will of God.) Again obviously there are philosophical questions at stake. The *Euthyphro* question mainly—is the good automatically the Will of God, or is the Will of God that we should do the good? It seems to me that the natural law position scotches this problem. God made us as we are and what He wants of us is that we do the natural. It is not arbitrary but follows from our nature. It is not natural to eat our own feces and God is not being capricious in saying that we should not do such disgusting things. Conversely, it is natural for folk to hitch up and have kids, and God is in favor of this. It is a morally good thing to do.

Again the scientific kicks in because the scientific can tell us much about what is natural. Take male homosexuality (Ruse 1988). Prima facie, anal intercourse is unnatural. Anuses are for defecating not for sexual pleasure, and such intercourse does not lead to children. However, compared to Aquinas—who was pretty strong on this issue—today we know a lot more about the biology of sexuality. We know that sex, especially sex between humans, is a lot more than simply copulating and having babies. In heterosexuals, for instance, it has much to do with pair bonding and keeping the male around during the arduous years of child rearing. In the case of homosexuals, there is now much evidence that, as an orientation compared to heterosexuality, it too is biologically caused and may well have lots of good evolutionary reasons to do with helping family members and the like. Note that I am not arguing that this is necessarily so. What I am arguing is that the natural law position demands that we take science seriously and think about its content and implications. Science and religion must negotiate their boundaries.

What is man that thou art mindful of him? Well, most importantly that we are made in the image of God, meaning that we are thinking beings with a capacity for right and wrong. We have the obligation to study and enjoy the world that God has made for us and to do good to our fellows (where increasingly we are starting to realize that our fellows are not just other human beings). So sentience is in some sense the divine within us—not that we are gods, but that we are god-like in this sense. Even getting this far seems to me to demand some philosophy, about the nature of analogical reasoning and so forth. And, speeding things up a little, scientific questions are not going to be so far behind either. Remember, religion is not going to solve the mind-brain problem. It is not going to tell us how thinking emerges from a soft, wet, soppy organ like the brain—a computer made of meat. But having given the religious answer, there is more work to be done. I take it that using science to explore the dimensions of freedom that humans have is important here: Do childhood experiences determine what the grown man or woman is bound to do? Is childhood sexual abuse enough to explain and forgive an adult sexual transgressor? So science and religion engage here too.

Finally, meaning. Again the Christian has an answer. The world exists so that we might share eternal bliss with our Creator, and the Christian story of the Incarnation and the Atonement is part of this. Obviously there are philosophical-cum-theological issues about the possibility and meaning of eternal life. I would think science is important here too. For instance, I suspect that the problem of evil might be significant here (elsewhere also possibly)—trying to understand human evil and also the role of natural evil. What about Darwinian evolutionary theory with its central role for the struggle for existence? How do you reconcile this with a loving Creator and how does this affect matters to do with salvation? Again, I am not trying to solve these problems now. This is simply to say that religion has answers but that the very answers themselves call for much more work.

Additional Issues

This then is the approach I advocate for true understanding of the science-religion relationship. Where science can answer, then it must answer. Religion must give way. Adam and Eve as a unique founding couple is simply incompatible with modern paleoanthropology. They must go.[3] And the same is true of Noah's Flood and much more. Does this mean that I am ruling out all miracles? Not necessarily. The approach I am taking says that if science can do the job then science should do the job—including areas (like the origin of life) where science is still working on it. That is why Intelligent Design Theory is ruled out, because the examples it holds up as inexplicable are either already explained or of a type that science can explain. But if someone says that, since God created the world, He is able to intervene and did do so for our salvation—the Resurrection, for instance—then I am not sure that the scientist can stop such a move. A miracle thus understood is to have little time for people like Wolfhart Pannenberg (1968) who try to show the reasonableness of the stone being moved and so forth. Instead one says simply that it is something outside the course of nature. It is believed on faith not empirical evidence. As a general approach, however, I would suggest it is probably a good thing not to overdo the miracle claims—although that perhaps reflects the fact that, although I am a non-believer, I am a very conservative Protestant non-believer! Make John Henry Newman a saint by all means, but do it on the basis of his merits and not because of rather iffy physical cures of co-religionists.

Talk of reason and faith rather raises the question of natural theology. Where does that stand on the position I have taken? Again, I would probably say that for me the theology is paramount. I do not see that faith backed by evidence is worth that much. I am with Kierkegaard and of course more recently Karl Barth in think-ing that genuine faith requires a leap, not so much into the absurd but into the non-provable. Newman had it about right. Of the Argument from Design, he wrote: "I believe in design because I believe in God; not in a God because I see design" (Newman 1973, 97). He continued: "Design teaches me power, skill and good-ness—not sanctity, not mercy, not a future judgment, which three are of the essence of religion." Here, however, I am not offering any definitive argument against natural theology. Obviously it goes against the spirit of the position I am taking, namely keep science and religion separate unless it is necessary to bring them together. (As you will have seen, this leaves a great deal of scope for interaction of some kind or level.) Also, I would point out that every attempt to do natural theology has run into severe difficulties. The current fondness for some kind of anthropic principle—the laws of nature must be designed or the world would not function in such a way as to support intelligent life—seems no more promising than the rest of the arguments. How anyone can argue for probabilities on the evidence of one example (our world) completely mystifies me. But as I say, I am not offering any definitive argument so will leave matters at that.

One final point. Am I not putting down religion against science? I am sug-gesting that science must be given full license and only when it cannot answer questions—or refuses to answer questions—can religion be allowed to try its hand. And always looms the possibility that science might in the future move its boundaries and another place for religion is closed off forever. What kind of fair resolution is this? To which I can only reply that I am not trying to be fair but to be right. And if this is the way of things, then so be it. Although I would point out that for the

Christian the power of reason and observation is precisely what makes us beings in the image of God, and that finding out about His creation is surely part of the work, the task, that God has set us. In other words, for the believer doing science is doing God's work. Do not think of science and religion as antagonists but as complements, doing their separate tasks. Once perhaps religion did much of the heavy lifting. Now science does more and more. But as Saint Paul taught us, this is precisely what Christians should expect and welcome. "When I was a child, I spake as a child, I understood as a child, I thought as a child: but when I became a man, I put away childish things." It is not that religion is childish and science grownup activity, but that childish is to think the two at odds and grownup is to see that a proper division of labor is possible and desirable.

And now you have my resolution of the science-religion conflict, a resolution that seems so right and obvious that I am sure it must be in Plato somewhere!

Florida State University

Notes

I dedicate this paper to the memory of Jay Newman, my long-time colleague and friend at the University of Guelph in Canada. Jay was for many years a member of and faithful attendee at meetings of the American Catholic Philosophical Association.

1. The basic ideas in this paper are to be found in my book, *Science and Spirituality: Making Room for Faith in the Age of Science* (2010). As always, when you try to express your thoughts succinctly, you find yourself rethinking things and getting new ways of viewing problems. What I will do is use the book as the backup for information on which many of my claims rely, starting with more details about the present-day clash between science and religion.

2. I want to stress that I am not invoking multiverses on grounds of scientific plausibility, although there are those who would argue this. Mine is a purely theological speculation. God if He so wished could create as many universes as He wanted to, and He could keep doing so until humans appear.

3. Go in the literal sense, that is. It amazes me to think that many Americans think that unless one abides by the literal sense, whatever that might be in the light of the two creation stories, one can find no deep theological value in the early chapters of Genesis.

Bibliography

Barnes, J., ed. 1984. *The Complete Works of Aristotle.* Princeton: Princeton University Press.

Boyle, R. 1996. *A Free Enquiry into the Vulgarly Received Notion of Nature.* Edited by E. B. Davis and M. Hunter. Cambridge: Cambridge University Press.

Churchland, P. M. 1995. *The Engine of Reason, The Seat of the Soul.* Cambridge, Mass.: MIT Press.

Clark, A. 2000. *Mindware: An Introduction to the Philosophy of Cognitive Science.* New York: Oxford University Press.

Conway-Morris, S. 2003. *Life's Solution: Inevitable Humans in a Lonely Universe.* Cambridge: Cambridge University Press.

Darwin, C. 1859. *On the Origin of Species by Means of Natural Selection, or the Preservation of Favoured Races in the Struggle for Life.* London: John Murray.

Dawkins, R. 1986. *The Blind Watchmaker.* New York, N.Y.: Norton.

Descartes, R. 1964. "Discourse on Method." *Philosophical Essays*, 1–57. Indianapolis: Bobbs-Merrill.

Dijksterhuis, E. J. 1961. *The Mechanization of the World Picture.* Oxford: Oxford University Press.

Farlow, J. O., C. V. Thompson, and D. E. Rosner. 1976. "Plates of the Dinosaur Stegosaurus: Forced Convection Heat Loss Fins?" *Science* 192: 1123–1125.

Gould, S. J. 1985. *The Flamingo's Smile: Reflections in Natural History.* New York: Norton.

———. 1999. *Rocks of Ages: Science and Religion in the Fullness of Life.* New York: Ballantine.

Heidegger, M. 1959. *An Introduction to Metaphysics.* New Haven: Yale University Press.

Hesse, M. 1966. *Models and Analogies in Science.* Notre Dame: University of Notre Dame Press.

Hume, D. 1739–1940. *A Treatise of Human Nature.* Oxford : Oxford University Press.

Kant, I. 1951. *Critique of Judgement.* New York: Haffner.

Kuhn, T. 1977. *The Essential Tension: Selected Studies in Scientific Tradition and Change.* Chicago: University of Chicago Press.

Lakoff, G., and M. Johnson. 1980. *Metaphors We Live By.* Chicago : University of Chicago Press.

Leibniz, G. F. W. 1714. *Monadology and other Philosophical Essays.* New York: Bobbs-Merrill.

McGinn, C. 2000. *The Mysterious Flame: Conscious Minds In A Material World.* New York: Basic Books.

Newman, J. H. 1973. *The Letters and Diaries of John Henry Newman, XXV.* Edited by C. S. Dessain and T. Gornall. Oxford: Clarendon Press.

Pannenberg, W. 1968. *Jesus—God and Man.* London: SCM Press.

Ruse, M. 1988. *Homosexuality: A Philosophical Inquiry.* Oxford: Blackwell.

———. 2001. *Can a Darwinian Be a Christian? The Relationship between Science and Religion.* Cambridge: Cambridge University Press.

———. 2003. *Darwin and Design: Does Evolution Have a Purpose?* Cambridge, Mass.: Harvard University Press.

————. 2005. *The Evolution-Creation Struggle*. Cambridge, Mass.: Harvard University Press.

————. 2010. *Science and Spirituality: Making Room for Faith in the Age of Science*. Cambridge: Cambridge University Press.

Weinberg, S. 1977. *The First Three Minutes: A Modern View of the Origin of the Universe*. New York: Basic Books.

Darwin, Faith, and Critical Intelligence

John F. Haught

Abstract: Evolutionary biology has considerably altered our understanding of life, and it now promises to enhance our understanding of human existence by providing new insights into the meaning of intelligence, ethical aspiration and religious life. For some scientific thinkers, especially those who espouse a physicalist worldview, Darwin's science seems so impressive that it now replaces theology by providing the deepest available explanation of all manifestations of life, including human intelligence. By focusing on human intelligence this essay asks whether a theological perspective on the universe can still have an illuminating role to play alongside of biology (and other scientific perspectives) in contemporary attempts to understand human intelligence.

C harles Darwin's theory of evolution, updated by genetics, is probably more intellectually influential today than ever before. Evolutionary biology has now become foundational to much moral philosophy and cognitive science. It also comprises much of the intellectual basis of the "new atheism" of Richard Dawkins and Daniel Dennett.[1] "Evolutionary naturalism," the amalgam of Darwinian ideas and materialist metaphysics, claims that evolutionary biology provides the ultimate explanation—not just scientifically but also metaphysically—of the instincts, habits and behavioral traits of everything living, including human beings. Darwin's famous advocate, Thomas H. Huxley (1825–1895) used the expression "scientific naturalism" to remind his readers that science must never invoke supernatural explanations.[2] Today, however, scientific naturalism has become a sweeping worldview, endorsed especially by academic scientists, philosophers and an increasing number of those working in the humanities. It claims that outside of nature, which includes human beings and their cultural creations, there is literally nothing. Nature is self-originating. Neither God nor souls exist. The universe has no purpose, and no reasonable prospect exists of conscious human survival after our deaths.[3]

Evolutionary naturalism, a subspecies of scientific naturalism, has become increasingly prominent in contemporary intellectual circles lately. Its best-known defender is the evolutionist Richard Dawkins, who claims that the natural selection

© 2012, *Proceedings of the ACPA*, Vol. 85
DOI: 10.5840/acpaproc2011856

of minute chance genetic variations in the cells of living beings over an unfathomable depth of time can account fully for all living traits including those of human beings. Not only human mental faculties, but also ethical and religious aspirations can be adequately explained as either evolutionary adaptations or as byproducts of other adaptations. Evolutionary naturalists claim that biological factors *rather than* divine influence account *ultimately* for why people tend to be intelligent, moral and religious. The "Darwinian recipe" that consists of three main ingredients—genetic accidents, natural selection, and an immensity of time—provides the deepest available understanding of all organic design, diversity, instincts, behavior and other features of life.[4]

The explanatory confidence of evolutionary naturalism is captured nicely in novelist Ian McEwan's ode to evolution:

> What better creation myth? An unimaginable sweep of time, numberless generations spawning by infinitesimal steps complex living beauty out of inert matter, driven on by the blind furies of random mutation, natural selection and environmental change, with the tragedy of forms continually dying, and lately the wonder of minds emerging and with them morality, love, art, cities—and the unprecedented bonus of this story happening to be demonstrably true.[5]

Before Darwin, according to Dawkins, our ancestors' invocation of mythic creation myths and divine interventions to account for living phenomena was understandable and forgivable. But such leniency is no longer allowed. Darwin's ideas, brought up to date by genetics, can provide a purely natural account of all living phenomena. In the sphere of human life, cultural and social factors are merely secondary specifications of a purely biological infrastructure. After Darwin, Dawkins adds, we now realize that the universe in which life occurs and evolves is governed not by divine providence but by pitiless indifference.[6] Moreover, one cannot be a serious evolutionist without also being a materialist (and of course that means an atheist).

Here Dawkins shows how much he has in common with his evolutionary adversary Stephen Jay Gould, the late Harvard paleontologist. Although Gould tried to make peace with religious believers late in his life, he saw no way around a purely materialist interpretation of life.[7] Many other contemporary biologists and philosophers embrace the metaphysical materialism of Dawkins and Gould, even though they are usually not inclined to say so publicly. A materialist reading of nature, they quietly suppose, can render all evolutionary outcomes fully intelligible, at least in principle. Such a metaphysical stance obviously makes Darwin's science irreconcilable with belief in God.[8]

Is Evolutionary Naturalism Reasonable?

The main point I want to make here is that evolutionary naturalism (or, if you prefer, evolutionary materialism) is not only theologically objectionable but also logically self-contradictory. I wish to emphasize at the outset, however, that I fully accept the scientific research and information that contributes to the formation and confirmation of contemporary evolutionary theory. What I object to is the belief system I am referring to as evolutionary naturalism. This brand of metaphysics is tacitly and uncritically imported into biological discourse quite often as though it were essential to making the science of biology itself fully intelligible. I argue on the contrary that evolutionary naturalism is logically self-subversive and hence unreasonable. In the final analysis, evolutionary naturalism makes life's evolution less, rather than more, intelligible. By claiming that Darwinian science provides the ultimate explanation of human intelligence, this belief system implicitly calls into question the truth-status of its own assumptions and conclusions. Most Catholic philosophers do not need to be reminded of this self-contradiction, but the intellectual world in general remains largely uncritical of the fundamental unreasonableness of the naturalistic worldview. Here I can offer only one of many possible ways of bringing to light this unreasonableness.

I begin by calling to mind the evolutionary naturalist's typical claim that the natural history leading to the appearance of the human mind is itself *essentially* mindless. The cosmic and biological chain of events leading to life and mind, the naturalists claim, bears not the slightest trace of directionality or intentionality, even though evolutionary process has recently brought about intelligent, intentional human subjects. The Duke University philosopher Owen Flanagan, for example, has no doubt that human intelligence, even though it is a marvelous evolutionary outcome, does not require intelligence—by which he means divine intelligence—as an explanatory factor at any point in its emergence. "Evolution," he announces, "*demonstrates* how intelligence arose from totally insensate origins."[9] Dennett echoes this claim: "the designs in nature are nothing short of brilliant, but the process of design that generates them is utterly lacking in intelligence of its own."[10]

Is it reasonable, however, to posit a completely mindless process as the ultimate and adequate explanation of human cognitional life? Let me ask you the reader to respond to this question yourself. As a starting point for your reflections, I request that you examine in several steps your own cognitional activity as it is taking place right now in the act of reading and trying to understand the present essay. Here I am inviting you to undertake an exercise in self-awareness proposed by the Jesuit philosopher Bernard Lonergan.[11]

Step 1: As you have been reading what I have written so far, have you noticed that your mind has been performing three distinct cognitional acts? First, you have been attending to the words and sentences I am writing. You have had the *experience* of looking at the words and sentences on the pages you are reading. Second, you have spontaneously tried to *understand* this set of data. Third, you have wondered whether what I am writing is correct or true, or perhaps you have reflected on the question of whether your understanding of what I am writing is correct or true. Such reflection may lead, at least eventually, to a third cognitional act, that of *judgment*. It is only in the act judgment, and not in the acts of experience and understanding alone, that you formally contact *truth*.

Since you are capable not only of attending, understanding and judging, but also of acting in the world, you also at times engage in acts of *decision*, a fourth cognitional act. For simplicity's sake, however, let us focus here only on the first three cognitional acts: experience, understanding and judgment.

In undertaking this task of questioning and reflection you are becoming aware not only of the objectifiable world "out there," but also of your cognitional activity which is also part of the real world. In becoming aware of your cognitional acts you are bringing into the range of your experience a dimension of the real world to which the natural sciences and most other kinds of inquiry generally pay no attention. Indeed, by paying *close* attention right now to your own cognitional performance—which may be a completely new venture for you—you are being more empirical than ever. Attending not only to data in nature to which your mind normally directs its attention but also to the sheer givenness of your own cognitional performance is to follow what Bernard Lonergan calls "generalized empirical method."[12]

Step 2: Observe now that your mind cannot help engaging in the three distinct acts of experience, understanding and judging. If you are questioning this assertion you are demonstrating its accuracy even in the act of expressing such suspicion. You are being obedient to a set of directives, or transcendental imperatives, that constitute the motivating core of your cognitional life. These imperatives are constantly directing you to actualize your intelligence in a patterned way. The imperatives, along with their associated cognitional acts are:

(1) Be attentive!   → experience

(2) Be intelligent! → understanding

(3) Be critical!   → judgment

A fourth set (which I shall not consider here) is:

(4) Be responsible! → decision[13]

Step 3: Notice next that underlying the imperatives of your mind and their corresponding cognitional acts is an unrestricted desire to know.[14] It is such a desire that may be leading you to ask for evidence about what I am saying right now. The evidence, therefore, is immediately available.

Step 4: Let us now give a name to the whole complex of desiring, imperatives and cognitional acts that you have just brought to your attention. Call it *critical intelligence* (this is my own, not Lonergan's label). Scientific method is perhaps the clearest illustration of critical intelligence since scientists invariably experience the imperatives to be attentive, intelligent and critical—even if at times they fall short of heeding their call. Scientists, that is, begin their work in a state of wonder awakened by the imperative to be attentive (or open) to a range of data. Then they attempt to make sense of this data as it is given in sense experience or in data mediated by instruments of experience (such as microscopes or telescopes). The imperative to be intelligent leads scientists first to description and then to explanation of the data they have been observing, and they bring this understanding to expression in the form of hypotheses and theories. Finally, the imperative to be critically reflective prods scientists to keep asking whether their hypotheses or theories correspond accurately to the data of experience. For not every ingenious scientific theory is necessarily true. Only after subjecting their ideas to critical reflection—and possible refutation or revision—do scientists arrive at the point where they can make truly scientific judgments about the truth or falsity of their hypotheses and theories.[15]

What you are doing right now, however, is practicing what Lonergan calls "generalized empirical method."[16] You are looking not only at the world of things "out there" but also at the cognitional activity taking place in your inquiring subjectivity. Keep in mind that your critical intelligence is just as much part of the natural world as rocks and rivers. Human cognition is seamlessly tied into the whole universe that science has recently exposed as a nearly fourteen billion year old narrative of creativity. Your own critical intelligence is part of this universe, and so the failure to make a prominent place for it in your cosmology would be decidedly unempirical and unintelligent on your part. Unless you decide arbitrarily to exile your mind from nature or deny the existence of your critical consciousness altogether, you are obliged to make it an important ingredient in the whole range of data that go into your understanding and knowing the universe of which you are a part. By leaving your own critical intelligence out of your survey of nature and life, you end up, along with the evolutionary naturalists, not only subverting your own cognitional life but also shrinking the world you are trying to understand.

Step 5: The next, and most important, item to notice is that the activation of your critical intelligence is impossible without an implicit and deeply personal *trust* in the imperatives of your mind. Lonergan does not focus on the word "trust," as I am doing here, but his awareness of the role of trust in our cognitional performance is implicit in his citing the need for "self-affirmation" as a condition for making judgments.[17]

Perhaps after attending to what I am saying in this essay, and after trying to understand and judge whether my claims are right or wrong, you may still doubt and even attempt to refute what I am saying. In doing so, however, I hope you will agree that in the act of refutation you will still be trusting in your own mind's imperatives to be attentive, intelligent and critical. In other words, you will find that the pattern of your cognitional performance, along with the trust needed to activate it, is not revisable. I am asking that you acknowledge this invariance of cognitional structure and performance, as you reflect on the reasonableness or unreasonableness of the view of nature, life and mind that I am calling evolutionary naturalism.

Intellectual consistency should lead evolutionary naturalists to admit that if their minds are purely adaptive and ultimately explainable ontologically in terms of mindless events spread out over an immensely long time, there is no reason inherent in such an account for trusting their own minds as they make their bold claims? For example, if Owen Flanagan is correct in claiming that a cosmic and evolutionary process completely devoid of intelligence is an adequate explanation of human intellectual faculties, how can he avoid logically undermining the very confidence required to activate the thought processes that lead him to make this claim.

Evolutionary naturalists seldom if ever notice that Charles Darwin himself raised the same question I am asking here:

> With me [Darwin writes] the horrid doubt always arises whether the convictions of man's mind, which has been developed from the mind of the lower animals, are of any value or at all trustworthy. Would any one trust in the convictions of a monkey's mind, if there are any convictions in such a mind?[18]

The claim that natural selection is the ultimate explanation of the human desire to know, including the evolutionist's own longing for truth, is intellectually troubling. As regards the mind's attraction to truth, the philosopher Richard Rorty, no friend of theology, has righty remarked: "The idea that one species of organism is, unlike all the others, oriented not just toward its own increased prosperity [that is, toward "fitness"] but toward Truth, is as un-Darwinian as the idea that every human being has a built-in moral compass—a conscience that swings free of both social history and individual luck."[19]

Neither Rorty nor Darwin, however, seems to have grasped the gravity or implications of his own retorsive suspicion. Each would explicitly claim to be a lover of truth, and each would spontaneously trust his mind as it makes the claims I have just quoted. Moreover, every scientific naturalist must agree in principle that the human mind is fully embedded in the natural world. Yet, can a purely Darwinian account of life, important informationally as it may be in telling the story of mind's emergence, adequately justify the trust underlying the deployment of critical intelligence? Would not a formal acceptance of evolutionary naturalism (as distinct from evolutionary biology) logically sabotage the trust that underlies the evolutionary naturalist's own cognitional performance as it seeks to understand and make accurate judgments about the world?[20] Commenting on Sigmund Freud, Lonergan writes: "If enthusiasm for the achievement of Freud were to lead me to affirm that all thought and affirmation is just a byproduct of the libido . . . this very assertion of mine would have to be mere assertion from a suspect source."[21] He might also have written regarding purely Darwinian accounts of cognition: "If enthusiasm for the achievement of [Darwin] were to lead me to affirm that all thought and affirmation is just a byproduct of [natural selection] then . . . this very assertion of mine would be suspect."

Implications for Cosmology

I believe evolutionary naturalists fail to notice this inconsistency and their own unreasonableness because at heart they do not really believe their own minds are part of nature. A tacit dualism exempts their own intellectual performance from the mindless universe they are trying to understand. However, if we adopt Lonergan's widely empirical view of nature, a survey that is inclusive of critical intelligence, our understanding of the universe will differ considerably from that presupposed by the naturalist. Naturalists assume that critical intelligence, and for that matter subjectivity of any degree or kind, is either nonexistent or at most epiphenomenal. Consequently, an inescapable and irresolvable dissonance persists between naturalism's formal view of nature as essentially mindless on the one hand, and the enormous confidence naturalists typically place in their own intellectual performance on the other. Even though they embrace the scientific conclusion that an unbroken chain of physical causes leads from mindless nature to the recent emergence of human beings, they fail to make sense of this physical and evolutionary continuum (which, by definition, includes their own cognitional performance) in a way that avoids obvious self-contradiction.

The cosmic story cannot be told accurately, after all, if it leaves out any mention or understanding of the recent emergence in evolution of critical intelligence as I have been describing it. Evolutionary naturalism, however, fails to take seriously and consistently the ontological and physical inseparability of critical intelligence and its cosmic matrix. No doubt naturalists will reply that mind, of course, is part of nature. But what exactly do they mean by "mind" and "nature" when they make this assertion? How much have they had to abstract from actual cognitional structure and performance to fit what they call mind into what they simultaneously take to be nature's mindlessness? I believe it is safe to say that scientific naturalists in general fail to be truly empirical about the natural world. Their characteristic portraits of the universe have their point of departure in a picture of nature as a seamless continuum of allegedly mindless stuff and processes. The irony is that their exceptionally self-confident intellectual projects can find no intelligible place, and their inordinate cognitional confidence no justification, in their portrayals of an essentially lifeless and mindless universe.

Assuming nature to be fundamentally unintelligent, and intelligence merely epiphenomenal, evolutionary naturalists invariably make nature's recent secretion of critical consciousness appear magical or alchemical rather than intelligible. In effect they fall back on an inadmissible metaphysical dualism—implicitly segregating their own minds from mindless nature—even while at the same time they deny to their own intelligence any real existence, let alone trustworthiness. The richer empiricism I am advocating, on the other hand, is so sensitive to the mind's imperative to be open to the full range of experience that it keeps critical intelligence in the foreground as it looks into mind's evolutionary arrival. Exiling critical consciousness formally from their restrictive field of experiential data at the outset, naturalistic interpretations of consciousness can only meet defeat when they seek to make a place for what we all immediately experience as critical consciousness. More sober philosophers of mind admit that we do not and perhaps never will possess the conceptual tools to bridge the gap between physicalist accounts of mind on the one hand and the first person discourse of critically intelligent subjects on the other.[22]

A Theological Proposal

Is there any coherent way, therefore, of locating critical intelligence seamlessly within the evolution of the universe while at the same time justifying the trust we spontaneously place in the performance of our minds? To establish such coherence I propose that nothing less than a revolution in cosmology is essential. Such an expansive vision of the universe can emerge only from a wider empirical approach to the cosmos than the one undertaken by scientific naturalists. A sufficiently rich understanding of the universe must begin with a general empirical survey of the world, one that is inclusive of the critical intelligence that is taking the survey, while at the same time embracing the story that evolutionary biology, geology and cosmology have told us about the gradual emergence of life and mind. How, though, can we tell the story of how critical intelligence evolved out of early cosmic states where life and mind were absent and at the same time justify the spontaneous trust we place in our minds when we tell this story here and now?

I propose that even though science has an essential role to play in narrating the astrophysical, chemical and biological processes that have led to the emergence of mind, this narrative alone is neither sufficiently explanatory of critical intelligence nor supportive of the confidence we have to place in our minds if they are to function as reliable sources of understanding and truth. A richer explanatory toolbox than that provided by evolutionary naturalism is needed to avoid gaps and miraculous leaps. It is no help to our understanding of either the mind or the universe to reply that critical intelligence may be one of many unintended *byproducts* of other evolutionary adaptations. Concluding that critical intelligence is merely an evolutionary fluke can hardly explain or justify trust in the mind that makes such a claim. Positing a chain of blind efficient and material causes alone, no matter how temporally prolonged and gradual in cumulative effect, can never add up to a sufficient reason for putting the kind of confidence in their own intellectual functioning that naturalists actually do when they offer such an account.

A richer and wider empiricism, on the other hand, in obedience to the mind's first imperative (to be open and attentive to the full range of data available to us), allows us to leave nothing out of the range of data to be rendered intelligible—and this includes our own critical intelligence. In my proposal, the wide range of data we need includes the *anticipatory* character of critical intelligence as it reaches out toward an inexhaustible horizon of meaning (intelligibility) and truth (here I put aside consideration of the other transcendentals, goodness and beauty).

To account adequately for both the element of anticipation and the component of trust involved in the actual performance of critical consciousness, I believe a biblically based theological worldview is essential.[23] Rather than reducing the mind's spontaneous intention or anticipation of intelligibility and truth to a ghostly shadow hovering over a mindless universe, an appropriate theology of nature after Darwin (and Einstein) emphasizes that the intentionality and anticipation that emerge explicitly with the arrival of critical intelligence is seamlessly knitted into the fabric of the entire universe (or, as the case may be, a "multiverse"). Anticipation in the natural world apparently becomes explicitly conscious for the first time only with the emergence of critical intelligence. However, by virtue of the complicity of physical, chemical and biological processes in the cosmic process of making minds, our own anticipation—of being, meaning and truth—may be understood correctly as a generic characteristic of the whole universe rather than a "fluke" or epiphenomenon that does not belong to nature essentially. Moreover, in light of contemporary astrophysics, we may now more than ever understand the universe's spatial and temporal magnitude as inseparable from the existence of critical intelligence.

When critical intelligence emerged recently the universe became explicitly aware for the first time of the transcendental horizon toward which it had always been oriented. Historically speaking, of course, critically intelligent subjects arrived only recently in evolution, but in our human response to the transcendental horizon of being, meaning and truth, the whole universe is narratively, and indeed physically, involved. Contemporary astrophysics, cosmology, and biology allow us to interpret critical intelligence as extending its roots deep down into the physical and chemical specifics of the still emerging cosmos. Instead of interpreting the mind's cosmic prehistory as either indifferent or hostile to the fact of critical intelligence, science itself now allows us to read the whole of cosmic and evolutionary history as inseparable from the drama of the mind's emergence. Theologically speaking, I suggest, in the acts of allowing ourselves to be grasped by the infinite horizon of being, intelligibility, and truth we have a very good reason to trust, not only in the universe's intelligibility, but also in the fundamental integrity of the transcendental imperatives to be attentive, intelligent, and critical.

This ultimate environment of being, meaning, and truth, moreover, is inherently resistant to ever being fully "naturalized." It is the transcendental condition of the possibility of the emergence of mind. Furthermore, it is the metaphysical prerequisite of the ongoing creation of a universe that has always been pregnant with mind—and other outcomes such as hope and love. Without this transcendental horizon, critical intelligence could never have become actual in this or any other universe. Apart from the anticipated horizon of being, meaning, and truth, moreover, we would at present have no good reason to trust our minds.

Woodstock Theological Center, Georgetown University

Notes

1. Richard Dawkins, *The Blind Watchmaker* (New York: W. W. Norton & Co., 1986); *The God Delusion* (New York: Houghton Mifflin, 2006); Daniel Dennett, *Breaking the Spell: Religion as a Natural Phenomenon* (New York: Viking, 2006).

2. Ronald Numbers, "Science without God: Natural Laws and Christian Belief," *When Science and Christianity Meet*, ed. David C. Lindberg and Ronald Numbers (Chicago: University of Chicago Press, 2003), 266.

3. Charley Hardwick, *Events of Grace: Naturalism, Existentialism, and Theology* (Cambridge: Cambridge University Press, 1996).

4. See the above-mentioned books by Dawkins and Dennett.

5. Ian McEwan, *Saturday* (Toronto: Alfred A. Knopf), 56.

6. Richard Dawkins, *River Out of Eden* (New York: Basic Books, 19950, 133.

7. Stephen Jay Gould, *Ever Since Darwin* (New York: W. W. Norton, 1977), 12–13.

8. For example, Michael R. Rose, *Darwin's Spectre: Evolutionary Biology in the Modern World* (Princeton: Princeton University Press, 1998); William Provine, "Evolution and the Foundation of Ethics," in *Science, Technology and Social Progress*, ed. Steven L. Goldman (Bethlehem, Pa.: Lehigh University Press, 1989); E. O. Wilson, *Consilience: The Unity of Knowledge* (New York: Vintage Books, 1999); and Philip Kitcher, *Living With Darwin: Evolution, Design, and the Future of Faith* (New York: Oxford University Press, 2007).

9. Owen Flanagan, *The Problem of the Soul: Two Visions of Mind and How to Reconcile Them* (New York: Basic Books, 2002), 11 (emphasis added).

10. Daniel Dennett, "Intelligent Thought," in *The Third Culture*, ed. John Brockman (New York: Touchstone Books, 2006), 87.

11. Bernard Lonergan, "Cognitional Structure," in *Collection*, ed. F. E. Crowe, S. J. (New York: Herder and Herder, 1967), 221–239.

12. Bernard Lonergan, *Insight: A Study of Human Understanding*, 3rd. ed. (New York: Philosophical Library, 1970), 72, 243.

13. Lonergan, "Cognitional Structure," XXX.

14. Ibid.

15. Ibid., 72, 243.

16. Ibid., 328–332.

17. Ibid., 335–336.

18. Charles Darwin, "Letter to W. Graham, July 3rd, 1881," in *The Life and Letters of Charles Darwin*, ed. Francis Darwin (New York: Basic Books 1959), 285.

19. Richard Rorty, "Untruth and Consequences," *The New Republic* (July 31, 1995): 32–36. I owe this reference to an online essay entitled "Darwin, Mind and Meaning" (1996) by Alvin Plantinga: http://idwww.ucsb.edu/fscf/library/plantinga/dennett.html.

20. For elaboration on this point see my books *Is Nature Enough? Meaning and Truth in the Age of Science* (Cambridge: Cambridge University Press, 2006; and *Deeper than Darwin: The Prospect for Religion in the Age of Evolution* (Boulder, Colo: Westview Press, 2003).

21. Lonergan, *Insight*, 329.

22. Colin McGinn, *The Mysterious Flame: Conscious Minds in a Material World* (New York: Basic Books, 1999).

23. I have developed this proposal at book length in *Is Nature Enough?*

Why Thomistic Philosophy of Nature Implies (Something Like) Big-Bang Cosmology

Travis Dumsday

Abstract: I argue that two components of Thomistic philosophy of nature (specifically, hylomorphism combined with a relational ontology of space) entail a core claim of big-bang cosmology. I then consider some implications of this fact for natural theology.

1. Introduction

According to the big-bang model in cosmology, the universe as we know it today, with its myriad of distinct physical entities, took its origin from a single, incredibly high-energy physical entity which for some reason "exploded," resulting in the expansion of space and with it mass/energy.[1] What may have happened before this explosion, and even whether there was a "before" this event or whether time began with it, is a matter of some controversy. But the basic model is now standard fare in cosmology (though like any scientific model it could of course be overturned). One of the core components of this model is the idea that there was a first material entity; that is, a material substance which existed alongside no other such entities, was preceded by no other such entities,[2] and which was temporally prior to any of the subsequent entities that surround us today. I am going to argue that this core component is implied by Thomistic philosophy of nature. More specifically, I will argue that Aquinas's hylomorphism combined with his relationist theory of space implies that there must have been such an entity—at least, implies it if one looks at the question strictly from the standpoint of the philosophy of nature, prescinding from theism.[3]

The paper proceeds as follows. In the next section I briefly review a few salient aspects of both Aquinas's hylomorphism and his relationist theories of space and time. Then in section three I argue that hylomorphism, combined with relationism about space, entails that there must have been a first material object. Having concluded to that important component of the big-bang model, in section four I go on to consider whether that conclusion, combined with Aquinas's relationist theory of time, might entail what some cosmologists take to be a further component of that

© 2012, *Proceedings of the ACPA*, Vol. 85
DOI: 10.5840/acpaproc2011857

model, namely the idea that time itself has a beginning. I argue that this further conclusion does not follow. Having focused solely on philosophy of nature in the first four sections, section five is then devoted to examining these results in relation to natural theology: both the possible implications for cosmological arguments on behalf of theism, and also how plugging theism into the picture from the outset might impact the course of the argument.

A couple of provisos before beginning: first, the argument I make here could be run on a number of the major scholastic hylomorphisms, but I am going to limit my discussion to Thomistic hylomorphism. I do so not just because Aquinas's formulation is the most plausible of the versions on offer, but also because I cannot afford the space needed to show that my argument runs just as well on alternate hylomorphisms that (for instance) affirm the possibility of unformed prime matter, or a plurality of substantial forms, or a single basic type of *forma corporeitatis* (like *lux* in the hylomorphisms of Bonaventure and Grosseteste). It does in fact run just as well on these, but I will have to leave the proof of this as an exercise for the reader.[4] Second, I do *not* intend the argument to be taken as being of purely historical interest; if it works, it provides new reason to think that there was a first material object in the sense outlined above, and hence provides us an interesting a priori reason to think that a central component of big-bang cosmology is true. I expect many readers of this piece will themselves be Thomists or Thomist-sympathizers and will hardly need to be told this. For them, Aquinas's system is already a live option for contemporary philosophical reflection. But for readers who may have stumbled upon this piece armed with nothing but an interest in the philosophy of space-time or perhaps looking for further fuel to support a cosmological argument, this may not be obvious. So I will state it plainly: Thomistic hylomorphism should be seen as very much a live option in substance ontology, and it has not been lacking in contemporary defenders.[5] Similarly, relationism about space and time (and space-time) is unquestionably a live option in the recent metaphysics literature.[6] I do not have room to present a properly thorough summary or defense of these views, so for those readers who are not familiar with this material I encourage a perusal of these and other readily available sources.

2. Thomistic Hylomorphism and Relationism: A Quick and Targeted Review

Again, I cannot lay out these views in any detail, and will have to restrict myself to summarizing some central commitments that bear directly on the discussion to follow. With respect to Thomistic hylomorphism: according to Aquinas, a physical object or substance is a compound of a basic principle of potency (prime matter) and a basic principle of act (substantial form). These are really distinct but also really inseparable. In this respect hylomorphism may sound reminiscent of the substratum / attribute theory of contemporary substance ontology. However, a substantial form is not an attribute or property; indeed, it is not in the category of "accident" at all. Moreover, the substantial form has a certain ontological priority over prime matter in a way that the attributes do not have over the substratum. The substantial form in a sense actualizes the prime matter; the form is that by which the prime matter, and indeed the compound substance as a whole, exists at all. In actualizing prime matter the substantial form also gives rise (instantaneously, not in a temporal process) to the intrinsic properties[7] we associate with a natural kind of object. This includes both its dispositional properties (i.e., its causal powers) and its categorical properties (i.e., its geometrical / structural properties, like shape and size). It therefore constitutes the origin point and principle of unity of an object's varied intrinsic traits, explaining why it has the properties it does and how those properties are unified as properties of one coherent substance. Since the substantial form is that which gives rise to properties, it is not itself characterizable in property-terms. Consequently it is simple, inaccessible to the senses, and cognizable only by an operation of the intellect.[8]

With respect to a relationist ontology of space: space is generally taken by Thomists to supervene on objects with categorical properties, and on the resultant distance relations between those objects.[9] Indeed, one could more simply say that space supervenes on categorical properties and their relations; for present purposes nothing hangs on the different formulation. At any rate, space is not a reality "over and above," or independent of, these objects and their relations. As Clarke (*The One and the Many*, 176) puts it, "physical bodies do have real extension within themselves [and] these bodies, in relation to each other, are really distant from each other, and take time to move toward and away from each other. What is real, then, is the set of relations of bodies to each other as regards distance and motion. And all that needs to be said about 'space' can be said in terms of these relations of bodies towards each other. There is no need at all to speak of these bodies as located 'in' something, or moving 'through' something, or out 'into' something which we call space." Space, and spatial location, therefore supervene on the categorical properties of objects and on the resultant relations between those objects, which properties in turn arise from the substantial forms of the objects to which those properties belong.

Finally, with respect to the relationist ontology of time: time is the measure of motion. That is, time supervenes on change and the potential measurement of that change. As with space, it is not a substance or accident that exists "over and above" or independently from objects. Hence, in a changeless universe, time would not exist. Owens (*An Elementary Christian Metaphysics*, 207) describes the Thomistic view of time as follows: "The unit of time, like any other accepted unit of measure, is conventional. . . . As a measure in this way, time exists extrinsically to the sensible thing that it measures. 'When any sensible thing exists,' therefore, is a category taken from something extrinsic. It follows upon the relations of before and after in the unilinear spread of sensible existence. . . . Since time is the measure of motion, it does not apply to immobile or purely spiritual natures, any more than does place." Clarke (op. cit., 162) concurs, writing that time "implies real successive change in some real being or beings. Without real succession of some kind there is simply no basis for distinguishing 'before' and 'after,' which are essential ingredients of all our time language. Time is opposed in its very meaning . . . to simultaneous, motionless presence. . . . It does not make sense to treat it, as some have tried to do, as though time were some entity in its own right prior to change."

Obviously all three of these ideas are highly contentious, but as noted they all have advocates in the recent literature, and they will be assumed in what follows.

3. Thomistic Hylomorphism and a First Material Substance

Since on a Thomistic philosophy of nature all the categorical properties of physical objects arise from their constituent substantial forms, and space supervenes specifically on objects with categorical properties and on the relations between those objects, any complete explanation of the existence and nature of space must make reference ultimately to substantial form. Having recognized this point we can now conduct a thought experiment that will draw out a potential worry for this picture.

Imagine a set of physical objects co-existing within a certain proximity to each another. On a Thomistic hylomorphism, each of these objects is a compound of substantial form and prime matter, with the substantial form actualizing the prime matter and thereby constantly giving rise to the object's assorted dispositional and categorical properties. So again, the categorical properties are ontologically posterior to, thoroughly dependent upon, the substantial form. Now, according to Aquinas two physical objects cannot coexist at the same place at the same time. This means that a necessary condition for the existence of these physical objects is that they not be located at the same place as any of their fellows. But what determines their location? On Aquinas's relationist theory of space, spatial location depends upon categorical properties and their relations. Spatial location supervenes on categorical properties, categorical properties are ontologically posterior to substantial forms, yet the successful instantiation of the substantial forms depends on their having certain determinate spatial locations—namely, locations that differ from those of their fellow objects. Now, if *every* substantial form presupposed a categorical property in this way, the priority relation between substantial form and categorical properties supposed in Thomistic hylomorphism would be compromised. The implication would be either that, taking the whole set of material objects into account, categorical properties are in fact prior to substantial forms, or that there is a vicious circularity in dependence relations (every substantial form which gives rise to a categorical property presupposes a specified spatial location which does not overlap that of a fellow material object, which locations are determined by categorical properties and their relations, which are in turn rooted in substantial forms, which are in turn reliant on prior categorical properties . . .). In order for the substantial form-which-gives-rise-to-categorical-properties to be instantiated, it seems the resultant object must already have a determinate spatial location, i.e., that it must already have a categorical property, that the categorical property has priority over the substantial form in some sense. Again though, this is only a real worry if the point applies to *every* object in the group. If there were at least one object for which the successful instantiation of its substantial form in no way relied on ontologically prior facts about location, then on the whole the priority relation between substantial form and categorical property could be preserved, for it would be clear that, in principle, the categorical property depends on the substantial form and not vice versa.

To make sure the argument is clear, let's break it down:

1. Aquinas affirms two independently plausible theories: hylomorphism and a relational theory of space.

2. On hylomorphism, categorical properties arise from and are therefore ontologically posterior to substantial forms.

3. On a relational theory of space, spatial locations supervene on the categorical properties of objects and their interrelations.

4. Two material objects (hence two substantial forms) cannot exist at the same place at the same time.

5. If two material objects (hence two substantial forms) cannot exist at the same place at the same time, then the successful instantiation of a substantial form must somehow take into account facts about the locations of other material objects (provided there are other material objects).

6. Therefore the successful instantiation of a substantial form must somehow take into account facts about the spatial locations of other material objects (provided there are other material objects).

7. If the successful instantiation of a substantial form must take into account facts about the spatial locations of other material objects (provided there are other material objects), and spatial locations supervene on the categorical properties of objects and their interrelations, then the successful instantiation of a substantial form is dependent on ontologically prior (not necessarily temporally prior) categorical properties.

8. The successful instantiation of a substantial form must take into account facts about the locations of other material objects (provided there are other material objects), and the locations of material objects supervene on the categorical properties of those objects and their interrelations.

9. Therefore the successful instantiation of a substantial form is dependent on ontologically prior (not necessarily temporally prior) categorical properties.

10. But this contradicts premise two, for now categorical properties are ontologically prior to substantial forms. So it seems Aquinas must give up hylomorphism or a relational theory of space or both.

Thomists will of course not want to give up either view, so we must look for a way around the difficulty. To that end, let's imagine a different state of affairs: one material object, existing alone with no fellow objects. Will it run into any comparable difficulty? Certainly not. I have already hinted at this with the "provided there are other material objects" provisos above. For if there is only one material object, then obviously its substantial form can give rise to its categorical properties without itself being in any way dependent upon the categorical properties of other objects. If there is only one material object, the successful instantiation of its substantial form can come about without any reference to the categorical properties of other entities. So, as long as there is a first material object (in the sense of an object which initially coexists with no others, is preceded by no others,[10] and which is temporally prior to any others that may subsequently come into being), then the desired priority relation between substantial form and categorical properties is preserved and Aquinas's hylomorphism remains consistent with his relationist ontology of space. For there remains at least one material object which does not in any way rely on ontologically prior categorical properties. And the dependence of any other, subsequently created objects on these properties will tie back in a non-circular fashion to the first material object and its underlying substantial form. That is, any subsequent objects will have to be created in relation to the location of the first object, but that first object has its location founded on the categorical properties dependent on its substantial form, which substantial form is not in turn dependent on any prior categorical properties for its successful instantiation. Looked at from the perspective of the physical system as a whole, substantial form retains priority over categorical properties, since there is a first object whose form is in no way dependent on ontologically prior categorical properties.[11]

The upshot: granting a relationist ontology of space, and Thomistic hylomorphism, we have new reason to think that a core component of big-bang cosmology is true, namely that there was a first material object. Could the argument be extended from a first material object to a first moment in time?

4. Thomistic Hylomorphism and First Moment?

To affirm a first material object is not automatically to affirm a first moment, even on a relationist view of time. For one might think that that first object had no beginning; that no other object preceded it, but that the object has been sitting there forever, its substantial form constantly entailing its intrinsic properties in an instantaneous manner implying no temporal process and hence no change. On a relationist view of space and time, this seems a possible scenario. And in fact Aquinas allows for the possibility of a material universe created and conserved by God without beginning and in which no motions take place.[12] Such would be a literally timeless world, because a world devoid of change. Hence also a world in which time, being unreal, does not have a beginning.

So Thomistic hylomorphism does not strictly entail that time has a beginning. However, even if it does not entail this for every possible world, might it not entail this conclusion for our world, one in which time exists? As we have seen, there must have been a first material object. Either that first material object itself had a beginning, or it did not. If it did, then time began with it (given a relationist view of time). If it did not, if instead the first object was beginningless, then one of two scenarios would obtain with respect to that object:

(1) On one scenario, the one just considered above, the first object is wholly static. If the first and beginningless object of our world had been like that, then

clearly time must have had a beginning, for our world is one of multiple material objects and continual change. Something new must have happened at some point, or else we would not be in our present state of affairs. And with that first change came the advent of time. Hence time has a beginning.

(2) On another scenario, the first object is once again beginningless, but rather than being static it is dynamic. That is, it is involved in some sort of ongoing process on which time supervenes. One candidate for such a process would just be local motion: something like a lone photon accelerating continually and eternally through space. Another option might be some sort of internal temporal processes going on continually within the object.

Are either of these scenarios possible? It is difficult to say, and a proper evaluation would require more space than I can devote to the question here. But suffice it to say that I see nothing in Thomistic hylomorphism that would rule out this second scenario. In consequence I see no reason to think that Aquinas is committed to holding that time must have a beginning. And this is hardly a surprising result: it is well-known that he critiques a number of traditional arguments for backwards temporal finitude, including some that are still used in discussions of the kalam cosmological argument.[13] Moreover, according to him the fact that the physical universe had a beginning is an article of faith, one which right reason cannot contradict but also cannot prove.[14]

So far we have been working solely from within the confines of philosophy of nature. I would like to conclude by looking briefly at how some of this material plays out in relation to natural theology.

5. Bringing Theism into Play

An argument that concludes to a first material object is not as congenial to the construction of a cosmological argument for theism as an argument concluding that the universe itself had a beginning in time. Still, it may be of some value. Even if one conceives of that first material object as beginningless (whether static or dynamic), there is still a need to explain the radical change which took place in the coming-to-be of objects distinct from that first material object. The big-bang model takes those subsequent objects to be derived from that first object, to *be* that first object in spread-out-exploded form. But if that first object is beginningless, the obvious question is: what accounts for the shift from eternally-not-exploding to exploding? If all the ingredients were there, through an infinite past, what accounts for the shift? One way to get around this question is to turn to a certain variety of oscillation model in which our big-bang was just one of an infinite series of big-bangs. However, as we have seen, from the perspective of hylomorphism such an oscillation model is problematic. Consequently, there is reason to think that if that first material object was beginningless, an external cause would still be needed to account adequately for subsequent cosmic history. This is a modest point in favor of theism (or at least some form of metaphysical non-naturalism involving non-physical causal agency), but it is still worth making.

Another way in which theism is relevant to the preceding discussion has to do with the internal problem I raised for Thomistic philosophy of nature: namely, it likely ceases to be a problem if one situates that philosophy within Aquinas's broader theistic system. Prescinding from that system, one must rely on the notion of a first material object to get around the apparently viciously circular dependence relations between substantial forms and categorical properties. But if one can make reference to an intelligent designer who plans out the locations of objects, then the apparent dependence of substantial forms on categorical properties for successful instantiation really becomes a dependence on God's plan of creation / conservation. And God can certainly decide to create objects such that no one of them is created at the same time and place as another. God's design breaks the circle of co-dependence, as it were. This is of some significance, for if (1) you happen to think that Thomistic hylomorphism and a relationist theory of space are both independently plausible, and (2) that the worry I have raised for the compatibility of these two views is a genuine problem, and (3) you also think that my posit-a-first-object reply is in some way faulty (certainly it is open to a number of objections I have not had the space to consider here),[15] and (4) you fail to see another way out of the problem within the confines of philosophy of nature, then (5) you have a new (if convoluted) reason to affirm theism.

So, to recap this final section: on the one hand, if Thomistic hylomorphism and a relationist theory of space are both plausible, and I've identified and *solved* a potential problem for these views, then we have a new reason to think that there was a literally first material object. As we have seen, this could be taken to lend some mild support for a certain familiar sort of cosmological argument for theism (or at least for metaphysical non-naturalism). If on the other hand Thomistic hylomorphism and a relationist theory of space are both plausible and I've identified and *failed* to solve a potential problem for these views, and if no other solution within the philosophy of nature presents itself, then we have a new form of cosmological argument for theism. Either way, this is an interesting result for natural theology.[16]

Philosophy & Religious Studies, Livingstone College

Notes

1. Consider for instance the following description: "The entire universe, the sum of all substance . . . began as an impossibly small, impossibly dense, impossibly hot speck in the midst of nothing. Like a fertilized egg, this self-contained germ of a universe carried within itself everything that was yet to come, either actual or latent. . . . The universe must have started out as a very small, very compressed, and very hot concentration of energy." Michael Munowitz, *Knowing: The Nature of Physical Law* (Oxford: Oxford University Press, 2005), 293.

2. This is actually a controversial aspect of some but not all models of the big-bang; oscillation models that posit a series of big-bangs might not share this component, unless

they take the oscillations to be finite in number. My argument, if successful, will end up constituting an objection to oscillation models that posit an infinite number of big-bangs.

3. Obviously one can question whether it would really be possible to divorce Thomistic philosophy of nature from wider metaphysics in general or from natural theology in particular; I suspect not, given its commitments to inherent teleology. All I am supposing is that one can at least provisionally consider a portion of his philosophy of nature apart from theism, which seems doable. (Indeed, it seems doable even if there are ways in which one can derive theism directly from hylomorphism, as Norris Clarke suggests in *The One and the Many: An Elementary Thomistic Metaphysics* [Notre Dame: University of Notre Dame Press, 2001], 183–184.)

4. The argument would not run on the hylomorphisms of Scotus and Ockham, since, unlike Aquinas and many others, they affirm the metaphysical possibility of two numerically distinct material objects existing at the same place and time. They also affirm the idea that a substantial form of a material object could be instantiated without entailing any quantitative extension on the part of the object. As we shall see, these affirmations would derail the initial argument.

5. See for instance Norris Clarke, *The One and the Many*; Lawrence Dewan, *Form and Being: Studies in Thomistic Metaphysics* (Washington, D.C.: Catholic University of America Press, 2006); Leo Elders, *The Philosophy of Nature of St. Thomas Aquinas: Nature, the Universe, Man* (Frankfurt: Peter Lang, 1997); Terence Nichols, "Aquinas's Concept of Substantial Form and Modern Science," *International Philosophical Quarterly* 36 (1996): 303–318; David Oderberg, *Real Essentialism* (London: Routledge, 2007); Joseph Owens, *An Elementary Christian Metaphysics* (Houston: Center for Thomistic Studies, 1985); and William Wallace, *The Modeling of Nature: Philosophy of Science and Philosophy of Nature in Synthesis* (Washington, D.C.: Catholic University of America Press, 1996).

6. See for instance Gordon Belot, "Rehabilitating Relationalism," *International Studies in the Philosophy of Science* 13 (1999): 35–52; D. Dieks, "Space-Time Relationism in Newtonian and Relativistic Physics," *International Studies in the Philosophy of Science* 15 (2001): 5–17, and "Space and Time in Particle and Field Physics," *Studies in History and Philosophy of Modern Physics* 32 (2001): 217–241; Graeme Forbes, "Places as Possibilities of Location," *Noûs* 21 (1987): 295–318; Nick Huggett, "The Regularity Account of Relational Spacetime," *Mind* 115 (2006): 41–73; Brent Mundy, "On Quantitative Relationist Theories," *Philosophy of Science* 56 (1989): 582–600; Henrik Zinkernagel, "Did Time Have a Beginning?" *International Studies in the Philosophy of Science* 22 (2008): 237–258.

7. I here use "properties" to indicate necessary accidents, or "propria."

8. Again, I am going through this very quickly; for detailed expositions see again the sources cited in note 5, and for Aquinas's own summaries see especially the opuscula *De Ente et Essentia* and *De Principiis Naturae*.

9. Aquinas himself had little to say on what we would think of as space, focusing instead on the Aristotelian conception of "place," i.e., the surface of a containing body. With a bit of creative license, later Thomists have adapted his original ideas into a Thomistic theory of space. I take it to be a fitting adaptation, reflective of Aquinas's own thought, though this could be questioned.

10. If the object had been preceded by a group of coexisting objects which then went out of existence (or were somehow incorporated into the object, as on oscillation models of the big-bang), leaving it alone, then its substantial form would be such as to have been

previously dependent on the categorical properties of other objects for its successful instantiation. That would still grant ontological priority to categorical properties over and against substantial form. So the first material object must have been preceded by no others.

11. It is worth noting that there is another, distinct problem of ontological priority between substantial forms and categorical properties, one I will not discuss here. It runs like this: Aquinas holds that only individuals really exist—universals exist *qua* universals only in the mind. He also holds that the substantial forms of material objects are individuated by their signate matter, matter as determined by quantitative properties like extension. (Or, on the terminology used here, matter as determined by categorical properties.) So material substances rely on quantitative accidents for individuation, hence also existence, and yet the category of "substance" is supposed to be ontologically prior to the category of "accident." Scotus takes Aquinas to task for this seeming conflict, and later Thomists have sought to address it. See for instance the treatment by Joseph Bobik in his "St. Thomas on the Individuation of Bodily Substances," in *Readings in the Philosophy of Nature*, Henry Koren (Maryland: The Newman Press, 1961), 327–340. For a very different treatment of this issue see David Oderberg's "Hylomorphism and Individuation," in *Mind, Metaphysics and Value in the Thomistic and Analytical Traditions*, ed. John Haldane (Notre Dame: University of Notre Dame Press, 2002), 125–142.

12. This point relies on the idea that even though all physical things are changeable by nature, it is not absolutely necessary that they actually undergo changes; God could preserve them in a static state. I do not know of anywhere that Aquinas explicitly affirms this of bodily change in general, but he does affirm it of bodily corruption (see the *Summa Theologica*, III (suppl.), q. 82, art. 1; *Summa Contra Gentiles*, bk. 4, ch. 97; *Sentences*, bk. 1, dist. 8, q. 3, art.2), and I see no reason why the conclusion could not be extended.

13. See for instance the *Summa Contra Gentiles*, bk. 2, ch. 38.

14. See for instance the *Summa Theologica*, Ia, q. 46, art. 1 and art. 2; *De Potentia Dei*, q. 3, art. 13 and art. 14; and the opusculum *De Aeternitate Mundi*.

15. For instance, Thomas McLaughlin suggests an alternative way out of the problem for a Thomist: maintain that the universe contains not a *temporally* first body, but instead a body that is primary in the sense that it functions to determine the locations of all other bodies. He further suggests that the outermost celestial sphere plays something like this role for Aquinas, as laid out in the *Commentary on the Physics*, book IV. However, I don't think this alternative quite works, for it appears as if the successful instantiation of the primary body's substantial form would then be dependent not on a categorical property, but on a dispositional property (namely the universal locator power, which guarantees that the primary body is not located at the same time and place as any of the subordinate bodies). Either way the priority relation demanded by Thomistic hylomorphism, the priority relation between a substantial form and its propria, is overturned.

16. I would like to express my sincere thanks to Marilyn McCord Adams, Michael Krom, and Thomas McLaughlin for their many helpful comments on an earlier draft.

St. Thomas Aquinas on Intelligent Design

Robert C. Koons and Logan Paul Gage

Abstract: Recently, the Intelligent Design (ID) movement has challenged the claim of many in the scientific establishment that nature gives no empirical signs of having been deliberately designed. In particular, ID arguments in biology dispute the notion that neo-Darwinian evolution is the only viable scientific explanation of the origin of biological novelty, arguing that there are telltale signs of the activity of intelligence which can be recognized and studied empirically. In recent years, a number of Catholic philosophers, theologians, and scientists have expressed opposition to ID. Some of these critics claim that there is a conflict between the philosophy of St. Thomas Aquinas and that of the ID movement, and even an affinity between Aquinas's ideas and theistic Darwinism. We consider six such criticisms and find each wanting.

T he Intelligent Design (ID) movement—which includes figures such as Phillip E. Johnson, William A. Dembski, and Michael Behe—has challenged the claim of many in the scientific establishment that nature gives no empirical signs of having been deliberately designed. In particular, ID arguments in biology (on which this paper will focus) dispute the notion that neo-Darwinian evolution is the only viable scientific explanation of the origin of biological novelty.[1] Defenders of ID argue that there are telltale signs of the activity of intelligence that can be recognized and studied empirically, such as the "specified complexity" of DNA or the "irreducible complexity" of micro-biological systems. In recent years, a number of Catholic intellectuals (philosophers, theologians, and scientists) have joined with philosophical naturalists in attacking the scientific *bona fides* of ID. Some of these Catholic critics have claimed that there is a conflict between the philosophy of St. Thomas Aquinas and that of the ID movement, and even an affinity between Aquinas's ideas and theistic Darwinism.

These critics include:

Edward T. Oakes, S.J., a theologian at University of St. Mary of the Lake;

Edward Feser, a philosopher at Pasadena City College;

Francis J. Beckwith, a philosopher at Baylor University;

© 2012, *Proceedings of the ACPA*, Vol. 85
DOI: 10.5840/acpaproc2011858

Stephen M. Barr, a physicist at the University of Delaware;

and Michael W. Tkacz, a philosopher at Gonzaga University.

The critics have offered six major objections to ID from a (purportedly) Thomistic perspective.[2]

1. ID has a materialistic, mechanistic or modernist conception of life/science and consequently mis-describes God's act of creation by using the model of a human artisan.

2. ID fails to take into account the pervasive immanence of God's activity in creation and so wrongly argues for discrete interventions. Aquinas requires no such interventions and recognizes God's use of secondary causation.

3. Aquinas's design argument is superior to that of ID, because he appeals only to the regularity of nature. Complexity is, and should be irrelevant, contrary to the thrust of the ID movement.

4. While ID focuses on probabilities and inferences to the best explanation, Thomists have no need of such devices. The arguments of Aquinas establish their conclusions with deductive certainty. Besides, end-directed function without an intelligent cause is not just improbable, as ID theorists suppose, but metaphysically impossible.

5. Dembski's three-part filter (necessity, chance, or design) is flawed, since God can use both necessity and chance in creating.

6. Design and teleology belong to *a priori* metaphysics, not to empirical science.

We'll take these criticisms up one at a time.

1. Is ID "Materialistic," "Mechanistic" or "Modernist"?

Oftentimes, the critics are unclear as to what they mean by this charge. There are several possibilities. The charge of mechanism might mean that ID proponents accept the modern rejection of formal and final causation in favor of efficient and material analyses. First, note that this criticism is *certainly* true of Darwinian theory, which seeks to explain the diversification of life via solely material processes of mutation and differential reproduction. Yet, one rarely sees the critics' ire directed toward Darwinism. Second, given that ID seeks signs of intelligent causation/agency, it is not at all apparent that this criticism hits the mark. Take Stephen C. Meyer's argument for intelligent design (Meyer 2009). His argument, inspired by Polanyi (1967), focuses on the formal properties of DNA which go beyond the mere physical arrangement of molecules. This semantic content points beyond itself to the only currently known cause of semantic content: minds. Meyer's focus, unlike that of the Darwinians, is thinking scientifically about the properties of life beyond those of physics and chemistry. Meyer may not be doing Thomistic philosophy, but if his argument holds, it may well open the door to renewed thinking about formal and final causation—even within the sciences.

By this charge, however, some critics seem to have reductionism in mind. But in the debate over the origin of the informational content of DNA, clearly, the Darwinians are the reductionists. In contrast to ID proponents, Darwinians, by and large, rarely consider (immaterial) information content as a separate entity to be studied scientifically and philosophically. They are focused on bottom-up causation and have reduced life to physics and chemistry alone. The centrality of information to the ID paradigm is an important link to the Aristotelian and Thomistic tradition. The very word points back to the centrality of the concept of form in Aristotle's system and to its irreducibility to matter.

Furthermore, ID proponents have been a lonely voice decrying the reductionistic approach to life. ID proponents argue that life is not matter only but also needs immaterial in*form*ation. This information exists both inside and outside of the DNA (Meyer 2009, 473–477; Sternberg forthcoming). Organismal parts are integrated into coordinated systems in a top-down fashion where multiple parts must be present for function and survival (Behe 1996; 2007). And whereas Darwinians often reduce life not merely to DNA, but to only coding DNA, ID proponents argue that organismal structures are designed with a purpose. The Darwinian myth of so-called "Junk DNA" is just that—a myth (Wells 2011, 89–96).

Some critics seem upset that Michael Behe would refer to some micro-biological systems as being composed of "molecular machines" (Behe 1996). But these criticisms fail to recognize that St. Thomas himself often used analogies between living things and man-made artifacts. In fact, for Thomas, "all creatures are related to God as art products are to an artist, as is clear from the foregoing. Consequently, the whole of nature is like an artifact of the divine artistic mind" (*SCG* 3.100).[3] Behe and others in the ID movement—unlike their Darwinian counter-parts (e.g., Dawkins 2006)—have not forgotten that living creatures are much more than machines or human artifacts.

By arguing that (at least) some features of the universe are best explained by intelligent rather than mere material and efficient causes, ID proponents are reintroducing teleology into the study of nature rather than accepting the anti-Thomistic, Baconian partition of academic disciplines.[4] ID proponents claim to be doing science under a broad definition of science as the systematic study of nature via careful observation.[5] They do this not, as some Thomists fear, because they have conceded that all knowledge is ultimately empirical knowledge, but because nineteenth-century science drove teleology out of nature more by definition than by observation.[6] To the question of whether there are empirical markers of design in nature, ID proponents say yes, and Darwinists say no. To classify two projects with different answers to the same question as different disciplines is unwarranted, and, in our scientist culture, it puts ID at an unnecessary rhetorical disadvantage. That said, ID proponents have never disowned philosophical knowledge. ID proponents are not afraid to be classified as doing philosophy, so long as other equivalent theories are also so categorized.[7]

The critics fail to distinguish the essence of the ID movement from various accidents of argumentation on its behalf. Prudent advocates take into account the metaphysical assumptions of their audience. Most contemporary scientists are not metaphysical Aristotelians. So, it makes sense, *arguendo*, not to challenge every aspect of modern scientific thinking at once.

Often, the critics seriously misrepresent the actual position of key ID proponents, especially William Dembski, on this point. Dembski explicitly insists on the complementarity of physical and intelligent causes, which he describes as two modes of explanation that are "distinct without prejudicing each other" (Dembski 1999, 90). Dembski himself criticizes the view of American theologian B. B. Warfield on the grounds that Warfield adopts a "virtually mechanistic account of nature" with "occasional supernatural intervention," which Dembski describes as a "muddle" and "exactly the worst of both worlds" (ibid.). In contrast, Dembski endorses the view of Charles Hodge, who talked of physical and intelligent causation as "acting in tandem" (Dembski 1999, 87–88). Dembski insists that intelligent agency does not violate natural law, while not being reducible to it (Dembski 1999, 89).

Even if the critics were right about Dembski's allegiance to a modern and un-Thomistic conception of the physical world, this would be far from sufficient to prove that ID is essentially anti-Thomistic. The ID movement is, metaphysically speaking, a big tent. What unifies the members of the movement are commitments to certain relatively narrow scientific questions, especially: are non-intelligent mechanisms (including the Darwinian mechanism) capable of explaining the sort of functionality we find in the biological order? This question is every bit as legitimate from the perspective of Thomism as it is from the perspective of mechanism. Indeed, it is more legitimate for Thomists, since Thomists are already committed to the reality of irreducible, intelligent agency.

2. Is Divine Agency Exclusively Immanent?

Thomists rightly call attention to the intrinsic or immanent teleology evident in living things. However, this focus leaves some Thomists with an Aristotelian blindspot. Given the temporality of the world (i.e., its finite past), creation—including its irreducible teleology—has an *extrinsic* source for Aquinas. It's true that, had God created an eternal, beginningless universe, creation would have involved no temporal intervention (Aquinas 1997, 43–44). However, we know, both from revelation and (now) from empirical evidence, that the universe is not infinitely old, but had its origin in time. Such origins in time require direct divine action.

Aquinas shows no inclination to avoid miraculous creation. He does not share the aversion of Enlightenment thinkers like Spinoza to interruptions or discontinuities in the fabric of nature due to direct divine agency. For example, Aquinas believed that Adam was miraculously created from the "slime of the earth," and that Eve was miraculously formed from his rib (*ST* 1.92.4).

Yet, the critics often recoil at the idea of God "intervening" in nature. Some seem to think that this implies that God is going against nature—or worse, that God did not get things right the first time, and so he has to wind his clock back up.[8] In this vein, Michael W. Tkacz wonders if God must poke his finger in the pre-biotic soup—as though he were an intruder upon foreign territory, rather than its rightful ruler (Tkacz 2007, 275). But according to Aquinas, miracles are *beyond*, but not *contrary to*, nature:

> Since God is prime agent, all things inferior to Him are as His instruments. But instruments are made to serve the end of the prime agent, according as they are moved by Him: therefore it is <u>not contrary to, but very much in accordance with</u>, the nature of the instrument, for it to be moved by the prime agent. Neither is it contrary to nature for created things to be moved in any way whatsoever [*qualitercunque*] by God: for they were made to serve Him. (*SCG* 3.100)

Fr. Oakes similarly complains that ID makes God into a "Celestial Cell Constructor" or a "Divine *Bauplan* Architect" (Oakes 2001b, 52). In great contrast to St. Thomas, we are told, God does not intervene in the natural order to manage his creation as though he were "the traffic cop of cellular evolution" (Oakes 2001a, 10). "The idea that God swooshed down from heaven 3.5 billion years ago to toggle some organic-soup chemicals into self-replicating molecules and thereafter, as occasion warranted, had to intervene to jump-start new species is, quite literally, incredible." It is offensive, he thinks, to believe that God "intervenes *every now and again*" (Oakes 2001a, 11). Thinking that God intervenes "directly," we are told, has "grotesque" "theological implications." (Oakes 2001a, 8).

But, *pace* the critics, for Thomas—someone who knew a thing or two about orthodox theology—lack of "intervention" was no virtue of an account of divine creation. More than this, according to Thomas, God sometimes purposely acts contrary to the regular, divinely ordained workings of nature so as to show that he is the Almighty, that he is not constrained by necessity, but stands above the created order. Notice that this necessarily involves our observation of God's "intervention," or what Del Ratzsch calls "counterflow" in nature (Ratzsch 2001, 4–6, 41–43). Thomas writes:

> So, if by means of a created power it can happen that the natural order is changed from what is usually so to what occurs rarely—without any change of divine providence—then it is more certain that <u>divine power can sometimes produce an effect, without prejudice to its providence, apart from the order implanted in natural things by God. In fact, He does this at times to manifest His power</u>. For it can be manifested in no better way, that the whole of nature is subject to the divine will, than by the fact that <u>sometimes He does something outside the order of nature</u>. Indeed, this makes it evident that the order of things has proceeded from Him, not by natural necessity, but by free will. (*SCG* 3.99; see also *SCG* 2.3)

In addition, Aquinas's commitment to essentialism rules out most meanings of "evolution." According to Aquinas, the semen of one species lacks the natural power to produce a plant or animal of another species. So, if a new species appears, it must come "immediately from God" (*ST* 1.65.4). Mere chance lacks the power to jump the gulf from one form to another.

> But in the first production of corporeal creatures no transmutation from potentiality to act can have taken place, and accordingly, the corporeal forms that bodies had when first produced came immediately from God, whose bidding alone matter obeys, as its own proper cause. To signify this, Moses prefaces each work with the words, "God said, Let this thing be," or "that." (*ST* 1.65.4)

As one can see, the critics' focus on God's use of secondary causes—or as one critic revealingly puts it, "the autonomy of nature" (Tkacz 2007, 279)—exaggerates Thomas's view of the role of secondary causes regarding the origin of species. True enough, Thomas (1) rejected occasionalism, holding that creatures are true causes of their effects, and (2) believed that God created living things to operate according to the nature he gave them. However, the idea that "God's action in the world is exhausted by creation and conservation" was, according to Freddoso, "regarded as too weak by almost all medieval Aristotelians" (Freddoso 1988, 77). For Thomas and others, God must also be a concurrent cause of every action. In this sense, it is misleading for the critics to speak of secondary causes as though this means nature is just "doing its own thing." Rather, concurrence entails divine action at every level.[9]

What is more, Thomas specifically considers and rejects the notion that humanity was created via secondary causation: "The first formation of the human body could not be by the instrumentality of any created power, but was immediately from God" (*ST* 1.91.2). Thomas believes God must be directly involved in the creation of the first human form. He likens this involvement to direct miraculous activities like raising the dead to life or restoring sight to the blind. He thinks "the human soul is 'breathed into' the materials of earth" (McMullin 1985, 18). Aquinas was aware that the Biblical text may indicate some secondary causes in life's development when it speaks of what the earth brought forth. But for Thomas, one thing is certain: as regards the human soul, "God had to intervene in a more radical way" (McMullin 1985, 19).

Moreover, this exaggerated focus on secondary causation is also seen in the utter absence of Thomas's doctrine of exemplar causation—a crucial part of Thomistic metaphysics—in the critics' writings.[10] Given that creatures are a combination of form and matter, the crucial question as regards the origin of species is where form comes from. Darwin, denying Aristotelian essentialism, saw organisms' traits as accidental properties of living things that change with the winds of time (Darwin 1993, 78–79; Wiker 2002, 218).[11] Not so St. Thomas.

An exemplar cause is a type of formal cause—a sort of blueprint; the idea according to which something is organized.[12] For Thomas, these ideas exist *separately* from the things they cause. For instance, if a boy is going to build a soap-box derby car, the idea in his mind is separate from the form of the car; yet the car's form expresses the idea, or exemplar cause, in the boy's mind. Herein lies the important point: for Thomas, a creature's form comes from a similar form *in the divine intellect*. In other words, the cause of each species' form is *extrinsic*. In fact, writes Thomas, "God is the first exemplar cause of all things" (*ST* 1.44.3). Creatures do possess the causal powers proper to the nature God granted them, but creatures most certainly do *not* possess the power to create the form of their (or any other) species.

For instance, frog parents have the proper ability to generate tadpoles. They are able to bring out the natural form that is present in the potentiality of matter. However, the frog parents cannot create the form *frog*. After all, Thomas reasons, if frog parents could create the form *frog*, they would be the creators of their own form, and this is clearly a contradiction. Natural things can *generate* forms of the same species, but they cannot *create* the form of a species in general.

More than this, while the critics find intervention unseemly, Thomas specifically considers the idea that God may continue his creative activity with creatures even after he has given them their form—i.e., intervene creatively—and finds it perfectly acceptable. Thomas writes:

> It is not contrary to the essential character of an artist if he should work in a different way on his product, <u>even after he has given it its first form</u>. Neither, then, is it against nature if <u>God does something to natural things</u> in a different way from that to which the course of nature is accustomed (*SCG* 3.100).

Secondary causes are certainly real. But, to repeat, they are not the whole story. Not only did Thomas not share the critics' aversion to God's intervention; his metaphysics is fundamentally opposed to it. For Thomas, "God . . . can cause any effect to result in anything whatsoever independently of middle causes" (*SCG* 2.99). Only God has the power to create novel form. He is truly the creator "of all things visible and invisible."

While Aquinas did not shy away from intervention—and even thought God purposely intervened in a detectable way—ID is a very minimal claim which does not *require* intervention. Dembski points out that his heroes, Reid, Paley and Hodge, "made no appeal to miracles in the production of design" (Dembski 1999, 87). Dembski, following Thomas Reid, locates Cicero and the Stoics as precursors of ID, despite their lack of belief in a "personal, let alone transcendent and miracle-working, God" (Dembski 1999, 88). Dembski insists that design does not require miraculous intervention (Dembski 2002, 326), and he admits that it is logically possible that all design was front-loaded into the Big Bang. As he puts it, "A designer is not in the business of moving particles but of imparting information" (Dembski 2002, 335). Dembski is not alone. Behe concurs:

> the assumption that design unavoidably requires "interference" rests mostly on a lack of imagination. There's no reason that the extended fine-tuning view . . . necessarily requires active meddling with nature. .. . . One simply has to envision that the agent who caused the universe

was able to specify from the start not only laws, but much more (Behe 2007, 231).

3. Is Complexity Relevant to an Inference to Design?

Contrary to the claims of Feser (2010, 154–155), the presence of complexity is relevant to Aquinas's argument for design:

> To signify this, Moses prefaces each work with the words, "God said, Let this thing be," or "that," to denote the formation of all things by the Word of God, from Whom, according to Augustine [Tract. i. *in Joan.* and *Gen. ad Lit.* i. 4], is "all form and fitness and <u>concord of parts</u>" (*ST* 1.65.4).

> It is impossible for things contrary and discordant to fall into <u>one harmonious order</u> always or for the most part, except under some one guidance, assigning to each and all a tendency to a fixed end. But in the world we see things of different natures falling into harmonious order, not rarely and fortuitously, but always or for the most part. Therefore there must be some Power by whose providence the world is governed; and that we call God. (*SCG* 1.13)

This accords well with Behe's straightforward definition of design: "Design is simply the *purposeful arrangement of parts*" (Behe 1996, 193).

Feser has not shown complexity to be absent from Thomas's argument for design. Even if he did, it would only demonstrate that there is more than one kind of design argument. Thomas's paradigm for "harmonious order" may well be the Ptolemaic system of astronomy—hardly a simple picture.

Contemporary readers should keep in mind that with the advance of information science, there exist today even more refined categories of explanation for what Thomas called "order." Thomas generally contrasts order—or great or "harmonious" order—with chaos and disorder. But contemporary ID arguments take advantage of categories which distinguish relatively simple order (such as is often seen in physics) from the highly ordered or "specified complexity" such as is seen in DNA (cf. Dembski 1998). In this instance, ID theorists have retained the same basic distinctions made by Thomas, but accommodated the insights of modern science to strengthen the conclusion that order requires an intelligent orderer.

4. Is the Use of Probabilities Legitimate in Detecting Intelligence?

Feser (2010, 155) also contends that probabilities are irrelevant to Aristotelian-Thomists' arguments for the existence of irreducible teleology in nature. But Thomists surely need to consider the measure of the improbability of chance-generated design simulacra. They are right to assert that it is metaphysically impossible for something with a *real* telos to exist apart from the activity of an intelligent cause. However, it is possible for a "heap" of merely physical things, assembled by chance, to *mimic* real teleology and purpose. We encounter many examples: clouds or rocks that resemble sculptures of human beings or animals, pancakes that look like profiles of JFK, etc. We can sensibly ask, is the Old Faithful geyser a living organism, with its own form and telos, or is its regularity a mere by-product of a chance conjunction of various geological conditions? To answer these questions with confidence, we must ask how likely the observed conjunction would be in the absence of a unifying and ordering immanent form.

To rigorously distinguish between real and merely apparent design, then, it is best to consult probabilities. It is true that in many ordinary situations, it is unnecessary to consult probabilities to distinguish design from apparent design. In most cases, we simply perceive design using our reliable faculties to do so (cf. Ratzsch 2003, 107). Dembski himself merely claims to formalize what is involved in everyday perceptions of design with his notion of specified complexity. But while they may not be strictly necessary for detecting design, these probability assessments serve to tighten up our objective certainty regarding perceptions of design. Thus, Dembski's work is vital to the modern realization of the Thomistic project.

5. Can God "Use" Chance?

The critics have also taken aim at Dembski's "explanatory filter" (Barr 2010; Beckwith 2010, 437–438; Beckwith forthcoming). The usual criticism is that Dembski's filter implies that things which are attributable to "law" are not attributable to God's design. But this is a gross misunderstanding—one the critics should have noticed, given that Dembski and other ID theorists have consistently supported design arguments from the fine-tuning of the laws of physics. Dembski has long noted that law, chance and design are not mutually exclusive categories (Dembski 2004, 93). When detecting design, one might conclude that known laws of nature are insufficient to produce the phenomenon in question. But this in no way implies that the known laws are not themselves designed.[13]

While Dembski's filter is only one possible way of framing ID arguments—and not necessary to any such argument—it is interesting that Aquinas seems to anticipate this tripartite schema: necessity, chance or design. There is one difference in terminology: Aquinas would speak not of "necessity" or "law of nature," but of the *powers* of natural or created beings. Every effect must be the product either of some unintelligent agent or of chance or of some intelligent agent. Aquinas follows the Aristotelian definition of "chance":

> A chance event arises from a coincidence of two or more causes, in that an end not intended is gained by the coming in of some collateral cause, as the finding of a debtor by him who went to market to make a purchase, when his debtor also came to market (*SCG* 3.74).

> Good fortune is said to befall a man, when something good happens to him beyond his intention, as when one digging a field finds a treasure that he was not looking for (*SCG* 3.92).

According to Thomas, the order of creation, including the distinction of species, is not a result of chance.

> And again, the form of anything proceeding from an intellectual and voluntary agent is intended by that agent. But, as we have already seen, the universe of creatures has as its author God, who is a voluntary and intellectual agent. Nor can there be any defect in His power so that He might fail in accomplishing His intention; for, as we proved in Book I of this work, His power is infinite. It therefore follows of necessity that the form of the universe is intended and willed by God, and for that reason it is not the result of chance. For it is things outside the scope of the agent's intention that we say are fortuitous. Now, the form of the universe consists in the distinction and order of its parts. The distinction of things, therefore, is not the result of chance. (*SCG* 2.40)

In fact, nothing in creation is, ultimately (in reference to God), due to chance.

> It is further to be observed that good or ill fortune may befall a man as a matter of luck, so far as his intention goes, and so far as the working of the prime forces of nature (*corpora coelestia*) goes, and so far as the mind of the angels goes, but not in regard of God: for in reference to God nothing is by chance, nothing unforeseen, either in human life or anywhere else in creation. (*SCG* 3.92)

But couldn't God use a stochastic or chancy process in creating? No, for three reasons:

1. God does not in fact leave anything up to chance (as just seen in *SCG* 3.92).

2. God could not leave anything up to chance: every particular contingent fact depends on God's providential will, as a matter of necessity (*ST* 1.22.2).[14]

3. If a chance process did occur *per impossibile*, it would be incapable of creating a new form.

Couldn't God use chance to produce a specific result intentionally? No. By the Aristotelian (and Thomistic) definition of chance, chance is whatever is caused by a confluence of causes outside the intention of anyone. So, by definition, God cannot use chance to produce a specific result. This would make the result both outside anyone's intention and inside God's intention—a self-contradiction.

This is not to say that Thomas thinks it nonsensical to speak of chance or fortune. Quite the opposite (*SCG* 100.74). There is contingency in nature. And chance certainly exists in the sense of interacting causal chains apart from any creature's intention. But this is chance only in reference to creatures, or perhaps more accurately, in reference to the limited knowledge of creatures. As Thomas says, "in reference to God nothing is by chance, nothing unforeseen, either in human life or anywhere else in creation" (*SCG* 3.92). As regards God's creation of creatures, chance has no place. Creatures are *intended* by God, for they come from a corresponding form in the divine intellect.

Still, there have been clever attempts to integrate divine action with the Darwinian definition of chance. Peter van Inwagen, for instance, claims that chance processes can be used by an intelligent agent. Van Inwagen correctly points out that the inference from the chanciness of every part of an ensemble of events to the chanciness of the whole ensemble commits the fallacy of composition. The individual events in some set of events can be random, and can be random because the agent made them so, in order to fulfill some purpose. For example, an agent can make use of an intentionally random sampling of points in order to estimate the area under a curve (van Inwagen 2003, 353–354). Van Inwagen's observation is correct, but not relevant to the case in which God is the agent, at least not according to Aquinas. God does intend each and every natural event, not merely some global pattern.

Van Inwagen also asks what "random" means in the context of Darwinism. His answer, on behalf of Darwinian biologists, is to claim that "randomness" merely refers to a lack of correlation between the probability of the occurrence of a mutation and its functionality or adaptiveness. This is compatible with frequent, purposeful intervention by God, guiding the process of evolution toward a desired result.

We have three responses. First, van Inwagen is right that neo-Darwinians often claim that the randomness they have in mind when referring to "random mutations" only means that there is no correlation between mutations and beneficial adaptations. But this could be taken in two ways. On one hand, it might mean that specific mutations do not happen *because* they are adaptive. On the other, it might mean that, on the whole, there is no correlation between mutations and adaptive functions. Notice, however that the former understanding is not amenable to van Inwagen's argument. In his postulation of divine action the guided mutations would indeed happen because God knew that they were adaptive. The latter interpretation is more amenable to van Inwagen's argument, but this sort of evolution would not be Thomistic. It faces both the challenge of essentialism (seen earlier) and the fact that Thomas thought divine action would be evident to all. Plus, if God is actively intervening at critical points in the history of life with sufficient frequency to shape the course of evolution, what grounds do we have for thinking that his doing so would not induce some correlation between the occurrence of mutations and their adaptiveness? *Prima facie*, we would expect some such correlation to result. In addition, what possible motive would God have to respect the Darwinian no-correlation constraint?

Second, truth be told, Darwinians typically advance a much stronger claim than this minimal assertion of a lack of correlation. The whole point of Darwinism in the first place was to exclude intelligent agency from the details of the process altogether. As Darwin himself said, "If I were convinced that I required such additions to the theory of natural selection, I would reject it as rubbish . . . I would give absolutely nothing for the theory of nat. selection, if it require miraculous additions at any one stage of descent" (Darwin 1991, 345).

Third, if van Inwagen is correct, God is (inexplicably) acting directly in such a way as to mimic the power of non-intelligent mechanisms to mimic intelligent agents. This is not the scientific theory Darwin or the chief neo-Darwinians had in mind. Not only is it convoluted, but it is drastically removed from the spirit of Thomas's claim that God sometimes acts apart from the natural order so as to reveal his power in a detectable fashion. (*SCG* 3.99)

6. Is Design Empirically Detectable?

Critics like Feser also contend that "Aquinas's argument is intended as a metaphysical demonstration," not as a "quasi-scientific empirical hypothesis" like that on offer from ID (Feser 2009, 111). To be sure, there are differences between Thomas's Fifth Way and, say, Behe's argument for irreducible complexity. But Aquinas clearly thought that the activity of intelligence can be empirically detected. For instance, there could be no spontaneous generation of living forms without intelligence. Thus:

> It was laid down by Avicenna that animals of all kinds can be generated by various minglings of the elements, and naturally, without any kind of seed. This, however, seems repugnant to the fact that nature produces its effects by determinate means, and consequently, those things that are naturally generated from seed cannot be generated naturally in any other way. It ought, then, rather to be said that in the natural generation of all animals that are generated from seed, the active principle lies in the formative power of the seed, but that in the case of animals generated from putrefaction, the formative power is the influence of the heavenly bodies. (*ST* 1.71.1)

Aquinas refers to the formative power of the heavenly bodies precisely because these bodies were thought to be animated by celestial or angelic intelligences. Thus, Aquinas affirms the soundness of inferring intelligent design from the spontaneous generation of life. But this is not the only place in which it is clear that Aquinas thought that the activity of intelligence could be empirically detected.

> Everything that tends definitely to an end, either fixes its own end, or has its end fixed for it by another: otherwise it would not tend rather to this end than to that. But the operations of nature tend to definite ends: the gains of nature are not made by chance: for if they were, they would not be the rule, but the exception, for chance is of exceptional cases. Since then physical agents do not fix their own end, because they have no idea of an end, they must have an end fixed for them by another, who is the author of nature. But He could not fix an end for nature, had He not Himself understanding. (*SCG* 1.44)

> The fifth way is taken from the governance of the world. We see that things which lack intelligence, such as natural bodies, act for an end, and

this is evident from their acting always, or nearly always, in the same way, so as to obtain the best result. <u>Hence it is plain that not fortuitously, but designedly, do they achieve their end</u>. Now whatever lacks intelligence cannot move towards an end, unless it be <u>directed by some being endowed with knowledge and intelligence</u>; as the arrow is shot to its mark by the archer. Therefore some intelligent being exists by whom all natural things are directed to their end; and this being we call God. (*ST* 1.2.3)[15]

Often the critics implicitly accept the identification of science with methodological naturalism: according to the critics, immanent teleology cannot be empirically identified. Since ID theorists seek to frame arguments that fall within the purview of natural science, the critics erroneously jump to the conclusion that ID theorists have unwittingly embraced naturalism or mechanism (Feser 2009, 110–115; Beckwith 2010, 435–439). Once we recognize that ID theorists believe teleology to be empirically detectable (as did Aristotle and Aquinas), this bizarre misattribution to them of "mechanistic philosophy" falls flat.

In addition, the critics import into their interpretation of Aquinas an Enlightenment dichotomy of philosophy from empirical science.[16] Aquinas was no Rationalist, like Descartes or Spinoza. Physics and metaphysics formed a continuum for Aristotelians like Aquinas. Both are equally rooted in the knowledge that comes to us through the senses. Aquinas assigns a very modest role to purely *a priori* (in the Kantian sense) or introspectible axioms.

Thomists are right to insist that *knowledge* can be derived from philosophy, theology and other disciplines—not merely from science. But, contrary to the critics, ID proponents have never claimed otherwise (Beckwith 2009, 443–444). In fact, ID proponents have fought this misconception tooth and nail (Johnson 1995, 89–131; Pearcey 2004). They insist their work is scientific, not because it must be scientific to be knowledge, but because it is scientific under any neutral definition. When some critics take issue with ID's claim to be scientific, they unwittingly concede an anti-theistic definition of science (Plantinga 2001, 341). What metaphysically neutral rule would keep scientists from searching for empirical signs of purpose and agency?[17] Why should the Thomist concede that God's design cannot be empirically detectable? Why not remain open-minded, especially when Aquinas himself thought that God's acts are detectable via observation of the natural world?

Conclusion: The Thomist Critics' Central Misunderstanding

The Thomistic critics of ID understand neither ID nor the heart of Darwinian evolution. Darwinism and Neo-Darwinism are instances of reductive materialism. That's their whole point, their *raison d'être*. Again, Darwin was emphatic that natural selection was worthless if it needed to be supplemented by divine action. Natural selection was meant to be a designer substitute; nature could, given enough time, mimic the effects of intelligence.

Darwinism contends that the ultimate cause of the origin of all biological functionality is the result of chance genetic mutations. Natural selection is not a second, parallel cause. It is not a force or mathematically precise natural law like gravity. Forces may be guided or unguided. Laws are teleological. In contrast, natural selection merely means that living things die and reproduce at different rates; this in turn affects the composition of the next generation. Natural selection merely increases nature's probabilistic resources by progressively fixing "beneficial" innovations in a much larger population. Chance and chance alone must be responsible for the emergence of each new form and function. The Darwinian process as a whole is impersonal, non-intentional, and reduces the evolutionary process to material and efficient causes. If Darwinism is correct, the Thomist must hold that mere material and efficient causes have the power to, and did in fact, give rise to formal and final causes.

If Darwinism is true, then Thomism must be false. Thomists claim that the biological world is populated by things with irreducible biological natures, each of which must be the product of an intelligent cause. ID is not a competing metaphysical system for the simple reason that it is not a metaphysical system. With respect to the origin of species, at least, Thomism is a form of intelligent design, not an alternative to it.[18]

University of Texas at Austin
Baylor University

Notes

1. We focus on *biological* design arguments, even though proponents have made arguments in various scientific disciplines, simply because these arguments are the center of the critics' ire. The critics show little awareness of design arguments in other disciplines (e.g., Gonzalez and Richards 2004).

2. The critics, taken collectively, have leveled these six objections. It should not be implied, however, that each ID-critic endorses each objection.

3. Cardinal Joseph Ratzinger, now Pope Benedict XVI, agrees: "If creation cannot be recognized as the metaphysical middle term between nature and artificiality, then the plunge into nothingness is unavoidable" (Ratzinger 1995, 93). Thomas's *Summa Contra Gentiles* will be abbreviated *SCG* and his *Summa Theologiae ST*. All SCG quotations are from the translation of Anton C. Pegis, et al., while all *ST* quotations are from the Fathers of the English Dominican Province translation.

4. This should not be taken as implying that ID proponents think teleology, natures, essences, or universals cannot be grasped in non-empirical ways (contra Beckwith 2009, 443).

5. Such a broad definition is easily justified given the well-acknowledged failure of proposed demarcation criteria (Laudan 1982).

6. Fortunately, there has been some recent movement away from principled methodological naturalism, even among metaphysical naturalists. As one recent paper argues,

"Evolutionary scientists are on firmer ground if they discard supernatural explanations on purely evidential grounds, and not by philosophical fiat" (Boudry et al. 2010, 241).

7. Stephen C. Meyer, for instance, argues persuasively for the scientific status of ID and the methodological equivalence of ID and Darwinian theory. He insists most strongly, however, not that ID is science but that if it is not going to be called science, then neither should theories with the same logical structure. He writes:

> Perhaps, however, one just really does not want to call intelligent design a scientific theory. Perhaps one prefers the designation 'quasi-scientific historical speculation with strong metaphysical overtones.' Fine. Call it [ID] what you will, provided the same appellation is applied to other forms of inquiry that have the same methodological and logical character and limitations. In particular, make sure both design and descent [Darwinian theory] are called 'quasi-scientific historical speculation with strong metaphysical overtones.' (Meyer 2000, 193)

8. Because the critics often claim that ID, in great opposition to St. Thomas, views God as a Clockmaker, the following passage is noteworthy:

> Accordingly, in all things moved by reason, the order of reason which moves them is evident, although the things themselves are without reason: for an arrow through the motion of the archer goes straight towards the target, as though it were endowed with reason to direct its course. The same may be seen in the movements of clocks and all engines put together by the art of man. Now as artificial things are in comparison to human art, so are all natural things in comparison to the Divine art. And accordingly order is to be seen in things moved by nature, just as in things moved by reason, as is stated in *Phys.* ii. And thus it is that in the works of irrational animals we notice certain marks of sagacity, in so far as they have a natural inclination to set about their actions in a most orderly manner through being ordained by the Supreme art." (*ST* 1-2.13.2) [all underlined emphases are ours]

While there is surely a helpful distinction between natural and artificial objects, Thomas is not averse to viewing God as acting analogously to a human artificer, even a clockmaker. For Thomas, it is evident that intelligent agency lies behind the order seen in natural entities which lack reason. Such order is the exclusive hallmark of rational agents. ID proponents, with the knowledge modern science affords, extend such reasoning to, among other things, the highly ordered nature of DNA and the microbiological world.

9. God and his creatures are both wholly causes of the same events, not partial causes (*SCG* 3.70).

10. Even in the one instance in which exemplar causation is alluded to, Edward Feser fails to notice its centrality to the debate about whether God "intervenes" in nature (Feser 2010). Much of what follows in this discussion of exemplar causation is also to be found in Gage (2010).

11. Neo-Darwinians also advocate a nominalist conception of species (Dawkins 2006, 34).

12. For the most extensive treatment of Thomas's doctrine of exemplar causation to date, see (Doolan 2008).

13. One must be careful, however, as assuming that the laws of nature are designed when making an ID argument may beg the question (cf. Richards 2010, 254–258).

14. Thomas is quite clear that everything is subject to the providence of God. He writes:

> But the causality of God, Who is the first agent, extends to all being, not only as to constituent principles of species, but also as to the individualizing principles; not only of things incorruptible, but also of things corruptible. Hence all things that exist in whatsoever manner are necessarily directed by God towards some end; as the Apostle says: "Those things that are of God are well ordered (Romans 13:1). Since, therefore, as the providence of God is nothing less than the type of the order of things towards an end, as we have said; it necessarily follows that all things, inasmuch as they participate in existence, must likewise be subject to divine providence. It has also been shown (Q. 14, A. 6, 11) that God knows all things, both universal and particular. And since His knowledge may be compared to the things themselves, as the knowledge of art to the objects of art, all things must of necessity come under His ordering; as all things wrought by art are subject to the ordering of that art.

And further:

> So far then as an effect escapes the order of a particular cause, it is said to be casual or fortuitous in respect to that cause; but if we regard the universal cause, outside whose range no effect can happen, it is said to be foreseen. Thus, for instance, the meeting of two servants, although to them it appears a chance circumstance, has been fully foreseen by their master, who has purposely sent to meet at the one place, in such a way that the one knows not about the other. (*ST* 1.22.2)

In this way, "The order of divine providence is unchangeable and certain, so far as all things foreseen happen as they have been foreseen, whether from necessity or from contingency" (*ST* 1.22.4).

15. Often the critics complain that Thomas's Fifth Way is not really a design argument at all. Feser (2008; 2010), for instance, pits ID arguments, and even those of William Paley, against Thomas's Fifth Way. Supposedly, Paley is concerned with the end-directedness of things like watches, but Aquinas is only interested in the "immanent end-directedness" of natural things. But, as Marie George points out, "Feser's overemphasis on the difference in natural and artificial teleology results in" this error (George 2010, 446). Feser's "emphasis on the intrinsic directedness to an end of natural things leads him [Feser] to be unduly critical of Paley's argument, when in fact there are many striking similarities between Paley's argument and the Fifth Way" (George 2010, 449). Both Paley and Aquinas see the end-directedness of artifacts as an extension of the intelligence of intelligent agents. So too, they both see the end-directedness of living things as pointing to an intelligent being. In this regard, note that Feser (2011, 4) argues that Paley's argument (and, by extension, ID arguments) are "incompatible" with Thomas's metaphysics of immanent finality. Yet this incompatibility claim is unsupported by Feser. He points to what he takes to be several differences between the two types of arguments, but it would take a contradiction, not mere differences, to support an incompatibility claim.

16. For more on the critics' strange amalgamation of Aristotle's four causes with a Baconian demarcation of the disciplines, see Richards (2010, 260–270).

17. On methodological naturalism, see Meyer (2000), Plantinga (2001), Ratzsch (2004), and Menuge (2010).

18. The authors wish to thank Jay Richards, Lydia McGrew and attendees of the 2011 meeting of the American Catholic Philosophical Association (especially Robert Delfino, our commentator) for their comments and suggestions.

Bibliography

Aquinas, Thomas. 1997. *On the Eternality of the World*. In *Aquinas on Creation*. Trans. Steven E. Baldner and William E. Carroll, 114–122. Toronto: Pontifical Institute of Medieval Studies.

Barr, Stephen M. 2005. "The Design of Evolution." *First Things*. October. http://www.firstthings.com/article/2007/01/the-design-of-evolution-22.

———. 2010. "The End of Intelligent Design?" *First Things: On the Square*. February. http://www.firstthings.com/onthesquare/2010/02/the-end-of-intelligent-design.

Beckwith, Francis J. 2009. "The Courts, Natural Rights, and Religious Claims as Knowledge." *Santa Clara Law Review* 49.2: 429–458.

———. 2010. "Guidance for Doting and Peeping Thomists: A Review Essay of Aquinas: A Beginner's Guide, by Edward Feser." *Philosophia Christi* 12.2: 429–439.

———. Forthcoming. "Or We Can Be Philosophers: A Response to Barbara Forrest." *Synthese*.

Behe, Michael. 1996. *Darwin's Black Box*. New York: Free Press.

———. 2007. *The Edge of Evolution: The Search for the Limits of Darwinism*. New York: Free Press.

Boudry, Maarten, Stefaan Blancke, and Johan Braeckman. 2010. "How Not to Attack Intelligent Design Creationism: Philosophical Misconceptions About Methodological Naturalism." *Foundations of Science* 15.3: 227–244.

Darwin, Charles. 1991. "To Sir Charles Lyell 11 October [1859]." In *The Correspondence of Charles Darwin, Volume 7: 1858–1859*, ed. Frederick Burkhardt and Sydney Smith, 345. Cambridge: Cambridge University Press.

———. 1993. *The Origin of Species*. New York: The Modern Library.

Dawkins, Richard. 2006. *The Selfish Gene*. New York: Oxford University Press.

Dembski, William A. 1998. *The Design Inference: Eliminating Chance through Small Probabilities*. New York: Cambridge University Press.

———. 1999. *Intelligent Design: The Bridge between Science and Theology*. Downers Grove, IL: InterVarsity Press.

———. 2002. *No Free Lunch: Why Specified Complexity Cannot Be Purchased without Intelligence*. Lanham, MD: Rowman & Littlefield.

———. 2004. *The Design Revolution: Answering the Toughest Questions about Intelligent Design*. Downers Grove, IL: InterVarsity Press.

Doolan, Gregory T. 2008. *Aquinas on the Divine Ideas as Exemplar Causes*. Washington, D.C.: Catholic University of America Press.

Feser, Edward. 2008. *The Last Superstition: A Refutation of the New Atheism*. South Bend, IN: St. Augustine's Press.

———. 2009. *Aquinas: A Beginner's Guide*. Oxford: Oneworld.

———. 2010. "Teleology: A Shopper's Guide." *Philosophia Christi* 12.1: 142–159.

———. 2011. "On Aristotle, Aquinas, and Paley: A Reply to Marie George." *Evangelical Philosophical Society Online Article Library*, 1–9. http://www.epsociety .org/userfiles/Feser-Reply%20to%20Marie%20George%20_revised_.pdf.

Freddoso, Alfred J. 1988. "Medieval Aristotelianism and the Case against Secondary Causation in Nature." In *Divine and Human Action: Essays in the Metaphysics of Theism*, ed. Thomas V. Morris, 74–118. Ithaca: Cornell University Press.

Gage, Logan Paul. 2010. "Can a Thomist Be a Darwinist?" In *God and Evolution*, ed. Jay W. Richards, 187–202. Seattle: Discovery Institute Press.

George, Marie. 2010. "An Aristotelian-Thomist Responds to Edward Feser's 'Teleology.'" *Philosophia Christi* 12.2: 441–449.

Gilson, Etienne. 1984. *From Aristotle to Darwin and Back Again: A Journey in Final Causality, Species, and Evolution*, trans. John Lyon. Notre Dame, IN: University of Notre Dame Press.

Gonzalez, Guillermo, and Jay W. Richards. 2004. *The Privileged Planet: How Our Place in the Cosmos Is Designed for Discovery*. Washington, D.C.: Regnery.

Johnson, Phillip E. 1995. *Reason in the Balance: The Case Against Naturalism in Science, Law, and Education*. Downers Grove, IL: InterVarsity Press.

Laudan, Larry. 1983. "The Demise of the Demarcation Problem." In *Physics, Philosophy, and Psychoanalysis*, ed. R. S. Cohen, 111–128. Dordrecht, Holland: D. Reidel.

McMullin, Ernan. 1985. "Introduction: Evolution and Creation." In *Evolution and Creation*, ed. Ernan McMullin, 1–56. Notre Dame, IN: University of Notre Dame Press.

Menuge, Angus. 2010. "Against Methodological Materialism." In *The Waning of Materialism*, ed. Robert C. Koons and George Bealer, 375–394. New York: Oxford University Press.

Meyer, Stephen C. 2000. "The Scientific Status of Intelligent Design: The Methodological Equivalence of Naturalistic and Non-Naturalistic Origins Theories." In *Science and Evidence for Design in the Universe, The Proceedings of the Wethersfield Institute* 9: 151–211. San Francisco: Ignatius Press.

———. 2009. *Signature in the Cell: DNA and the Evidence for Intelligent Design*. New York: HarperOne.

Oakes, Edward T., S.J. 2001a. "Edward T. Oakes and His Critics: An Exchange." *First Things* 112: 5–13.

———. 2001b. "Newman, Yes; Paley, No." Review of The Wedge of Truth, by Phillip E. Johnson." *First Things* 109: 48–52.

Pearcey, Nancy R. 2004. *Total Truth: Liberating Christianity from Its Cultural Captivity*. Wheaton, IL: Crossway Books.

Plantinga, Alvin. 2001. "Methodological Naturalism?" In *Intelligent Design Creationism and Its Critics: Philosophical, Theological, and Scientific Perspectives*, ed. Robert T. Pennock, 339–361. Cambridge, MA: MIT Press.

Polanyi, Michael. 1967. "Life Transcending Physics and Chemistry." *Chemical and Engineering News* 45: 54–66.

Ratzinger, Joseph. 1995. *"In the Beginning . . .": A Catholic Understanding of the Story of Creation and the Fall*. Grand Rapids, MI: William B. Eerdmans.

Ratzsch, Del. 2001. *Nature, Design, and Science*. Albany: State University of New York Press.

———. 2003. "Perceiving Design." In *God and Design: The Teleological Argument and Modern Science*, ed. Neil A. Manson, 124–44. London: Routledge.

———. 2004. "Natural Theology, Methodological Naturalism, and 'Turtles All the Way Down.'" *Faith and Philosophy* 21.4: 436–455.

Richards, Jay W. 2010. "Understanding Intelligent Design." In *God and Evolution*, ed. Jay W. Richards, 247–271. Seattle: Discovery Institute Press.

Sternberg, Richard W. Forthcoming. *The Immaterial Genome*.

Tkacz, Michael W. 2007. "Thomas Aquinas vs. The Intelligent Designers: What Is God's Finger Doing in My Pre-Biotic Soup?" In *Intelligent Design: Science or Religion?* ed. Robert M. Baird and Stuart E. Rosembaum, 275–282. Amherst, NY: Prometheus Books.

van Inwagen, Peter. 2003. "The Compatibility of Darwinism and Design." In *God and Design: The Teleological Argument and Modern Science*, ed. Neil A. Manson, 348–367. London: Routledge.

Wells, Jonathan. 2011. *The Myth of Junk DNA*. Seattle: Discovery Institute Press.

Wiker, Benjamin. 2002. *Moral Darwinism: How We Became Hedonists*. Downers Grove, IL: InterVarsity Press.

Thomistic Hylomorphism, Self-Determination, Neuroplasticity, and Grace: The Case of Addiction

Daniel D. De Haan

Abstract: This paper presents a Thomistic analysis of addiction that incorporates scientific, philosophical, and theological features of addiction. I will argue first, that a Thomistic hylomorphic anthropology provides a cogent explanation of the causal interactions between human action and neuroplasticity. I will employ Karol Wojtyła's account of self-determination to further clarify the kind of neuroplasticity involved in addiction. Next, I will elucidate how a Thomistic anthropology can accommodate, without reductionism, both the neurophysiological and psychological elements of addiction, and finally, I will make clear how Thomism can provide an ethics and a theology of grace that can be integrated with these ontological and scientific considerations into a holistic theory of addiction.

> *"Psychological motives and bodily occasions may overlap*
> *because there is not a single impulse in a living body which is*
> *entirely fortuitous in relation to psychic intentions, not a single*
> *mental act which has not found at least its germ or its general*
> *outline in physiological tendencies"*[1]
>
> —Maurice Merleau-Ponty

The theme of this year's *ACPA* conference, "Science, Reason, and Religion" provides an opportunity to engage a problem which demands an integrated answer, that is, an answer which requires a consideration of what science, philosophy, and religion can contribute to a particular problem. Addiction is just this sort of problem. This paper will adopt a unified psychosomatic approach to addiction and will attempt to articulate some of the diverse ways in which addictions involve neurological, psychological, moral, and spiritual aspects of the human person.[2] This holistic approach to addiction in terms of science, philosophy, and theology will be developed within the context of a Thomistic philosophical anthropology.

© 2012, *Proceedings of the ACPA*, Vol. 85
DOI: 10.5840/acpaproc2011859

This paper will argue that a Thomistic hylomorphic anthropology provides a cogent explanation of the causal interactions between human action and neuroplasticity, can accommodate, without reductionism, both the neurophysiological and psychological elements of addiction, and is also able to show how ethics and a theology of grace can be integrated along with these ontological and scientific considerations into a holistic theory of addiction. This is an ambitious task for such a short space, and so many important details have been omitted for the sake of a holistic and unified account of addiction.

The paper is divided into four parts. The first part of this paper will show how a Thomistic doctrine of self-determination applies beyond the order of the psychological and can account for various alterations of our neurophysiology. We argue that by acting, persons not only become psychically inclined to good or evil activities, they also become *physiologically* ordered to these activities. This is because, on a hylomorphic view of man, a human person can be psychosomatically altered through acts of self-determination. In the second section we will contend that some instances of neuroplasticity are the neurophysiological results of human action as self-determination, which is made especially clear in the case of addictions. In short, addiction provides a clear case of what happens to the nervous system and psychological faculties of a human person who partakes in acts that are often deprived of moral goodness. The results are the numerous psychosomatic operational privations that are acquired by the addicted person. In the third part we will provide a holistic account of addiction within a Thomistic anthropology. We will present a sketch of how Thomism can provide a robust descriptive and explanatory philosophical anthropology that can give unity and clarity to the numerous ways that addictions introduce different operational privations within the human person. After suggesting a few of the ways in which addictions can be treated through pharmacology, moral formation and the solidarity of community, the final part of this paper will address the role that grace can play in the life of an addict.

I. Self-Determination and Thomistic Philosophical Anthropology

Thomism is committed to the incarnate dimension of the person as a psychosomatic hylomorphic unity. The intellectual soul is the substantial form of the organic body with the potentiality for life. But to what degree do the accidental formal determinations of human action really alter our material substrate? A central topic in Karol Wojtyła's *The Acting Person* is the nature of *self-determination*.[3] The horizontal transcendence proper to the intentionality of conscious voluntary human action is well established in the Thomistic tradition. Consciously acting is always oriented towards some object; human persons transcend their own subjectivity in virtue of such intentional objects. In the *Acting Person*, Wojtyła seeks to emphasize and articulate more clearly the nature of vertical transcendence as well.[4] Through the efficacy of the will, the person transcends the natural determinations of the physical order and *becomes* the sort of person who chooses and performs certain axiologically specified activities. In acting, the person is self-determining. A person is able to determine himself because he is able to act beyond the determinations of nature and become responsible for the activities he wills. One becomes good by doing good, and one becomes evil by doing evil.

> The engagement in freedom is objectified—because of its lastingly repetitive effects, and conformably to the structure of self-determination—in the person and not only in the action, which is the transitive effect. It is in the modality of morality that this objectification becomes clearly apparent, when through an action that is either morally good or morally bad, man, as the person, himself becomes either morally good or morally evil. . . . [H]uman actions once performed do not vanish without a trace: they leave their moral value, which constitutes an objective reality intrinsically cohesive with the person, and thus a reality also profoundly subjective. Being a person, man is "somebody," and being somebody, he may be either *good* or *bad*.[5]

The axiological character of the objects and activities that we determine ourselves to become through the efficacy of our free choices make us into what we are. But in what way do we become the activities we choose? How far down does the psychosomatic integration of the person through self-determination extend? Obviously there is a determination of the human person at the spiritual, moral and psychological order, but what about the body? Is it really reasonable to suppose that through our ordinary acts of free choice we are not only laying down tracks of a psychological character, but also of a physiological character?

It seems that anyone committed to a Thomistic anthropology must take seriously the penetrating dynamism of human action, that is, the transformative efficacy of self-determination that occurs in a human person who is consciously acting.[6] This integrated dynamism of the whole person finds its core in the Thomistic doctrine of the existential unification of form and matter as well as accidents and subject within the essential order of being.[7]

> "To be" is to be cause, that is, both immanent cause of its own being and transitive cause of other beings through efficient causality. Matter itself is no longer here as a mere obstacle, blindly aspiring to form; it is also a help. Actively engaged in it, the soul is giving itself the body which it needs; it progressively builds it up through physiological operations which pave the way for intellectual operations.[8]

If our accidental acts did not formally alter and determine our substance, that is both our form and matter, then there would be a real vitiation of the hylomorphic unity of the person. All moral acts would involve nothing more than a purely formal alteration of the spiritual and psychic order of man. Such a thesis has more in common with dualism than Thomism. The human person in Aquinas's anthropology is an almost completely integrated form and matter composite substance. That is, we are psychically incarnate, and all of our psychological activities—except acts that essentially occur without matter and so have their being entirely separate from matter—have some physiological substrate and manifestation.[9]

But if this is true, then we should expect to find some manifestation of formal determinations within the material substrate. Indeed we do. Disciplined activities (intentionally and unintentionally developed dispositions and *habitus*) bestow proficiency and increased capacities at both the physiological and psychological levels. Those who exercise various muscle groups gain superior endurance, flexibility and dexterity in these muscles. Various activities can also heighten our sensory attention to the more subtle details present in different sensibilia, for instance, in musicians with audition and sommeliers in olfaction and gustation. These are all putative instances of psychosomatic sensory plasticity, that is, cases of physiological development or deterioration as the result of decisions to participate or not in various sorts of activities that involve the adaptation of our peripheral as well as of our central nervous system. But what provides our brain with the efficacy and formal unity to adapt in these ways? Do our self-determining human acts also significantly alter central features of our neurophysiology?

Addictions suggest an interesting case because they do not appear to fall clearly on the side of free choice or neuro-chemically determined compulsive behavior. It seems obvious in the majority of cases that addictions are initiated by non-compulsive decisions, yet they seem to result in motivations and cravings that undermine the person's ability to rationally deliberate and freely decide how to act. Addiction involves a kind of dialectic between initially voluntary choices and the whittling down of free choice to apparently compulsive behavior, which in extreme cases can even undermine choice. Even after years of treatment and abstinence, why is it that many "former" addicts can relapse following an encounter with a single evocative cue?[10] The choices we make that bring about our addictions to various activities or substances do alter us in very significant psychosomatic ways, but it is not entirely clear how this should be understood. If it is merely a matter of choice, why are addictive activities so difficult to avoid and overcome? The addict no longer appears to be in control of their behavior. This is why many theorists on addiction are inclined to conclude that for many addicts the causal gravity has shifted entirely to the central nervous system. On such an account, the person is no longer a causal actor; the brain alone seems to be the causal origin of the addict's behavior. But this cannot be the whole story. How is the nervous system so altered? Addictive behavior is acquired; it is not native to human persons from birth, let alone to their nervous system. We are not born with addictions to Internet browsing, pornography, drugs or gambling. Just as there are psychic alterations, there also seem to be some adaptations in the nervous system *because* and *in response to* the activities and decisions of the person.[11]

What we have articulated thus far should suggest the importance of the metaphysical axiom: an object is received into a recipient according to the mode of the recipient.[12] For instance, human action not only inculcates the inclinations of our practical reason and will; it also affects the inclinations of our emotions with respect to the objects of our actions. Our self-determining activities instill within our psychological faculties dispositions or *habitus* that lead to disciplines and virtues or vices in our concupiscible and irascible powers.[13] Furthermore, on the physiological dimension, just as on the psychological dimension, these human actions of self-determination are received into the underlying material substrate of these powers, and there follows the alteration of various neural networks. In the next section we will clarify the nature of these neurological adaptations by turning to the phenomenon of neuroplasticity.

II. Neuroplasticity, Hylomorphism, and Addiction

We have just presented a number of theses about the nature of self-determination in human persons and argued that, even in cases of addictive human behavior, human action alters significant features of the whole person as a hylomorphic entity, including the brain. In this section of the paper we will examine the empirical evidence on neuroplasticity, which, we argue, supports our claims about hylomorphism and self-determination, and is also resistant to reductionistic interpretations, especially in the case of addiction.

Our nervous system's capacity to be altered in virtue of human experience through actions and activations results in various neurophysiological adaptations. This phenomenon is commonly referred to as *neuroplasticity* or Hebbian learning, named after Donald Hebb, one of the earliest theorists on neurological adaptation. His theory is summarized in the often-quoted paraphrase, "neurons that fire together, wire together."[14] In what follows I will briefly summarize a number of the characteristics of neuroplasticity as it is presented by contemporary neuroscientists.

Empirical evidence has shown that the central and peripheral nervous system is able to adapt, not only to endogenous stimulation, but also to the exogenous stimulations of ordinary human experiences and behaviors. Early studies in the neurophysiology undergirding memory, such as inquiries about the hippocampus, motivated theoretical postulates about neural adaptation. Not only has this been confirmed, but numerous empirical investigations have also discovered other kinds of neural adaptation. The field of research dedicated to neuroplasticity has focused on uncovering the electrochemical mechanisms that underlie the transformative abilities of our nervous system to respond to experience. Neuroplasticity is found in such phenomena as the strengthening and growth of synaptic connections and the genesis of new neurons.[15] Furthermore, in some experimental cases with primates and ferrets, neuroscientists have even discovered rather surprising instances of cortical substitutions.[16] In short, the brain is not an isolated, predetermined structure; it is significantly altered by a myriad of extra-neural stimuli that determine the brain in a variety of different ways.

Empirical research on neuroplasticity is, like neuroscience itself, still very much in its infancy. The majority of positive empirical confirmations for studies on human beings are limited, although there is a considerable amount of evidence drawn from other mammalian brains.[17] Some neuroscientists have postulated that certain mechanisms of plasticity might be ubiquitous to the nervous system in all mammals.[18] What is especially significant for the purposes of our hylomorphic proposal are the interlocking schemes of recurrence and inter-organizational manifestations of plasticity found within the biological hierarchical of any animal.

> Given the ... mutuality of feedback between levels, alterations at the genetic level can ultimately propagate up to the behavioral level. ... In the same way, responses to the sensory environment and experience can percolate back down through the various levels to impact ultimately on the genetic level, leading, potentially, to changes in gene expression. ... [E]ach level is acted upon directly by those above and below, and indirectly by all the others. This is true even at the two ends of the continuum, at both the gene and the behavioral level: the gene level is affected by the molecular/synapse level above it in the web, and by free radicals, toxins, radiation, and other energies at the 'extra'-gene level. By the same token, the behavioral level is directly affected by the whole [central nervous system] level below and the effects of the environment above. Since the whole system is nested, in some sense behavioral and environmental events must make their ways down through the levels to the genome ... to affect genetic expression in at least some fraction of genes, perhaps as a function of age.[19]

Thomas Aquinas would not be surprised to see such a manifest instance of his favorite hylomorphically interpreted Dionysian principle.[20] There is a form matter causal order found within any physical hierarchy. The activities of the highest in a lower genus will be ordered to the formal principle that is lowest in the immediately higher genus. The neural substrate of our psychological faculties materially conditions the potential range of formal activities carried out by our faculties. But these activities also formally determine the whole central nervous system as the substrate these activities organize and pattern. By seeing, perceiving, desiring and acting towards some object, our psychic faculties cooperatively enlist the coordination and integration of different neural systems, e.g., the visual cortex, limbic system, sensorimotor cortex, etc. These latter systems are nested within networks of plastic neural circuitry that are variably patterned by the variable patterning of intramodal and intermodal systems interactions. "Interactions within a neural circuit also include cell to cell feedforward and feedback excitation and inhibition, lateral inhibition, etc. Alterations in the activity of any neuron in the circuit impacts circuit activity as a whole and, as a result, the activity of other component neurons."[21] These interlocking patterns of formally ordering and materially ordered causal principles continue to cascade down beyond the neuronal level to synaptic, genetic, molecular and further chemical and physical levels of interaction.[22]

We have just offered a brief account of how the phenomenon of neuroplasticity relates to hylomorphism. Let us now turn to the problem of how addiction fits into our account of human self-determination and neuroplasticity.

Among the different fields of neurophysiological inquiry, neuroscientists have dedicated a great deal of research into the mechanisms of neuroplasticity involved in drug addictions. Addiction, like memory, is a clear instance of acquired capacities or appetites, and so offers promising avenues for investigating neuroplasticity.[23] The evidence in support of neuroplasticity in the case of drug addictions is extensive. It has been shown that "Addictive drugs induce long-term neuroadaptations at the structural, cellular, molecular, and genomic levels."[24]

Empirical evidence has even recently challenged the predominant theoretical position that addiction is essentially a brain disease.[25] The problem with the brain disease theory is that the reward centers of the brain that are stimulated and modified through prolonged uses of addictive substances function in many of the same ways as reward centers function for all other pleasurable activities. The neural genesis and plasticity that takes place in response to a person who regularly participates in pleasurable activities like exercise, eating and drinking, reading, sex, gambling, shopping, browsing the internet, etc. is often indiscernible *in kind* from the similar phenomena found in substance addictions.[26] Such evidence goes a long way in supporting both that there are similar neurophysiological mechanisms involved in non-substance addictions (like pornography, gambling and video games), and that addictions must be approached in a holistic way that recognizes various addictions as phenomena that are not reducible to the brain.

Despite the fact that such evidence suggests that more is involved in neuroplasticity than the internal electrochemistry of the brain, many thinkers continue to interpret the phenomenon of neuroplasticity in a reductionist way. Joseph LeDoux concludes his impressive study on the synaptic self with the astonishingly reductionist assertion: "You are your synapses. They are who you are."[27] Of course, there are exceptions to this reductionist interpretation of neuroplasticity. Richard Davidson, of the Laboratory for Affective Neuroscience, has stated otherwise:

> [T]he fact of biological differences among individuals says nothing about the origins of those differences. A large corpus of neuroscience research over the past decade has underscored the importance of experiential determinants of the structure and function of the circuitry that has been featured here. Social influences on brain structure, activation patterns, neurogenesis, and even gene expression have all been demonstrated. . . . Although heritable influences surely occur, environmental influences, particularly when they occur repetitively over time, can be extremely powerful and produce lasting changes in the brain. The fact that such experiential influences occur provides an impetus for the development of neurally inspired training programs to transform dysfunctional affective styles into ones that may be more adaptive. . . . This is only a promissory note at the present time and requires much additional study and validation.[28]

It is surprising that those manifestations of neuroplasticity that occur as the *result* of addictive behaviors could be interpreted in any other way.[29] But this is a not a recent philosophical mistake. And since the reductionistic objections have remained largely the same over the more than two thousand years of philosophical history, it is not surprising that the response of Socrates is still as formidable as any.

If someone said that without bones and sinews and all such things, I should not be able to do what I decided, he would be right, but surely to say that they are the cause of what I do, and not that I have chosen the best course, even though I act with my mind, is to speak very lazily and carelessly. Imagine not being able to distinguish the real cause from that without which the cause would not be able to act as a cause. It is what the majority appear to do, like people groping in the dark; they call it a cause, thus giving it a name that does not belong to it.[30]

Substituting the more known with the less known remains the spirit of materialism. Such thinkers continue to refuse to be *informed* by the insights found outside the caverns of the cranium. We should instead take seriously the advice that was given to us by Socrates in his last attempt to bring us outside the labyrinth of philosophical perplexity about the soul. I hope to show that our efforts at neuro-spelunking will not be in vain if we also allow our inquiries to be conducted under the light of formal causality.[31]

Thus far we have illustrated how many neural systems in the brain are plastic; i.e., they are able to be modified and to develop according to both intrinsic and extrinsic formal determinations. An overwhelming body of empirical evidence has substantiated the Hebbian theoretical axiom, "neurons that fire together, wire together." But how and why they fire together remains a disputed point. How is the unusual synchrony of diverse cerebral parts causally coordinated? The nature of addiction presents us with a case of neuroplasticity that is resistant to reductionist interpretations. This resistance motivates our non-reductionist hylomorphic interpretation. What is involved in such an interpretation?

If we take seriously the phenomenon of addiction, we cannot accept proposals that entail its theoretical reduction or elimination. To capture the complex nature of addiction, we must adopt a holistic understanding of the integrated structure of the human person's psychosomatic unity. We must have an ontology of the human person that is able to account for the complex but unified interaction that occurs within our psychosomatic constitution. The putative character of the neuroplasticity that is caused by addictions reveals that these physiological adaptations are determined, in the majority of cases, by the decisions and activities performed by human persons. The causal gravity does not find its source in the brain, but in the activities of the person, which require the brain, but also can transcend and determine it. I could not agree more with Eric LaRock that

> The relationship between body and soul on Aquinas's composite view may better be understood as the soul's capacity to organize neurons (and other physical parts of the body) into definite living structures. The higher cognitive functions of the soul inform the brain to be definite neural patterns in acts of cognition. If living organization is a metaphysical feature of soul exhibited, at least in part, by the activities of neurons, then it is a feature associated with but not identical to neurons. The neural machinery

of the brain has living organization through the soul, not vice versa. The soul holds genuine causal control over the material parts of the material component of human nature and hence the rational soul of the human composite cannot be a supervenient or derivative, epiphenomenal effect of neural activity. Matter depends on form for its actuality, i.e., structure, organizing activities, and causal powers. From Aquinas's perspective, the human body exhibits many levels of organization—from elementary constituents of the brain's nucleons and electrons on up to atoms, molecular structures, neurons, and the cerebral excitation associated with higher cognition—because of the causal activity of form.[32]

Interpreting the scientific discoveries of neuroplasticity in terms of formal and material causality provides a promising answer to our initial question concerning self-determination. But we must also ask, to what extent do human activities determine the material substrate? How does the activity of formal action, in particular, through the operations of our powers, affect our neurophysiology?

Human action is able determine a number of aspects of our psychosomatic constitution, including the re-organization of our nervous system in a variety of significant and empirically measurable ways. Likewise, just as this latter line of philosophical reasoning is complemented by scientific discoveries, so also Karol Wojtyła's account of self-determination, set, as it is, within a Thomistic philosophical anthropology, can provide explanations to these questions about the cause of the neurological adaptations manifested in the phenomenon of addiction.

A formal act is always received into the recipient according to the mode of the recipient, and when that recipient is the brain, it involves the neurological adaptation known as neuroplasticity. The repetitious activities that constitute the repertoire of human actions also determine the adaptation of different neurological pathways, which, in their own way, as material recipients, reinforce the physiological dimension of the actions of a human person, who is a psychosomatic whole. Addictions as disordered, acquired, autonomic drives are the result of psychic *habitus* of behavior that have also become dense physiologically inlaid neural systems. The outcome is that our material body comes to be appetitively inclined towards the same objects and actions that we have persistantly chosen to perform over an extended period of time. Like our natural appetites for food and water, our body comes to depend upon the objects of the acquired autonomic drives. Appetition for such objects becomes a constitutional part of a complete human person, who has engrafted certain psychosomatic activities or behaviors into their hylomorphic constitution.

A lot more work needs to be done in order to show how hylomorphism would account for all the available empirical evidence, as well as how it would to respond to various scientific and philosophical objections. These important questions and problems cannot be taken up here. This paper only aims to show how a Thomistic hylomorphism provides a fruitful way for understanding neuroplasticity in general, but especially with respect to particular cases of neuroplasticity, like addiction, that clearly result from human acts of self-determination.

Thus far, our analysis has left two important questions untouched. Why do addictions seem to be compulsive, and why are they so difficult to overcome? Can philosophy and science offer an integrated answer to why rationally chosen activities can become apparently compulsive and irreversible behaviors? This paper cannot give a complete answer to these crucial questions, but it will suggest the outline of an answer to both of them in the next section. This will require first clarifying what an addiction is.

III. Addiction, Self-Determination, and Thomistic Philosophical Anthropology

There are a number of competing theories on addiction. This paper's holistic account integrates a number of features found in these different theories of addiction, but it has more in common with the visceral factor perspective of addiction than strong emotions, weak-willed, erroneous belief, or brain disease models of addiction.[33] Attempting to define and defend our notion of addiction in such a brief space would add more confusions than clarification. Instead, we will begin with a tentative account of addiction and an explanation of our terms; we will then proceed to show how this account fits within a Thomistic philosophical anthropology. For the purposes of this paper, *addiction* will be taken as an *acquired dysordered drive*; this will require a brief explanation.[34]

Aquinas distinguishes three *appetitus* or affective appetites, (1) natural concupiscence, what we will call *drives*,[35] (2) somatic affections (*passio corporalis*),[36] and (3) passions or emotions (*passio animalis*), what we will often call *psychic affections*.[37] While Aquinas provides us with a detailed account of passions, his treatment of drives and somatic affections is not developed at length. The underdeveloped treatment of the Thomistic doctrine of drives and somatic affections requires a further articulation of how these distinct orders are integrated into each other, as well as how they are related to practical reason and addiction.

Drives are pre-conscious powers that serve our vegetative powers by activating other sensitive powers that bring into consciousness various vital needs for nourishment, sleep, and reproduction. Plants do not have vital drives, but many animals do. Drives have the distinctive function of placing *telic demands* of vital appetites into consciousness.[38] Drives are the psychological pivot between the nonconscious vegetative powers—which formally pattern the autonomic nervous system—and the activities of sentient consciousness—which also pattern, and yet are conditioned by, various features of our nervous system. Unlike the vegetative powers of growth, nutrition, metabolism, and reproduction, which are all ordered towards organic vital ends, drives are teleologically ordered towards conscious manifestations via various activation channels that bring to the conscious attention of the animal some telic demand or need for satiation. The telic specification of a drive does not presuppose the animal's cognition, and it is underdetermined with respect to the means of satiation. That is, drives indicate a vital appetitive need, but do not specify unconditionally the objects or activities that will satiate the vital appetite.

Drives are teleologically connected to different activation channels of conscious emergence, i.e., they have different avenues for being presented into our conscious life. There are two generic spheres of sentient consciousness that are principally activated by drives: interoceptive somatic affections and non-observational perceptions by the cogitative power. Somatic affections are as various as aches, pains, tickles, and other hedonic bodily affects, many of which pertain to the viscera. Cogitative perception involves spontaneous, non-introspective, aspectual, actional, and affectional apprehensions and judgments that in turn activate *psychic affections* (e.g., love, concupiscence, aversion, fear). The activation of both somatic affections and cogitative apprehensions by drives, make present unspecified telic demands to satiate some vital physiological needs. The telic demands communicated through visceral affections and cogitative apprehensions are often ambiguous and require a hermeneutical investigation before any pragmatic solution can be enacted.[39] In other cases there is no apparent ambiguity, and the telic demands are non-inferentially identified and cogitatively associated with the behavioral activities ordered to nourishment, sleep or sexual reproduction, because these activities normatively satiate the vital drive. This cogitative association of objects and activities with certain vital drives is a learned developmental association and specification of a multi-specifiable and poly-satisfied telic demand. Normatively, abdominal somatic affections are cogitatively associated with a vital drive for hunger, grogginess and fatigue are cogitatively associated with a vital drive for sleep, and cutaneous somatic affections in erogenous zones are cogitatively associated with reproductive drives. Again, because these cogitative associations are learned specifications of vital drives, they can be mistaken. For example, not all abdominal affections are activated by a drive for nourishment: some are caused by illness or organ malfunctions like appendicitis.

Vegetative powers and the vital drives they activate are autonomic; i.e., they are self-regulating and can function without any exogenous or other direct interjections by conscious human action.[40] However, most of them do require maintenance by activities carried out through conscious interactions with the environment, like acquiring nourishment or reproductive mates. Activated drives are acts of a human (*actus hominis*) that episodically recur in various degrees of intensity and are normatively satiated by actions that fulfill the specified vital drive. The intensity of a vital drive is often proportionate to the somatic affections it activates. When one prolongs the satiation of a vital appetite, it often increases the intensity of a drive and the activation channels it is teleologically connected with. A protracted vital drive for nourishment increases the intensity of the telic demand and activates further somatic affections beyond the visceral, like dizziness, headaches, fatigue, etc.

There are natural and acquired drives; some acquired drives are addictions because they are *dysordered*. They are *dysordered* because they are acquired autonomic drives that are both 1) contrary to the ends and proper order of the psychosomatic unity of the human person of which they perform a functional *part*, and 2) upon *acquisition*, they are difficult or arduous to overcome and reform. Addictions should be understood according to the psychological model of drives connected with our vegetative powers for nourishment, sleep, and sex. There is also neurophysiological evidence to support that addictions co-opt the same behavior reinforcement centers that are involved in motivating the activities which satisfy our vital physiological needs for nourishment, sleep, and sex.[41]

This categorization of addiction preserves the truth that we can be morally culpable for our addictions and proto-addictions insofar as they deprive us of the goods proper to human persons. This account rejects the reductionist theory that addictions are brain diseases, although it recognizes and is able to account for why many addictions can cause biological and psychological diseases. It also allows us to identify a wide variety of activities as addictions, thus going beyond the conception that we can only be addicted to chemical substances.[42] Further, addictions are not vices, even though in most cases they are introduced into our psychosomatic constitution due to incontinent and vicious activities, especially when the latter become psychological *habitus* of our will and other cognitive or affective faculties. By denying that addiction is a vice, we are also contending that addiction falls outside of the psychological faculties where we might at first glance believe it is to be found, like as an emotion in the concupiscible power.[43]

Nonetheless it is important to see how this account of addiction preserves the fact that most addictions are the result of vice. Recall that our nutritive-reproductive drives, the seat of addiction, are the causal sources for many of our somatic affections and emotions. Hunger, thirst, and somatic exhaustion are all the results of our natural autonomic vital drives. These drives are able to cause or activate somatic affections and/or the cogitative power's activation of emotions that attract our conscious attention to some telic need for satiation. Natural drives for nourishment and sleep are not themselves conscious, but by evoking, say, somatic affections in one's stomach, we become consciously aware of such visceral factors. The activation of somatic affections alone, such as aches, pains, itches, vasomotor alterations, etc., however, is not sufficient for the conscious identification of them as hunger, thirst, etc. This is a further apprehension achieved by the cogitative power, which first aspectually or categorically perceives such visceral affections as "hunger," "thirst," "sexual arousal," and then evaluates or estimates such affections within a repertoire of actional-cum-affectional or axiological judgments as an object to be pragmatically sought or avoided by such-and-such an activity.[44] Only after the actional and affectional judgment of the cogitative power is there any activation on the part of the emotions.[45] The emotions react to the evaluation of the actional-cum-affectional percept, and this reaction often results in further somatic affections and an emotively affected fixation of our cogitative awareness upon our visceral feelings.

This point is important because the cogitative power is also able to participate in practical reasoning. In fact, in his treatments of practical reason, Aquinas often calls it the particular reason, because it provides the singular operable object, which is the term of practical reason.[46] In this way the cogitative power participates in and is integrated within consciousness by apprehending our somatic affections and providing the object of our emotions, and, also, through its subordination to universal reason, provides us with the minor premise of the practical syllogism. If this subordination is inverted, as occurs in instances where our conscious cogitative awareness is distracted by, if not bound to, somatic aches or pains, then the person will begin subordinating universal and particular reason to the end of satiating such irrepressible visceral factors. Many will recognize this inverted subordination of intellect and will to the cogitative judgment and passions of the inner senses as the phenomenon of incontinence or *akrasia*. But what is characteristic of the peculiar kind of incontinence found in addictions?

Addictions, as dysordered acquired drives, can, like natural drives, act on our visceral affections. Yet they do so without a natural limit. Addictive appetites can become so dysordered that they activate vehement somatic affections that significantly reduce, if not eliminate, our ability to reason truthfully about practical matters. Drew Leder has written especially well on the variety of ways in which the body is present or absent. With respect to vehement somatic and visceral affections he writes:

> When normal physiology reaches certain functional limits it seizes our attention. We remember the body at times of hunger, thirst, strong excretory needs, and the like. It is biologically adaptive that we recall our situation at such moments and that their unpleasantness exert a telic demand for removal. Cases of weakness, dizziness, or fatigue operate similarly.[47]

This paper contends that addictions co-opt the system of autonomic drives and their activation channels for somatic affections. The vehement presence of a somatic affection that one instinctually, or, more precisely, cogitatively associates with addictive cravings for certain substances or activities will narrow our conscious attention by imperatively directing us towards considering means for satiation. Vehement somatic affections are unpleasant, if not unbearable. Addictions that activate somatic affections of this kind involve reductions in the sphere of human action to a limited scope of attention, often dedicated to considering possible satiating behaviors. One's addictive cravings for the associated vicious activities are often manifested dynamically at the somatic level as nearly irrepressible visceral affections that seem to unconditionally demand satiation. The cogitative evaluation of these pains becomes so spontaneous and compulsive that the vehement antecedent passions restrict any further cognitive estimation, and there is limited fixation of awareness upon a particular object and the means by which to remove it.[48] By bringing into relief how the dynamism of our cognitive and affective powers of action and activation are etiologically related, we find a more amplified context for analyzing such problems as the apparent, if not real, compulsive character of addictive cravings, continence and incontinence, and antecedent and consequent passions.

For the serious addict, the field of evaluation and practical reason becomes truncated, and the attendance to right reason is diminished, if not omitted, by the telic demands communicated through painful somatic affections.[49] Satiating the telic demand appears as a good next-to-no-other; i.e., practical reason terminates in a judgment that this is good "and nothing else,"[50] and the object of the will is thereby bound by a disordered rationality to affirm or deny without the ability to attend to alternative goods.[51] In such cases, the human person has been reduced as a moral being. Human persons should seek goods that are truly ordered within the teleological complex of human well-being (*eudaimonia*). Instead, such addicted persons become viciously neurotic, since their ability to reason practically, i.e., to consciously attend to alternative ends and means to these ends, is so impaired that they only seem able to use reason to subordinate other ends to their addiction and to give pseudo-justifications for their narrowing sphere of false goods. In this way, addiction can diminish our ability to form *true* rational evaluations and free-choices. However, addictions *as such* do not *eliminate* these operations, although addiction caused *diseases* can. In such extreme cases, the human person ceases to be an agent of truth and goodness, because the person has become incapable of distinguishing true from only apparently true reasons for action, and all of their behavior is determined without any voluntary choice with respect to some good.

Finally, we must briefly respond to the question, "why are addictions so difficult to overcome?" On the side of material causality, we must take note that despite the flexible range of neuroplasticity, some adaptations are more rigid than others. It may be that some addictions formally and materially determine the psychosomatic constitution of the person in such a way that addictions and their cue-dependent perceptions by the cogitative power reach points of no return. Cue-dependent cravings can be activated years after an addict has been abstinent from their addictive behavior. "Successful quitting is thus likely to require a substantial investment in change of environment and lifestyle because addiction 'poisons' person, places and things associated with it in the sense of imparting them with the ability to induce craving."[52]

Addictions go deep. They infiltrate and affect our basic psychological abilities to categorically and axiologically identify patterns of behavior with respect to various objects in the world, as well as bind these perceptual cues with neurologically seated autonomic drives. These autonomic drives are able to operate independently of conscious interjections and can initiate cravings without exogenous stimulation. In the case of addictions we have manifest instances that display our autonomic drives ability to submit our conscious operations to the telic demands of electro-chemical equilibria and recurrent schemes of activity proper to the peripheral and central nervous systems.

Overcoming addictions requires a proper diagnosis of the problem. One must make clear both its etiological root as well as the salient impediments to recovery, which, if not removed, can take the unwary sober addict by surprise, who then, often enough, relapses. Without a holistic approach to addictions, diagnostic omissions will be common, and recovery will only be partial. In other words, there will normally be numerous means of treatment for addictions that are required, so as to target and reform the numerous ways in which addictions affect us. Pharmacological treatments of addictions are often helpful and sometimes essential. Nevertheless, treatment of addiction requires more than pharmacological inhibitions, it also requires re-forming our perceptual repertoire of categorical and actional percepts or cues that stimulate cravings within an addict's acquired drives. This is difficult because such perceptions are integrated into our very way of life. To reform the matter, we must also reform the form, and this requires changing one's life by re-ordaining the values and goods that one chooses to seek by placing them within their proper teleological order.[53] In many cases it also requires uncovering and correcting the initial impetus that led to and started their addictive behavior in the first place.

Addicts, like all human persons, are dependent rational animals and the likelihood of recovery is increased through human solidarity in a community that acknowledges a true teleological order of values and goods. Addicts have dug themselves into a pit; without the help of family, friends, and a community who participate in a common set of goods, the addict is unlikely to find the social and psychological resources that are a necessary and essential complement to pharmacological treatments. We repeat, to reform the matter, one must also reform the form. As much as the neurological and psychological mutually condition each other, the psychological and the social also mutually condition one another. Nonetheless, even with the best treatment resources available, recovery is very difficult, and success is rarely achieved in extreme cases of addiction.

IV. Addiction and Grace

We hope that this paper has made clear a few of the ways that a Thomistic hylomorphic ontology of the human person provides a robust and unified philosophical framework for analyzing the complex interlocking causal orders involved in the moral psychology of human action, self-determination, addiction, and neural plasticity, and offers a promising alternative to dualism or reductive physicalism. Nevertheless, this integrated discussion of how Thomistic philosophical anthropology and neuroscience are related to addiction would not be complete without mentioning how the religious sphere offers us some hope in extreme cases of addiction. In addition to philosophical analysis, Thomism also provides us with a powerful theological doctrine on the grace that perfects nature, even in its most deteriorated and dejected forms.[54] The grace of Christ is a free gift, which is needed by us all, but it is needed in a special way for those suffering from addictions. Philosophy and science only bring us so far, and both remain open to theological insight and guidance. Without the intervention of Divine grace, some humans would never be able to achieve even the most minimal natural ends. We cannot expect it, but God can enter in and restore the horizon of human practical reason and action by returning it to its natural course.

We must also recognize that addictions are often the result of sin. Even though not all addictions are caused by evil actions and vice, most are. Inasmuch as addictions are related to sin, they can and do disorder us with respect to our supernatural end. The depravity of the objects and activities which such persons have chosen, have corrupted not only their practical reasoning and emotions; they have also infiltrated their bodies, rendering entire persons deprived of their full natural vitality. It is through their evil choices that their entire being, as psychosomatic, has taken on the characteristic privations that are so many manifestations of evil. This is especially so in the case of addictions that have caused diseases, either physiological, like liver disease, or psychological, like psychosis.

Despite such dire circumstances, we must recognize that not all of these incapacities are absolute. Where human optimism would be foolhardy, one's hope in Christ will not be in vain. Grace is able to give life again to an otherwise operationally diminished practical reason. Where sin has abounded, grace is able to abound even more. Dependent rational animals are able to find solace in suffering and liberty in the grace of Christ, which is most especially given to us through living within the *Ecclesia* and partaking of Her sacraments. Through charity, addicts are able to receive the infused virtues, which, though they do not necessarily remove the acquired inclinations towards objects of evil, they do miraculously give one the ability to avoid such temptations.[55] Even with grace, overcoming an addiction remains an upward battle with a vector well beyond the addict's deficient natural capacities. But such is the vector of Calvary for us all. And sometimes, the way of the cross is only taken up because one has finally come to see that truly it is His yoke that is easy, and that such burdens, by his grace alone, are able to become light.[56]

Center for Thomistic Studies
University of St. Thomas, TX

Notes

1. Maurice Merleau-Ponty, *Phenomenology of Perception*, trans. Colin Smith (New York: Routledge, 1962, Reprint 2002), 101.

2. I will not take up refuting the numerous reductionist accounts of addiction, such as the disease theory. A substantial amount of literature exists which has sufficiently addressed the problems with the disease theory of addiction. Cf. Jon Elster, *Strong Feelings: Emotion, Addiction, and Human Behavior* (Cambridge, Mass.: The MIT Press, 1999; George Loewenstein, "A Visceral Account of Addiction" In *Getting Hooked: Rationality and Addiction*, ed. J. Elster and O. J. Skog (Cambridge: Cambridge University Press, 1999), 235–264; Bennett Foddy and Julian Savulescu "A Liberal Account of Addiction" *Philosophy, Psychiatry, and Psychology* 17.1 (March 2010): 1–22.

3. Karol Wojtyła *The Acting Person*, definitive ed., trans. Andrzej Potocki, in *Analecta Husserliana: The Yearbook of Phenomenological Research* 10, ed. AnnaTeresa Tymieniecka (Boston: D. Reidel Publishing, 1977), xiii. Translated and revised from *Osoba i czyn* (Krakow: Polskie Towarzystwo Teologiczne, 1969). See also, Norris Clarke, *Person and Being (Aquinas Lecture)* (Marquette University Press, 1993).

4. "The transcendence we are now considering is the fruit of self-determination; the person transcends his structural boundaries through the capacity to exercise freedom; of being free in the process of *acting*, and not only in the intentional direction of willing toward an external object. This kind of transcendence we shall call 'vertical transcendences,' in contrast to the other kind of transcendence that we have called horizontal" *The Acting Person*, 119. Cf. Karol Wojtyła, "The Personal Structure of Self-Determination" in *Person and Community: Selected Essays*, volume 4 of Catholic Thought from Lublin, trans. Theresa Sandok and ed. Andrew N. Woznicki (New York: Peter Lang, 1993), 190–193.

5. Wojtyła, *The Acting Person*, 151. See also, Yves Simon, *Freedom of Choice*, ed. Peter Wolf (New York: Fordham University Press, 1969, 1987).

6. "We find a great wealth of various types of dynamisms at both the somatic and the psychical levels; and it is due to integration that these dynamisms become 'personal' and related as well as subordinated to the transcendence of the person in the action. They thus find their place in the integral structure of the self-governance and self-possession of the person. Our analysis of the integration of the acting person on both the psychical and the somatic levels has . . . revealed the complexity in man." Wojtyła, *The Acting Person*, 256. Cf. Thomas Aquinas, *ST* I-II.17.1; 17.4; 18.6; 20.1–3; *de Malo* 2.2ad5, ad11.

7. Cf. Wojtyła, *The Acting Person*, 71–85ff. "[T]he human being as the person—seen in its ontological basic structure—is the subject of both existence and acting, though it is important to note that the existence proper to him is *personal* and not merely individual—unlike that of an ontologically founded merely individual type of being. Consequently, the action—whereby is meant all the dynamism of man including his acting as well as what happens in him—is also personal" p. 74. "There is a real difference between the two manifestations of man, 'man as existing' and 'man acting,' even though it is the same man who exists and who acts. When man acts, his acting also has a kind of derivative existence of its own. The existence of the acting depends indeed on the existence of man, and it is here that there lies the proper moment of their existential causality. The existence of acting flows from and is subsequent to the existence of man; it is its consequence or effect" p. 82.

8. Etienne Gilson, *Being and Some Philosophers*, 2nd ed. (Toronto: PIMS, 1952), 186.

9. Cf. Thomas Aquinas, *Summa theologiae* (=*ST*) I.75.1, 2; 76.1, 8; 85.7.

10. Cf. Hugh Garavan, et al. "Cue-Induced Cocaine Craving: Neuroanatomical Specificity for Drug Users and Drug Stimuli" *American Journal of Psychiatry* 157 (2000): 1789–1798; Goldstein, et al. "Dopaminergic Response to Drug Words in Cocaine Addiction" *The Journal of Neuroscience* 29.1) (May 6 2009): 6001– 6006. More philosophically integrated accounts of cue-dependent cravings can be found in Loewenstein, "A Visceral Account of Addiction"; Foddy and Savulescu "A Liberal Account of Addiction"; and Elster, *Strong Feelings*.

11. These claims are defended at length in Elster, *Strong Feelings*, esp. chap. 5.

12. Cf. Thomas Aquinas, *de Veritate* (=*DV*) 2.2.ad5; 20.4ad1; *de Malo* 3.13ad 2; *In de Anima* II. lt. 24, n.2; *ST* I.79.6; 89.4; I-II.67.2; III.54.2ad1; *In Liber de Causis* 12.

13. Cf. Thomas Aquinas, *ST* I.81.3; I-II.17.7; 17.9; 30.3; 77.1–2.

14. Donald Hebb, *The Organization of Behavior: A Neuropsychological Theory*, (New York: John Wiley and Sons, Reprinted 1961; 1967, Originally published in 1949).

15. Cf. Eric Kandel, et al. *Principles of Neural Science*, 4th ed. (McGraw-Hill Medical, 2000) 34ff.

16. J. Sharma, A. Angelucci, and M. Sur, "Induction of Visual Orientation Modules in Auditory Cortex," *Nature* 404 (2000): 841–847. For psychological discussions of neuroplasticity see: Jeffrey Schwartz, "A Role for Volition and Attention in the Generation of New Brain Circuitry: Toward A Neurobiology of Mental Force" *Journal of Consciousness Studies* 6.8/9 (1999): 115–142; Jeffrey Schwartz and Sharon Begley, *The Mind and the Brain: Neuroplasticity and the Power of Mental Force* (New York: Regan Books, 2002). Schwartz's work is significant both for its scientific and philosophical challenges and for its practical results, especially for OCD. However, despite the important practical outcomes of Schwartz's treatment methods, there are problems with his homunculus interpretations of mindfulness and neural plasticity, and his reliance on William James's confused accounts of attention and will. For criticism of these approaches to philosophy and cognitive neuroscience, see M. R. Bennett and P. M. S.

Hacker, *The Philosophical Foundations of Neuroscience* (Malden, Mass.: Blackwell, 2003). Even though there are many important parallels between Schwartz's account of "mental force" and our notion of "self-determination," nonetheless, a Thomistic account of self-determination, especially when interpreted through the insights of Anscombe, presents a very different theoretical account of intentional human action from Schwartz's Jamesian-inspired account of volition. For further significant philosophical discussions on neuroplasticity, which also address the results of Sur's studies on ferrets see, Alva Noë, *Out of Our Heads: Why You are Not Your Brain, and Other Lessons from the Biology of Consciousness* (New York: Hill and Wang, 2009); Alva Noë and Evan Thompson, "Are There Neural Correlates of Consciousness?" *Journal of Consciousness Studies* 11.1 (2004): 3–28; Alva Noë and Susan Hurley, "Neural Plasticity and Consciousness" *Biology and Philosophy* 18 (2003): 131–168.

17. Cf. S. F. Cooke and T. V. P. Bliss, "Plasticity In the Human Central Nervous System" *Brain* 129 (2006): 1659–1673; Mark R. Rosenzweig and Edward L. Bennett, "Psychobiology of Plasticity: Effects of Training and Experience on Brain and Behavior" *Behavioural Brain Research* 78 (1996): 57–65. For an attempt to evaluate this research program systematically, see Christopher A. Shaw and Jill McEachern (eds.) *Toward a Theory of Neuroplasticity* (Psychology Press, 2001).

18. "LTP and LTD, the long-term potentiation and depression of excitatory synaptic transmission, are widespread phenomena expressed at possibly every excitatory synapse in the mammalian brain" Robert C. Malenka and Mark F. Bear "LTP and LTD: An Embarrassment of Riches" *Neuron* 44 (September 2004): 5–21, p. 5.

19. Christopher Shaw and Jill McEachern "Traversing Levels of Organization: A Theory of Neuronal Plasticity and Stability" in *Toward a Theory of Neuroplasticity*, chap. 29, 427–447 at 441.

20. "*Supremum infimi ordinis attingit infimum supremi*" Aquinas, *De Spir. Crea.* 2; *In III Sent.*, 25. 1.2; *DV* 15.1; 16. 1; *Summa Contra Gentiles* (=*SCG*) I. 57. 480; II. 91. 1775; III. 49. 2271; *ST* I. 78.2; *In Divinis Nominibus* VII. 4. 733; *In de Causis* 19, 352. Cf. Fran O'Rourke, *Pseudo-Dionysius and the Metaphysics of Aquinas* (Indiana: University of Notre Dame Press, 2005), 263–274.

21. Cf. Shaw and McEachern "Traversing Levels of Organization," 438.

22. Ibid., 438–443. Philosophically we would contend that such causal hierarchies should be understood hylomorphically or in terms of something like Lonergan's systematic and non-systematic causal schemas within different explanatory genera. Lonergan has argued that, "an acknowledgement of the non-systematic leads to an affirmation of successive levels of scientific inquiry. If the non-systematic exists on the level of physics, then on that level there are coincidental manifolds that can be systematized by a higher chemical level without violating any physical law. If the non-systematic exists on the level of chemistry, then on that level there are coincidental manifolds that can be systematized by a higher biological level without violating any chemical law. If the non-systematic exists on the level of biology, then on that level there are coincidental manifolds that can be systematized by a higher psychic level without violating any biological law. If the non-systematic exists on the level of the psyche, then on that level there are coincidental manifolds that can be systematized by a higher level of insight and reflection, deliberation and choice, without violating any law of the psyche. . . . Again, an acknowledgement that the real is the verified makes it possible to affirm the reality no less of the higher system than of the underlying manifold. The chemical is as real as the physical; the biological as real as the chemical; the psychic as real as the biological; and

insight as real as the psychic. At once the psychogenic ceases to be merely a name, for the psychic becomes a real source of organization that controls underlying manifolds in a manner beyond the reach of their laws." Bernard Lonergan, *Insight: A Study of Human Understanding* (Revised 2nd ed., Philosophical Library, 1957), 205–206, cf. chaps. 6, 8, and 15.

23. Cf. Richard J. Davidson, et al., "Emotion, Plasticity, Context, and Regulation: Perspectives From Affective Neuroscience" *Psychological Bulletin* 126.6 (2000): 890–909; Richard J. Davidson, "Affective Neuroscience and Psychophysiology: Toward a Synthesis" (Presidential Address, 2000)" *Psychophysiology* 40 (2003): 655–665; Anne-Noël Samaha, et al., "The Rate of Cocaine Administration Alters Gene Regulation and Behavioral Plasticity: Implications for Addiction" *The Journal of Neuroscience* 24, no. 28 (July 14, 2004): 6362–6370; Francis J. White, "A Behavioral/Systems Approach to the Neuroscience of Drug Addiction" *The Journal of Neuroscience* 22.9 (May 1, 2002): 3303–3305; Ann E. Kelley and Kent C. Berridge, "The Neuroscience of Natural Rewards: Relevance to Addictive Drugs" *The Journal of Neuroscience* 22.9 (May 1, 2002): 3306–3311; Steven E. Hyman, "The Neurobiology of Addiction: Implications for Voluntary Control of Behavior," *The American Journal of Bioethics* 7.1 (2007): 8–11.

24. Kelley and Berridge, "The Neuroscience of Natural Rewards: Relevance to Addictive Drugs," 3308.

25. For a series of articles which take up this contention see "Addiction, Adherence, and Awareness," *Philosophy, Psychiatry, and Psychology* 17.1 (2010); especially Foddy and Savulescu "A Liberal Account of Addiction, 1–22.

26. Most studies in substance abuse focus on the mesolimbic dopamine receptors, which are the central neurophysiological systems that regulate the reinforcement of behavior. However, not just addictive substances involve the stimulation of dopamine receptors and reuptakes, "any pleasurable experience [like sex, gambling, consumption of foods, etc.] causes dopamine to be released within the brain, activating these 'reward' pathways" "A Liberal Account of Addiction," 4. Both addictive substances and behaviors, as well as any pleasurable activities, can sensitize receptors and so result in the reinforcement of synaptic connections that are neurologically involved in the biological substrates of our human experiences. Though it remains true that addictive substances, unlike non-substance based behavioral addictions, often introduce foreign or alternative ways for stimulating these neural networks. Cocaine, for example, blocks pre-synaptic reuptake of dopamine causing a flood of dopamine transmitters to remain in the synaptic cleft without being recycled.

27. Joseph LeDoux *The Synaptic Self: How Our Brains Become Who We Are* (Viking, 2002), 324.

28. Richard Davidson, "Toward a Biology of Personality and Emotion" *Annals of the New York Academy of Sciences* 935 (2001):191–207; 206–207.

29. Cf. Alva Noë, *Out of Our Heads*, esp. chap. 3. See also the related critiques of reductionism in Bennett and Hacker, *The Philosophical Foundations of Neuroscience*; David Braine, *The Human Person: Animal and Spirit* (Indiana: Notre Dame University Press, 1992); and David Oderberg, *Real Essentialism* (New York: Routledge, 2007).

30. Plato, *Phaedo*, trans. G. M. A. Grube (Hackett, 1977) 99e.

31. Eric LaRock's recent work also avails Aristotelian formal causality to resolve problems in neuroscience (especially in visual consciousness and human emotions), which cannot be resolved on reductionistic models. Eric LaRock, "Is Consciousness *Really* a Brain Process?" *International Philosophical Quarterly* 48 (2008): 201–229; eadem, "Intrinsic Perspectives,

Object Feature Binding, and Visual Consciousness" *Theory and Psychology* 17 (2007): 799–809; eadem, "Disambiguation, Binding, and the Unity of Visual Consciousness" *Theory and Psychology* 17 (2007): 747–777; eadem, "Why Neural Synchrony Fails to Explain the Unity of Visual Consciousness" *Behavior and Philosophy* 34 (2006): 39–58; Eric LaRock and Konstantinos Kafetsios, "Cognition and Emotion: Aristotelian Affinities with Contemporary Emotion Research" *Theory and Psychology* 15 (2005): 639–657; eadem, "Against the Functionalist Reading of Aristotle's Philosophy of Perception and Emotion" *International Philosophical Quarterly* 42 (2002): 231–258; eadem, "Dualistic Interaction, Neural Dependence, and Aquinas's Composite View" *Philosophia Christi* 3, (2001): 459–472. See also the recent monograph of William Jaworski, *Philosophy of Mind: A Comprehensive Introduction.* (Malden, Mass.: Wiley-Blackwell, 2011), chaps. 10–11.

32. LaRock, "Dualistic Interaction, Neural Dependence, and Aquinas's Composite View," 271–272.

33. Cf. Elster, *Strong Feelings*, chap. 3.3, 58–76; Lowenstein "A Visceral Account of Addiction." This paper's Thomistic account of addiction has more in common with Elster's presentation than with Lowenstein's. It also resembles, though to a lesser degree, the doctrine presented in Gerald May, *Addiction and Grace: Love and Spirituality in the Healing of Addictions* (San Francisco: HarperOne, Reprint, 2007).

34. The account of addiction adopted in this paper is treated and defended at length in the forthcoming article, "The *Ratio* of Addiction within a Thomistic Philosophical Anthropology: A Proposal."

35. Cf. *ST* I.78.1 (esp. ad3); I-II.26.1; 30.1ad3; 30.3; 35.2; 35.7.

36. Cf. Aquinas, *DV* 26. 1–3; 9; *ST* I-II. 22.2ad3; 28.5; 35.2; III. 15.4.

37. Aquinas's most extended treatment of the emotions is found in the treatise on the passion, *ST* I-II. qq. 22–48. Let us also note here that the details and telescopic analysis of psychology faculties and their operations should not cause the reader to overlook the fact that, properly speaking, it is not the cogitative that perceives, the concupiscible power that desires, or the will that acts, but it is the human person that perceives, has desires, and acts, in virtue of such powers. The synecdochical expressions we employ within our discussions of faculties and operations should not be taken as challenges to the integrated unity of the human person and his operations.

38. The notion of a *telic demand* is from Drew Leder, *The Absent Body* (Chicago: University of Chicago, 1990): "Pain exerts a *telic demand* upon us. While calling us to the now, its distasteful quality also establishes a futural goal: to be free of pain. . . . The sensory aversiveness and world disruptions effected by pain cry out for removal" (77). Leder subdivides telic demands into two moments, the hermenutical and the pragmatic, which I integrate into aspectual and actional intentions formed by the inner sense faculty Aquinas calls the cogitative power. I use telic demands in a way that synthesizes features of both Leder's idea and Lonergan's account of *neural demand functions* in *Insight,* chap.6.

39. Cf. Drew Leder, *The Absent Body*, 77–78ff.

40. Though causally coordinated with the autonomic nervous system in a number of respects, these autonomic psychological *powers* should not be identified with the autonomic nervous system.

41. Cf. George Loewenstein, "Out of control: Visceral Influences on Behavior" *Organizational Behavior and Human Decision Processes* 65 (1996): 272–292 and, eadem, "A Visceral Account of Addiction."

42. Substance based addictions like nicotine, alcohol, and cocaine were thought to be normative, but recently the notion of addiction has been, and I believe should be, extended to include gambling, aberrant sexual behavior, pornography, cutting, exercise, video games, T.V. watching, internet browsing, and perhaps even eating disorders such as anorexia or bulimia. Though the latter are certainly kinds of behavioral disorders, it is not clear if they should be classified as addictions. Concerning the distinction between substance and behavioral addictions, and its potential deficiencies see Elster, *Strong Feelings*, 58; Foddy and Savulescu "A Liberal Account of Addiction," passim.

43. There are extreme instances where addictions are involuntarily acquired, such as when the consumption of addictive substances is forced upon victims. This unfortunately occurs too frequently in cases of sex slave prostitution and as a means of torture. Also, many addicts who are trying to quit no longer desire, i.e., have an emotional attraction to the addictive substance or activity, yet the addict still has a strong drive or inclination for it. These are just a few of the many reasons why we have not placed the locus of addiction in the concupiscible power.

44. Cf. *DV* 10.5; *ST* I.78.4; *In DA* II.13. In these passages Aquinas makes it clear that the proper object of the cogitative power is a singular *per accidens* sensible which is neither the colored, moving, shaped magnitude of *per se* proper and common sensibles, but is *this man*, which happens to be *per se* sensible as white, a certain shaped magnitude, and in motion. Essentially speaking, the proper object of the cogitative power is a singular intention. These intentions admit of a division into aspectual, actional, and affectional intentions, which are taken up in detail in the forthcoming paper, "Perception and the *Vis Cogitativa*: A Thomistic Analysis of Aspectual, Actional, and Affectional Percepts."

45. Cf. Thomas Aquinas, *In II Sent.* 24.2.1; ad2; *In III Sent.*, 17.1.1.2ad 2; *In IV Sent.* 49.2.2; *ST* I.81.3 (esp. ad.2); *ST* I-II.22.2; *DSC* 9; *DQVC* I.4. There are a number of recent articles and books that treat this feature of the cogitative power and the object of the passions. My account differs considerably with Robert Miner, but is quite similar to the doctrine expressed by Diana Cates and Michael Stock. See: Diana Cates, *Aquinas on the Emotions: A Religious-Ethical Inquiry* (Georgetown University Press, 2009); Peter King, "Aquinas on the Passions" in *Aquinas's Moral Theory*, ed. Scott MacDonald and Eleonore Stump (Cornell University Press, 1998), 101–132; Robert Miner, *Thomas Aquinas on the Passions* (Cambridge University Press, 2009); Michael Stock, "Sense Consciousness According to St. Thomas" *The Thomist* 21.4 (1958): 415–486.

46. "Ratio autem practica quedam est *uniuersalis* et quedam *particularis* (universalis quidem sicut que *dicit quod oportet talem tale agere*, sicut quod oportet filium honorare parentem; ratio autem particularis, *quod hoc quidem tale et ego talis*, puta quod ego filius hunc honorem nunc debeo exhibere parenti)" *In DA* III. 10 (434a16) (Leonine, 251:128–133); "ut sic fiat quidam syllogismus cuius maior sit universalis quae est sententia mentis, minor autem singularis quae est apprehensio particularis rationis, conclusio vero electio singularis operis, ut patet per id quod habertur in III De anima." *DV* 10.5, (Leonine, 309:94–99). Both in his commentary on this text from the *De Anima* and in *De Veritate*, Aquinas distributes practical reason into the "universal reason" and the "particular reason," which is one of many ways in which Aquinas distinguishes the intellect from the cogitative power. Cf. Aquinas, *ST* I.81.3; 86.1; II-II. 49.2; 5; *In VI Ethics*, lt. 1, n. 1123; lt. 7 nn. 1213–1215; lt. 9, nn. 1247–1256.

47. Drew Leder, *The Absent Body*, 84.

48. Cf. Aquinas, *De Malo* 3.4; *ST* I-II. 77.6.

49. Addictions range in intensity throughout their development just as psychic *habitus* do. Likewise, just as natural appetites for nourishment, sleep and sex can be resisted and ignored by various means, so too with acquired proto-addictions, like excessive acquired drives for exercise, caffeine, and social stimulation or solitude. Just as one can quell hunger or a sexual urge, we can ignore or put out of mind appetitive promptings. We can do this prudently or imprudently. *Dysorder* with respect to these appetites' appropriate function is revealed when we are no longer able to do this with relative ease. It should be noted, however, that moderately intense drives in one's acquired appetites for exercise or hygiene could be rationally ordered and so be signs of virtue, not vice, and especially not of disease.

50. Cf. Steve Jensen, "The Error of the Passions," *The Thomist* 73 (2009): 349–79.

51. Even if an addictive appetite is evaluated as one to be avoided, the somatic affections caused by the addictive appetites might manifest a vehement need and telic demand to overcome the pain, which is often physiologically debilitating, recurrent and sometimes incapacitating if avoided and not satiated. Such extreme cases of addiction can often further result in diseases that are caused by addictions.

52. Elster, *Strong Feelings*, 245.

53. This is difficult to achieve, especially in the absence of the support provided by friends and family. In *Dependent Rational Animals*, Alasdair MacIntyre discusses how solidarity and communities are needed for human beings to practice the virtues and for ordering their lives towards their proper ends. The importance of solidarity has proved to be especially fruitful for treating addictions, as has been demonstrated by the success of groups like AA.

54. For Aquinas's principal treatment of grace, see *ST* I-II. 109–114. He then takes up the nature of grace throughout the rest of the *Summa theologiae*, but especially in his extended treatments of the theological virtues, Christology, and sacramental theology.

55. "Those emotions that incline us towards evil are not completely removed either through acquired or through infused virtue, except, maybe, by a miracle. For the struggle of the flesh against the spirit always remains, even when we possess moral virtue. St Paul says about this in Galatians, 5:17 'The flesh lusts against the spirit, and the spirit against the flesh.' But emotions of this sort are modified both by acquired and by infused virtues, so that we are not stirred by them in an unrestrained way. However, (i) acquired virtue achieves this in one way and (ii) infused virtue in another. (i) For *acquired* virtue is effective to the extent that the struggle is felt less. This comes about from its own particular cause: when someone becomes accustomed to virtue through repeated actions, they then become unaccustomed to obey those emotions, and accustomed to resist them. The consequence of this is that they feel less troubled by them. (ii) *Infused* virtue, by contrast, is effective to the extent that even if emotions of this sort are felt, they do not take control. For infused virtue means that we refrain totally from obeying sinful desires, and as long as it remains in us, we do so unfailingly. (Acquired virtue can fail in this way, but rarely, in the way that all natural inclinations occasionally let us down.)" Thomas Aquinas, *On the Virtues in Common*, 10 ad14, in *Disputed Questions on the Virtues*, ed., and trans., E. M. Atkins (New York: Cambridge University Press, 2005).

56. I would like to thank my friend Ann-Therese Gardner for suggesting the idea of analyzing addiction from a Thomistic perspective as well as her subsequent comments and suggestions. I should especially thank Bernard Prusak as well the other participants at the ACPA conference for their helpful criticisms, comments, and questions. Finally, I must acknowledge the invaluable, detailed feedback that I have received on this paper and the problem of addiction from Brandon Dahm, Domenic D'Ettore, Eric Mabry, Geoffrey Meadows, Theodore Rebard and Jeremy Wilkins.

What Is Seeing? A Phenomenological Approach to Neuro-Psychology

Robert E. Wood

Abstract: With a myriad of others, Francis Crick has sought the nature of the soul in the observable functioning of the nervous system, beginning with seeing. In contrast, this paper explores the nature of the soul through the grounding of the act of seeing in the power of seeing as its "soul" and folds in the kinds of attention we pay through seeing. We begin with the eidetic characteristics of the visual field. We then explore three theoretical positions on where what is seen presents itself: within the brain, on things, or between awareness and things. What makes possible the appearance of things is the self-presence of the seer revealed in the nature of touch which suffuses the functional, self-directive body. Objectifying the eyes by the ophthalmologist abstracts from their essential expressivity and from the speech that can explain that expression. In the situation of encounter, focus upon the empirical features breaks the character of the encounter where we live "outside" ourselves and within the space of common meaning expressed in language. Even in the empirical focus, the ophthalmologist recognizes, through her seeing, deviations from normality of functioning and uses techniques that follow from her having intellectually mastered the field of practice. As a native power, seeing is a universal orientation towards all instances of the colored kind, cutting through the problem of universals by finding them in powers and correlative kinds. Recognition of this is made possible by the functioning of the notion of Being that grounds both intellectual and volitional activities. A concluding section explores several tasks for neuro-psychological research and expands into the grounds of a general cosmology centered upon the free and intelligent commitment of neuro-psychologists.

> *"What is most obvious and universal in experience is most*
> *frequently overlooked, probably because it is too familiar to evoke*
> *special comment."*
>
> —Errol Harris, *Nature, Mind and Modern Science*

© 2012, *Proceedings of the ACPA*, Vol. 85   pp. 121–134
DOI: 10.5840/acpaproc20118510

In one of my recent classes, an ophthalmologist with forty years' experience in his practise was listening to my discussion of awareness. I began with a philosophic analysis of seeing, and when I ended he exclaimed: "I never really thought about that!" I was as surprised as he was, but for different reasons. I assumed that specializing in eye-care would naturally include reflection upon the nature of seeing; I found it does not. This assumption was as naïve as my undergraduate assumption that a Ph.D. in a field meant you not only knew the basic discoveries in the field and how to work with the investigative methods involved in order to further the discipline, but you would have entered into the exploration of the *philosophy* of the field, how its basic concepts fit within the Whole. After all, "Ph.D." abbreviates *Philosophiae Doctor*, one learned in philosophy. Both realities made me more aware of how fractured the universe of knowing is today. I offer the following as a modest aid in healing that fracture. I will proceed by laying out the parameters of a phenomenological psychology, i.e., a description of the essential features of human awareness. I will conclude by expanding the field of interrelation between the neural and the conscious.

* * *

Well, what then *is* seeing? Physicists can trace the route of light radiating outwards from light-sources as it is partially absorbed and partially reflected off of bodies in the environment until it arrives at a seeing organism. Physiologists can investigate light's passage through the pupils and the lenses through which it impacts the rods and cones of the retina, setting off the electronic transmission of the impact via a set of electro-chemical switches by means of which it ends up in the visual cortex at the back of the brain.

One typical approach to seeing occurred a few years back when Francis Crick (of Crick and Watson double-helical DNA fame) wrote a book called *The Astonishing Hypothesis: The Scientific Search for the Soul*.[1] The book zeroed in on seeing as the initial focus in a long-range project of examining the functioning of the brain in order to explain awareness through the "astonishing hypothesis" that eliminates the soul in favor of observable mechanisms. He presented a detailed but also a somewhat scattered report on what was known about the process of physiological functioning with regard to seeing in conjunction with something of experimental psychology and suggestions for lines of research. Crick rightly claimed that we had better know something about visual consciousness in order to explain it in terms of neural functioning, but what he brought forth attended only to isolated studies in experimental psychology such as Gestalt shifting or the binding of moments involved in minimal awareness but not the total field of awareness within which visual presentation occurs. Further, what he presented did not draw upon the experimental psychological reports. In fact, his whole procedure is peppered with anthropomorphic descriptions of knowings, preferrings and seekings on the part of the neurons. My claim is that what is needed first and foremost in the "search for the soul" is an inventory of the overall structure of the full field of awareness involved in human visual functioning.[2]

From examining neural functioning, it is not uncommon, in fact it is "natural" to conclude, as Crick does, that what we are seeing when we see are images in the visual cortex. (I will have something to say later about why I think the conclusion seems natural, even obvious.) If we granted the last claim, not one thing has been said about seeing, except that, whatever it is, it takes place in the back of the cortex, and what are viewed are images resulting from the highly complex neuro-physiological process. What then *is* seeing?

Let's come at it first from the essential features of what is seen. The generic object of seeing is color. Even the so-called "color-blind" see black, white, and gray, often (oxymoronically) called 'achromatic colors.' And color necessarily involves extension. One cannot even imagine a color that is not extended. And in things extension appears terminated by shape surrounded by the encompassing extension of the sky. But color is not a thing; it is rather a dependent feature of a given thing: the tree, the sky, the friend. Visible things move within the field of awareness, so the shape and motion of things are co-given with the visual object.

When we open our eyes from a fixed position, a 180 degree arc opens up, revealing a panoply of things that remain marginally present when we focus attention successively upon different things appearing within that field. Such focal attention is central to human psychological functioning. We are passive to what we receive from the environment, but we are active in paying attention in various ways that we will consider throughout this paper.

Another aspect of the field of vision as the condition for seeing colored objects is light filling what, in fact, is only apparently empty space between the eyes of the seer and what is seen. A little reflection shows that the apparently empty space between me and the computer on which I am working is full of the sound of the music that plays in the background, though it is not seen. And that I can turn on a classical music station means that, not only are sound waves filling the apparently empty space, so also are the unhearable radio waves. Think also about television and then about the irradiations that form the electro-magnetic spectrum. All of that is streaming through the environment within which vision operates, not seen, invisible, and that precisely as a condition for seeing anything. Paradoxically, could we see all that is "under" or "behind" that phenomenally empty space, we could see nothing because there would be no phenomenal distance between seer and what would be seen. Seeing operates in function of the organic need to identify what fosters and inhibits the ends of the organism. To do that the organism must be built to screen out those features of the surrounding space that would inhibit seeing the things we need to see across that space that gives the illusion of emptiness.

Plato provided a great image for reflecting upon this situation. He said we are like prisoners in a cave, chained so we cannot turn our heads but only stare straight ahead at the cave wall.[3] Behind us is a wall and behind that a fire. And what we see are shadows of things carried on the wall behind us and projected upon the wall in front of us by the fire. Knowing what is known through simple reflection, but even more astonishing through the immense underlying complexity that physics and physiology continue to unveil, and meditating on Plato's image in relation to all that, provides a place of reflective distance for us to consider the oddity of what we take for granted. We live within the way the senses enable us to be tuned in to the things we need in the environment. But the senses' way of revealing conceals what does not lie within their range. Not animals, but only we, as reflective beings, can come to be aware of that and how strange and marvelous the taken-for-granted actually is. The senses as it were blow a luminous bubble, opaque to sensation on the outside, within which we live our unreflective lives and that, even as we reflect upon its strangeness, continues to present the solid sensory world, full sensory actuality with no crack of negativity such as the underlying but in-visible powers of the things seen and the in-principle un-seeable awareness itself.

Two rather odd things also characterize how things are seen. Objects shrink in size as they recede from the viewer's position, so that each three-dimensional thing is perspectivally distorted. A one-foot cube lying on a table looks square on the face frontally and statically viewed, with the top and one side appearing as somewhat flat rhombuses. What is odd is that we do not typically notice the distortion. That is because the psycho-neural system that underpins the field of awareness automatically discounts it by reason of having learned from the past what the actual shape and size of the objects are by our having moved around objects or by having handled and ro-tated them. Our perceptual system has built up within us anticipatory motor schemes that direct our attention away from the factual distortions as we move through the environment. That fact of pre-personal learning on the part of our nervous system from the showing of things in the environment opens up a region of experience that must be explained wholly in terms of the nervous system and its interplay with the level of awareness that emerges from it. What the neuro-psychological system learns is pre-personal, providing the manifest context within which each of us freely directs her-or himself, let's say to engage in research into neuro-psychological functioning. In doing so, we initiate a programming of ourselves that we freely take up and freely continue. As we rely upon the automatic learning by our psycho-neurological system to negotiate our environments, we also rely upon our previous self-programming to advance in our chosen fields of research and practice.

Besides the spontaneous assimilation of perspectival distortion, the other oddity is that everything appears within a horizon that is the limit of the field of vision. The horizon is like a psychic hoopskirt that goes out ahead of and around us and that moves as we move. The horizon is not in me, but is out there as the limit of the field of vision. Developing perspectival drawings consists in elongating the lines of things like a cube that stand progressively away from the viewer in the direction of a point on the horizon where the lines would meet. This allows the progressive shrink-ing of objects to be represented as they stand progressively away from the viewer.

These two considerations, of perspective and horizon, join a third: the question of the status of color. The position that emerged since Galileo was that color, along with other sensory features, are effects within awareness arising out of the brain and caused by wave agitation across the space surrounding one's body—exactly the position "naturally" suggested by developed knowledge of the physiological recep-tion of light. But as Berkeley pointed out, since we have access to the wave agitation only through the color in our visual field, wave agitation is as subjective, that is, essentially related to perception as the allegedly merely subjective sensory features.[4]

Of course, the position of common sense is that color is clearly presented "on" things "out there." Well, that means that we are not seeing things in the back of our brains. And that is the only way we could have gotten the data that show us the wave agitation: from their registration on the scopes "out there," presented across visual space on the screens of mechanisms that scientists have constructed to register in our visual field the effects of light waves. Scientists, both in their practice in looking at and manipulating the objects appropriate to their field and in their everyday lives are common-sense realists. It is only when they buy into the enclosure of awareness inside the brain that they undercut philosophically the basis for their evidence.

There is a third position, which, I would claim, is actually that of both Plato and Aristotle: that sensory features are a special kind of occurrence *between* perceiver and perceived.[5] Aristotle's was the now familiar question: if a tree falls in the forest and there is no one to hear it, is there sound? His answer was that there is agitation of the air, but no sound until it strikes a hearer.[6] And considering the senses as such, he further noted, the sensory power when it is activated has a distinctive *cognitive identity* with the sensible thing as its sensibility is activated. He said, "The sensory power in act is the sensible thing in act."[7] Like common sense, this position holds that we are cognitively outside our physiological inside, but in a distinctive kind of relation: one of *manifestation* or *appearance* that is *sui generis* and that co-modifies the seer and the seen. That co-modifying act used to be called *immaterial*—but, of course, that depends upon what is meant by "matter."

But to return to the status of sensory features, the Galilean position that what we see are images inside our brains cancels its own presupposition: we must be cognitively outside our physiological inside, else we could not know what happens outside in examining the physiology of some organism other than our own—and, indeed, even our own as a visual object. The upshot of the analysis is that color, like perspective and horizon, is neither wholly objective nor wholly subjective, neither simply "out there" nor simply "in here." The color of things exists as a peculiar relation between the seeing subject and visible object: that of *manifestation* or *appearing*. And that is the real heart of the nature of seeing: it brings us *cognitively* outside of our physiological inside in the mode of *manifestation* that is *sui generis*, totally different than what appears as object of seeing or of any other sense. No imaginative picturing can display the peculiarity of the non-seeable character of seeing. We can see the seeable but we cannot see seeing, though we are intimately acquainted with it.

I want to consider further what makes such manifestation possible. To arrive at that, I want to consider the nature of touch. What will seem like a detour will actually bring us to the crucial insight. Unlike other senses, touch has no localized organ. Rather, the whole organic surface with its subcutaneous sensors is the organ. This requires that the one who can touch and feel itself being touched is cognitively, consciously "in touch with" its own organism as a functioning whole. This "being in touch" occurs when the "consciousness switch" in the reticular activating system of the brain-stem is in the "on" position. When that occurs, awareness suffuses the functional body. I say "functional" because being awake is not being in touch with one's brain or one's liver, much less with one's cells, but with what is involved in the self-direction of the organism. One feels awake and thus can feel something that one touches and feel something that touches oneself. Being awake and feeling are equivalent: feeling is non-reflective self-presence.

Relevant to our discussion of seeing, here is the point arrived at through considering touch: what makes the manifestation of something other than oneself possible is the manifestation of oneself as that non-reflective self-presence, other than which the other is manifest. Though it may sound gobble-de-gookey, it is the case: in being focally aware of something other than myself, visually of a set of colored, extended things in the environment, I am non-focally present to myself as the one who is seeing. In the act of seeing, I know that it is I that sees. Being aware at all is a mode of felt self-presence: in animals it is the self-feeling of appetite and of satisfaction or frustration, of pleasure and pain when the animal is absorbed in its relation to the environmentally given. But in seeing and in sensing generally, one's conscious self is not the focus of one's attention; the focus is rather upon the objects given "out there" in the environment. Consciousness is a self-present non-object that is the locus of the manifestation of any object—not "in" oneself, but "out there" in the environment. We live for the most part in animal extroversion. What makes that possible is the causal series of physical and physiological events whose integral functioning is a necessary but not sufficient condition for seeing. What is sufficient is the felt self-presence of the sensing being.

Focused upon, and thinking in terms of visual objects, I said we are "naturally" inclined to think of an organism that sees as confined within the seeable limits of the organism. By reason of tracing the physiological route of transmission of the effect of light upon the retina and then upon the optic nerve, where seeing occurs is in the visual cortex and, "naturally," what is seen is an image that results from the transmission. Beyond the seeable inside and outside, there is nothing—or so we are naturally inclined to think. Seeing leads us on pragmatically, but systematically misleads us speculatively. We are seduced by the richness available through seeing, instrumentally aided or not, and the marvelous things that such knowledge enables us to do, that we neglect to notice that what is deepest, namely our own awareness, is not available through seeing it. What is known is not reducible to a set of visual objects or to imaginative models fashioned upon visual objectivity. We are seduced by visual models into neglecting the true character of the act of seeing. Seeing itself is a different kind of "object" than what is seen; in seeing, the being that sees is brought *outside* its visually observable insides, outside its brain, neural networks, and eyeballs. Grounded "here" inside the organism and in the visual cortex, seeing nonetheless brings the seer *outside* its own visually available inside to be cognitively "with" what is seen outside, given precisely *as outside* the seer's body and as *other than* the awareness that sees. Seeing itself is not seeable and thus not imaginable in terms of some visual model.

Let us add another feature. Consider the ophthalmologist who greets her patient. They meet and exchange pleasantries. She then gets to work, focusing upon the eyes of the patient. In looking at the eyeballs, she *looks away* from the looking of the patient and looks at the full visual actuality of his eyeballs. Her work entails *abstracting* from the concrete presence of the patient, no matter how sensorily "concrete" such experience is. In meeting one another, the eyes of the other appear within an overall facial gestalt that is gestural, expressive in character. In living interchange, one does not focus upon the sensory as such but upon the person with whom one is conversing and/or the matters about which they are conversing. One enters a space of communication in which sensory features play only a subsidiary role. In fact, focus upon some sensory feature of the other breaks the living connection. In living interchange, the state of mind of the other is expressed in the sensory presentation that is strictly subsidiary to that expression. We see that the other is sad or tired or cheery or just in an ordinary, everyday mood. The eyeball as a visual object is subsidiary or non-focally present within one's attention to the person as a live subject, present primarily through the expressive appearance of the face. According to an old Platonic saying, "the eyes are the windows of the soul."[8]

There is a fundamental distinction then between the *lived body* and the *body-object*, the body as felt and lived "from within" by the person who is embodied and that same body looked upon by the scientist. But there is also a distinction between the body objectified in scientific investigation and in medical practice and the body as *expressive* of the disposition of the person whose eyes are being observed scientifically. Expressivity indicates the lived body. Physical science systematically abstracts or looks away from expressivity and thus from *meaning* or how a given thing is to be *read* or *interpreted*. One could consider any living body as *aimed* at its full flourishing and at the endurance of its species. Mechanistic science systematically looks away from teleology or goal-directedness as a fundamental characteristic of life. And so we get a fundamental distinction between fact and value: facts that we can see and values that *we* are said to attribute to things. However, what is given in the case of living things is not simply factually observable mechanisms but also goal-directedness on account of which organisms can succeed or fail. So, when we find living things, we find values: on the one hand, there are the *intrinsic values* of growth to maturity, sustenance, and, following the attainment of maturity, reproduction and nurturing of offspring. On the other hand, there are the *extrinsic values* of things in the environment that serve the intrinsic values, as a given organism may also have extrinsic value for its mate, its parent, or its prey. So human goal projection is not a stranger in a strange land, but a carrying on at a level of deliberateness what had already been going on in both phylogeny and ontogeny, in both the coming into being of the species and the development of the individual human organism.

Parallel to the abstract looking away from meaning is what is involved in the act of reading the E-chart. When the patient scans the E-chart, the letters have been taken out of their typical function of providing a text for reading and are put together in such a way as to invite being focused upon all by themselves. In reading an actual text the letters are, like the eyeballs of other persons in our encountering them, strictly subsidiary to the activity of following what they express: the meaning indicated by the conventional configurations. Focusing upon the eyeballs and focusing upon letters de-focuses the expressive meaning of the look of the other through the eyes and the meaning of the letters in words. We abstractly attend away from the meaningful interchange within which we live our lives.

Further, in the ophthalmologist-patient relation, while looking at the patient's eyes as visual objects, the doctor continues *talking* to the patient. In examining a patient, for example for lens prescriptions, the patient's verbal input is essential. He is asked which in each of a series of two lenses yields a clearer vision of the E-chart.[9] Here we have sound available through one's ears functioning subsidiarily in carrying the meaning of the words, like the visible eyeball of the other is subsidiary in relation to one's focus upon the gaze of the other or like the printed letter subsidiary to reading. The primary presence of the person, going along with his or her gestural style, is in what he or she says. This expresses, not primarily the *disposition*, but rather the *mind* of the patient, what he or she thinks and out of which she or he lives. So the human body that we see is not simply a visible object upon which we can act, guided by science; the human body is first and foremost the expression of the dispositions and thoughts of the person or, in Hegel's terms, the human body comes to be penetrated by, and expressive of, Spirit.

Further still, the doctor is not just looking at the full actuality of the eyes but focusing on them in function of an attempt to understand what is present as a symptom of what she intends to fix. She knows what constitutes regularity of structure and function and can take notice of deviations from typicality. She not only sees the eyes but sees them *as instances of types.* She is focusing *with developed intelligence* that recognizes patterns that call for standard procedures in bringing the eyes to normality of functioning. She is a skilled practitioner of ophthalmology. She brings her intellectual experience to bear upon her sensory experience.

In the development of her skills, she uses optical instruments, scopes that magnify the visual objects, devices that test peripheral vision, glaucoma testing devises and the like. All this is possible because those who first invented such instruments knew the laws of the relation between light, diffracting media, and visual presentation. This entails advancement beyond the skillful coping of animals with the visual environment driven by organic need. It entails advancement beyond the immediacy of visual givenness of *individuals* in the environment to the *universal types* of structure and function that are the objects of scientific investigation, independent of organic needs. Though the physician is interested in curing the ailments of her patients, understanding types of structure and function can occur apart from that interest and in function of the pure desire to understand and even stand in awe of the miracle of seeing, its astonishing difference from the things we see.

It is important, but a bit more difficult, to notice that there are several features of sensory objects in general, and not just visual objects, which help us to understand better the character of seeing. Sensory objects are all *individual* and *actual.* That means that what we cannot visually see is the *potentiality* or the *power behind,* so-to-speak, or *beneath* the manifest surface. And what is peculiar about the native power of any entity is that each individual power, for example my own power of seeing, is not simply individual but is a *universal* orientation that requires individuals of a natural *kind* of object in the environment. Seeing as a power is oriented towards *all* individual features of the kind we call colored. And the capacity to be seen is oriented toward *all* organisms that can see. Now kinds are universal: a kind is found in *all* individual instances. But sensory objects are all individual. We have the capacity to move beyond individuals and recognize the universality of the orientation of powers and the universality of object-types as such. That is why we can have science, and, indeed, why we can have language where the sound or visual shape of a word is a sensorily available stand-in for the intellectual apprehension of the type in a concept. Concepts function like glasses: we normally and unreflectively look *through* them and not *at* them. But we are now attending reflectively *to* them.

What is true of native powers is true also of acquired skills. A skill is a capacity to deal with *all* the individuals of the kind correlative to the skill. If I become a skilled carpenter, I can deal with all individual instances requiring the work of a carpenter correlative with the level of skill I acquire. An ophthalmologist is one who has mastered the skill of curing problems with the eyes *as such*, that is, not just the eyes of the patient with whom he/she is dealing in any given instance, but of any and every individual who comes to the doctor with eye problems. The universality involved on the part of the skilled physician and on the part of the patients whom she cures is not something one can see, but clearly something one can and does come to know—even though one might say, metaphorically speaking, "I *see* what the problem is."

In summary of some of the major features noted above, what cannot be visually inspected or imaged is seeing itself and the general awareness involved, the powers that underlie or stand behind visible actuality, and the universal types we can come to recognize within each sensory field. What cannot be seen is the mind of human beings that is nonetheless present to us in the speech and action that we can hear and see, and is present as the mind of the one who sees, hears, thinks, acts, and speaks as a responsibly self-present human agent. These observations give us new ears to hear the claim of Aristotle: If the eyeball were an organism rather than an organ within an organism, its soul would be the power of seeing and its act would be factual seeing.[10] The holistic character of awareness expresses the holistic principle that underpins it as a metabolic process furnishing the instruments for seeing. The power of vision is not a feature of a kind of ghostly substance haunting the nervous system; it is a second-stage emergent out of a prior and enduring metabolic process. The ground of that process and of emergent consciousness is what Aristotle called the *psyche* or soul. Francis Crick is looking in the wrong direction to find the soul, which he considers a hangover from antiquated ways of thinking.[11] Crick's thinking is rather a degeneration of a richer tradition that he chooses to ignore. The soul is found operative in the power of awareness underpinned by the constructive power of the organism.

Let me add one more observation—a bit more difficult to see, but of primary importance in human life. My first consideration is easy to observe, but it leads to the more difficult point. Beyond visual functioning and coping with the environment, science, through seeing and manipulating, can aim at understanding the nature of organism as such and at a general theory of how the current inhabitants of various ecosystems have come on the scene. It can aim at understanding the system of the underlying subatomic particles embedded in the space-time-energy matrix that underpins and encompasses whatever appears within the sphere of ordinary awareness. It can aim at a general cosmology that extends to the evolution of the entire space-time system that encompasses everything material. It can even raise the question if there might be something beyond such a system. And that very questioning indicates the "being beyond" of the questioner. That is the observation.

Here is the point: science can aim at all that because the human mind is by its nature aimed at absolutely everything by reason of the operation of the *notion of Being* and, along with it, the unrestricted character of the principles of non-contradiction and identity. We know ahead of time that whatever is cannot have and not have a given attribute at the same time and in the same respect. For this to be the case, things and their properties must have distinct identities that endure through time and in place. As a long line of philosophers going back to ancient Greece have noted, what makes the human mind to be such is the *notion of Being*. "Being" includes absolutely everything, for outside being there is nothing.[12] But for us it includes everything only *in principle* since we can actually include *in fact* only what we are able to discover by using the proper methods and dispositions or are able to learn from those who did discover things by reading their reports.

At some undetermined point in the development of the human individual, the *notion of Being* arises in the mind and grounds the question about our place within the whole scheme of things. We exist as *the question of Being* as such and as a whole. Such a question is built into our nature. It is that upon which is based our ability to think of meanings that apply always and everywhere in time and space where individuals of a given type may be found. It is the *notion of Being* that gives us inward distance from the Here-and-Now where our senses operate and within which we direct ourselves. The *notion of Being* gives us distance from what continues to determine us as genetic endowment, cultural upbringing, and the history of our own choices. As we noted, all that is Me for every I. It opens and limits my concrete possibilities. But I as a responsible agent am at a distance from all that and must, by nature, choose what to do with myself. Reference to the Whole via the initially empty *notion of Being* forces each of us to take responsibility for what we become. Both *intellect*, as the ability to apprehend universal meanings, and *will*, as the capacity to choose, are grounded in the operation of the *notion of Being*. It functions not only to ground our distinctively human operations; it functions to draw us beyond our current hold on things and our current modes of operation to modes of thinking and acting that correspond more and more to our place in the scheme of things.

It is all of this that any specialist as a human being should understand. He or she will thereby be enabled to resist the reductionist temptation into which Crick, like so many others, falls. He or she will become increasingly aware of the way we humans are responsibly positioned within the Whole as scientists, as physicians, as friends, as members of a community, and ultimately as members of the community of all human beings.

****

In this concluding section, I want to open up a more wide-ranging battlefront in coming to terms with those who would reduce awareness to material processes. Along the same lines as Crick, there is an earlier book by Dean Wooldridge called *Mechanical Man* that is a refreshingly frank statement of the reductionist program and its central difficulty. The author deliberately hearkens back to La Mettrie's *L'homme machine* published in1748.[13] For Wooldridge, in that work La Mettrie had issued a promissory note, and subsequent research had succeeded by 1968 in paying out about 80 percent of the promise.[14] But then, with admirable honesty, Wooldridge admitted that consciousness isn't anything like the focal mechanisms. However, from what is now known about human mechanisms, all it can be is a purely passive byproduct of the nervous system, "a sort of window through which we can observe a part of the workings of the brain."[15] This says nothing about who "we" are or what "watching" is. John Searle in his *Recovery of Consciousness* remarked that, if consciousness has no function, it is a very expensive evolutionary product that contributes nothing to survival.[16] Wooldridge is a typical epi-phenomenalist whose position on consciousness as a secondary phenomenon is a scientific embarrassment. Our reflections upon all the essential features of human consciousness involved in seeing show the way to overcome the embarrassment.

It is the pre-personal functioning of the perceptual system that calls for a neuro-physiological explanation. An experiment with prisms that inverted the images on the retina led initially to seeing everything upside down. But after a certain period of time, *the psycho-neural system*, correlating the visual images with the other sensory reports developed in terms of the motor habits formed for negotiating the environment, learned to re-invert the images so that they appeared normally.[17] If a photo-electric cell were linked to the proper motor system, such learning could, in principle, be explained without the awareness, although I think that animal/human learning at this level would involve the synthesis of *conscious experience* derived from holistic interaction with the environment. What then is the function of awareness at that level? I think animal awareness must be considered *en route* to human awareness as having a kind of self-determination, but one governed wholly by biological needs. Animal awareness allows for a more flexible adaptability than is the case further down the evolutionary line, for example, in the case of insects where the character of awareness, if existent, is dim. But distinctively *human* awareness can detach itself from being wholly governed by those needs, though human free functioning also has it neurological correlates.

An athlete or a ballet dancer or a musician through practice learns to align him- or herself with the gift of spontaneous performance that they let their bodies execute. The distance of objective awareness and deliberate control (so-called acts of intellect and will) have to be given up in the performance situation so that, as the Zen masters say, *it* acts in me when I achieve "no mind."[18] This alignment with the gift occurs in such a way that the agent simultaneously takes responsibility for what she or he allows to happen spontaneously through him- or herself as a psycho-physical whole. Future brain research has to target the neurological basis for that state of maximum free performance where responsibility and necessity, choice and gift intersect.

Reaching the skill level involved in excellent bodily performance involves having freely programmed oneself by practice. There are actually three basic levels of programming upon which we rely in our free self-dedication. First is the genetic level that delimits each of our particular possibilities. It is open not only to our psychoneural system's automatic learning that allows us to negotiate the environment; it is also open to our being programmed by primary care-givers, most especially in language-use through which all distinctively human learning takes place. The on-going impact of our interplay with others and our being saturated by communications media continues the programming process. But at some point, each of us began to take responsibility for his or her own programs, choosing to follow paths to various skills. We then became free self-programmers within the parameters of our previous tri-leveled programming. The future of brain research should show how these programs are formed, stored, and made available to us as conscious agents, always with the awareness that there is a level of programs that we freely take up, many of which, like the pursuit of neuro-psychology, we choose to form and will continue to choose.

As a concluding remark, I want to extend our considerations to the widest context of the cosmos. The rational freedom to choose the pursuit of the acquisition of different skills has to find its place in an evolutionary universe. I hold that if we accept "whole-hog" evolution, a view that everything, ourselves included, is a product of nothing but the evolutionary process, what has to be changed is not simply our view of mind as a separate thing but, in a sense more important but too often overlooked, what has to be changed is our view of matter as other than mind. If we attend carefully to awareness, we see transparently that science is one of the glorious achievements of the human spirit, using one's freedom to focus one's powers in the pursuit of truth. If that comes out of the initial stages of the universe we inhabit, the early stages have to be understood, not only in terms of visual evidences, but also in terms of the unseeable potentiality for the awareness, and thus the science, that emerges out of it. That places the shoe on the other foot of the reductionists. It is not those who hold for the distinctive character of mind that have to yield the field; it is the reductionists who ignore the peculiarities of mind and who are popularly thought to command the field. The view of mind changes the view of matter as well as of mind as a separate thing, but it does not change the immediately given view of mind as a center of self-directive intelligence oriented toward the Whole. The king and queen of philosophic reductionists, Paul and Patricia Churchland,[19] whom Francis Crick especially admires, have no clothes. Like Crick, they fail to attend to their own practice, aimed at the Whole and freely choosing a reductionist program. The big fuss about reductionism that has unnecessarily dogged science and appears all too often in the popular press is based upon abstracting from the practice of scientists and the intelligent and responsible activity of ordinary human beings. The reductionists are involved in a performative contradiction, using their rational freedom to argue against such freedom.[20]

So, reflection upon what is present in awareness when we see gives us a basis for coming to terms with the all-too-common tendency to reductionism that follows in the train of scientific developments in neuro-physiology. Our presentation has focused most basically upon the free self-determination that follows from our being referred, beyond our current state, to the encompassing Totality. Such reference founds the capacity for apprehending the universal that is operative in ordinary language and in the specialized languages of the sciences; it founds as well our capacity for freely committing ourselves to searching out our place in the Whole, and especially the role of our neural systems in underpinning that search.

Institute of Philosophic Studies
University of Dallas

Notes

1. *The Astonishing Hypothesis: The Scientific Search for the Soul* (New York: Simon and Schuster, 1994).

2. In an extended confrontation with reductionists, P. M. S. Hacker and Maxwell Bennett, in *The Philosophical Foundations of Neuroscience* (Oxford: Blackwells 2003), set ordinary language use over against reductionist attempts. Their direct encounter with David Dennett and John Searle drew a huge crowd at a recent convention of the American Philosophical Association and was made available in print as P. M. S. Hacker, Maxwell Bennett, Daniel Dennett, and John Searle, *Neuroscience and Philosophy—Language, Mind, and Brain* (Columbia University Press, New York, 2007). The approach I am taking here gives the phenomenological underpinnings of an ordinary language approach.

3. Plato, *Republic* VII, 514Aff.

4. *Three Dialogues Between Hylas and Philonous* in George Berkeley, *The Philosophical Works*, ed. M. R. Ayers (London: Orion, 1996).

5. Plato, *Theaetetus*, 153D.

6. Aristotle, *On the Soul*, trans. W. Hett (Cambridge: Harvard University Press, 1975), III, 426a.

7. Ibid., 429b27.

8. Plato, *Phaedrus*, 255C.

9. One of my colleagues wondered how an ophthalmologist might correct a dog's vision.

10. Aristotle, *On the Soul*, 412b19.

11. One of the best philosophical works on medicine is Leon Kass, *Toward a More Natural Science* (New York: The Free Press, 2008).

12. One of the clearest treatments of the notion of Being is Bernard Lonergan's in *Insight: An Essay on Human Understanding* (London: Longmans Green, 1964), 348–374.

13. We should note that LaMettrie was not a pure mechanist; he also published in 1748 a work entitled, *L'homme plante, L'Homme plus que Machine.*

14. If 80 percent was secured at that time, research to the present has advanced significantly further and thus further encourages the reductionist position.

15. Dean Wooldridge, *Mechanical Man: The Physical Basis of Intelligent Life* (New York: McGraw-Hill, 1968), 85, 160–161, 167.

16. John Searle, *Rationality in Action* (Cambridge: MIT Press, 2001), 296.

17. The classic locus is George M. Stratton "Some Preliminary Experiments on Vision Without Inversion of the Retinal Image," *Psychological Review* 4 (1897): 182–187.

18. "The Zen Doctrine of No-Mind," *Zen Buddhism: Selected Writings of D. T. Zuzuki,* ed. W. Barrett (Garden City, N. Y. : Doubleday, 1956), 157–226.

19. Paul and Patricia Smith Churchland, *On The Contrary* (Cambridge: MIT Press, 1998).

20. See my "Five Bodies and a Sixth: On the Place of Awareness in an Evolutionary Universe," *American Catholic Philosophcial Quarterly* 83.1 (Winter, 2009): 95–105.

"Fifthly, or Rather First"[1]: Why Aristotle takes Public Religious Worship to be Crucial to the Activity of Science

Erin Stackle

Abstract: In his *Politics*, Aristotle identifies the public worship of the gods as the most important element of the city, but then immediately follows this claim with the claim that justice is the most important element of the city. I first consider the various possible ways of interpreting this claim on the basis of Aristotle's metaphysical commitments. I then consider what Aristotle actually says about religious worship. The things Aristotle says when elaborating public worship in the city indicate that the importance of this public worship to the city is in establishing the leisure necessary for, and which turns the citizens toward, contemplation. This contemplation, the activity of science, is, as Aristotle elaborates in the *Nicomachean Ethics*, the most divine activity in which we can engage. Public religious worship, then, is essential to the activity of science in a city.

At a seminar at Boston College this past February, Daniel Garber made the provocative claim that instead of referring to the flurry of scientific development of the sixteenth through eighteenth centuries as the Scientific Revolution, which would suggest that the extant science was replaced with some new regime, we ought instead term it the Scientific Reformation, because what all these new models had in common was a rejection of the dominant Aristotelian model.[2]

This proposal, in conjunction with the theme of this year's conference, made me wonder what Aristotle thought was the appropriate relation between religion and science, since one of the crucial changes occasioned by this reformation was the splitting of science from the guidance of religion. Did Aristotle think the two were integrally connected? Or was this new split actually consistent with Aristotle's position? Was there something in Aristotle's thought about the relation between the two that was not sufficiently considered in the somewhat hasty division of science from religion?

The typical instinctive reaction to the question of the relation of science and religion in Aristotle's thought is either to reformulate the question as one about the

© 2012, *Proceedings of the ACPA*, Vol. 85
DOI: 10.5840/acpaproc20118511

relation between thought (*nous*) and the unmoved mover (thought thinking itself), or to dismiss the question as one not particularly relevant to Aristotle's work. Father of many sciences he may be, but father of liturgy or of the structure of religious community he is not. Those with some interest in the Greek philosophical response to this question instead turn their attention to Plato's *Phaedo, Euthyphro* or the second book of his *Republic,* and immerse themselves in questions of our belonging to the gods, our owing them sacrifice, or a proper view of them as crucial to a successful orientation in the world.

A) Aristotle makes the perplexing claim that religious worship and justice are both the most important civic element.

I happily contented myself a member of this group until I came across a provocative claim in Aristotle's *Politics* as he is listing the "elements . . . necessary for the existence of the city"[3] (*episkepteon de kai posa tauti estin hon aneu polis ouk an eie*) (VII.8.1328b2–3).[4] He enumerates the necessary elements of the city as the provision of: (1) food, (2) crafts, (3) arms for internal and external protection, and (4) property for domestic and military use. But Aristotle then remarks: "fifthly, or rather first, there must be a care of religion, which is commonly called worship" (*pempton de kai prôton ten peri to theion epimeleian, hen kaloûsin hierateian*) (VII.8.1328b11–12).

Rather than providing an explanation for this provocative interjection, however, Aristotle simply continues his enumeration with the sixth element necessary to a city, i.e., "a power of deciding what is for the public interest, and what is just in men's dealings with one another" (VII.8.1328b14–15). What makes this sixth item even more confusing for our purpose than that its immediate proximity to the preceding item prevents any explanation of it, is that Aristotle describes this sixth element as "the most necessary of all" of the six (*kai panton anagkaiotaton*) (VII.8.1328b14).

Were we to want to take Aristotle's interjection that the establishment of public worship is "rather first," to mean that this is the most important of the six necessary elements of a city, this remark about the sixth element being the most necessary must at least give us pause. The fifth and sixth elements certainly cannot both be the most important, or, at the very least, they cannot be the most important in the same respect.

Because Aristotle does not modify the claim that the sixth is "most vitally necessary" in some particular respect, and since his insistence thereupon is more explicit than upon the former, it seems reasonable to assume that this sixth element he actually takes to be the most necessary to the city, and that the fifth, the service of the gods, must be first in some other way. The fact that this sixth element is essentially justice, which Aristotle explicitly defends as central to the city in his *Nicomachean Ethics* and in his *Politics,* coupled with the fact that the *Republic*'s author was Aristotle's teacher and friend, even further motivates taking this claim to unambiguously place the sixth element—justice—at the center of the city's existence.

So, if the service to the gods, the fifth "or, rather first" element of the city is not first in order of essential necessity, as the structure of the formulation "elements

. . . necessary for the existence of the city" would otherwise suggest, in what way does Aristotle mean it to be first? The interjection that this fifth element is instead first could be a claim limited to the already mentioned elements. Worship of the gods he could mean to be prior in civic importance to the provision of food, of crafts, of protection, and of property. His assertion about the sixth element being most important could mean, then, that, while the worship of the gods is the most necessary so far, in comparison, justice is even more necessary. Or, perhaps the last two elements are both prior, but in different respects.

But how, precisely, is the fifth element first, that is, prior, to the others? The case for the priority of the sixth element—the determination of what is best for the city, both as a whole, and for its individual members, can be straightforwardly made as being the underlying structure of the city's good, which Plato identifies as "justice" in his *Republic* (*Republic* I, IV).

Or, the two claims of priority could indicate a deep ambivalence in Aristotle's position, parallel to his ambiguity about the priority of both the contemplative and the political life. Or the first five necessary elements of the city could be subsets of the sixth, justice, and the fifth, public worship of the gods, could be the most important of these.

B) Aristotle enumerates in his Metaphysics the various possible meanings of priority.

Perhaps a consideration of the various possible meanings of priority Aristotle enumerates in his *Metaphysics* can help solve this problem. Aristotle identifies the many possible ways we mean "prior" (*protera*) in the eleventh chapter of the fifth book, the book of definitions, of his *Metaphysics*. Something can be prior in place (*kata topon*), in time (*kata nun*), in motion (*kata kinêsin*), in power (*kata dunamin*), in ordering (*kata tina logon*), in knowledge (*to tê gnôsei*), in substance (*kata ousian*), in potency (*kata dunamin*),[5] and in activity (*kat' entelekheian*) (*Metaphysics* V.11).[6]

The notable lack of discussion of service to the civic gods in Aristotle's metaphysical thought[7] suggests it wildly unlikely to rank prior in either substance or activity, the central elements of his metaphysics, and, most probably, not prior in potency, determined as it always is by activity. Nor, given the priority universals take in knowledge (V.11.1018b31), does the worship of the gods, who are concrete particulars worshiped in particular situations, seem prior in knowledge. This leaves priority of place, of time, of motion, and of ordering as plausible ways Aristotle could mean that worship of the gods is first of the six elements necessary to a city.

Since Aristotle identifies the genus of 'priority' as that which is "nearer to some beginning," (V.11.1018b10) and since "all causes are sources" (*archai*) (V.1.1013a18), it also seems helpful to consider the possibility that the relevant priority is in one of the four causes. Of these four, the formal cause seems solidly disqualified by the competition justice presents. But the worship of the gods could be prior to justice as "that from which each thing might best come into being," "that [nonconstituent] from which something first comes into being," or "that for the sake of which," what are commonly termed the material, efficient, and final causes (V.1.1013a1–21).

So, to summarize our position: either Aristotle is not sure whether justice or the worship of the gods is more necessary to a city; or the worship of the gods is more necessary than providing food, crafts, protection and property, but not more necessary to a city than justice; or, the first five necessary elements of the city are subsets of justice, and the worship of the gods is the most important of these; or, while justice is essentially prior to the worship of the gods in the structure of a city, the worship of the gods is prior to justice in some other way with respect to the city. The leading candidates for this other way are: priority in place, in time, in motion, or in ordering; or priority in one of the three basic causes left after formal cause is excluded.

C) Aristotle's further remarks in his Politics about organizing the city suggest religious worship is not a subset of justice, but rather grouped with the other four civic elements.

Some of Aristotle's further remarks about the organization of the various functions of the city give some further insight about which of these possibilities we ought most seriously consider.[8] When considering "the right distribution of the executive offices," in *Politics*, Book VI, chapter 8, Aristotle distinguishes between "the main political offices" (*hai men oûn politikai tôn archon skhedon tosaûtai tines eisin*) and "another province of affairs, which is concerned with the cult of the civic deities; and this requires officers such as priests and custodians of temples—custodians charged with the maintenance and repair of fabrics and the management of any other property assigned to the service of the gods" (*d' eîdos epimeleias he peri tous theous, hoîon hiereîs te kai epimeletai tôn peri ta hiera toû sozesthai t eta huparkhonta kai anorthoûsthai ta piptonta tôn oikodomematon kai tôn allon hosa tetaktai pros tous theous*) (*Politics* VI.8.1322b17–19). This distinction indicates a separation in kind between the preceding group of responsibilities for ensuring the public good and public religious worship.

This separation is further indicated by his insistence, in enumerating the offices required to manage public religious worship, that there would need to be a "separate office, charged with the management of all public sacrifices which have the distinction of being celebrated on the city's common hearth, and, as such, are not legally assigned to the priests" (*ekhomene de tautes he pros tas thusias aphorismene tas koinas pasas, hosas me tous hiereusin apodidosin ho nomos, all' apo tês koinês hestias ekhousi ten timen*) (VI.8.1322b26–28). The law divides the realm of "the city's common hearth" from explicitly religious property.

But what does this separation between civic responsibilities and public worship mean with respect to Aristotle's previous ordering of justice and public religious worship? Should we consider the preceding civic responsibilities the concerns of justice? Aristotle's subsequent summary of "the necessary offices of superintendence" (*hai . . . anagkaîai epimeleiai*) "on the basis of their various functions" helps to answer this question (VI.8.1322b29–30).

Here Aristotle does list public religious worship (*peri t eta daimonia*) as one of the charges, or offices, of the state, though he uses the term for 'charges' (*hai epimeleiai*), rather than 'ruling' (*archon*). This time, Aristotle lists public religious worship first in its group. Aristotle groups these charges into three sets. Public religious worship is grouped with military matters, revenue and expenditure, care of the marketplace, of the city center, of the harbours and of the countryside.

The second group includes the law courts, contract regulation, enforcement of penalties, custody of prisoners, and auditing of the officials—those offices that ensure the appropriate order is maintained by identifying and punishing those who threaten to undermine it. While Aristotle explicitly uses the term 'justice' (*peri tôn dikaion*) in reference to the execution of sentences (VI.8.1322a6–7), the implication is that all these offices are explicitly necessary to ensure that justice means something.

The third and final group consists only of that office that deliberates on public affairs. This office, when Aristotle introduced it earlier in the chapter, he identified as the one "that controls, more than any other office, the whole range of public affairs" (*para pasas de tautas tas arkhas he malista kuria panton estin*) (VI.8.1322b12). If any group is to qualify as the practitioners of justice, this group will be it.

As concerned with the proper ordering and subsequent thriving of a city, all these offices are concerned with justice, if we take justice to be the characteristic excellence of a city. Insofar as Aristotle is distinguishing justice as an element of the city from other essential elements, we have to consider that some offices in the city will focus more explicitly on justice than others will.

If we are to arrange the necessary offices of the city alongside what Aristotle has identified earlier as the necessary elements of the city, the first four elements—food, crafts, defense and property—seem addressed by the first group of offices just mentioned. The sixth element, justice, seems explicitly addressed in different ways by the second and third groups of offices—the third with its deliberations and the second with its enforcement. The fact that the fifth ("or rather, first") element, public religious worship, is grouped here with the offices addressing the first four elements, suggests that when Aristotle says public religious worship is "rather first," it must be in relation to the preceding four elements.

In sum, Aristotle's arrangement of public offices indicates that the necessary civic element of public religious worship is *not* a subset of justice, and *is* first with respect to the four preceding elements of the original list. He differentiates public religious worship from other offices by indicating: 1) that it is not one of the "main political offices"; 2) that there is a clear legal distinction between public property and religious property; and 3) that religious worship belongs in the set that includes the offices concerned with the first four necessary elements of a city.

So, is public religious worship, while first with respect to its set of elements, still second to justice? Is it first, but in a different way than justice is? Or, is Aristotle ambivalent about the priority between the two, in a way similar to his apparent ambivalence about the priority between political excellence and contemplation?

Aristotle's civic categorization does not seem adequate to further decide this. Instead, we must now turn to what Aristotle says in his *Politics* about just *why* the worship of the gods is so important.

D) The worship of the gods is consistently valued in terms of its relation to leisure.

A strong connection to leisure emerges from a consideration of why public religious worship is so important to the city. The things Aristotle says when elaborating public worship in the city indicate that the importance of this public worship to the city is in establishing leisure and turning the citizens toward contemplation.

1) The worship of the gods is a structurally leisured activity.

First, the worship of the gods is a structurally leisured activity.

In dividing the various functions of the city amongst its inhabitants, Aristotle concludes that the farmers and craftsmen cannot be citizens, because a citizen needs a leisure which neither of these functions allows. This leisure is a necessary criterion of citizens, because the best city is the one that "can attain the greatest happiness; and that, as we have already stated, cannot exist without goodness" (VII.9.1328b35–37).[9] The lives of farmers, mechanics, and shopkeepers, however, are "ignoble and inimical to goodness" (VII.9.1328b40–41). "[L]eisure is a necessity, both for growth in goodness and for the pursuit of political activities" (VII.9. 1329a1–3). This leisure is necessary for the happiness and goodness that orient a good city. To have the kinds of citizens that could make a good city, these people must have leisure.

These citizens engage in the activity of the city in three basic ways as they age. Aristotle divides the functions of military defense, deliberation, and religious worship between these leisured citizens, insisting that the same people ought perform the various functions of the city at various ages. When they are young and strong, they should serve in the military; when they are older and wiser, they should serve in the deliberations of the city. When they have completed both services, they may then take up the remaining service of the priesthood (VII.9.1329a28–34). The officers of the priesthood, those concerned with the city's public worship, must, therefore, as citizens, be people of leisure.

The priests, however, must have even more leisure than ordinary citizens. The worship of the gods is thus even more a structurally leisured activity than either military defense or the deliberations of justice. "[I]t is appropriate," Aristotle explains, "for the service of the gods and the relaxation which it brings to be assigned to those who have given up [these tasks—those of military defense and deliberation] through age" (VII.9.1329a31–34). Those qualified for the service of the gods no longer have even the responsibilities of deliberation or those of military defense that citizens of leisure in their respectively younger years must bear.[10]

2) The worship of the gods is also crucial to developing contemplative leisure in the city.

But not only is the worship of the gods a structurally leisured activity, it is crucial to developing leisure in the city, and this a leisure that is directed toward contemplation, rather than justice. This is first evident in Aristotle's discussion of the temple's role in the physical arrangement of the city.

When laying out the physical order of the city most conducive to its goodness, Aristotle determines that "the buildings appropriated to religious worship" (VII.12.1331a24–25) ought be placed on "a spot seen far and wide" (VII.12.1331a28). This should be a spot, he claims "which gives due elevation to excellence and towers over the neighbourhood" (*eiê d' an toioûtos ho topos hostis epiphaneian te ekhei pros tên tês theseôs aretên hikanôs kai pros ta geitniônta merê tês poleôs erumnoterôs.*) (VII.12.1331a28–30).

This description makes two interesting claims about these sites of religious worship. First, these buildings of public religious worship serve as seats of excellence, and make this excellence evident to the citizens by the physical elevation at which they are located. They "give due elevation to excellence." Given how central excellence is to Aristotle's discussion of happiness, happiness being the criterion by which we can call a city good, the claim that these buildings of public worship serve as seats of excellence indicates that they are crucial to the city's goodness.

In a footnote, Jowett[11] indicates that the Greek text here is uncertain, so one cannot put undue weight upon the precision of any particular translation. Rackham[12] translates it "the site would be suitable if it is one that is sufficiently conspicuous in regard to the excellence of its position." Barker[13] translates it as, "This site should be on an eminence, conspicuous as a seat of goodness." The common consensus in English translations, therefore, seems to be that the best way to make sense of the passage is to emphasize the making conspicuous, the drawing attention to themselves that these sites serve to accomplish, and the excellence revealed, whether merely by being an excellent position, with Rackham, or by serving to situate excellence. The gist seems to be, then, that this site makes conspicuous to the citizens something about excellence. It draws their attention to it.

The second interesting claim in Aristotle's description is that this elevation also allows these houses of religious worship to command the areas surrounding them. These places can be seen from the lower surrounding areas, and these surrounding areas can be seen from the temples. It is a place that oversees its surroundings, and that is visible to the surrounding inhabitants. The being visible seems helpful to the prior project of making conspicuous. Because everyone can see the building, it can command their attention.

Because the surrounding citizens also realize that they can be seen from this commanding position, their attention to their own behavior and appearance is heightened. It reminds them that they can be watched, that they are being watched, perhaps immediately by those at the sites of worship, but perhaps more relevantly, by those gods whose worship these buildings house. This seems likely to effect an increased care in governing themselves.

By making excellence evident, these places of worship can inspire imitation of this excellence in the surrounding citizens. By their evident command of the surrounding area, these places of worship can increase the self-conscious attention with which the surrounding citizenry engage in this imitation.

Because these places of worship are explicitly devoted to the gods, there is some reason to think that there would be a particular emphasis on the most divine of the excellences. As Aristotle makes clear in the tenth book of his *Nicomachean Ethics*, the characteristic divine excellence is that of contemplation.[14]

The way in which these places of public worship of the gods are at work in structuring the city is further supported by the claim immediately following this one, in which Aristotle asserts that, "Below this spot should be established an agora, such as that which the Thessalians call the 'freemen's agora'; from this all trade should be excluded, and no artisan, farmer, or any such person allowed to enter, unless he be summoned by the magistrates" (VII.12.1331a31–36). Aristotle explicitly excludes anything unleisurely from this place. No non-leisured activities can be performed here, and no people who lack leisure are permitted to enter. The place most immediately commanded by the place of public worship of the gods must be explicitly a place of leisure. As Aristotle says, this "upper agora we devote to the life of leisure, the other [a lower marketplace] is intended for the necessities of trade" (VII.12.1331b12–13).

Aristotle's description of the leisure activities that commence here shows *how* he understands the commanding place of public worship to inspire leisure in the citizenry. He says, "It would be a pleasing use of the place, if the gymnastic exercises of the elder men were performed there" (VII.12.1331a37–38). He terms this a "noble practice," which ought be performed in the presence of the magistrates, "for the presence of the magistrates is the best mode of inspiring true modesty and ingenuous fear" (VII.12.1331a38–b1). These qualities, of modesty and appropriate fear, he takes to be those of free citizens, rather than of people without leisure. The purpose of gymnastic exercise, Plato insists, is to make a person beautiful,[15] and these people are able to perform this practice in a better way because of the presence of the magistrates. Their presence inspires the appropriate emotions from the citizens.

It seems this must support the immediately prior description of the places of public worship making excellence conspicuous and commanding their surroundings. If this is how the activities in this place of leisure will be facilitated, by the observation of those who hold standards of excellence inspiring those standards in those being observed and aware they are being observed, it makes sense that the places of public religious worship, commanding these public gathering places, would work similarly to facilitate leisure. In fact, it seems like the effectiveness of the magistrate's observation is predicated on the power of the temple's observation. While the magistrates may be paragons of human excellence, the temples house the higher divine excellence.

This distinction between human and divine excellence should call our attention to the fact that, while in some other places in the *Politics* in which leisure is discussed,[16] Aristotle explicitly links it to political excellence, he does not do so here. None of the activities he describes as particularly appropriate to this free public space are those of political excellence, or justice. This 'freeman's agora' seems to be committed to leisure that is not directed beyond itself to justice. It is conducted for its own sake.

Aristotle's emphasis on leisure that is not political is furthered by his emphasis here on the exercise of the elderly, insisting that "different ages should be separated, and some of the magistrates should stay with the boys, while the grown-up men remain with the magistrates" (VII.12.1331a39–40). This echoes the division of ages he made earlier,[17] when dividing the functions of the city between the same leisured citizens, as their age made them suitable. This evokes the emphasis on the leisure of the elderly being greater than that of the younger, and the special emphasis on the elderly here suggests this emphasis on the greater amount of leisure being appropriate to this space, the leisure that follows the cessation of political responsibility.[18]

So, the temple placement inspires and enforces excellence, particularly the most divine excellence, and the *agora* its placement commands is, by extension, structured to inspire leisured excellence. This leisured excellence seems particularly appropriate to contemplation, rather than to justice.

E) The city's happiness relies on good starting points, for which we must pray to the gods.

This completes Aristotle's explicit discussion of public religious worship in the *Politics*. A few more remarks in the text, however, directly pertain to this discussion of how divine worship is integral to a flourishing city. The city's happiness, we discover, relies on good starting points, for which we must pray to the gods.[19]

Another way to consider precisely how the public worship of the gods can effectively cultivate leisure is to examine Aristotle's preliminary remarks when establishing how to make a good city. A good city is one that is happy, just as a good person is one that is happy. So, in identifying what a good city needs, since a city is an agglomeration of people, we ought consider what a good person needs (*Politics*, VII.13.1331b24–38). "A city," Aristotle says, "can be excellent only when the citizens who have a share in the government are excellent, and in our state all the citizens share in the government . . . for in the excellence of each the excellence of all is involved" (VII.13.1332a35–38).

"The happiness and well-being which all men manifestly desire," Aristotle says, "some have the power of attaining, but to others, from some accident or defect of nature, the attainment of them is not granted; for a good life requires a supply of external goods, in a less degree when men are in a good state, in a greater degree when they are in a lower state. Others again, who possess the conditions of happiness, go utterly wrong from the first in the pursuit of it" (VII.13.1331b39–a1).

Unless a person is gifted with the right starting point, she is not able to accomplish the happiness she seeks. Similarly, unless a city is gifted with the right starting point, it is not able to accomplish the happiness it seeks. Once we have this good starting point, the work of the city begins. It attempts to accomplish its project of the goodness that embraces happiness. Without this good starting point, though, the work is fruitless, or even destructive. We can work continuously without ever accomplishing what we most need, because our disordered desires fail to lead us to what would genuinely satisfy us. If this were so, we would be utterly incapable of leisure.

We can know that we want to, and need to, accomplish happiness, and even know what is necessary to accomplish it, but be utterly powerless to do so. This crucial good starting point is not something for which we can rely upon ourselves. Of course we cannot accomplish a good city without the "knowledge and purpose" of its citizenry (VII.13.1332a33). Our knowledge and work are, however, alone insufficient to accomplish that without which we are perpetually dissatisfied.

Thus, we must turn for help to higher powers. We must pray. In Aristotle's words, "we can only say: may our state be constituted in such a manner as to be blessed with the goods of which fortune disposes (for we acknowledge her power)" (VII.13.1332a30–31).[20] We enjoin the gods. "A city," he says, "can be excellent only when the citizens who have a share in the government are excellent, and in our state all the citizens share in the government . . . for in the excellence of each the excellence of all is involved" (VII.13.1332a35–38). We must pray for the good starting conditions of the city, which means praying for the good starting conditions of each of its members. Once these good starting conditions are attained, the necessary excellence of the citizens can be communicated by the temple making excellence conspicuous.

The worship of the gods, then, allows us some confidence that we can rely for these essential foundations, which we cannot provide for ourselves, but which we absolutely need, on more powerful beings than we are. Without this, we cannot afford the leisure that is crucial to a satisfied city. We can only engage in activities that are not for the sake of some further benefit when we are confident that the necessary conditions of a satisfying life are provided us.

F) The worship of the gods is crucial to establishing the leisured activity of contemplation.

The leisure made possible by this public worship of the gods makes possible the activity of contemplation, the activity that is, unlike any other, entirely for its own sake. In the seventh chapter of the tenth book of his *Nicomachean Ethics*, Aristotle explains that the qualities of contemplation "evidently are self-sufficiency, leisure, as much freedom from fatigue as a human being can have, and whatever else falls to the lot of a supremely happy man" (*EN* X.7.1177b21–23).[21] The person engaged in contemplation "requires the necessities of life . . . [to] have been adequately provided" (X.7.1177a29–30). Without these, contemplation is impossible.

This leisure also, of course, makes possible political activity, the excellence of which, justice, consists in harmonizing the appetitive soul with the rational soul. But having been provided with leisure, "a just man still needs people toward whom and in company with whom to act justly" (X.7.1177a31–32). The "wise man," the one practicing contemplation, however, "is able to study even by himself" (X.7.1177a34). This higher degree of self-sufficiency indicates a higher level of leisure. "[S]tudy seems to be the only activity which is loved for its own sake" (X.7.1177b1).

Also, although practical virtue requires leisure, the practical virtues are activated in political and military pursuits, . . . the actions involved in these pursuits seem to be unleisurely. This is completely true of military pursuits, since no one chooses to wage war or foments war for the sake of war; he would have to be utterly bloodthirsty if he were to make enemies of his friends simply in order to have battle and slaughter. But the activity of the statesman, too, has no leisure. It attempts to gain advantages beyond political action, advantages such as political power, prestige, or at least happiness for the statesman himself and his fellow citizens, and that is something other than political activity. (X.7.1177b6–15)

Practical excellence involves some unleisurely engagements. The activities of contemplation, on the other hand, are ends in themselves, entirely leisurely (X.7.1177b15–23).

Even external goods are much less necessary to contemplation than they are to the practice of practical virtue. To be generous requires money. To be courageous requires physical strength, to be self-controlled requires "the possibility of indulgence" (X.8.1178a23–34). "But a man engaged in study has no need of any of these things, at least not for the active exercise of studying; in fact one might even go so far as to say that they are a hindrance to study" (X.8.1178b3–4). Contemplation, therefore, by requiring fewer external goods, is an even more leisured activity than political virtue is.

This most leisured activity is also the one by which we are most akin to the gods. Contemplation, Aristotle takes to be the distinctive activity engaged in by the gods. The gods, if they exist, must be active, and since "a concern with actions is petty and unworthy of the gods," as is a concern with production, "what is left except contemplation?" (X.7.1178b17–21). A person who lives such a contemplative life, Aristotle says, "would do so . . . because there is a divine element within him" (X.7.1177b28).

"The gods enjoy a life blessed in its entirety; men enjoy it to the extent that they attain something resembling the divine activity; but none of the other living beings can be happy, because they have no share at all in contemplation or study" (X.8.1178b26–28). We enjoy a blessed life insofar as we engage in contemplation, this activity that distinguishes the gods.

In fact, it seems that those who engage in contemplation are "most beloved by the gods" (X.8.1179a23–24). "For if the gods have any concern for human affairs—and they seem to have—it is to be expected that they rejoice in what is best and most akin to them, and that is our intelligence" (X.8.1179a24–27). The gods, who Aristotle takes to be interested in our affairs, are specifically interested in our contemplative exercise.

This indication that the gods are particularly interested in those who practice contemplation, who "most love and honor intelligence," suggests a further correlation between the kind of leisure made possible by public religious worship and the activity of contemplation (X.8.1179a28). Our worship of the gods allows us to develop those activities that endear us to them.

G) Our distinctively scientific activities belong to the activity of contemplation.

The distinctively intellectual life, the activities that are exclusively rational, and make up the contemplative life, are three in number: science (*epistêmê*), intelligence (*nous*), and theoretical wisdom (*sophia*) (*EN* VI). All three of these fit into what we currently term 'science,' and consider to be the study of the things that are in such a way that they do not change. All intellectual activity, including that focused on more practical concerns, is concerned with "the attainment of truth" (VI.2.1139a28–9). The practical applications of intelligence are either applied science (*tekhnê*) or practical wisdom (*phronêsis*). Their concern with truth, however, is with respect to action. The intellectual activities concerned only with truth, those that are involved in contemplation, since their objects are sufficiently unchanging to allow continuous consideration, are those we consider to be authentically scientific.

The particular correlation between leisure and contemplation is supported in Aristotle's *Metaphysics* by the strong correlation Aristotle draws between the activities of science, the requisite leisure, and the priestly class. He writes there:

> And as more and more arts were discovered, some relating to the necessities and some to the pastimes of life, the inventors of the latter were always considered wiser than those of the former, because their branches of knowledge did not aim at utility. Hence when all the discoveries of this kind were fully developed, the sciences which relate neither to pleasure nor yet to the necessities of life were invented, and first in those places where men had leisure. Thus the mathematical sciences originated in the neighborhood of Egypt, because there the priestly class was allowed leisure. (*Metaphysics* I.1.981b18–24)[22]

H) Public religious worship facilitates in a city the leisure necessary for scientific activity.

Aristotle clearly takes the public worship of the gods to be integral to a happy city. Our investigation of the provocative claim that public religious worship is both the fifth and the first element essential to a good city, has revealed that Aristotle intends this worship to be considered first with respect to the preceding four essential civic elements. His discussion of this public religious worship shows *why* it is so important to a city. At least in part, this public religious worship is important because it specifically facilitates the leisure necessary for contemplative scientific activity. Without public religious worship, a city cannot develop the scientific activity that Aristotle insists in his *Metaphysics* is so crucial to satisfying our most basic desire to understand (I.1).

What remains to be determined is precisely how this importance of public religious worship is related to the importance of justice in a city's overall good. Is public religious worship first with respect to its own set, but second with respect to justice? Is it coordinate with justice?

The strong connection between this religious worship and contemplation suggests that we might explain the two claims of importance in the introductory passage by the continual tension in Aristotle's thought between the priority of justice and the priority of contemplation. The claim that religious worship is first might also refer to the emphasis Aristotle places on the need for a good starting point for any person or city to be happy, and the complete reliance for this starting point on the blessings of the gods. It could be prior in place, as the temple must command and orient the city, and this orientation could correspond with a priority in ordering, though the priority in ordering seems more likely to belong to justice. It could be prior in time, in that the good starting point must be provided before we can begin to bother about justice. This temporal priority could fit with a priority in motion, the gods beginning the lives that we then lead. A case could also be made for the causal priority of religious worship over justice in the realms of material, efficient, and final causality. It could point to the city's material cause, by turning our attention to that out of which the city comes to be, the starting point provided by the gods, without which no city could be construed. It could similarly point to the city's efficient cause, by turning our attention to the origination of the city by these same gods. And it could serve as the final cause, by inspiring in us the activity in which we are most akin to the gods, the contemplation that is that for the sake of which we ultimately live.

Religious worship is clearly crucial to the city in ways that justice cannot be. And this is why Aristotle insists, as he closes his discussion of how a city ought be organized, that "the country should be studded with temples" (*Politics* VII.13.1331b17).

Loyola Marymount University

Notes

1. Aristotle, *Politics, The Complete Works of Aristotle*, vol. 1, ed. Jonathan Barnes, trans. Benjamin Jowett, VII.8.1328b12.

2. Daniel Garber, "What Really Happened During the Scientific Revolution: Aristotelieans vs. Anti-Aristotelians," February 18, 2011, Boston College.

3. Aristotle, *Politics*, trans Jowett.

4. Aristotle, *Politica* (Oxford: Ross, 1957); all Greek text is from the Oxford Classical text.

5. The repetition of *kata dunamin* arises because Aristotle takes up this version of priority again when he considers it in relation to activity.

6. Aristotle, *Metaphysics*, trans. Joseph Sachs (Santa Fe: Green Lion Press, 2002); all English translations are from this volume.

7. Richard Bodéüs addresses some helpful ways to make sense of Aristotle's understanding of the Greek gods in his book, *Aristotle and the Theology of the Living Immortals* (Albany, N.Y.: State University of New York Press, 2000).

7. The reader must keep in mind how very little Aristotle explicitly discusses public religious worship in his *Politics*.

8. R. F. Stalley, in the Oxford World's Classics translation, draws our attention here to the passage at *Politics* VII.I.1323b29–36, where Aristotle makes this claim a bit more thoroughly. Aristotle, *Metaphysica* (Oxford: Jaeger, 1957); all Greet text is from this volume.

9. *To hoplitikon* (military class); *to bouleutikon* (concillor class); *ton khronon apeirêkotas* (the time of retirement).

10. Aristotle, *Politics, The Complete Works of Aristotle*, vol. 1, ed. Jonathan Barnes, trans. Jowett.

11. Aristotle, *Politics*, trans. H. Rackham, Loeb Classical Library, vol. XXI (Cambridge, Mass.: Harvard University Press) 1998.

12. Aristotle, *Politics*, trans. Ernest Barker (Oxford: World's Classics, 1995).

13. I elaborate this point further in sections F and G.

14. Plato, *Gorgias* 452.

15. For instance, VII.9.1329a1.

16. At VII.9.

17. As Aristotle describes at *Politics* VII.9.1329a32.

18. A question might arise, based on the assumption that Aristotle only seriously considers the 'Unmoved Mover' divine, about how it could make sense for Aristotle to believe in prayer. Certainly the 'Unmoved Mover' would not be moved by our pleas. For a fascinating argument about the seriousness with which Aristotle considers the Greek deities, read Richard Bodéüs's book, *Aristotle and the Theology of the Living Immortals*.

19. Barker translates this: "we pray that the establishment of the city be blessed with fortune, in matters where fortune is sovereign" (VII.13.1332a30–31).

20. All citations from the *Nicomachean Ethics* are from Martin Ostwald's translation: (Prentice Hall, 1999).

22. I thank Arthur Madigan, S.J., for kindly suggesting this connection..

The Status of Laws of Nature in the Philosophy of Leibniz

Karen R. Zwier

Abstract: Is it possible to take the enterprise of physics seriously while also holding the belief that the world contains an order beyond the reach of that physics? Is it possible to simultaneously believe in objective laws of nature and in miracles? Is it possible to search for the truths of physics while also acknowledging the limitations of that search as it is carried out by limited human knowers? As a philosopher, as a Christian, and as a participant in the physics of his day, Leibniz had an interesting view that bears on all of these questions. This paper examines the status of laws of nature in Leibniz's philosophy and how the status of these laws fits into his larger philosophical picture of the limits of human knowledge and the wise and omniscient God who created the actual world.

Introduction

I t seems plausible to think that anyone who takes the science of physics seriously would believe that that science has the potential for arriving at objective fact about the world—i.e., that the methodology of physics and its typical modes of reasoning have the potential for determining *how things really are*. It would seem absurd, for example, for a physicist to choose his or her career out of a desire to study in detail what humans *think* is the case, with no attention to whether or not such a conception corresponds to matters of fact about the world. I begin this paper, then, with the assumption that physics is an interesting and worthwhile study precisely because we believe it to have some hope of arriving at a characterization of the way things *are*, not because we believe it to tell us something about ourselves as human knowers or what we *think* is the case. (At least, we would not expect this latter goal to be one's *only* goal in the study of physics—surely there are much more direct ways of understanding the human condition and the limits of human knowledge than the study of physics.)

The *prima facie* distinction I draw upon in the above observations is a distinction between two sets of questions. One set of questions—those of the objective sort—concerns the way things are. These questions ask: "What is so? What is the actual world really like?" The other set of questions—those of the subjective

© 2012, *Proceedings of the ACPA*, Vol. 85
DOI: 10.5840/acpaproc20118512

sort—concern what is *thought* to be so. These questions ask: "How do we think and know? How is our knowledge shaped and constrained by our cognitive capacities and our particular position with respect to the world?" In this paper, I attempt to determine what kind of status—objective or subjective—laws of nature have in Leibniz's philosophy.

Leibniz was both interested in and involved in the science of physics of his day.[1] It would therefore be surprising if he did *not* think that the science of physics could reveal objective fact about the world. And there is plenty of textual evidence that he did hold that laws of nature—which, for Leibniz, were the important results of physics—were indeed objectively true of the world. However, there is also some compelling evidence that Leibniz was particularly sensitive to a sense in which the laws of nature have a subjective character. Laws of nature in this subjective sense are, at best, shaped by human knowers, and, at worst, outright false because of human limitations in conceptualizing reality.

In what follows, I will examine the tension between the objective and subjective understanding of laws of nature in Leibniz's philosophy. In Section 1, I will lay out the case for an objective understanding of laws of nature within Leibniz's philosophy. In Section 2, I will argue that, when we dig into the details of Leibniz's opinion on the matter, we find he takes the view that the laws at which physics arrives are subjective—i.e., necessarily adapted to and peculiar to human cognition. I will also come to the surprising conclusion that in Leibniz's philosophy, laws of nature must be, in the strictest sense, false. In Section 3, I will discuss Leibniz's peculiar solution for reconciling both the objective and subjective aspects of laws of nature. How can one believe that the laws of nature are false (in the strictest sense) but still be serious about the enterprise of physics? Leibniz's solution to this problem will be of interest to anyone who wishes to have a serious attitude toward physics while also acknowledging the limitations of human knowledge, the possibility of miracles, and the inscrutable ways of God.

1. The Case for Objective Laws of Nature

1.1. Laws of Nature as True Relations and Orderings

As is well known of Leibniz's philosophy, neither relations nor the phenomena of physics are real in a strict sense. Relations and physical phenomena are not substances in themselves; rather, they are *entia rationis*.[2] Since laws of nature are relations among entities and orderings of events to which these entities are subject, and since they deal with physical phenomena, it might seem at first glance that there would be nothing objective about a law of nature. After all, the physical interactions to which such laws pertain are not real in a causal sense, as there can be no interactions between or among "windowless" monads.[3] But on closer examination, Leibniz certainly thinks that relations and orderings can be true or false, and also real, in a sense. The foundation for the truth of relations and orderings lies in the substances related, and whether or not the relation or ordering in fact holds of them:

> Relations and orderings are to some extent "beings of reason," although they have their foundations in things; for one can say that their reality, like that of eternal truths and of possibilities, comes from the Supreme Reason.[4]

Each monad has an internal program, a sequence of states that defines and identifies it as the entity it is. Inasmuch as there are regularities in the programming of any individual monad, we can say that there is a true ordering of its states. And inasmuch as there are regularities in the way that the sequence of one monad aligns with that of others, it can be said that there are true relations that hold among monads. Facts about the monads themselves, including their internal progression and the alignment of their progression with that of other monads, are the foundation for the truth or falsity of relations and orderings. And since laws of nature are relations and orderings, we can say that there is a truth or falsity as to whether or not any stipulated law matches the facts of the actual world—i.e., whether or not the phenomena described by the law are "well-founded." These facts, being decidable independent of human knowers, can be said to be objective. Physical laws are attuned to, derived from, and inherent in the operation of monads.

Beyond relations having a foundation in the monads and sequences of which they are true, Leibniz tells us that relations have a reality in that God knows and sees them:

> God not only sees individual monads and the modifications of every monad whatsoever, but he also sees their relations, and in this consists the reality of relations and of truth.[5]

The divine mind, which sees all substances exactly as they are in their complete concept, can also see any laws that supervene on the sequence of states that inevitably unfolds within any individual monad *as well as* any laws that supervene on the alignment of all monadic sequences in the world across world history. For God to know and see these laws in the world that he actually creates is for them to be true and real and objective. In order to create *ex nihilo*, there must be a complete determination of the complete concept of every monad created (and hence every sequence and every natural law). Hence there must be some fact of the matter about the laws that supervene on the actual sequence of the world. God must make decisions as to how he is to create the world and what order it will exhibit, and these decisions form a basis for objectivity.

1.2. The Hierarchy of Order

But is it not trivial to say that God created an orderly world? Is it even possible for any collection of substances to *lack* order? No matter what the sequence of events pertaining to each and every substance, is it not possible to describe some (possibly arbitrary and contrived) rules or laws that are true of that sequence? Leibniz was well aware of this trivial sense of order:

> Not only does nothing completely irregular occur in the world, but we
> would not even be able to imagine such a thing. Thus, let us assume, for
> example, that someone jots down a number of points at random on a piece
> of paper, as do those who practice the ridiculous art of geomancy. I main-
> tain that it is possible to find a geometric line whose notion is constant
> and uniform, following a certain rule, such that this line passes through
> all the points in the same order in which the hand jotted them down.[6]

> No possible series of things and no way of creating the world can be
> conceived which is so disordered that it does not have its own fixed and
> determinate order and its laws of progression.[7]

It seems that, for Leibniz, order is a metaphysical necessity. There *cannot* be a group
of monads such that some sort of order cannot be identified that relates their internal progression of states to one another. Order, then, must be a matter of degree.

Lest it seem that the laws of nature are determined only by an arbitrary choice
of God, Leibniz explicitly clarifies that God chooses the laws that he does according
to a standard of wisdom and perfection.

> Some very able philosophers of our day have held that the laws of motion
> are purely arbitrary. They are right in this if they take *arbitrary* to mean
> coming from choice and not from geometric necessity, but it is wrong
> to extend this concept to mean that laws are entirely indifferent, since it
> can be shown that they originate in the wisdom of their Author or in the
> principle of greatest perfection, which has led to their choice.[8]

Thus, the laws of nature are not objective *only* because God chose them as those to
which the actual world would conform, but also because they themselves were chosen
to meet certain standards. Leibniz thinks that there *is* an answer to the question of
why the laws of nature are as they are—an answer that is rationalistic rather than
voluntaristic. To deny that there is such a rationalistic explanation would be to deny
God's glory and wisdom in having chosen such excellent laws.[9]

In fact, the project of Leibnizian rational mechanics is precisely this: to examine, discover, and reconstruct the principles that unite the laws of nature.[10] Leibniz
thinks that above and beyond the laws of nature that order physical phenomena,
there are general, metaphysical laws that order—and by the creative act of God
supervene on—the laws of nature themselves. Metaphysical considerations can give
us an account of why physical laws are a certain way; metaphysics provides "the
foundation of the laws of nature."[11]

> And indeed, we observe that everything in the world takes place in
> accordance with laws that are eternally true, laws that are not merely
> geometrical, but also metaphysical, that is, not only in accordance with
> material necessities, but also in accordance with formal reasons. . . . We
> also see the wonderful way in which metaphysical laws of cause, power

and action, have their place in the whole of nature, and we see that these metaphysical laws prevail over the purely geometrical laws of matter.[12]

Metaphysical principles (e.g., simplicity, economy, continuity, least action) are imposed as structural constraints within which nature must operate to achieve her ends. For example:

> The laws of motion ought to be formulated in such a way that there is no need for special laws for equal bodies and bodies at rest. Rather, these laws arise *per se* from the laws of [un]equal bodies and motions, or if we want to formulate special laws for rest and equality, we must be careful not to formulate laws that are inconsistent with the hypothesis that takes rest as the limit of motion or equality as the least inequality, otherwise we will violate the harmony of things, and our laws will not be consistent with one another.[13]

Laws of nature are objective not only because they have their foundation in the real entities of the world and in the mind of God, but also because they belong to a hierarchy that orders and constrains them; they have their foundation in metaphysical principles that are subject to rational consideration.

2. The Case for Subjective Laws of Nature

2.1. Harmony as a cognitive aid for humans

The fact that there are *exactly these* laws of nature is a contingent feature of the world; it is not metaphysically necessary for the phenomenal order of the world to be subject to the actual laws, because the world that God chose to create could have had just a bare minimum of order (in the trivial sense discussed above in Section 1.2). The actual laws of the world are not true by necessity, but rather because of the harmony that God willed to instill in the world:

> The laws of motion and nature have been established, not with absolute necessity, but from the will of a wise cause, not from a pure exercise of will, but from the fitness [*convenientia*] of things.[14]

As we also saw above in Section 1.2, metaphysical principles provide an objective standard against which various possible laws of nature (or rather, sets of laws of nature) can be measured.

But how does God make the choice of one particular set of laws? Are metaphysical principles sufficient to narrow down the possibilities to just one most perfect world? Are there other criteria outside of these principles? First of all, let us begin with Leibniz's view that the actual world is the most perfect of all possible worlds:

> As the design of a building may be the best of all in respect of its purpose, of expense and of circumstances; and as an arrangement of some figured

representations of bodies which is given to you may be the best that one can find, it is easy to imagine likewise that a structure of the universe may be the best of all.[15]

The best world is the one that optimizes or maximizes all of the metaphysical considerations:

We can already understand in a wondrous way how a certain Divine Mathematics or Metaphysical Mechanism is used in the very origination of things, and how the determination of a maximum finds a place.[16]

Leibniz compares God to an architect who is able to weigh the various considerations against one another. In describing this optimization calculation, Leibniz repeatedly mentions two principles that appear to be the dominant considerations: simplicity and variety.

In whatever manner God might have created the world, it would always have been regular and in accordance with a certain general order. But God has chosen the most perfect world, that is, the one which is at the same time the simplest in hypotheses and the richest in phenomena, as might be a line in geometry whose construction is easy and whose properties and effects are extremely remarkable and widespread.[17]

Notice that these two prime values, simplicity and variety, are at odds with one another. There is a somewhat intuitive appeal to the idea of a world with much variety and abundance,[18] but presumably, to maximize only with respect to variety would greatly reduce simplicity. But why should simplicity be of such great value? Why not discard simplicity as a value and simply make the most abundant and varied possible world?

The answer lies in the special care that God has for spirits (i.e., humans) as rational creatures:

We mustn't doubt that the happiness of minds is the principle aim of God and that he puts this into practice to the extent that general harmony permits it.[19]

Humans are limited, both in thought and interpersonal communication, to language that consists in symbols—a language which, as a consequence, is both discrete and finite. Human language is thus inadequate for describing the world, which, on the contrary, is continuous and infinitely detailed. Therefore, it is necessary that the order perceived by humans be an oversimplification of reality. If reality is continuous and consists in an actual infinity of monads, there must be a discrepancy between human language and reality.

Now, since all human knowledge can be expressed by the letters of the alphabet, . . . it follows from this that one could calculate the number of truths of which human beings are capable. . . . This investigation serves to let us understand better how small man is in relation to the infinite substance. Then the number of all the truths which all men together are able to know is small enough even if there be an infinity of men who throughout all eternity strive towards the advancement of knowledge . . . this number is almost nothing in relation to that of all truths.[20]

Humans, being limited, use approximations to deal with the infinity of reality, since reality doesn't fit our conventionalities. God knows that finite intelligences such as ourselves need to be able to get by with suboptimal procedures. It is important to God, who cares for us, that we live in a "user-friendly" world, where our approximations and discrete mechanisms of thought are sufficient. The more complex and varied the world, the greater the mismatch will be between the human capacity for knowledge and the object of that knowledge. And so God chose the actual world from all possible worlds using a standard of simplicity; this way, human methods of ordering and categorizing *do* give us some access to *approximate* truth about the world.[21] This intelligibility makes spirits feel at home in the world; cognitive dissonance would be painful to intelligent beings.

For Leibniz, the concept of harmony is relative to human epistemology. Harmony is not just any order; harmony requires some minimum amount of order, and this minimum amount of order is one in which the relations that hold among a set of things allow for those things to be distinguished from one another by a finite mind.[22] Despite there being no hope that a finite mind will be able to distinguish among an actual infinity of monads, a certain level of order—i.e., a harmonious order—among monads might give rise to phenomenal unities such that humans can make clear and useful distinctions among those unities. God's choice to create the actual world with laws of nature that are harmonious, then, is an epistemic aid for humans. However, despite the epistemic sufficiency of human perception, it still remains at the phenomenal level; the regularities and distinctions that we manage to pick up on are not faithful to the infinite subtlety and continuity of the actual world. For Leibniz, then, the truth we are able to grasp is only an approximate one, and that we are even able to grasp this approximate truth is by design. These considerations would seem to favor the case for a subjective view of the laws of nature.

2.2. Laws of Nature Are Not without Exception

Leibniz divides occurrences into two categories: those that are natural (for which he also uses the term "ordinary"), and those that are miraculous (for which he also uses the terms "extraordinary" or "supernatural").[23] Although we might expect that miracles violate any specifiable order of nature, Leibniz repeatedly explains that *both* natural and miraculous occurrences belong to a certain orderliness of the world.

Now, since nothing can happen which is not in the order, one can say that miracles are as much within the order as are natural operations, operations which are called natural because they are in conformity with certain subordinate maxims that we call the nature of things. For one can say that this nature is only God's custom, with which he can dispense for any stronger reason than the one which moved him to make use of these maxims. . . . We can say that God does everything following his most general will, which is in conformity with the most perfect order he has chosen, but we can also say that he has particular volitions which are exceptions to these aforementioned subordinate maxims. For the most general of God's laws, the one that rules the whole course of the universe, is without exception.[24]

Miracles are indeed exceptions to the laws of nature (they are "above the subordinate maxims"), but they *are* in accord with a higher-order law: the "universal law of the general order."[25] So laws of nature are not the highest order regularity; the highest order regularities in the mind of God also include miracles. Laws of nature are merely the regularities that are accessible to created minds, there being a higher order of true, unbroken regularity that is incomprehensible to men:

Miracles in the universe . . . are always in conformity with the universal law of the general order, even though they may be above the subordinate maxims. . . . God's miracles and extraordinary concourse have the peculiarity that they cannot be foreseen by the reasoning of any created mind, no matter how enlightened, because the distinct comprehension of the general order surpasses all of them. On the other hand, everything that we call natural depends on the less general maxims that creatures can understand.[26]

In a discussion of a paradox relating to God's foreknowledge of the sin of Adam, Leibniz again confirms that laws of nature have exceptions, and that there is a higher level of order to the world:

Everything is in conformity with this order [the general and inviolable order], even miracles, which are, no doubt, in conformity with God's principal plans, although they do not always observe the particular maxims that are called laws of nature.[27]

The above comments are evidence that, on Leibniz's view, the laws of nature on which humans focus in the study of physics apply only to a limited range of phenomena. Phenomena outside of that range—phenomena that are supernatural or miraculous—can be observed and witnessed by humans, but fail to be explainable on the basis of limited human knowledge. This is perfectly consistent with God's concern for the welfare of spirits, since, presumably, an ability to identify and explain regularities beyond certain limits is not necessary for spirits to understand and feel at home in their world. That there are higher-level regularities that are even more robust than the laws of nature need be of no concern to humans. Again, we have seen that, because of miracles that are exceptions to the laws of nature, the laws of nature must be understood as subjective—i.e., laws of nature must be a peculiarly *human* way of conceiving the world, and in the strictest sense, an erroneous one.

3. A Reconciliation of the
Subjective and Objective Aspects of Laws of Nature?

Let us recapitulate the results of the previous sections. Laws of nature, as relations and orderings of monads and their successive states, have the potential for being objectively true of the world on the basis of facts about succession of states in the actual world. This basis for truth is doubly founded because of the presence of these relations in the mind of God. Secondly, it is Leibniz's view that laws of nature belong to a hierarchy in which metaphysical principles explain and provide a foundation for physics. Since these metaphysical principles are subject to rationalistic consideration, they are objective, and thus the laws of nature must also be objective if decided on the basis of these principles.

By other considerations, however, laws of nature must be subjective. Physics, as an enterprise carried out by human knowers, is limited by the discrete and finite cognitive abilities of humans, and of necessity can only be an approximation to the infinite detail of the world. Fortunately, this does not prevent humans from having *any* access to truth; it merely limits humans to approximate truth. So far, the subjective and objective aspects of the laws of nature are reconcilable.

But the tricky point is this: laws of nature, as humans understand them, have exceptions. The order of the world that is in fact exceptionless is beyond the realm of physics and beyond the realm of *any* human ability to explain, because it requires infinite knowledge and the total world view that only God can have. So we cannot get around the fact that the laws of nature are, in the strictest sense, false.

The question arises: how can one believe that the laws of nature at which physics has arrived (or at which it has any chance of arriving in the future) are false, and still be serious about the enterprise of physics? Allowing for miracles, the only sense in which physics can be said to reach objective truth is that the laws of nature professed by physics are true of a large subset of phenomena that are the object of human experience. Leibniz's solution is the following: the objective and subjective senses of a law of nature are united by the fact that, by the design of God, *laws of nature apply to exactly that subset of phenomena that spirits are concerned with for the purposes of intelligibility.* The fact that knowers are spirits, and that these same spirits are of paramount concern to God, guarantees that the subjective and objective laws of nature are one and the same.

Leibniz's solution, which relies on God as a lynchpin, is an elegant and interesting one. However, it may be a bit difficult to swallow. A physicist who adheres to Leibniz's metaphysical views is forced into the belief that physics is merely a discovery of what God left for humans to discover, and nothing more. Such a physicist must accept that there is an absolute limit to his method, such that no amount of future time or thought will pull back the curtain to the exceptionless realm of truly universal law.

University of Pittsburgh, Department of History and Philosophy of Science

Abbreviations

I. Collections of Leibniz's Works in English Translation

[AG] 1989. *G. W. Leibniz: Philosophical Essays*. Ed. and trans. Roger Ariew and Daniel Garber. Indianapolis: Hackett Publishing Company.

[L] 1969. *Philosophical Papers and Letters*. Ed. and trans. Leroy E. Loemker. Second Edition. Dordrecht: D. Reidel Publishing Company.

[PM] 1973. *Philosophical Writings*. Ed. and trans. G. H. R. Parkinson and Mary Morris. London: Dent.

[S] 2006. *The Shorter Leibniz Texts: A Collection of New Translations*. Ed. and trans. Lloyd Strickland. London: Continuum.

II. Leibniz's Works

DM *Discourse on Metaphysics*. Cited by section number and page number in [AG].

M 1991. *Monadology*. Cited by section number and page number in Nicholas Rescher, *G. W. Leibniz's Monadology: An Edition for Students*. Pittsburgh: University of Pittsburgh Press.

NE 1996. *New Essays on Human Understanding*. Cited by chapter, section number, and page number in Peter Remnant and Jonathan Bennett (eds. and trans.), *New Essays on Human Understanding*. Cambridge: Cambridge University Press.

T 1985. *Theodicy*. Cited by page number in Austin Farrer (ed.), *Theodicy: Essays on the Goodness of God, the Freedom of Man, and the Origin of Evil*. Trans. E. M. Huggard. La Salle, IL: Open Court.

TA *Tentamen Anagogicum: An Anagogical Essay in the Investigation of Causes*. Cited by page number in [L].

Notes

My reflections in this paper originated from a seminar on Leibniz's philosophy taught by Nicholas Rescher. I thank him for his lectures and his deep exploration of Leibniz's life and thought. I also thank James Madden and Peter Distelzweig who provided me with helpful comments and feedback.

1. His serious interest is obviously implicit in his essays on physics (e.g., "A Specimen of Dynamics" [AG 118–138]; "Dynamics: On Power and the Laws of Corporeal Nature" [AG 105–111]; "Tantamen Anagogicum: An Anagogical Essay in the Investigation of Causes" [L 477–485]). In addition, many expressions of the worthiness of the enterprise of physics occur in Leibniz's works. Often, these occur in the context of a defense of the study of both mechanical principles and the metaphysics of substance, which founds those mechanical principles. For example:

> It is useless to mention the unity, notion, or substantial form of bodies when we are concerned with explaining the particular phenomena of nature, just as it is useless for the geometers to examine the difficulties concerning the composition of the continuum when they are working on resolving some problem. These things are still important and worthy of consideration in their place. All the

phenomena of bodies can be explained mechanically, that is, by the corpuscular philosophy, following certain principles of mechanics posited without troubling oneself over whether there are souls or not (Letter to Arnauld, 1686 [AG 80]).

For similar passages, see: *DM* §11 [AG 43]; *DM* §22 [AG 54–55]; "On Body and Force, Against the Cartesians" (esp. [AG 254–255]); "Against Barbaric Physics" (esp. [AG 318–319]).

2. See quotation in note 4 below.

3. See *M*, §7, p. 58.

4. *NE*, 227.

5. Notes for Leibniz to Des Bosses, 1712, [AG 199]. See also *NE*, ch. XXX, §4, p. 265.

6. *DM*, §6 [AG 39].

7. "A Specimen of Discoveries about Marvelous Secrets" [PM, 78–79].

8. *TA* [L, 478]. See also Leibniz's complaint against Malebranche in "On a general principle useful in explaining the laws of nature through a consideration of the divine wisdom," [S, 131–134]; *T*, §359 p. 341; *TA* [L 477]; *DM*, §2 [AG 36].

9. See *DM*, §2 [AG 36].

10. See Chapter 5 in Nicholas Rescher, *Studies in Leibniz's Cosmology* (Piscataway, N.J.: Transaction Books, 2006) for a discussion of the project of Leibnizian physics and its search for metaphysical principles which serve as laws for the laws of nature. Rescher states that "the insistence not just on the lawfulness of nature but on the higher-order lawfulness of nature's laws is the hallmark of Leibnizian physics" (103).

11. "On Nature Itself," [AG, 157].

12. "On the Ultimate Origination of Things," [AG, 152].

13. "A Specimen of Dynamics," [AG, 133]. Note that Leibniz's language here of "formulating" laws is not an indication of a lack of objectivity. It is evident in the context that his concern with how laws are formulated is a concern that they reflect the way that the actual world really is. Laws should be formulated in a harmonious and consistent way, not for the sake of the formulation itself, but because the world is organized in a harmonious way and the laws should reflect this reality.

14. "Against Barbaric Physics" [AG, 319]. See also Letter to Bernard le Bovier de Fontenelle (1703) [S, 136–137]; *TA* [L, 478, 484].

15. *T*, §200, p. 252.

16. "On the ultimate origination of things" [AG, 151]. See also *TA* [L, 484]; Letter to Malebranche (1679) [L, 211].

17. *DM*, §6 [AG, 39]. See also *DM*, §5 [AG, 38–39]; *M*, §58, p. 203; *PNG*, §10 [AG, 210]; Letter to Malebranche (1679) [L, 211].

18. See "On the ultimate origination of things" [AG, 151], where Leibniz compares the tendency of heavy things to descend to the "greatest number of possibles" which strives for existence.

19. *DM*, §5 [AG, 38]. See also "On the ultimate origination of things" [AG, 152–153].

20. Philip Beeley, "Leibniz on the Limits of Human Knowledge: With a Critical Edition of *Sur la calculabilité du nombre de toutes les connaissances possibles* and English Translation,"

The Leibniz Review 13 (2003): 100. See also Chapter 8 in Nicholas Rescher, *Studies in Leibniz's Cosmology*.

21. Nicholas Rescher reflects on the fact that the natural limitations of human knowledge and its mismatch with the world do not create a hopeless situation. We can still access truth by making vague statements: "it is not the truth *per se*, but the *detailed* truth that is bound to be inaccessible to beings afflicted by cognitive myopia" (*Studies in Leibniz's Cosmology*, chap. 8, 183).

22. See Laurence Carlin, "On the Very Concept of Harmony in Leibniz," *The Review of Metaphysics* 54.1 (2000): 99–125. Carlin argues convincingly that Leibniz defines harmony in terms of "distinctive relations" and cogitability. However, it remains somewhat unclear what the "things" are that must be distinguishable to satisfy the criterion for harmony. Carlin frequently refers to the distinguishable "things" as "entities," which might be taken to suggest that they are monads. This can't be the case, however, since there should be no hope that a finite mind would be able to distinguish among an actual infinity of monads. The best candidate for the "things" distinguished seems to be phenomenal unities such as, e.g., societies, bodies, and colors.

23. See *DM*, §6–7 [AG, 39–40], §16 [AG, 48–49]; Letter to Arnauld (1686) [AG, 71–72]; (1687) [AG, 82–84].

24. *DM*, §7 [AG, 40].

25. See quotation below (*DM*, §16 [AG, 48–49]).

26. *DM*, §16 [AG, 48–49].

27. Letter to Arnauld (1686) [AG, 72].

Mental Causation as Teleological Causation

Andrew Jaeger

Abstract: I argue that the Causal Closure Argument (CCA) and the Explanatory Exclusion Argument (EEA) fail to show that mental causes must either be *reduced/ identical* to physical causes or that mental causes are epiphenomenal. I begin by granting the soundness of CCA and EEA and go on to argue that they only rule out irreducible mental *efficient* causes/explanations. A proponent of irreducible mental causation can, therefore, grant the soundness of CCA and EEA, provided she holds mental causation/explanation to be teleological. I go on to argue that, in light of these two objections, such an account of mental causation is possible. I conclude by giving a cursory sketch of how such a picture of mental causation as non-reductive teleological causation would work. The upshot being that this general approach to mental causation, as non-reductive and non-epiphenomenal, *cannot* be undermined by the CCA and EEA.

W̶e take there to be instances of mental causation all around us: you decide to get a drink of water and so walk towards the kitchen. Few people will tell you that your decision is irrelevant in regards to causing you to walk towards the kitchen. What is contentious is the metaphysics that grounds statements like these. In discussing what is at issue in the debate about mental causation, Jaegwon Kim writes, "It is the problem of showing *how* mental causation is possible, not *whether* it is possible."[1] Following Kim, our starting point should grant there to be cases of mental causation. However, this is just the beginning of the beginning of the story. Depending on the explanation we give of *how* mental causation is possible, some serious metaphysical consequences are sure to follow. It might be that mental causation is possible *only if* it turns out that mental causes are physical causes, or perhaps emergent on physical causes, or perhaps entirely distinct from physical causes.

One common approach to this question attempts to show that mental causation is possible *only if* mental causes are identical to physical causes. This argument appeals to two commonly held principles: the "Causal Closure Principle" (CCP) and the "Non-Overdetermination Principle" (NOP).[2] These principles have been formulated by E. J. Lowe as follows:[3]

© 2012, *Proceedings of the ACPA*, Vol. 85
DOI: 10.5840/acpaproc20118513

CCP: For any physical event, e, if e has a cause at time t, then e has a wholly physical sufficient cause at t.

NOP: If physical event, e, has a wholly physical sufficient cause at t, then e does not also have a mental cause at t which is wholly distinct from that physical cause.[4]

In clarifying what "sufficient" in CCP and "wholly distinct" in NOP mean, Lowe writes, "One or more events constitute a *sufficient* cause of an event e just in case *the conjunction of those events causally necessitates the occurrence of e*,"[5] and a bit later, "two events are 'wholly distinct' just in case *there is no event that is a common part of both events*."[6] The truth of both these principles remains a matter of much inquiry; however, in this paper I will not be concerned with how those debates pan out. I will assume, for the sake of argument, what many physicalists take to be *the* deal breaker for non-reductive mental causation (i.e., CCP and NOP) and argue that these principles do not necessarily show that *non-reductive* mental causation is impossible.

It is easy to see how the argument, from CCP and NOP to the conclusion that mental causes are identical to physical causes, is supposed to run by considering the following scenario. Enter the "Causal Closure Argument" (CCA). Suppose some physical event (the movement of my foot as I start towards the kitchen) occurs. Call this physical event, e. Also, suppose that e has a mental cause at time t, say the intention to get a drink of water in the kitchen. So, in light of NOP, this yields e not having a wholly physical sufficient cause at t, which is wholly distinct from that mental cause. However, e is a physical event with a cause at t. Given CCP, e must also have a wholly physical sufficient cause at t. Therefore, e's mental cause at t must *not* be wholly distinct from e's wholly physical sufficient cause at t. So, e's mental cause is *a part* of e's *wholly* physical sufficient cause. But, it seems that to be a part of something that is *wholly* physical entails that that part too is physical. This is to say that e's mental cause is physical. Those that adhere to this type of argument do not renounce the existence of mental causation, rather they take these arguments to show that mental causation is something other than we thought—it is physical. If this argument is sound, it is often taken to show that there is no room for intentional explanations of physical events *unless* those explanations are reducible to purely physical explanations.

Many things can be said regarding possible ways of responding to the CCA. Clearly, if one rejects either CCP or NOP one can reject CCA. Whether one can, or should, reasonably reject them remains a matter of dispute.[7] It is important to note that, in this paper, I will not entertain whether we can or should reject CCP and NOP. Instead, I will argue that non-reductive mental causation and the CCA are *not* incompatible. To show this, I will assume the soundness of the CCA (with a slight clarification) and argue that there is still plenty of explanatory/causal room for genuine, non-reductive intentional explanations/causes. In short, I will argue that the CCA does *not* necessarily show that mental causes are epiphenomenal.

I will begin by arguing that CCA is *only* able to show that whenever there is a wholly physical sufficient *efficient cause* of some event e at time t, there cannot also be a wholly distinct mental *efficient cause* of e at t. In light of this clarification, I argue that one can readily grant the physicalist both CCP and NOP, and acknowledge genuine intentional explanations of physical events which are *not reducible* to physical explanations. This is due to the fact that intentional explanations are grounded in irreducible teleology. Given that CCA is only able to rule out mental causation consisting in an intentional *efficient* cause, wholly distinct from the sufficient physical *efficient* cause, there remains room for couching mental causation in terms of teleological causation. The upshot of this argument is that the success of a teleological account of mental causation *cannot* be undermined by the CCA.

The CCA and Efficient Causation

I will call purported mental *efficient* causes, which are not reducible to physical *efficient* causes, "downward causes." Downward causation will then be used to refer to non-reductive mental-to-physical *efficient* causation. In this section, I will argue that the CCA as presented by Kim, and reformulated by Lowe, is only capable of showing that downward causation is impossible.[8] To see why this is, let us turn to what it is for a cause to be an *efficient* cause.

In *De Principiis Naturae*, after arguing that there are three principles of nature (matter, form and privation), St. Thomas Aquinas argues that something can "come to be" (be generated) *only if* there is some efficient cause that is the initiator of the change. Aquinas writes,

> What is in potency cannot bring itself to actuality, as the bronze which is potentially an idol does not make itself to be an idol, but needs an agent to bring the form of the idol from potentiality to act. The form does not bring itself from potentiality to act: I mean the form of what is generated, which we call the term of generation, for the form is only in that which has come to be, but while it is being made it is in becoming, that is while the thing comes to be. Therefore besides matter and form there must be a principle which acts, and this is called the effects or moving agent or that whence motion begins.[9]

A lump of bronze is potentially a statue, but a lump of bronze cannot carve itself. It cannot bring *itself* to become an actual statue. Lumps of bronze are made into statues only by the work of efficient causes. In speaking of one of the four different ways in which something can be said to be a cause, Aristotle writes, the efficient cause is "that from which the change or the freedom from change first begins, e.g., the man who has deliberated is a cause, and the father a cause of the child, and in general the maker a cause of the thing made and the change-producing of the changing."[10]

I take it that of the four Aristotelian causes, the one (if any) that has survived is the efficient cause. When discussing causation in the pool hall, people often talk about what caused the billiard ball to move. A common answer is that the cue ball's striking it caused it to move. It was from the cue ball (or an event containing the cue ball[11]) that the 8-ball's motion came. People then say things like, if the cue ball had not been moving/struck the 8-ball/etc. then the 8-ball would not have moved. We take these counterfactuals to highlight (at least when the counterfactual is not taken as the truth maker of the causal statement) the fact that the cue ball was the efficient cause of the 8-balls moving. It was the thing that produced the change in the 8-ball. Clearly, matters only get murkier when we try to spell out the details; however, what should be gathered from this is that the "common" notion of causation, used by philosophers in pool halls and bars, is the notion of efficient causation.

When the contemporary philosopher of mind asks us to suppose that some physical event has a cause, what exactly are we supposed to be supposing? Presumably, it is that some physical event has an *efficient* cause. Namely, that there is something from which that physical event came, just as the statue came from the sculpture. If we are to suppose that some physical event (say the raising of my arm) has a cause, we are being asked to consider that there is something that brought about the raising of my arm. This, I hope, should be uncontroversial. If so, I take the following revisions of CCP and NOP to merely make explicit something that is there implicitly: the type of causation in play in CCP an NOP is *efficient* causation.

CCP*: For any physical event, e, if e has a cause at time t, then e has a wholly physical sufficient *efficient* cause at t.

NOP*: If physical event, e, has a wholly physical sufficient *efficient* cause at t, then e does not also have a mental *efficient* cause at t which is wholly distinct from that physical *efficient* cause.

I take CCP* and NOP* to be *as plausible as* CCP and NOP; therefore, they should be held for the exact same reasons as their originals. As mentioned above, I will assume CCP* is true for the sake of argument. However, I would like to offer a defense as to why we should think NOP* is true. NOP* appears to be just an instance of a more basic principle about efficient causation (ECP):

ECP: If event, e, has a sufficient efficient cause, c1, at time t, and e also has an efficient cause, c2, at t, then c2 is not wholly distinct from c1.[12]

The plausibility of ECP can be seen from considering some examples. First, however, it should be noted that ECP also implies that there cannot be two *sufficient efficient* causes of one event. Which is to say that ECP is just a general "no efficient causal overdetermination" principle. In attempting to explain why he thinks an overdetermination of causes for a single physical event is pernicious, Jaegwon Kim gives the following example of causal overdetermination. This example is supposed to be a clear-cut case of why we can't have two sufficient (efficient) causes of the same event. He writes,

Thus a car accident is explained by a highway designer as having been caused by the incorrect camber of the highway curve, and by the police officer as caused by the inattentive driving of an inexperienced driver. But in a case like this we naturally think of the offered causes as partial causes; they together help make up a full and sufficient cause of the accident.

As long as each claims to be a full cause of the event to be explained, a tension is created and we are entitled to ask, indeed compelled to ask, how the two purported causes are related to each other.[13]

Kim seems to be assuming the truth of ECP. If we insist that both reported causes are sufficient efficient causes of the accident, we are "compelled" to inquire about their relation to each other. Since ECP holds that they can't be wholly distinct, we know that they can't *both* be wholly distinct sufficient efficient causes of the accident. How could there be two distinct sufficient efficient causes of some one effect? This would mean that one action proceeds from two distinct agents, and it is not necessary that both agents act for the occurrence of that action (i.e., the action is not a collective action). Rather, *each agent is individually sufficient for that action*; in fact, each performs it. But, it does not seem possible for *one* action to be caused by two agents in this way. The burden of proof looks to be on those who reject ECP. Without any compelling reason to do so, we are justified in accepting ECP. A clarification of ECP is likely to yield much fruit.

St. Thomas, the CCA, and Causal Overdetermination

There was once (and perhaps still is) a debate over whether God immediately acts in every agent who acts. Here is how the worry arose. If God is the first cause then He is an efficient cause of every effect, since all causality originates in Him. However, this in light of ECP seems to lead us to conclude that for any putative instance of creaturely/secondary causation (e.g., a fire heats some body), either God partly causes the effect and the fire partly causes that same effect, or only one of the agents acts. But, if only one of the agents acts, then it will have to be God whom acts, given He is the first cause. So, *only* God causes the effect and the fire doesn't cause anything. In the opening paragraph of the *Summa Contra* III, chapter 69 ["On the opinion of those who take away proper actions from natural things"], St. Thomas writes, "From this conclusion [from 68.1, "He is in all things in the fashion of an *agent cause*"] some men have taken the opportunity to fall into error, thinking that no creature has an active role in the production of natural effects."[14] This is a natural reaction to have on the stipulation that God is the agent/efficient cause of all things, and it should be noted that this problem is grounded in an acceptance of ECP. Again, in the *Summa Theologiae*, St. Thomas raises the problem in the form of an objection,

> Further, the same work cannot proceed at the same time from two sources; as neither can one and the same movement belong to two movable things. Therefore if the creature's operation is from God operating in the creature, it cannot at the same time proceed from the creature; and so no creature works at all.[15]

One simple way to avoid this problem would be to simply reject ECP. But, this option is not the one St. Thomas takes. His reply comes by way of clarifying ECP, *not* rejecting it.

It seems that since one and the same movement cannot belong to two movable things, one and the same action cannot belong to two agents. St. Thomas responds to this objection by distinguishing between two ways a single action might be efficiently caused: primarily and secondarily. Aquinas apparently grants the truth of ECP, but with the proviso that it pertains *only* to efficient causes *of the same order* (i.e., it doesn't apply to efficient causes at different orders). He responds to our problem in the following way, "One action does not proceed from two agents of the same order. But nothing hinders the same action from proceeding from a primary and a secondary agent."[16] Granted, he simply asserts this without giving reasons, but why he holds it is perhaps not as important, for my purposes, than *that* he holds it. His reasons for making such a distinction aren't *ad hoc*, since elsewhere he has independent reasons for distinguishing between primary and secondary causation. I mention this historical debate for two reasons: (1) to highlight that St. Thomas held a principle sufficiently similar to ECP, and (2) ECP should be accepted barring reasons to the contrary.

It therefore looks reasonable to hold ECP to be true. If so, it will likely turn out that NOP* is true, on the grounds that it is just a specific instance of ECP. It looks like we are therefore committed to the truth of NOP*. As was mentioned above, I will take CCP* to be true. This means that for any event, e, that has an efficient cause at time t, e has a sufficient efficient *physical* cause at t. NOP* goes on to tell us that there can't be an efficient cause of e, either physical *or* mental, that is distinct from that sufficient efficient physical cause. The only type of efficient causal processes in play, then, are going to have to be physical, given CCP* and ECP.[17] But, putative downward causation (as I defined it above) *just is* irreducible *mental*-to-physical *efficient* causation, where "mental" here means non-physical. So, it follows that downward causation is not possible. With that said, this should not be taken to imply that mental causation is *reducible* to physical efficient causation, far from it. In the next section, I will argue that mental causation can reasonably be taken to be an instance of a more general type of non-efficient causation: teleological causation. The CCA is therefore incapable of telling us anything about mental causation so construed. The CCA is *only* capable of telling us about efficient causal processes. Therefore, if what I say in the next section is true, one can agree wholeheartedly with the CCA while countenancing irreducible mental causation.

Making Room for Mental Causation

In this section, I will take up the project of showing how it is possible for irreducible mental causation to be non-epiphenomenal, despite the findings of the previous section.[18] The details will unfortunately have to be worked out another day, but the general picture is itself sufficiently interesting as to merit a paper of its own. Irreducible mental causation is often thought of in terms of downward causation. This thought can be rejected, and perhaps must be rejected, given the concessions I made in the previous section. However, there is room yet for irreducible mental causation. I will briefly sketch a picture in which mental causation is cashed out in terms of *irreducible teleological causation* (TC). Granted, the tenability of irreducible teleology will certainly be questioned, but it should be noted that *if* we do have TC, then we at least have theoretical room for mental causation, while at the same time avoiding the worries of the CCA altogether.

Showing that X is *possible* is a far cry from showing that we should accept X as actual; but it is true that not being able to show that X is possible is an even farther cry from showing that X is actual. So, showing that irreducible mental causation is *possible* in terms of TC, brings us one step closer to an adequate account of mental causation. As small of a step as this is, it is still a step forward.

Unless we are going to be reductionists about mental causation we will need to ground it in something other than efficient causation. But, it will surely be argued, there is nothing else. Mental causation (or intentional/mental explanation of events) doesn't explain anything over and above what efficient physical explanations explain. And who needs two sufficient explanations explaining the exact same thing? Enter the problem of explanatory exclusion.[19] If we are inquiring as to why event e occurred and we are able to give a *sufficient* physical efficient explanation of e, have we thereby fully explained all there is regarding why e occurred? After all, isn't that what "sufficient" means? It will be argued, that the explanatory quest ends when we find the sufficient cause of e's occurring, and as we saw above, there is a sufficient physical efficient cause for any physical event e. So, what else needs to be explained in explaining why e occurred?

There is an age-old tradition which held that unless we know *that for the sake of which a thing is done* we do not have a full explanation of why that thing was done. According to this tradition, we can know everything there is to know about the efficient causal process culminating in me raising my arm, and yet not know anything about *that for the sake of which* I raised my arm. According to Aristotle, without knowing the *end* for which I acted, we do not have a *total* explanation of why I raised my arm. We might have a sufficient efficient causal explanation, but according to the tradition, that is not enough to make it a total explanation of the action. There is still something that cries out for an explanation. Aristotle writes, "'Why is he walking about?' We say: 'To be healthy', and, having said that, we think we have assigned the cause."[20]

This form of causal explanation (commonly called "teleological explanation") is consistent with saying that the raising of my arm was caused by the firing of neural networks in my brain in conjunction with muscle contractions, etc. I can offer an entirely physical efficient causal explanation of that action in terms of the latest neurobiological theory, but in offering this explanation, we cannot explain *that for the sake of which* I raised my arm. But, who cares about *that for the sake of which* a thing is done? Aren't those explanations/causes anachronistic anyway and rejected alongside with the ancient theories of physics, empirically proven to be false? Unfortunately, I will not be able to survey the reasons for thinking that teleological explanations are reasonable. But, it should be noted that there are some prominent philosophers who think we should at least take the possibility of teleological explanations very seriously. In fact, some think that teleological causation is far from anachronistic, and even farther from being empirically proven false.[21] For the purposes of this paper, I will have to simply assert that irreducible teleological causation (TC) is, at the very least, worth taking seriously.[22]

Supposing we have TC, how does it factor into mental causation? Let us begin with a general picture of TC. Consider a sunflower. It is a fact that young sunflowers "track" the sun. They continually adjust and face towards the sun as it moves across the sky.[23] Knowing the efficient casual processes that result in young sunflowers following the sun does not seem to give us the entire story regarding *why* young sunflowers do this. Young sunflowers do not turn randomly towards the sun. No, they do this for some reason. The most intuitive way of accounting for this phenomenon is in terms of it being a way that the young sunflower is able to achieve one of its needs (or goods). When we ask, "Why did that young sunflower move to face the sun earlier today?" We are likely looking for, and willing to accept, something in the ballpark of the following explanation, "Young sunflowers need a certain amount of sunlight in order to grow, and this is the way in which they are able to get the sunlight they need." *Prima facie*, this is one type of sufficient explanation of why the young sunflower did this. However, there is yet another explanation that can be given regarding why the young sunflower turns toward the sun.

> The plant equivalent of a muscle, the pulvinus consists of specialized extensor and flexor cells that swell or shrink with changes in turgor pressure (determined by the amount of water in the cell). As extensor cells swell and flexor cells shrink, the leaf blade is reoriented to track the changing position of the sun.[24]

An explanation of this sort does account for the efficient causal process of the sunflower's turning. In fact, if we were to fill it out a bit more, it could sufficiently explain how the sunflower turns. It explains how the "turning mechanism" of the plant functions, but it does not explain why it has such a function. In order to explain that, as the TC story goes, we would need to appeal to the needs/goals/ends of the plant. This type of explanation would be of the first sort—it functions as it does because of a certain need/end of the sunflower. Despite the fact that the event, the sunflower's turning, has a sufficient efficient causal explanation, there is yet an aspect of this event that needs to be explained. Thus, the presence of a sufficient efficient causal explanation of some event does not necessarily preclude the need for a teleological causal explanation of that event. With this in mind, let us turn to the picture of mental causation.

Recall how the story went: physical event e (the movement of my foot) occurs. What explains the occurrence of e? We can explain, *via* CCA, the occurrence of e by appeal to some sufficient physical efficient cause, namely the neural firings and muscle contractions.[25] However, like the young sunflower's turning toward the sun, merely stating an efficient causal explanation cannot adequately explain *why* that type of event occurred. It can explain *how* I, as a "foot moving mechanism," function on that specific occasion, but it can't explain *why* I have such a function in the first place. In order to explain this, we would need to appeal to the subject's needs/ends/goals. We can explain the occurrence of the turning of the sunflower by appealing to an end of the sunflower. Likewise, we can explain the occurrence of the moving of my foot by appealing to an end of mine. We explain this in the sunflower's motion by appealing to the needs/ends of the sunflower—e.g., growth. We explain this in me by appealing to my needs/ends—e.g., a drink of water.[26]

Teleological causal explanation is intentional explanation. Intentional explanation does not necessarily require mental states. Why? First off, there is somewhat of a resurgence in the dispositions/powers literature to argue that dispositions are fundamentally directed towards manifestation types. This directedness is something that many metaphysicians think cannot be reduced. Their battle cry—"The intentional is the mark of the dispositional *not* the mental."[27] In saying this, these metaphysicians have opened the door, albeit only a crack, for the possibility that sunflowers act intentionally (i.e., for some end) when they turn towards the sun. Likewise, when I move my foot in order to get a drink of water, I am acting intentionally (i.e., for some end). My action, like the sunflower, is directed. If a teleological causal explanation can explain *why* the sunflower acts for its end, then there is very good reason to think that a teleological causal explanation can explain *why* I acted for my end (in getting a drink of water).

If what I have said is true, or at least reasonable, then we can easily see how mental causation can be said to be teleological. Mental causes are teleological causes. Mental causes provide the *ends* for which we act. The sunflower's *ends* were provided naturally (by nature); my *ends* were provided by my mental states (e.g., my intentions). Mental causation should first and foremost be seen as teleological causation. On this general picture, mental causal explanation is not of a different explanatory category than the explanation of why the sunflower turns toward the sun. Therefore, the picture I have been painting—mental causation construed as irreducible teleological causation—*might* be one that the physicalist could accept, providing both the physicalists and the dualists with an alternative picture of mental causation.[28] Obviously, the success of this picture of mental causation will require details, something I am not able to do here. Nevertheless, it has been shown how mental causation understood as teleological causation is possible. This picture of mental causation is immune to the standard objections that presuppose mental causation to be downward (efficient) causation. Therefore, mental causes need not be epiphenomenal *regardless* of whether the CCA is sound or not.[29]

University of Nebraska-Lincoln

Notes

1. Jaegwon Kim, *Mind in a Physical World* (Cambridge: MIT Press, 2000), 61, original emphasis.

2. It is fairly difficult to come across non-question begging formulations of CCP and NOP. I take the ones I give here to be as good as any.

3. E. J. Lowe, *Personal Agency: The Metaphysics of Mind and Action* (Oxford: Oxford University Press, 2008), 63.

4. I use Lowe's "alternative" formulation of NOP, NOP#, because I take it to be more transparent than his official formulation. However, both are logically equivalent.

5. Lowe, *Personal Agency*, 63; emphasis added.

6. Ibid; emphasis added.

7. Lowe offers, what I take to be good reasons for rejecting both. (Or, perhaps not having to worry about both.) See Lowe, *Personal Agency*, 65–74.

8. Note: in saying that all CCA is *capable* of showing is the impossibility of downward causation, I do not intend to take a stand on whether CCA is successful in showing this. I merely point out that CCA's reach is *only* within the genera of *efficient* causation. Once again, I can remain neutral on this debate for the purposes of this paper.

9. St. Thomas Aquinas, *De principiis naturae*, III; in *Thomas Aquinas: Selected Writings*, trans. Ralph McInerny (New York: Penguin Books, 1998), 22.

10. Aristotle, *Meta.* 1013^{a}24ff., trans. Jonathan Barnes.

11. I would like it if I could remain neutral, in this paper at least, on the issues surrounding agent causation and event causation, but perhaps that is a fool's hope. I will continue with such a goal in mind.

12. It should be noted, and will be made clear in what follows, that ECP *only* pertains to efficient causes "of the same order." The significance of this addendum has been, at the very least, immensely historically important, as will become evident in what follows.

13. Kim, *Mind in a Physical World*, 66.

14. *SCG* III, 69.1.

15. *ST* I, q.105, a.5, ob.2.

16. *ST* I, q.105, a.5, ad.2.

17. It should be noted that I am only talking about secondary causes here.

18. "Non-epiphenomenal" here is used to mean that it plays some *real* causal role, but not necessarily an efficient causal role.

19. In fact, Kim raises the "explanatory exclusion argument" which makes this exact point. See: Kim, *Mind in a Physical World*, 60–67; and "Mechanism, Purpose, and Explanatory Exclusion" *Philosophical Perspectives* 3 (1989): 77–108.

20. *Physics* 194^{b}33ff.

21. For two prominent accounts of why we should see Jonathan Bennett, *Linguistic Behavior* (New York: Cambridge University Press, 1976); John Hawthorne and Daniel Nolan, "What Would Teleological Causation Be?" in *Metaphysical Essays* (New York: Oxford University Press, 2006), 265–284.

22. I fully acknowledge that this is far from uncontroversial and is a check that eventually will need to be cashed. That being said, I nevertheless think it is a perfectly good check to cash.

23. This phenomenon is called "heliotropism" and occurs in many plants. See G. S. G. Shell, A. R. G. Lang, and P. J. M. Sale, "Quantitative Measures of Leaf Orientation and

Heliotropic Response in Sunflower, Bean, Pepper and Cucumber" *Agricultural Meteorology* 3.1 (1974): 25–37.

24. Candace Galen, "Sun Stalkers" *Natural History* issue (1999). Accessed: 26 Mar, 2011. http://findarticles.com/p/articles/mi_m1134/is_4_108/ai_54574603/

25. Calling this efficient cause "sufficient" means that it is sufficient *qua* efficient causal explanation, not *qua* complete causal explanation.

26. Recall, that in the original example it was my intention to get a drink of water that caused me to move my foot.

27. See for example: George Molnar, *Powers* (New York: Oxford University Press, 2003), ch. 3; C. B. Martin and Karl Pfeifer, "Intentionality and the Non-Psychological" *Philosophy and Phenomenological Research*, 46. 4 (1986): 531–554; U. T. Place, "Intentionality and the Physical: A Reply to Mumford" *Philosophical Quarterly*, 49. 195 (1999): 225–231.

28. Whether a physicalist can accept this will depend upon whether teleology ultimately grounds out in something mental: a debate centered around St. Thomas's "Fifth Way," which I will not go into here.

29. I would like to thank Louis Mancha and Jean Rioux for their helpful correspondence on parts of this paper; I'd like to thank James Madden, John Haldane, and E. J. Lowe for helpful comments on an earlier draft, though any shortcomings are certainly not their doing; also, much thanks to Rev. James Brent, O.P., who provided helpful comments on my paper at the 2011 ACPA.

Hylomorphism: What It Is and What It Isn't

William Jaworski

Abstract: "Hylomorphism" has recently become a buzzword in metaphysics. Kit Fine, Kathryn Koslicki, and Mark Johnston, among others, have argued that hylomorphism provides an account of parthood and material constitution that has certain advantages over its competitors. But what exactly is it, and what are its implications for an account of what we are? Hylomorphism, I argue, is fundamentally a claim about structure. It says that structure is a basic ontological and explanatory principle. I argue that hylomorphism is compatible with physicalism, and also with substance dualism, and epiphenomenalism. The most interesting kinds of hylomorphism nevertheless reject these views. I describe one such hylomorphic theory. It is an empirically well-warranted theory, I argue, one based on work in biology and biological subdisciplines such as neuroscience.

1. Four Approaches to Structure

Hylomorphism" has recently become a buzzword in metaphysics. Kit Fine (1999), Kathryn Koslicki (2008), and Mark Johnston (2006), among others, have argued that hylomorphism provides an account of parthood and material constitution that has certain advantages over its competitors. But what exactly is it, and what are its implications for an account of what we are? I plan to describe a hylomorphic theory that is empirically well-warranted—a theory that the biological and social sciences give us good reason to believe is true. I've discussed this view in greater detail in Chapters 10 and 11 of Jaworski 2011, but in the interests of time I've had to leave out many details of that longer discussion, and focus on just a few of the points it covers.

Hylomorphism is fundamentally about structure. It says that structure, organization, form, arrangement, order, or configuration is a basic ontological and explanatory principle. Some individuals—living things, for instance—consist of materials that are structured or organized in various ways. You and I are not mere quantities of fundamental physical materials; we are quantities of fundamental physical materials with a certain organization or structure. That structure is responsible for you and I being humans as opposed to dogs or rocks, and it is responsible for

© 2012, *Proceedings of the ACPA*, Vol. 85
DOI: 10.5840/acpaproc20118514

you and I having the particular developmental, metabolic, reproductive, perceptive, and cognitive capacities we have. Understood in this way, hylomorphism appears to enjoy a good deal of empirical support.

Scientists frequently appeal to notions of structure, order, arrangement, organization, or configuration. At least some of these appeals appear to be ontologically serious; that is, they appear to posit structure as a real ontological and explanatory principle. Here is an example taken from a popular college-level biology textbook—note the references to organization, order, arrangement, and related notions:

> Life is highly organized into a hierarchy of structural levels, with each level building on the levels below it. . . . Biological order exists at all levels. . . . [A]toms . . . are ordered into complex biological molecules. Many of the molecules of life are arranged into minute structures called organelles, which are in turn the components of cells. Cells are [in turn] subunits of organisms. . . . The organism we recognize as an animal or plant is not a random collection of individual cells, but a multicellular cooperative. . . . [Moreover] there are tiers beyond the individual organism. . . . Identifying biological organization at its many levels is fundamental to the study of life. . . . With each step upward in the hierarchy of biological order, novel properties emerge that were not present at the simpler levels of organization. . . . A molecule such as a protein has attributes not exhibited by any of its component atoms, and a cell is certainly much more than a bag of molecules. If the intricate organization of the human brain is disrupted by a head injury, that organ will cease to function properly. . . . And an organism is a living whole greater than the sum of its parts. . . . [W]e cannot fully explain a higher level of order by breaking it down into its parts. (Campbell 1996, 2–4)

This passage suggests that organization, order, structure, or arrangement is a real feature of things, one that plays an important role in them being the kinds of things they are, and in explaining the kinds of things they can do. It suggests, in other words, that structure is a real ontological and explanatory principle. Consider likewise the biologist Ernst Mayr:

> [B]iologists . . . recognize no supernatural or immaterial forces, but only such that are physico-chemical. . . . [T]he modern biologist rejects in any form whatsoever the notion that a "vital force" exists in living organisms which does not obey the laws of physics and chemistry. All processes in organisms, from the interaction of molecules to the complex functions of the brain and other whole organs, strictly obey these physical laws. . . . But [modern biologists] do not accept the naïve mechanistic explanation of the seventeenth century and disagree with the statement that animals are "nothing but" machines. . . . Where organisms differ from inanimate matter is in the organization of their systems. Organismic biologists stress the fact that organisms have many characteristics that are without

parallel in the world of inanimate objects. The explanatory equipment of the physical sciences is insufficient to explain complex living systems. (1982, 2, 52)

The notion of structure is also central to many other branches of biological science. These appeals to structure provide a way of understanding what hylomorphism is. To articulate that understanding I'll put to one side questions about how best to understand the notion metaphysically, and come at it instead from the standpoint of what we want the notion of structure to do—especially the kinds of empirical work we want the notion of structure to perform.

Many philosophers find claims about organization or structure in the sciences obvious and unremarkable: "Clearly the notion of structure factors into descriptions and explanations of things," they think, and yet they fail to appreciate what this implies. The notion of structure does not come for free. If we are committed to the entities postulated by our best descriptions and explanations of reality, and we suppose that our best descriptions and explanations of reality derive from the sciences, then appeals to structure like the foregoing make a serious ontological demand. How are we to approach that demand? There are at least four ways of doing so. Three are committed to the idea that everything can be exhaustively described and explained *without* appeal to structure.

First, *structure eliminativists* claim there is no such thing as structure or organization, that talk of structure is not useful for serious descriptive and explanatory purposes—the sorts of purposes that drive scientific endeavor, for instance. *Structure reductivists*, on the other hand, claim that at least some statements about structure or organization are true, and that appeals to structure or organization do serious descriptive and explanatory work. Appeals to structure do that work, however, because the structures they postulate can be identified with things that can be exhaustively described and explained in nonstructural terms. Nonstructural discourse is thus capable in principle of taking over the descriptive and explanatory roles that appeals to structure play. Structural discourse is reducible, in other words, to nonstructural discourse.

Structure nonreductivists try to steer a middle course between reductivism and eliminativism. Like reductivists and unlike eliminativists, they try to countenance talk of structure, but like eliminativists and unlike reductivists, they try to avoid countenancing the entities to which structural discourse appears to commit us. Structural discourse has genuine descriptive and explanatory legitimacy, the structure nonreductivist says, but this legitimacy is not grounded in the identification of structures with nonstructural things, as reductivists claim. It is grounded instead in our descriptive and explanatory interests—interests that nonstructural discourse is incapable of satisfying. We appeal to the notion of structure because doing so enables us to satisfy descriptive and explanatory interests that would otherwise go unsatisfied.[1] Because structural discourse satisfies special interests, moreover, nonstructural discourse cannot take over the descriptive and explanatory roles we currently employ structural discourse to play. Consequently, structural discourse is irreducible to nonstructural discourse—not because there is something other than what can be exhaustively described and explained in nonstructural terms, but because we have interests that nonstructural discourse does not enable us to satisfy.

A fourth approach to structure denies the assumption the other three have in common; it denies that everything can be exhaustively described and explained without appeal to structure. Descriptions and explanations that appeal to structure are not all false, and they cannot be accurately paraphrased or reduced to nonstructural descriptions and explanations. Like the nonreductivist view, it denies that nonstructural discourse can take over the descriptive and explanatory roles of structural discourse, but unlike that view, it anchors its antireductionism in metaphysical soil. Exponents of this view do not offer paraphrases that aim at minimizing the ontological implications of appeals to structure; like reductivists, they take those implications at face value. Structure, they say, really does exist independent of whatever descriptive and explanatory interests we happen to have. Unlike reductivists, however, they deny that structures can be identified with things that can be exhaustively described and explained in nonstructural terms.

Exponents of this fourth option thus countenance talk of structure together with the entities to which that talk appears to commit us, but they do so by rejecting the idea that everything can be exhaustively described and explained without appeal to structure. Structure, they say, is a real feature of things distinct from any nonstructural phenomena that exist. Moreover, descriptions and explanations that appeal to structure cannot be reduced to claims about nonstructural phenomena, nor can they be accurately paraphrased in ways that do not appeal to structure. This commitment to *realism* about structure is what distinguishes hylomorphism from the other three views I've just described.[2] It claims that structure is a real and irreducible ontological and explanatory principle.

2. Hylomorphism, Physicalism, and Substance Dualism

Now that I've clarified the basic hylomorphic claim about structure, I want to discuss how that claim is related to physicalism and substance dualism. Contrary to what many people seem to think, hylomorphism is compatible with both. Let's start with physicalism. It claims that everything is physical; everything can be exhaustively described and explained by physics. Note that philosophers have sometimes used the term "physicalism" to refer to much weaker claims—the claim that everything has physical properties, or that everything is composed of physical parts or materials. These weaker claims do not express the core physicalist idea, however, since they are compatible with the existence of nonphysical things—nonphysical properties, for instance—and the existence of nonphysical things is what physicalism is supposed to rule out. If physicalism is true, every individual and event, as well as every feature they have, and every behavior they engage in can be described and explained using the conceptual resources of physics, and those descriptions and explanations are exhaustive; they leave out nothing, but give us the complete story about what there is, what it does, how it does it, and why.

Is physicalism compatible with hylomorphism? It should be evident that it is. Suppose that physicalism is true, and that everything can be exhaustively described and explained by physics. Suppose, moreover, that our best physics postulates structures that are real and irreducible. In that case, physicalists are committed to structures in the hylomorphic sense. Physicalism is thus compatible with the hylomorphic claim that structure is a basic ontological and explanatory principle. So is substance dualism. Substance dualism claims that persons, such as you and I, are distinct from bodies. The human bodies we see around us are not people; people are instead nonphysical entities that might be connected in some way to these bodies, but that are not identical to them. Suppose, then, that substance dualism is true, and that people such as you and I are nonphysical entities distinct from these bodies—these human organisms. Suppose, however, that these human organisms consist of physical materials that are structured a certain way. The upshot is a substance dualistic view that is committed to hylomorphism. Structure is a basic principle that factors into descriptions of what human bodies are and what they can do; it simply doesn't factor into descriptions of what we, nonphysical persons, are and what we can do. Hylomorphism is thus compatible with both physicalism and substance dualism.

This is not, however, the kind of hylomorphism suggested by the earlier quotes from biologists. The version of hylomorphism they suggest identifies us with human organisms, so it rejects substance dualism. Moreover, it distinguishes what physics by itself can describe and explain from what appeals to biological, or psychological, or social structure enable us to describe and explain. Because of that, exponents of this type of view often claim that organisms are not mere machines, as Ernst Mayr puts it, but have characteristics—emergent properties, to use Campbell's term—not found among nonliving things. The explanatory apparatus of physics is thus insufficient to describe and explain living behavior—the physico-chemical story gets at only half the truth, to use the cyberneticist Gerd Sommerhoff's (1969, 147–148) expression. Some things can only be described and explained by appeal to structure or organization at a biological, psychological, or social level.

When hylomorphists of this sort look at the world, they see the vast sea of matter and energy described by our best physics, but they see something more besides: structures of the sort postulated by biology, psychology, and other special sciences. Organisms are not just quantities of matter and energy; our best biology reveals instead that they are quantities of matter and energy that are structured or organized in various ways—knots of matter and energy, as Montgomery Furth (1978, 638–639) puts it. The structures these things have are responsible for their abilities to grow and develop, to reproduce, to move around the environment, and to perceive and think about its features. They are responsible, in short, for the capacities that qualify them as living beings as opposed to nonliving ones or perceptive, locomotive, cognitive beings as opposed to nonperceptive, nonlocomotive, noncognitive ones. This is a version of hylomorphism that rejects physicalism. It's the version on which I'll focus. Henceforth, when I use the term "hylomorphism," it will refer to this non-physicalistic, non-substance-dualistic version of the theory.

3. A Hylomorphic Worldview

The foregoing quotes from biologists suggest a hylomorphic view with at least five characteristics. First, hylomorphism takes the distinction between living things and nonliving ones (and also, as we'll see, mental beings and nonmental ones) to be grounded in the organization or structure of their components.[3] According to them, what distinguishes a living being from a nonliving one and a mental being from a nonmental one is not the entities that compose them, but the way those entities are structured or organized.

Second, living things such as human beings are exhaustively decomposable into particles or materials of the sort described by physics, the very same particles or materials found in nonliving things. Someone could endorse a hylomorphic view according to which living or mental beings have nonphysical components. Aquinas, for instance, may have endorsed a view of this sort. The hylomorphic view I have in mind, however, rejects this idea. It is committed instead to the empirical claim expressed in the quote from Ernst Mayr: living, mental beings such as humans have only physical components; they are exhaustively decomposable into the same fundamental physical materials found in nonliving things.

Third, because organisms consist of both structures and materials that are structured, hylomorphists claim that a complete account of living behavior must appeal to both. Consider an analogy: Suppose that a piano is not merely a heap of wood and metal, but wood and metal structured a certain way. If that is the case, and you are in the market for a piano and want to distinguish good pianos from bad ones, you'll have to know something both about piano materials and about how those materials are put together or arranged. Knowing only that the manufacturer used good materials to build this or that piano will be insufficient for determining whether it is a good one since good materials can be assembled in a shoddy way. Likewise, knowing only that the best craftsmen were employed to impose the best design on the available materials will be insufficient since good design and workmanship cannot overcome the limitations of shoddy materials. In a similar way, say hylomorphists, understanding the behavior of living things requires understanding something both about their structures and about the materials that are structured in those ways. This claim has at least two important implications. First, it implies a pluralism of properties.

On the hylomorphic view, living things have properties of at least two sorts: properties that are due to their structures (or their integration into individuals with structures), and properties that are due to their materials alone independent of the way those materials are structured. Consider an example. Subatomic particles, atoms, and molecules have physical properties such as mass irrespective of their surroundings. Under the right conditions, however, they can contribute to the activities of living things. Nucleic acids, hormones, and neural transmitters are examples; they are genes, growth factors, and metabolic and behavioral regulators. Each admits of two types of descriptions which are expressive of two types of properties. They can be described organically, in terms of the contributions they make to a structured system, but they are also independently describable in nonorganic, non-contribution-oriented terms. Descriptions of the former, organic sort are expressive of the properties characteristic of organisms and their parts. Descriptions of the latter, nonorganic sort are expressive of the properties things possess independent of their integration into organic wholes. A strand of DNA might always have various atomic or fundamental physical properties regardless of its environment, but it acquires new properties when it is integrated into a cell and begins making contributions to the cell's activities. It becomes a gene, a part of the cell that plays a role in, for instance, protein synthesis.

There are, then, properties that depend on something's structure and properties that things possess independent of a broader structure. According to hylomorphists, properties of both sorts make causal or explanatory contributions to the things having them. These contributions reflect a second implication of the idea that a complete account of living behavior must appeal to both structure and materials that are structured, namely, causal pluralism: there are different kinds of causal or explanatory factors. If you were, say, riding a roller coaster, we would be able to explain some of what you were experiencing purely by appeal to physical principles such as Newton's laws. Other aspects of your behavior, however, would require us to describe specific biological structures and capacities such as your vestibular system and how it enables you to maintain your balance and negotiate your environment, and yet other aspects of your behavior would require us to describe specific psycho-logical structures or patterns of behavior such as a penchant for thrill-seeking. On the hylomorphic view, then, there are different kinds of causal factors that contribute to explanations of their effects in different kinds of ways.

A fourth feature of the hylomorphic view is this: Because living things are composed of fundamental physical entities, their behavior never violates fundamental physical laws, the laws governing their fundamental physical constituents. In fact, the higher-level behavior in which they engage depends on those laws. It is because fundamental physical entities behave in stable, characteristic ways that they can be recruited to play in organisms the higher-level roles they do. It is because electrons have a characteristic mass and charge, for instance, that they are able to operate as membrane depolarizers within neural structures. According to hylomorphists, then, higher-level behavior depends on lower-level regularities.

Fifth, hylomorphism's view of structure is closely related to an account of composition or parthood. According to hylomorphists, lower-level entities such as atoms and electrons qualify as parts of higher-level entities such as organisms by virtue of contributing to their activities. An electron is a part of me, for instance, exactly if it contributes to my overall functioning—if, say, it contributes to depo-larizing one of my cellular membranes or plays a role in the metabolic processes of one of my cells. Consider again the strand of DNA. When it is integrated into a cell, it makes a goal-directed contribution to the activity of the whole. As a result, it gains the status of an organic part. It and parts like it are literally *organ-ized* in living things: they become organs. On the hylomorphic view of composition, then, parts contribute to the activities of the wholes they compose, and different parts of a whole contribute to its activities in different ways.

Peter van Inwagen (1990) has recently defended a similar account of composition. According to van Inwagen, something qualifies as a part if and only if it is "caught up in a life," an expression he borrows from the biologist J. Z. Young. He explains with an example:

> Alice drinks a cup of tea in which a lump of sugar has been dissolved. A certain carbon atom . . . is carried along with the rest of the sugar by Alice's digestive system to the intestine. It passes through the intestinal wall and into the bloodstream, whence it is carried to the biceps muscle of Alice's left arm. There it is oxidized in several indirect stages (yielding in the process energy . . . for muscular contraction) and is finally carried by Alice's circulatory system to her lungs and there breathed out as a part of a carbon dioxide molecule. . . . Here we have a case in which a thing, the carbon atom, was . . . caught up in the life of an organism, Alice. It is . . . a case in which a thing became however briefly, a *part* of a larger thing when it was a part of nothing before or after. (van Inwagen 1990, 94–95)

Hylomorphism's account of composition can be understood as a way of elaborating van Inwagen's basic idea: to be caught up in the life of something is to make a goal-directed contribution to its activities, where it is up to biologists, neuroscientists, and other empirical investigators to describe the nature of this goal-directed contribution.

An account of composition like this has also been articulated by several philosophers of biology including William Bechtel, a philosopher of neuroscience. According to Bechtel (2007; 2008), something qualifies as a component part of a complex system—what he calls a mechanism—only if it performs an operation that contributes to the activity of the whole.

Philosophers of biology and neuroscience, like Bechtel, have been attracted to a view of composition along these lines because this is the type of view suggested by *actual work in biology and neuroscience*—both the methods of those sciences and the kinds of explanations they employ. Of central importance is a method of scientific investigation philosophers have sometimes called *functional analysis*; other names include *mechanical decomposition* or *functional decomposition*. Biologists, cognitive scientists, engineers, and others frequently employ this method to understand how complex systems operate. They analyze the activities of those systems into simpler subactivities performed by simpler subsystems (Fodor 1968; Cummins 1975; Dennett 1978; Lycan 1987, chap 4; Bechtel 2007; 2008; Craver 2007, chap. 5; Jaworski 2011, section 10.3).

Consider a complex human activity such as running. Functional analysis reveals that running involves among other things a circulatory subsystem that is responsible for supplying oxygenated blood to the muscles. Analysis of that subsystem reveals that it has a component responsible for pumping the blood—a heart. Analysis of the heart's pumping activity shows that it is composed of muscle tissues that undergo frequent contraction and relaxation, and these activities can be analyzed into the subactivities of various cells. Analyses of these subactivities reveal the operation of various organelles that compose the cell and that are composed in turn of complex molecules. The cell membrane, for instance, is composed of a double layer of phospholipids. Analysis reveals that each phospholipid has a hydrophobic end that repels water, and a hydrophilic end that attracts it. Analysis of the water-attractive end further reveals that it is composed of a phosphate group with a distribution of electrons capable of attracting water molecules. The electrons are able to perform this role because they are negatively charged. If electrons have their charges not on account of the activities of some lower-level subsystems, but as an unanalyzable matter of fact, then no further functional analysis is possible. We reach a foundational level of functional parts.

Functional analysis provides a way of supplying empirical content to the idea that parts contribute to the activities of their respective wholes. If we want to know how a part contributes to the activity of a whole, hylomorphism leaves it to the relevant empirical disciplines to tell us.

Two clarifications are in order about functional analysis. First, a remark about the name: "Functional analysis" is a name that has been used by philosophers, but biologists have often called the method "reduction." This notion of reduction is different from the notion typically discussed in connection with the philosophy of mind. Reduction in the philosophical sense concerns the ability of one conceptual framework to take over the descriptive and explanatory roles of another. To say, for example, that Kepler's laws were reduced to Newton's laws is to say that Newtonian mechanics was able to take over all the descriptive and explanatory jobs Kepler's laws were previous employed to perform. When *biologists* speak of reduction, by contrast, they are typically not speaking of descriptive and explanatory take-over, but of a *method* for studying complex systems—what I have been calling "functional analysis." A commitment to employing this method does not imply a commitment to reduction in the philosophical sense. It might be impossible for neuroscience to take over the descriptive and explanatory roles of psychological discourse even though it is possible and even necessary to use functional analysis to understand how humans can engage in psychological activities.[4]

Second, the notion of function that gives functional analysis its name is different from the notion of function discussed in connection with functionalism in philosophy of mind. According to classic functionalist theories of mind, mental states are postulates of abstract descriptions framed in terms analogous to those used in computer science—descriptions that ignore the physical details of a system, and focus simply on a narrow profile of its features: inputs to it, outputs from it, and internal states that correlate the two (Putnam 1975, essays 18–21).[5] When it comes to functional analysis, by contrast, the notion of a function is not abstract in this way, and it has a teleological dimension: subsystems contribute to the activities of the wholes to which they belong, and that contribution is their reason or "purpose" for belonging to the system (Lycan 1987, chap. 4; Sober 1985, section 3): the purpose of the spark plug is to ignite the fuel; the purpose of the heart is to pump the blood, and so on.

Teleological functionalism is a type of functionalist theory that appeals to a teleological notion of function along these lines as well. Lycan's (1987, chap. 4) homunctionalism is an example. Like functionalist theories of all sorts, however, teleological functionalism claims that higher-level discourse is abstract discourse; higher-level properties are higher-*order* properties—logical constructions that quantify over lower-order properties. Saying that something has a belief, for instance, amounts merely to saying that it has *some* internal state that correlates inputs with outputs in appropriate ways. Hylomorphists reject this understanding of higher-level properties; they claim that higher-level properties are first-order properties in their own right. So although teleological functionalists and hylomorphists both claim that a system's components contribute teleologically to its overall operation, they disagree about how the notion of contribution is to be understood. According to teleological functionalists, descriptions of higher-level phenomena are simply abstract descriptions of lower-level occurrences. According to hylomorphists, by contrast, higher-level descriptions correspond to distinctive natural structures, ones that factor into descriptions and explanations of living behavior in ways that cannot be eliminated, reduced to, or paraphrased in favor of lower-level descriptions and explanations.

4. A Hylomorphic Theory of Mind

Let the foregoing remarks suffice for a description of the general hylomorphic worldview. I've discussed an empirically-based argument for it in detail elsewhere (Jaworski 2011, 296–302). Rather than rehearsing it here, I want to consider a hylomorphic approach to problems in the philosophy of mind—what I will call a *hylomorphic theory of mind*.

When people think of structures, they typically think of what we might call *mechanical structures* or *mechanisms*: spatial arrangements among a thing's parts that enable those parts to interact in novel ways that confer on the whole capacities not had by the parts taken in isolation. Hylomorphists acknowledge the existence of mechanisms, but they insist that mechanical structures are not the only kinds of structures that exist. Biological organization also comprises *patterns of behavior*—the characteristic ways that living things interact with each other and their environments (Jaworski 2011, 309–314).

Living things do not act at random. Birds build nests not webs, and lay eggs not acorns. Humans grow lungs instead of gills, and skin instead of scales. Dogs grow fur not feathers, and teeth not beaks. Squirrels bury nuts, and are active during the day; raccoons come out at night, and will rummage through our garbage if we do not take precautions. All of these are examples of patterns in living behavior. Just as the parts of living things are not assembled at random but have distinctive structures, so too the behavior of living things is characterized by distinctive *patterns of social and environmental interaction*.

Some of these patterns involve the ways organisms acquire and utilize energy from the environment to maintain their distinctive structures against entropy.

Others involve their abilities to respond to and interact with features of their environments—their capacities for sensation and movement, for instance. Yet other patterns involve states of motivation or arousal such as hunger, thirst, fear, anger, and disgust; and still others involve cognitive capacities such as memory, learning, reasoning, and problem solving.

According to hylomorphists, the patterns we find in the living world include mental phenomena. Thought, feeling, perception, and action are all patterns of social and environmental interaction. Some we describe in perceptual or sensory terms: seeing, hearing, tasting, feeling, having an itch. Others are more complex and incorporate perceptual or sensory patterns of these sorts. They include believing, wanting, knowing, and remembering. These higher-level patterns, moreover, are often integrated into behavioral patterns that are more complex still such as intellectual habits or personality or character traits. Consider an example: The interactions between a young child and the candy hidden in the cupboard are at first almost completely unstructured—or more precisely, they are structured in ways we can describe and explain merely by appeal to the conceptual resources of physics: the child and candy exert a gravitational influence on each other, for instance. But the interactions between the child and the candy become structured in more complex ways once the cupboard door is opened. We describe these ways by saying the child *wants* the candy, is *trying to get* it, and *remembers* that it is there once its mother has re-closed the cupboard door. The same is true of the child's interactions with its mother and with other people: it is *chagrined* and *frustrated* by her refusal to give the candy, but *knows* that its father is more pliable. Similarly, the father's *pliability* and the mother's *prudence* are also types of complex structured behavior. They represent broad patterns of choice, decision, thought, feeling, and action with long histories and long-term implications for future behavior.

The core idea of a hylomorphic theory of mind, then, is that sensations, feelings, thoughts, perceptions, actions, and other psychological phenomena are complex patterns of social and environmental interaction like the patterns just described. They are ways animals like us interact with each other and the environment—ways in which our behavior is structured or organized. According to hylomorphists, plants, animals, and other living things are not just organized assemblages of parts; they are zones of structured activities. These activities include muscular contractions, bodily movements, and other physiological states as lower-level contributing factors which are revealed through functional analysis, but they also include higher-level interactions with other animals and the environment. Organisms are thus multistructure complexes: each comprises a complex hierarchy of activities and subactivities, structures and substructures.

Human behavior in particular comprises biological activities and capacities that are incorporated into patterns of rational interaction, patterns that admit of evaluation in terms of rational, moral, aesthetic, and similar categories. What gets structured in these rational ways include the states and subactivities of the various organic parts, such as the parts that enable humans to perceive aspects of their social and physical environments and to feel and respond to those features. These forms of engagement and response, and the criteria we use to evaluate them are in part what we refer to and describe when using psychological predicates and terms. On the hylomorphic view, then, we use psychological discourse to describe high-level structured behaviors that have various organic states as lower-level contributing substructures.

Let me close by clarifying three points: how a hylomorphic approach to mental phenomena differs from behaviorism, how it differs from Dennett's (1991) real patterns, and how it treats qualia. The idea that mental phenomena can be understood as patterns of behavior is liable to remind some people either of behaviorism or of Dennett's real patterns. Hylomorphism nevertheless differs from both views in significant ways (Jaworski 2011, section 11.8). First, hylomorphism (at least the kind on which I've focused) rejects physicalism; behaviorism and Dennett do not. Second, hylomorphists do not conceive of behavior as narrowly as behaviorists do. Behaviorists tend to conceive of behavior merely in terms of bodily movements or utterances—something that can be given an exhaustive description by physics but that is observable under pedestrian circumstances (Jaworski 2011, 106). According to hylomorphists, however, behavior comprises more than this. Thoughts, feelings, perceptions, and actions all involve social and environmental factors in addition to physiological ones. Third, hylomorphists endorse a different semantics for psychological discourse (Jaworski 2011, section 11.7). Behaviorists claim that psychological expressions are abbreviations for longer physical descriptions of actual and potential bodily behavior. Hylomorphists deny that this is the case; we might initially learn how to use a psychological expression in the context of certain bodily movements or utterances, but psychological expressions are not shorthand for descriptions of these movements and utterances. Psychological language instead describes distinctive patterns of social and environmental interaction—patterns that cannot be analyzed or reduced to unstructured bodily movements, physiological states or dispositions. Hylomorphism also denies Dennett's idea that psychological discourse is merely a framework for predicting and explaining physical processes in a way that is more efficient (if less accurate) than physics. For hylomorphists, psychological discourse and the special sciences in general are conceptual frameworks for describing and explaining behavioral structures at levels higher than those described and explained by physics. We postulate patterns in nature not for predictive and explanatory convenience, but because there are structures in nature that exist independent of our predictive and explanatory interests. We might say that for hylomorphists, real patterns are more real than they are for Dennett, whose view is a form of structure nonreductivism (see Section 1).

What about qualia? Someone might wonder how hylomorphists can accommodate the existence of qualia—subjective, nonrelational, unanalyzable properties or events—if hylomorphists conceive of mental phenomena as patterns of social and environmental interaction, which are presumably relational, analyzable, and not subjective. Hylomorphists can respond to qualia exponents in at least two ways. First, they are free to endorse an epiphenomenalist approach to qualia; they are free to claim, in other words, that human patterns of social and environmental interaction produce or generate epiphenomenal qualia. The downside of this approach is that it saddles hylomorphists with the philosophical and empirical problems facing epiphenomenalists (Jaworski 2011, sections 8.8–8.9). Second, they can adopt an approach to qualia that denies that the qualitative aspects of experience consist in the instantiation or occurrence of subjective, nonrelational, unanalyzable properties or events. Sensorimotor contingency theory, for instance, claims that perception is a sensorimotor process of environmental exploration (Jaworski 2011, section 11.4).[6] The qualitative looks, tastes, and feels of things consist in distinctive patterns of sensorimotor interaction with features of the environment—in the various profiles objects present to us as we interact with them using our sensory and motor subsystems. The qualitative character of our experience consists not in there being subjective, nonrelational, unanalyzable properties or events, but in patterns of interaction between organisms and their environments.

I've tried to convey a rough sense of what a hylomorphic approach to mental phenomena involves and how it differs from some competing approaches to mental phenomena. I've also described how hylomorphists can start building an empirical case in their favor, and in what ways (or perhaps at what costs) the basic hylomorphic thesis can be squared with physicalism or substance dualism. There is obviously a great deal more to be said on these topics, and related ones. I haven't been able to describe how the hylomorphic view enables us to solve the mind-body problems facing its competitors—the problem of emergence, say, or the problem of mental causation (Jaworski 2011, sections 11.11–11.12). I nevertheless hope I've said enough for the time being to encourage you to keep structure in mind.

Fordham University

Notes

1. Option (c) is the kind of view Mark Johnston looks to reject when he ponders what might set apart those relations that are responsible for generating complex structured systems: "When certain items come to stand in certain relations . . . there then comes to be some further item which has those original items as parts. That is presumably how we have such complex items as model airplanes, trains, and molecules. Well, just why are those relations and their ilk, 'item-generators,' while other relations . . . seem impotent in the production of new items? Whence this invidious ontological distinction? . . . Could it just be a projection of our idiosyncratic way of experiencing and conceptualizing reality, so that things considered in themselves are not complex, but are so only relative to a scheme of clumping or bundling? Somehow, I doubt it" (Johnston 2006, 652).

2. I use the label "structure realism" to distinguish the view I have in mind from the view Ladyman and Ross (2007) call "structural realism." The view they have in mind is in some respects opposed to structure realism since they favor an ontology that rejects the existence of commonsense things. Structure realism, by contrast, is a view that can accommodate a commonsense notion of things. Ladyman and Ross's view also takes a stance on the empirical contents of physics. Structure realism does not. It claims simply that structure

is a real and irreducible ontological and explanatory principle, one that cannot be reduced to, paraphrased, or eliminated in favor of nonstructural discourse.

3. Hylomorphism is thus at odds with views that look to distinguish living things from nonliving ones or mental beings from nonmental ones purely on the basis of the entities that compose them. Examples include the views of Greek atomists such as Democritus who claimed that the differences between living things and nonliving ones could be explained by, say, the possession of a greater number of round atoms. More recently, Roger Penrose (1994) has made an analogous suggestion about consciousness: the difference between conscious beings and nonconscious ones, he suggests, is something that can be explained by differences among their quantum-level components. Hylomorphists, by contrast, reject a component-based account of these distinctions.

4. John Bickle (2003) refers to the philosophical sense of reduction as "ruthless reduction." Philosophers of neuroscience like William Bechtel have distinguished their notion of reduction from this one: "The theory reduction model . . . is much stronger than what scientists generally have in mind when they speak of reduction. For many scientists, research is reductionistic if it appeals to lower-level components of a system to explain why it behaves as it does under specified conditions. This sense of reduction is capture in the accounts of mechanistic explanation presented in the next section. . . . [T]he reductions achieved through mechanistic explanations are in fact compatible with a robust sense of autonomy for psychology and other special sciences, albeit a sense of autonomy no reductionist except one seeking hegemony for the lower level (Bickle . . .) should have any desire to deny" (Bechtel 2007, 173–174).

5. According to Putnam's original proposal, psychological descriptions are abstract descriptions that postulate relations among sensory inputs, motor outputs, and internal mental states. The only significant difference between Turing machine descriptions and psychological descriptions, Putnam suggested, was that psychological inputs, outputs, and internal states were related to each other probabilistically not deterministically. If, for instance, Eleanor believes there are exactly eight planets in our solar system, and she receives the auditory input, "Do you believe there are exactly eight planets in our solar system," then she will produce the verbal output, "Yes," not with a deterministic probability of 1, but with a probability between 1 and 0.

6. Noë and O'Regan (2002) defend a sensorimotor theory of consciousness. See also O'Regan (2009) and Noë (2004), chap. 4. For a discussion of how a sensorimotor theory of consciousness meshes with a hylomorphic theory of mind see Jaworski 2011, 321–324.

Bibliography

Bechtel, William. 2007. "Reducing Psychology while Maintaining its Autonomy via Mechanistic Explanations." In *The Matter of the Mind*, ed. Maurice Schouten and Huib Looren de Jong, 172–198. Blackwell Publishing, 2007.

———. 2008. *Mental Mechanisms: Philosophical Perspectives on Cognitive Neuroscience*. New York: Routledge.

Bickle, John. 2003. *Philosophy and Neuroscience: A Ruthlessly Reductive Account*. Boston: Kluwer Academic Publishers.

Campbell, Neil A. 1996. *Biology*, 4th Edition. San Francisco: The Benjamin Cummings Publishing Company, Inc.

Craver, Carl F. 2007. *Explaining the Brain: Mechanisms and the Mosaic Unity of Neuroscience*. New York: Oxford UP.

Cummins, Robert. 1975. "Functional Analysis." *Journal of Philosophy* 72: 741–764.

Dennett, Daniel C. 1978. "Toward a Cognitive Theory of Consciousness." In *Brainstorms: Philosophical Essays on Mind and Psychology*. Montgomery, Vt: Bradford Books.

———. 1991. "Real Patterns." *Journal of Philosophy* 88: 27–51.

Fine, Kit. 1999. "Things and Their Parts." *Midwest Studies in Philosophy* 23: 61–74.

Fodor, Jerry. 1968. "The Appeal to Tacit Knowledge in Psychological Explanation." *Journal of Philosophy* 65: 627–640

Furth, Montgomery. 1978. "Transtemporal Stability in Aristotelian Substances." *Journal of Philosophy* 75: 624–646.

Jaworski, William. 2011. *Philosophy of Mind: A Comprehensive Introduction*. Malden, MA: Wiley-Blackwell.

Johnston, Mark. 2006. "Hylomorphism." *Journal of Philosophy* 103: 652–698.

Koslicki, Kathrin. 2008. *The Structure of Objects*. New York: Oxford UP.

Ladyman, James, and Don Ross. 2007. *Every Thing Must Go: Metaphysics Naturalized*. New York: Oxford UP.

Lycan, William G. 1987. *Consciousness*. Cambridge, Mass.: MIT Press.

Mayr, Ernst. 1982. *The Growth of Biological Thought: Diversity, Evolution, and Inheritance*. Cambridge, Mass.: The Belknap Press of Harvard University.

Noë, Alva. 2004. *Action in Perception*. Cambridge, Mass.:The MIT Press.

Noë, Alva, and J. Kevin O'Regan. 2002. "On the Brain-Basis of Visual Consciousness: A Sensorimotor Account." In *Vision and Mind: Selected Readings in the Philosophy of Perception*, ed. Alva Noë and Evan Thompson, 567—98. Cambridge: MIT Press.

O'Regan, J. Kevin. 2009. "Sensorimotor Approach to (Phenomenal) Consciousness." In *Oxford Companion to Consciousness*, ed. T. Baynes, A. Cleeremans, and P. Wilken, 588–593 (Oxford University Press).

Penrose, Roger. 1994. *Shadows of the Mind: A Search for the Missing Science of Consciousness*. New York: Oxford University Press.

Putnam, Hilary. 1975. *Mind, Language, and Reality: Philosophical Papers, Vol.2*. New York: Cambridge UP.

Sober, Elliott. 1985. "Panglossian Functionalism and the Philosophy of Mind." *Synthese* 64: 165–193.

Sommerhoff, Gerd. 1969. "The Abstract Characteristics of Living Systems." In *Systems Thinking: Selected Readings*, ed. F. E. Emery, , 147–202. Harmondsworth: Penguin.

Van Inwagen, Peter. 1990. *Material Beings*. Ithaca, NY: Cornell UP.

Some Logical Problems for Scientism

Christopher M. Brown

Abstract: This paper looks at nine different ways of defining *scientism* in order to show that potential definitions of the term conform to a general pattern: a definition of *scientism* either is self-defeating or else cannot really count as a construal of scientism in the first place. Advocates for the experimental sciences would therefore be better off accepting a middle position—one might say *a broadly Thomistic approach to science*—between the extremes of scientism on the one hand and a religious fundamentalism that ignores the important contributions of the experimental sciences on the other. Such a middle position recognizes both the intellectual significance and the inherent limitations of the scientific method employed within the experimental sciences.

S cientism, roughly, is the notion that the only genuine kind of knowledge is scientific knowledge.[1] A commitment to scientism is rarely, if ever, expressly stated by a thinker, but scientism is a position that plays an implicit and foundational role in much of our contemporary academic and public discourse. But is scientism a credible philosophy? It is not hard to think of a number of reasons for thinking the answer is "no." For example, consider that scientific practice is not always *ethically* neutral. But science cannot give us moral knowledge and scientific practice often requires making momentous moral judgments (think, for example, of questions such as the following: "should we explode the atom bomb?" or "should we destroy human embryos to harvest their stem cells?"). A second argument notes that scientific practice is not always *metaphysically* or *religiously* neutral—and this seems to be particularly the case in those disciplines that study human beings.[2] Since metaphysical and religious questions are genuinely human questions, and metaphysical and religious questions lie beyond the competence of science, science cannot be the only kind of rational discourse. A third argument suggests that scientism constitutes a genuine threat to human flourishing. In his thought-provoking book *Technopoly: the Surrender of Culture to Technology*,[3] the sociologist Neil Postman argues that scientific imperialism can make no room for traditional religious or moral ways of making sense of the universe; but neither does it—indeed, it cannot—offer an alternative grand-narrative. Since a culture cannot

© 2012, *Proceedings of the ACPA*, Vol. 85
DOI: 10.5840/acpaproc20118515

survive without a grand-narrative, and human beings cannot be happy outside of a thriving culture, scientific imperialism leads to human misery. Finally, one might note that scientism constitutes a form of rationalism that (wrongly) suggests that we discover the truth about reality only by way of propositional discourse—and not also, for example, through the media of second-person encounters, narrative, and art.[4]

Whatever one might think of these sorts of arguments, this paper focuses on a different way of criticizing scientism, one to which a potential advocate of scientism should be particularly sensitive. By looking at nine different ways of defining *scientism*, I show that potential definitions of *scientism* conform to a general pattern: a definition of *scientism* either is self-defeating or else cannot really count as a construal of scientism in the first place. Advocates for the experimental sciences would therefore be better off accepting a middle position—one might say *a broadly Thomistic approach to science*—between the extremes of scientism on the one hand and a religious fundamentalism that ignores the important contributions of the experimental sciences on the other. Such a middle position recognizes both the intellectual significance *and* the inherent limitations of the scientific method employed within the experimental sciences.[5]

Scientism: The Strong Thesis

Consider the following proposition:

(S) [We *know* that all knowledge comes by way of scientific experiments] and [we possess some scientific knowledge, e.g., the earth revolves around the sun].[6]

(S) is a rather strong way of stating what one might mean by *scientism*. Of course, there is an advantage in defending a stronger thesis: a stronger thesis has more explanatory power than a weaker one. On the other hand, the stronger a thesis, the harder it is to defend and the easier it is to defeat. In fact, it is rather easy to show that (S) is false. To see this, first note that (S) has the following proposition as a component part:

(K) All knowledge comes by way of scientific experiments.

Like (S), (K) says that *all knowledge comes by way of scientific experiments*. But note a crucial difference between (S) and (K): (S)—but not (K)—says that we *know* that all knowledge comes by way of scientific experiments. Of course, if (K) were true, one of the things we might claim to know is (K) itself. Since (S) logically entails that we *do* know that (K) is true—see the left-hand component part of the conjunctive statement that is (S)—(S) also logically entails the following proposition:

(1) If (S) is true, then it is logically possible to come to know that (K) is true by way of scientific experiments [self-evident].

But (K) is a not a scientifically testable claim; it is a philosophical claim after-all. Therefore,

(2) It is logically impossible to come to know that (K) is true by way of scientific experiments [self-evident].

And from (1) and (2) it follows that:

> (3) Therefore, it is not the case that (S) is true, i.e., (S) is false [from (1) and (2), by modus tollens].

(S) is therefore in a boat similar to the now famous *verificationist criterion of meaning*:

> (V)A statement is meaningful only if it can be verified by a scientific experiment.

The logical positivists used (V) in an attempt to discredit God-talk, specifically, and the discipline of metaphysics more generally. Unfortunately (for the logical positivists), (V) discredits itself, since (V) itself is not a statement that can be verified by way of a scientific experiment. Likewise proposition (S) might be used to discredit God-talk and metaphysics. However, (S) too discredits itself, since (S) claims that we know that (K) is true and (K) says *all knowledge comes by way of scientific experiments.* But (K) is not the kind of statement that *can* be evaluated by way of a scientific experiment.

A Weaker Thesis

Since (S) is self-defeating, perhaps the critic of non-scientific knowledge claims—i.e., an advocate for scientism—would be better off making the following weaker claim:

> (S1) All knowledge comes by way of scientific experiments and we possess some scientific knowledge.

Believing (S1) apparently does not lead us into the same kind of trouble that believing (S) does. Recall that someone can *believe* some proposition *p* without thereby *knowing* that *p* is true. For example, say I believed in March of 2011 that the St. Louis Cardinals were going to win the World Series in October of 2011. From the fact that I *believe* in March of 2011 that the Cardinals are going to win the World Series in October of 2011, it does not follow that I *know* the Cardinals are going to win the World Series in October of 2011. Now consider propositions (S1) and (K). Susan can *believe* (K) is true without also claiming to *know* that (K) is true. And, whereas (S) logically entails that we know that (K) is true, (S1) does not. But it was the claim *we know that (K) is true* that caused problems for (S). And so it seems Susan will not run into logical problems believing (S1), *provided that* Susan does not also go on to claim to *know* that (K)—or (S1)—is true.

But there is another way to show that (S1) leads to self-defeat. To see how, consider the notion of *the reliability of a cognitive faculty.* We have a number of cognitive faculties, e.g., perception, memory, and reason. A cognitive faculty is reliable just in case it is *truth conducive.* As Moser, Mulder, and Trout put it, a reliable cognitive faculty tends "to cause true rather than false beliefs."[7] Say your Uncle John's memory is not what it used to be. But his amnesia is time-period specific. He remembers the good old days with crystal-clear precision. But you know from recent experience that when it comes to speaking truly about what he did, say, last week, Uncle John almost always gets it wrong. In addition, you have no reason to believe Uncle John is, in these reports, lying or stretching the truth; he seems to genuinely believe that his reports are accurate. Given such evidence, you have a good reason to doubt the reliability of Uncle John's memory—at least when it comes to recalling what he did last week. So, whenever Uncle John speaks about what he did last week, you (rationally) doubt that what he says is true.

Now, consider the following proposition:

(R) Human perception is a reliable cognitive faculty.

Can we know that (R) is true? One thing is for certain: we cannot come to know that (R) is true by way of a scientific experiment. This is because no scientific experiment could establish (R) without implicitly assuming its truth in the process. So it follows that

(4) If (S1) is true, then we cannot know that (R) is true.

But is it *rational* even to *believe* that all knowledge comes by way of scientific experiments and we possess some scientific knowledge if we cannot *know* perception to be a reliable cognitive faculty? It seems it is not rational to so believe—at least not for the person who has been apprised of the truth of (4). For, if we cannot know that (R) is true, then, for any proposition *p* that we care to believe on the basis of perception, the degree of confidence that we have that *p* is true would be far too low for us to rightly consider our belief that *p* is true to count as an instance of *knowledge*. So in order to know by perception that *p* is true, we need to be able to know that (R) is true. Since scientific knowledge involves believing propositions on the basis of perception, it follows that

(5) If we possess some scientific knowledge, then we can know that (R) is true.

But we now have said enough to show that (S1) leads to a contradiction. For from (S1) we can draw the following valid inference:

(6) If (S1) is true, then we possess some scientific knowledge [from (S1), conditional introduction].

And from (6) and (5) the following proposition follows by hypothetical syllogism:

(7) If (S1) is true, then we can know that (R) is true.

But that means (S1) entails both that we *can*—see proposition (7)—and we *cannot*—see proposition (4)—know that (R) is true. Now, any proposition that entails a contradiction is false. So, (S1) is false.

An Even Weaker Thesis?

Can we weaken (S) even further and still communicate a position that would be embraced by critics of non-scientific knowledge claims? How about the following:

(S2) All knowledge requires *good evidential support.*

Of course, if we simply identify *good evidential support* with *beliefs acquired by way of scientific experiments*, we are back to (S1). So, *good evidential support* has to mean something else. But in that case (S2) will turn out to be altogether *too* weak to satisfy the critic of non-scientific forms of knowing. For (S2) is compatible with there being *non-scientific* forms of good evidential support, e.g., philosophical, personal, religious, etc. So, (S2) cannot count as a legitimate construal of *scientism*.[8]

Scientism, Again

Let us consider a thesis that is stronger than (S2), but weaker than (S) or (S1). Perhaps the following can survive the sort of logical critique we have been mounting against more aggressive—and admittedly, rather naïve—forms of scientism:

> (S3) The only propositions the truth or falsity of which it is important to know are those that can be learned simply by way of scientific practices.

In evaluating this proposal, we should first ask ourselves whether the truth or falsity of (S3) itself is something important to know. It is hard to see how it *is not*. For someone who believes it, (S3) functions as a sort of epistemological gatekeeper, separating what is important to know from what is not. And presumably, it would be important to know whether such a gatekeeper is itself trustworthy. But, if the truth or falsity of (S3) counts as something important to know, then a belief in (S3) is in trouble, since the truth or falsity of (S3) is not something we could learn simply by way of scientific practices. (S3) therefore sets up a standard for what is important to know that it itself does not meet. So if (S3) is true, then (S3) itself is not something important to know. But we just proved that, if (S3) is true, then (S3) *is* something important to know. Believing (S3) leads to a contradiction and so (S3) is false.

Aside from being self-contradictory, (S3) suffers the misfortune of being subject to counter-example. Say I am studying the nature of the human mind. Some scientists believe the following:

> (8) Mental events (e.g., thinking about last night's baseball game) are not identical to brain events (e.g., some pattern of c-fibers firing in the brain).

Can we come to know the truth or falsity of (8)—or a proposition like (8)—by way of scientific practices alone? No. At best, what we learn about the brain by way of neurological and psychological studies will make an important *contribution* to our knowledge of the mind. Scientific knowledge of the brain cannot by itself be sufficient to rule out a thesis such as (8), if only because philosophers and scientists have plausible reasons for making a real distinction between mental and physical events, where the proper evaluation of such reasons necessarily involves engaging in a philosophical and not a scientific mode of reasoning, e.g., the evaluation of an argument for some sort of dualist approach to mind based on the apparent fact that mental and physical events have different essential properties.

So, if I accept (S3), given that (8) is not a proposition that can be known to be true or false by scientific practices alone, then it follows that (8) is not something important to know. In studying the mind, if you will forgive me for saying so, one need pay a proposition such as (8) no mind. But obviously, the truth or falsity of a proposition such as (8) has implications for the viability of various research programs. For example, some scientists believe (8) *and* are also *epiphenomenalists*. Epiphenominalists believe the following:

(EP) Mental events—although real and distinct from physical events—are nonetheless causally inert; although mental events necessarily accompany certain kinds of physical events, mental events themselves have no causal impact on the world.

Given the truth of (EP), psychologists—at least those who study beliefs—study a phenomenon that has absolutely no real effect on the behavior of human bodies. And that is probably going to come as some real (bad) news to those psychologists. As we have seen, (S3) entails that the truth or falsity of proposition (8) is *not* something important to know. (S3) also entails that the truth or falsity of the conjunct of (EP) and (8) is not important to know since the truth or falsity of the conjunct of (EP) and (8) is not the sort of thing one could know by scientific practices alone. But the truth or falsity of the conjunct of (8) and (EP) has implications for an important academic discipline such as psychology, and so it seems correct to say that the truth or falsity of the conjunct of (8) and (EP) *is* something important to know. Therefore, by *modus tollens*, (S3) is false.

Scientism as Global Methodological Naturalism

In a recent panel discussion with biologist David Sloan Wilson and theologian John F. Haught at the Graduate Center, CUNY, philosopher Daniel Dennett had the following to say about scientism (in response to a comment made by Haught):

> I don't know anyone who is guilty of it. It seems to me that "scientism" has been invented as a sort of straw man, . . . so that anytime anybody gets angry or anxious about science sticking its nose into something they think science has no business sticking its nose, they get to say "reductionism!," "scientism!" and these are epithets that are supposed to freeze everybody in their tracks. . . . I don't think I know any scientists who are really guilty of the caricature of scientism that you are describing. I do know scientists that (like me) are naturalists. We are methodological naturalists. But that's just built right into the scientific method. That's not to say there couldn't be supernatural things. But the burden of proof is on somebody who wants to invoke them.[9]

Let us grant, for the sake of argument, that the accounts of scientism discussed so far are mere caricatures of the position.[10] Can we do any better by way of scientism? Perhaps we can begin with professor Dennett's claim that scientists are committed to a doctrine known as *methodological naturalism*, here construed as *anti-supernaturalism in scientific practice*:

(S4) Scientism is the doctrine that says that true science is science committed to methodological naturalism, where methodological naturalism is the notion that *scientific* explanations are by definition *natural* explanations, where an explanation counts as natural just in case it appeals only to causes within nature, i.e., no supernatural causes allowed, e.g., God, spirits, souls, etc.

Now, by itself, (S4) will not work as a definition of *scientism*. For (S4) does not say anything about the proper *scope* of scientific practices. So consider an advocate of Intelligent Design Theory named Sam. Sam, say, believes in God and thinks that certain aspects of the nature of human beings lie outside the proper scope of scientific investigation. Sam can and does also accept (S4). Although Sam believes that God created the universe, Sam does not think that such a truth can be demonstrated by way of the experimental sciences. He does, however, think that *scientific* evidence shows that it is more probable than not that life on this planet has been *intelligently designed*. Since it seems correct to say that Sam is *not* an advocate of scientism, (S4) is obviously too weak to pick out what real advocates of (something such as) scientism have in mind by the doctrine.

Let us try to strengthen (S4) a bit. Consider the following suggestion:

(S5) Scientism is the doctrine that says that (a) a free-thinking person should be committed to a *global* methodological naturalism, i.e., an explanation of some phenomenon *P* is a good explanation of *P* only if it is a naturalistic explanation of *P* and (b) we possess some scientific knowledge.

One problem with (S5) is that the term *naturalistic* in the expression *naturalistic explanation* is ambiguous; *naturalistic* might be taken to mean *non-supernatural*, but it could also be taken to mean *non-personal* (in the sense of *without purpose* or *without intelligence*). Let us say we first take *naturalistic* to mean *non-supernatural* (as Dennett's remarks in his discussion with professors Haught and Sloan suggest that we do). In that case we are defining *scientism* as follows:

(S6) The doctrine that says that (a) a free-thinking person should be committed to a *global* methodological naturalism, i.e., an explanation of some phenomenon *P* is a good explanation of *P* only if it is a non-supernatural explanation of *P*, and (b) we possess some scientific knowledge.

Presumably, any advocate of scientism would defend the truth of (S6). In effect, such an advocate believes that we will arrive at a better understanding of the world as a whole only when we assume, in studying any given phenomenon in the world, that atheism is true.

That being said, we can note for our purposes that (S6) cannot be a good definition of *scientism*. (S6) suffers the same problem as (S4): it says nothing about the correct scope of *scientific* practices—which presumably is an essential element in any position that argues for the epistemic superiority of scientific practices over non-scientific ones. So, for example, consider the case of Jane the atheist. Jane believes (S6) but also thinks that the disciplines of psychology, sociology, and anthropology and are not in any real sense of the expression *scientific* disciplines, and so such disciplines are not productive of *scientific* knowledge. That being said, Jane believes that disciplines such as psychology and sociology (not to mention philosophy, religion, art, and literature) are indeed productive of genuine knowledge about human beings, knowledge that cannot, in principle, be discovered by way of the experimental sciences. Now, an advocate of scientism clearly sees the methods of the experimental sciences as directly applicable to the many different dimensions of *human* existence. Therefore, (S6)—the *supernaturalist* interpretation of (S5)—is too weak to capture what anyone means by *scientism*.[11]

What about reading *naturalistic* in (S5) as *non-personal*? If we take *naturalistic* in (S5) to mean *non-personal*, then we get the following definition of *scientism*:

> (S7) The doctrine that says that (a) a free-thinking person should be committed to a *global* methodological naturalism, i.e., an explanation of some phenomenon *P* is a good explanation of *P* only if it is a *non-personal* explanation of *P*, i.e., an explanation that appeals only to unguided, purposeless causes and not to intelligent causes and (b) we possess some scientific knowledge.

In evaluating (S7), we should first ask ourselves, "is (S7) itself an explanation?" The answer to this question is undoubtedly "Yes." For (S7) identifies a candidate for what counts as a necessary (although not sufficient) condition for an explanation counting as a *good* explanation. But (S7) itself does not explain what a good explanation is by positing non-personal causes. Instead, it explains what a good explanation is by using terms that invoke intelligent causation, e.g., (S7) implies that we should *believe* a theory because it is a good explanation for some phenomenon *P*; it entails that we have *knowledge* that some propositions are true, and therefore it implies that we *believe* some propositions are true, and that we are also *warranted* or *justified* in so believing, etc. But *believing*, *knowing*, and *being warranted* or *justified* are clear examples of intelligent and not non-personal causation. So, (S7) fails to satisfy its own criterion for what counts as a good definition of *explanation*. If we believe (S7), we ought to reject (S7). Like (S), (S1), and (S3), (S7) is self-defeating.

Scientism, One More Time

So far, our attempts to define *scientism* such that the experimental sciences constitute the *only* way of arriving at knowledge have resulted in definitions that are either self-defeating or too weak to satisfy the critic of non-scientific ways of knowing. Let us try a different strategy. Rather than claiming that *p* has a chance of being known only if it is believed on the basis of the practices of experimental science, let us suggest a definition that compares the relative value of the methods of the experimental sciences with the relative value of the methods of non-scientific disciplines or practices.[12] Consider the following:

> (S8) The experimental sciences offer us the most authoritative interpretation of reality and we have some scientific knowledge.

Note first that (S8) itself is not a deliverance of an experimental science; it is rather a philosophical claim. Assuming that *thought about reality* constitutes a part of reality, according to (S8), the degree of plausibility enjoyed by (S8) itself is not as high as the things known by way of the experimental sciences. But we might want to know from the advocate of (S8) just how plausible a deliverance from a non-scientific practice is. For, if we think the degree of plausibility of such deliverances is rather low, then (S8) itself will at best have a rather low degree of plausibility for the person who believes it. Such a position certainly sounds too weak to count as a correct construal of scientism. So let us rather imagine that the advocate of (S8) does not think the degree of plausibility of non-scientific statements is necessarily *low*; in fact, it might be quite high—simply not as high as the deliverances of the experimental sciences.

To see why (S8) too is open to the charge of self-defeat, consider first that scientism entails the truth of *evidentialism*, since scientism is presumably a species of evidentialism. We can roughly define *evidentialism* as follows:

(E) It is rational for person S to believe that p only if S has good evidence that p.

Second, consider the kinds of evidence that *could* be advanced for the truth of (S8): (a) the experimental sciences produce the fruit of technological wonders; (b) the practice of experimental science invites consensus about the nature of reality. But to invoke pragmatic reasons such as (a) and (b) as evidence for the truth of (S8) would seem to be question-begging, since offering such pragmatic reasons would assume that reality *as a whole* is such that it can be investigated by a method the careful and consistent use of which will, for example, invite consensus about its character and shape.[13] Clearly, some human questions treat aspects of reality that can and should be investigated by the experimental sciences. In such cases we might expect to win consensus about such questions over time, at least within a specific scientific paradigm. On the other hand, to take just one example, the question whether there is a God seems to be the sort of question that—at least given the current human condition—does not invite consensus among those who think long and hard about it. But the fact that there is no intellectual consensus about the existence of God gives us no reason to think that philosophy, faith, or unbelief has any less credibility or authority than the deliverances or practices of the experimental sciences, *unless* we are simply presupposing that only those disciplines or practices that naturally lead to technological advancement or intellectual consensus, i.e., the experimental sciences, have the greatest kind of credibility or authority. It seems to me that the only kinds of reasons it is possible to bring forward in support of (S8) presuppose its truth and so involve circular or question-begging reasoning.

Of course, to provide circular or question-begging reasoning as evidence that p is not to provide *good* evidence that p. So, given the soundness of my argument above, the only kind of evidence that could be brought forward in defense of (S8) does not count as good evidence. But in that case, given the advocate of scientism's acceptance of (E), the critic of non-scientific forms of knowledge ought to reject a belief in (S8) as irrational, since she does not possess good evidence that (S8) is true. So, if someone accepts (S8), then she ought to reject (S8). Therefore, (S8) is self-defeating.

Conclusion

As far as I can see, there is no way to formulate the position known as *scientism* so that it can be both coherent *and* really count as a construal of *scientism*. In other words, any viable alternative version of (S), say (S9), is either going to fall prey to the problem which plagues (S2), (S4), and (S6)—it simply will be too weak to satisfy the critic of non-scientific forms of knowledge—or else it will, like (S), (S1), (S3), (S7), and (S8), turn out to be self-defeating. Of course, nothing I have argued in this paper suggests that there is something wrong with the methods of the experimental sciences. There is a whole world of difference between *scientism* and *having a robust respect for the impressive contributions of the experimental sciences to our knowledge of the physical universe.* We do not really have to choose between scientific and non-scientific ways of knowing, as so many contemporary fundamentalists (theistic and atheistic alike) would like to have us believe. It goes without saying that we have learned—and continue to learn—much about the universe by way of the experimental sciences. But a tenable appreciation of the powers of the scientific enterprise requires that we also admit its inherent limitations. As I have shown in this paper, the experimental sciences cannot be the only way we come to know things about the world.[14]

The University of Tennessee at Martin

Notes

1. Craig Condella has suggested to me that the word *scientism* connotes a charge or a judgment, and not so much a position that someone would happily endorse. He might be right. But compare with the word *atheism*. *Atheist* is a label that few have wanted to wear. Indeed, it has often included a moral indictment (think of Socrates and the early Christians). Nonetheless, there are those who do gladly accept the label, and more important for my purposes, those for whom the label is entirely appropriate. Whether or not anyone likes being branded as someone who advocates scientism, there does seem to be a position Q on the proper scope of the scientific method—roughly, the position that says that scientific knowledge is the only kind of genuine knowledge—that some philosophers and scientists are only too glad to accept as true. For the purposes of this paper, consider the word *scientism* to be a term of philosophical art that refers to position Q.

2. For an argument of this sort, see, for example, Alvin Plantinga's "When Faith and Reason Clash: Evolution and the Bible," *Christian Scholar's Review* 21.1 (1991): 8–33.

3. New York: Vintage Books, 1993.

4. For a sophisticated defense of the view that there are forms of knowledge other than propositional—or third-person—forms of knowledge, see Eleonore Stump's *Wandering in Darkness: Narrative and the Problem of Suffering* (Oxford: Oxford University Press, 2010).

5. For different approaches to arguing for a conclusion similar to the one I advance here, see, for example: Barry Stroud, "The Charm of Naturalism," in *Naturalism in Question*, ed. Mario De Caro and David Macarthur (Cambridge, Mass.: Harvard University Press, 2004), 21–35, and Edward Feser, "Hayek and Scientism," *The City* 3 (2010): 54–62.

6. I include the second component part of the conjunctive proposition (S)—"we possess some scientific knowledge"—since, otherwise, scientism will be compatible with skepticism about scientific knowledge. But (I take it that) scientism is *not* compatible with skepticism about scientific knowledge.

7. Paul K. Moser, Dwayne H. Mulder, and J. D. Trout, *The Theory of Knowledge: A Thematic Introduction* (New York: Oxford University Press, 1998), 89.

8. In addition, we can mention the following problem for believing (S2): would an advocate of scientism claim to know that (S2) is true? If so, then the advocate of (S2) should not believe (S2). For what *good* evidence could we possibly possess to support the claim to know that (S2) is true?

9. "What is Religion? What is it for? How does it Change?" (Forum, Great Issues Forum, Graduate Center, City University of New York, New York, NY, November 17, 2009). A complete video documentation of the event can be viewed at the Great Issues Forum web-site: http://greatissuesforum.org/index.php?option=com_content&view=article&id=264:what-is-religion-what-is-it-for-how-does-it-change&catid=47:past-conversations-archive&Itemid=107.

10. But see the entry "scientism" in *The Skeptic's Dictionary*, which presumably has a vested interest in *not* offering a caricature of the position: "Scientism, in the strong sense, is the self-annihilating view that only scientific claims are meaningful, which is not a scientific claim and hence, if true, not meaningful. Thus, scientism is either false or meaningless. . . . In the weak sense, scientism is the view that the methods of the natural sciences should be applied to any subject matter" ("Scientism," *The Skeptic's Dictionary*, accessed December 13, 2011, http://www.skepdic.com/scientism.html). The entry admits that *scientism* in the strong sense is self-defeating. But by distinguishing a weak sense from a strong one, the entry implies that the weak sense of *scientism* escapes the problem of self-defeat. It does not. For defining a term such as *scientism* falls to philosophy. But philosophy—by definition—cannot employ the methods of the natural sciences. Since defining a term such as *scientism* is an act of philosophy, the act of defining *scientism* by the author involves a failure to do what the entry says ought to be done, i.e., stick to the methods of the natural sciences. Even this so-called *weak* definition of *scientism* ought to be rejected as self-defeating.

In addition, consider the following legitimate subject-matters: the nature of being, the nature of knowledge, and the nature of science. These subject-matters are properly philosophical and so the methods of the natural sciences should not be applied to them, if only because questions about the nature of being, knowledge, and science cannot be resolved by way of the methods of the natural sciences. But *weak scientism* says that the methods of the natural sciences should be applied to any subject-matter. Therefore, weak scientism is obviously a problematic methodology.

11. Note that if we modify (S6) so as to add to it a condition (c), perhaps, *all areas of human experience can be studied by the scientific method*, then we again run into the problem of self-defeat, since (S6) itself says something about human experience and (S6) is not a proposition that can be (properly) evaluated by the scientific method.

12. For this strategy, see, e.g., Tom Sorrell's *Scientism: Philosophy and the Infatuation with Science* (London: Routledge, 1991), 1.

13. If we *do not* assume that by the word "reality" in (S8) we are to understand *all of reality*, then (S8) simply will be too weak to pick out a position with which a critic of non-scientific forms of knowledge can be happy. For in that case (S8) will read as something such as the following: (S8') *The natural sciences offer the most authoritative interpretation of those aspects of reality—and only those aspects of reality—about which it makes sense to study using the methods of the natural sciences, i.e., material reality insofar as it can be measured quantitatively.* Now, say John believes that (H) *human persons are immaterial beings* and so he also believes

that human persons cannot be studied by the natural sciences. John could believe (H) and also believe (S8'). But advocates of scientism clearly reject (H). Therefore, (S8') is too weak to satisfy the critics of non-scientific forms of knowing.

14. I would like to thank the following people who heard and commented on earlier drafts of this paper: the participants in a UTM Philosophy Forum meeting on October 1, 2009; the members of the Martin Hobbit Club; the audience at a faculty colloquium at the University of Tennessee at Martin on April 19, 2010, and the participants at session V of the 2011 meeting of the American Catholic Philosophical Association. I'm especially grateful to the following people for providing helpful comments on earlier drafts of the paper: Brian Besong, Father Jim Brent, O.P., Merry Brown, Craig Condella, Bryan Cross, Jim Fieser, Norman Lillegard, Michael Rota, and John Schommer.

Modeling the Dialogue between Science, Philosophy, and Religion: Aquinas on the Origins and Development of the Universe

Michael P. Krom

Abstract: St. Thomas Aquinas is an acknowledged model for anyone who wants to understand the dynamics of faith and reason as compatible and collaborative partners in the search for Truth. Further, his extensive reflections over the course of his intellectual development on the theme of Creation make him a fruitful source for understanding the contemporary science and religion dialogue on the origins and development of the universe. What follows is a discussion of Aquinas's views on Creation with an eye toward contemporary scientific theory. It would be wrong-headed to attempt to "discover" that Aquinas was "the first Evolutionist/Big Bang Theorist" (as Lord Acton found him the "First Whig"), and yet we might be surprised to find how open his philosophical speculations are in this regard. And hopefully the lovers of Truth who wrongly reject Christianity as a result of this love are willing to be surprised by his perennial philosophy.

> *In no case should the appearance of a new dispute between natural science and faith be created, because in fact that is not at all what this dialogue is about. The real level of discourse is that of philosophical thought: when natural science becomes a philosophy, it is up to philosophy to grapple with it. Only in that way is the contentious issue framed correctly; only then does it remain clear what we are dealing with: a rational, philosophical debate that aims at the objectivity of rational knowledge, and not a protest of faith against reason.*[1]

—Pope Benedict XVI, preface to *Evolutionismus und Christentum*

In addition to being a delightful and gripping read, Walter M. Miller, Jr.'s *A Canticle for Leibowitz* is rich with insights into the uneasy relationship between the institutions of modern science and the Catholic Church. In the second part of the book a secular scientist visits a remote monastery where the

© 2012, *Proceedings of the ACPA*, Vol. 85
DOI: 10.5840/acpaproc20118516

remains of a lost generation's scientific findings have supposedly been wasting away. When the scientist arrives, he is astonished to discover a spirit of open-minded inquiry amenable to the scientific method. In particular, his reluctance to share his scientific understanding of "the refrangible property of light" (given that it might offend the monks' religious views) is met by hearty laughter. The abbot informs the good scientist that the source of this confusion was the speculation of an ignorant priest, who "is a good man, a good priest[;] but all men are apt to be incredible asses at times, especially outside their domains."[2] As it turns out, the contemplative monks are ignorant about the details of scientific theory and yet are wise enough to know their own ignorance. Like the scientist, they know a sham when they see it, but unlike the scientist they also know the distinction between faith and reason.

This is a wonderful parable for our times, for this is precisely what we witness in the public square: the New Atheists proclaim the death of God because they have trampled upon the uninformed speculations of "incredible asses" who come bearing crosses.[3] On the other side, those trained in and formed by the Christian tradition of inquiry are untouched by the attacks and yet frustratingly left out of the discussion because the dialogue is not really with them: the New Atheists seem to think they are arguing with the fundamentalists of Scopes Trial yore, unaware of the fact that the standard theological view from the Patristic era to our own sides more with Clarence Darrow than with William Jennings Bryan.[4] This is an unfortunate situation because it makes it all the more difficult for science and religion to benefit from one another's insights. What would be instructive for both sides is to reflect upon the relationship between science and religion in an era before they had begun to go their separate ways. By doing so, we might see that when the contemplative spirit of the lover of Wisdom is the source of one's scientific, philosophical, or theological investigations, one will find fellow travelers who know both how to stay within their domains as well as how to learn from those who have charted other territories.

St. Thomas Aquinas is an acknowledged model for anyone who wants to understand the dynamics of faith and reason as compatible and collaborative partners in the search for Truth. Further, his extensive reflections over the course of his intellectual development on the theme of Creation make him a fruitful source for understanding the contemporary science and religion dialogue on the origins and development of the universe. What follows is a discussion of Aquinas's views on Creation with an eye toward contemporary scientific theory. It would be wrongheaded to attempt to "discover" that Aquinas was "the first Evolutionist/Big Bang Theorist" (as Lord Acton found him the "First Whig"), and yet we might be surprised to find how open his philosophical speculations are in this regard. And hopefully the lovers of Truth who wrongly reject Christianity as a result of this love are willing to be surprised by his perennial philosophy.

1. Aquinas on Origins

When the Greco-Roman world and its philosophical traditions first encountered Christianity, among the many issues of dispute were the goodness of bodily existence in general, and the reasonableness of the Incarnation in particular. As Peter Brown says when speaking of St. Augustine's pagan friend, Volusianus, for him "to accept the Incarnation would have been like a modern European denying the evolution of the species: he would have had to abandon not only the most advanced, rationally based knowledge available to him, but, by implication, the whole culture permeated by such achievements."[5] As surprising as this might be in light of contemporary criticisms of Christianity, Augustine was charged with the task of convincing men of reason that *the body is good*, that our fleshly existence is not to be escaped from as from a prison.[6] Augustine's strategy was to show the limits of philosophical reasoning concerning the relationship between body and soul,[7] and thereby to open up a space for faith: since reason could not conclusively settle such matters, it has no grounds for rejecting the claims of faith so long as they are neither contrary to reason nor implausible given what reason can know.

A similar dispute, though held at a much later time and in a more hypothetical manner (since the disputants were Christians arguing over the value of pagan philosophy rather than members of competing traditions), was over the origins of the universe. Whereas the philosophers had asserted that the universe is necessary and eternal, Christian revelation posited both the contingency of the world upon God's will and its having a spatiotemporal beginning. To speak more precisely, the Neoplatonic metaphysical tradition's understanding of necessary emanation was at odds with God's *fiat*, and Aristotle's scientific claim that the universe is eternal rejected the claim that Creation had a beginning in time.[8]

Concerning the necessity of the universe, while the Neoplatonic system shared in common with Christianity an understanding of the universe as utterly-dependent upon and caused by God, it saw the emanation of the universe from the One as necessary: God did not freely will the universe into existence, for it emanates from Him eternally as a necessary outpouring of His Goodness.[9] While it is arguable that at least in Plato's *Timaeus* one finds a notion of the universe having a temporal beginning, not only does Plotinus's emanation model seem to deny this,[10] but he was also understood to reject the One's freedom to pour forth into becoming. This rejection of contingency, coupled with a general tendency to see matter as an evil by-product of this emanative process,[11] stood in stark contrast to the Christian understanding of divine free will and the "It was good" of Genesis.[12]

Regarding Aristotelian science, the assertion of the eternity of the universe could in no way be reconciled with Revelation. While there was doubt as to the nature of Aristotle's claim, i.e., whether it was to be taken as a matter of proof or simply of speculation, it was clear that at least on this point the incorporation of Aristotle into a Christian system of thought would be a challenge.

From Aquinas's first discussions of Creation in *Scriptum super libros Sententiarum*[13] (henceforth "*Sentences*") to arguably his last in *Super Librum de Causis* (henceforth "*Commentary on the Book of Causes*"),[14] he consistently affirmed the total dependence of the universe on God's *fiat*, and its having a temporal beginning. There was no doubt, then, that Aquinas would have to reject tenets of both the Neoplatonists and of Aristotle. That being said, he went as far with them as he could in an attempt to explore the nature of his Christian commitments.

The *Commentary on the Book of Causes* is of particular importance for assessing Aquinas's views on the Neoplatonic view of the origins of the universe. Written in the first half of 1272, and thus one of his last works, Aquinas was the first to recognize the *Book of Causes* as the work of an Arab thinker who was heavily indebted to Proclus's *Elements of Theology*. Whereas previously this work was attributed to Aristotle, Aquinas recognized its Neoplatonic roots. It is interesting, then, that he would return to an examination of Neoplatonic metaphysics at the end of his life as if to discern more closely its compatibility with Christianity.

According to Plotinus, bodily existence is the result of the contemplative activity of hypostases lower than the One.[15] The spatiotemporal order, then, comes into being from the One only indirectly. While as a Christian Aquinas cannot accept this strong claim, he finds that a certain truth is being conveyed in an obscure way: a particular human being, though not strictly speaking caused in its being (*esse*) by intelligences, is caused both to be *this* thing and to be actualized in respect of its nature. Only God can create the human soul and even impress it upon the body, and yet the disposition of this matter to receive this soul is in part the result of "the impression of an intelligence." And so, that God creates this soul is dependent on the intelligence's causal power which, to be sure, it derives from God. God alone creates the nature of things and all natures proceed from Him immediately (i.e., only God is Creator), for all forms exist *qua* potentiality in God;[16] yet that *this* thing becomes the particular form and matter which constitute its substance is at least partially a result of the causal power of intelligences insofar as they are movers of heavenly bodies that, in turn, make possible the generation of a human body.[17] While the *being* of this human is caused by God, its *becoming* this human being is dependent upon both its parents and the intelligences. Further, the actualization of its potency as a rational soul can take place through an intelligence,[18] and, since an intelligence "is most similar to God . . . through it God can be known in the highest possible way."[19] Finally, while the claim that lower intelligences are the cause of matter must be utterly rejected, Aquinas does not want to reject other Neoplatonic doctrines on the sole basis of Scripture's silence on the matter. In particular, like Pseudo-Dionysius Aquinas points out that "Catholic faith does not assert"[20] that heavenly bodies have souls; rather than simply reject this claim as contrary to dogma, in *Quaestio disputata de spiritualibus creaturis* he goes to great lengths to show that the circular motion of celestial bodies does require a spiritual mover, though such a mover is united *qua* mover and not *qua* form.[21] Once again, rather than reject what initially seems to be contrary to the faith, Aquinas acknowledges a speculative insight that needs correction.

In response to the Neoplatonic view of necessity, whereas it is necessary that any contingent thing be caused by God,[22] it is not necessary that there be a universe at all.[23] God's will is not necessitated save in relation to Himself in that He can only will what "would be suitable and just."[24] In *ST* 1aQ19A3, Aquinas distinguishes between necessity *absolute* (absolutely) and *ex suppositione* (by supposition). In the absolute sense, God wills of necessity His goodness; Creation, on the other hand, is only willed by supposition to the extent that it is ordered toward His goodness. But to say that Creation is necessary by supposition is only to say that God voluntarily wills Creation and, given that he wills it, "He is unable not to will it, as His will cannot change."[25] Put differently, God does not have free will with respect to Himself, but does with respect to Creation, for God's will is necessarily in accordance with His goodness but freely decides to be the cause of those things ordered to His goodness.[26]

Regarding Aristotle's claim that the universe is eternal, this was a topic that Aquinas returned to throughout his career.[27] For the purposes of this paper, focusing on *De aeternitate mundi* suffices given its relatively late composition (ca. 1270), and the fact that he takes up the distinction between scientific/philosophical and theological commitments that are of interest here. Regarding the polemical context, Aquinas is responding to his fellow theologians who contended that reason could prove the universe to have a temporal beginning. Such arguments, Aquinas maintained, went too far and failed to appreciate the nuanced distinction between what can be known by reason, on the one hand, or by Revelation, on the other.[28]

De aeternitate mundi begins with an acknowledgement of and endorsement of Catholic dogma: the world is of finite duration, having been created at some unspecified time in the past. Yet Aquinas immediately clarifies this dogma by distinguishing between possibility and necessity: the Church tells us *that* the world has a beginning but does not specify the *modality* of this beginning; the question is "Was the Universe *necessarily* created so as to have a beginning, or could God have created it to exist from eternity?" While it is necessary that God be the Creator of all that exists, "our task is to examine whether something that is made [by God] could have existed forever."[29]

In the primary sense, "eternal" is a predicate that belongs to God alone, for only God is His essence. Following Boethius's classical definition of eternity as "the simultaneously-whole and perfect possession of interminable life,"[30] Aquinas asserts that only God can possess this attribute in the absolute sense. Yet, as Cyril Vollert, S.J. explains, this does not prevent Aquinas from asserting an analogical sense of eternity that "excludes beginning or end or both, but not succession . . . [and asking] whether eternity is a communicable perfection somewhat in the way that God's goodness, wisdom, beauty and other attributes are communicable to creatures."[31] In this analogical sense, Aquinas concludes that it is logically possible for a thing to be both created and eternal. Endorsing a formula from Boethius, Aquinas points out that "it is one thing to be carried through an endless life [*per interminabilem vitam duci*], . . . and quite another to embrace the whole presence of endless life all at once [*interminabilis vitae totam pariter complexam esse praesentiam*]."[32] Even though nothing can be "co-eternal" (*coaeternum*) with God, it is possible though counterfactual for God to create a world that shares analogically in His eternity.[33]

To summarize what Aquinas has to say concerning the origins of the universe, consider how Vollert puts it: "The dogma of faith is no obstacle to scientific exploration. Revelation teaches that the world began, but does not date that beginning; science has unimpeded liberty to search for the initial state from which the universe took its origin. Likewise, the dogma offers no embarrassment to philosophical reflection"[34] given that Revelation does not close off any reasoned attempt to make sense of the possibility of an eternal world. In terms of contemporary science, it is striking that the first person to provide a serious alternative to the steady state model of the universe (which assumed an infinite universe), was Georges Lemaître, a Catholic priest who let his science rather than his religion dictate his science. In terms of contemporary philosophy, despite the fact that Lemaître's "Cosmic Egg" or Big Bang Theory reigns supreme and suggests a singularity, it is no threat to Revelation to speculate as to what is behind or before our observational range. As Aquinas might have put it, Revelation, far from closing off inquiry, actually makes reason more aware of its own limits and thus more free to pursue the Truth.

2. Aquinas on Development

The New Atheists generally advance the thesis that Christianity simply cannot be made compatible with the evolutionary theory that undergirds so much of contemporary science.[35] And it is hard to blame them for this misunderstanding given that the most vocal Christians to respond to such claims concede the point: Christianity and evolution are incompatible, and thus evolution must be incorrect. Such well-intentioned Christians build their science negatively as a protest against evolutionary theory. Another group of Christians tend to join the New Atheists in mocking their own forebears and unenlightened confreres in the faith: "yes, we agree that Christians accepted (and continue to accept) childish views on the age of the universe and of the origins of species! Of course, we sophisticated Christians are very different." This ignorance of the Christian intellectual tradition only adds credence to those who reject Christianity, and to those who would transform the Gospel message into a collection of moral sayings or naïve myths that have merely cultural value. The uninformed theist agrees that Christianity is constantly in retreat and only differs from the atheist on how far this retreat must go.[36] By contrast, when one discovers the incredible range of speculations and openness to truth wherever it may be found in the Christian tradition, one can be humbled before an earlier generation that has so much to teach us. Given the false scientific theories upon which the Patristic authors and Scholastics relied, it is startling to find them considering hypotheses about the development of Creation based merely on their awareness that all is possible to God. In Aquinas's case, when we consider his reflections on how to interpret the Creation account found in Genesis as well as his more philosophical insights into the possibility of new species arising over time are, we recognize that the Christian tradition is like "the master of a household who brings out of his treasure what is new and what is old."[37]

The first point to be made in understanding Aquinas's reflections on the six days of Creation[38] is that he thinks all scripture is to be taken *literally* and yet *not necessarily historically*: the literal meaning of the text is always the basis for the spiritual sense, but the literal is not necessarily the same thing as the physical. In the first question, 10th article of the *Summa Theologica*, Aquinas points out that a literal interpretation has to look toward "that which is figured" by the words; for example, "when Scripture speaks of God's arm, the literal sense is not that God has such a member, but only what is signified by this member, namely operative power."[39] Thus, while the six days of Creation are to be taken literally, this does not mean that there were six 24-hour days in which God created the universe.

Rather than work through Aquinas's reflections on the six individual days, only two points are essential for the purposes of this paper: (1) Aquinas does not intend to conclusively settle matters of natural history but to explain the metaphysical teachings about God as Creator and Creation's dependence on Him. His principal conclusion pertinent to evolution is that God created a universe intrinsically open to the development of potentialities not actualized in the beginning;[40] (2) Aquinas is primarily concerned with establishing the dependence of Creation on its Creator such that, while it changes over time, those changes are intelligible in light of God's causal power. As he says in *Sentences*, "God alone is the immediate cause of all things which come into being by creation, and these are things that cannot come into being by motion nor by generation."[41] More specifically, neither matter nor forms can be generated, but only created. What comes into being by generation is *this* composite of form and matter.

Given Aquinas's view that forms cannot be created save by God alone, it would seem that evolution is a non-starter: either all forms were present in the beginning, or we have to assert that God continues to create forms in the way that He did in the beginning. Neither of these options seems satisfactory, unless one makes a distinction between *actual* and *potential* forms. All forms were present in the beginning potentially, though the actualization of some forms can take place through the causal powers granted to the forms already themselves actualized.

There are two cases of physical change that must be considered: first, in some cases a creature gives rise to a creature of a different form that is equal to or less than it in terms of ordered structure. An example that Aquinas uses is a donkey and horse reproducing so as to actualize the potential form of mule.[42] Secondly, and more importantly from an evolutionary standpoint, in some cases a creature gives rise to one that is more ordered than itself. This seems problematic in light of the principle that something which is less perfect cannot cause something that is more perfect. If there are no resources in Aquinas for understanding such a case, then he would have nothing to contribute to the discussion of evolutionary theory.   Fortunately, Aquinas does address precisely this point, and while the scientific theory which he uses is incorrect, the philosophical principles are as applicable today as they were then.

In *ST* 2a-2aeQ51A.4, Aquinas uses the example of monstrous birth of an animal (*monstruosi partus animalium*) to explain his point that sometimes something of a higher order arises out of a lower order; since "the active seminal force" cannot account for the resulting animal in this case, one must turn to the causal power of a celestial body, or even to God's providence. Just as both the sun and the parent are co-operative causes in the generation of a creature with the same form as the parent, so too is the celestial body capable of co-operating with the parent to bring about a creature of a higher form than the parent but of a lower form than the celestial body. More technically, a celestial being (*qua* moved by an intelligence) is a participating efficient cause with the corporeal, terrestrial being in the *becoming* of this thing that differs in form from them both. However, since only that which is of a higher form can be a cause of being, the celestial being (unlike the terrestrial being) also is the efficient cause of the *being* of this thing, not by virtue of its own power, but insofar as it is an instrumental cause participating in God's principal causative power. While Aquinas does allow created substances to cause the being of something in this restricted case, he nonetheless maintains that God alone is the creator of forms: the causation here is simply the actualization of potentialities latent in creation.[43] While we clearly have a long way to go before we get a theory of sustained evolution over the course of time and in response to terrestrial conditions, the philosophical insights into the possibility of development over time are already present.

3. Contemporary Science and Religion

This is not the place to examine the nuances of contemporary scientific cosmology and evolutionary theory, yet it is important to avoid a precipitous conclusion: the fact that we are very confident that our universe's spatiotemporal development can be traced back to singularity does not *prove* that Christians are correct to assert that physical reality is created. Our range of experience is too limited to make such a claim, for we cannot "observe" the entirety of the universe either as it is now or as it was at its beginning. Further, using reason alone we cannot rule out the possibility of the infinite creation and destruction of universes, or of eternal multiverses.[44]

The same points could be made concerning evolution, for evolution is only a partial account of human origins, but this partiality does not establish the validity of the "let us make man." If we are honest with ourselves and humbled by the limits of our knowledge, we will recognize that scientists, philosophers, and theologians are equal partners in a dialogue about matters that reason cannot settle. To reject faith *a priori* or on the supposed basis of empirical evidence bespeaks a vanity that is ignorant of the human condition; yet to "find" proof for biblical cosmology in quantum uncertainty or Big Bang theory is to unintentionally become an incredible ass! The meeting space is philosophy, for science must turn to the metaphysical questions that its own activity raises and presupposes, and theologians must show the world that faith is the reasonable response to what we can and cannot know about the metaphysical structure of reality.

Aquinas's humility in pursuit of the Truth allowed him to distinguish between the essential and accidental: the Bible is not a scientific textbook but a Revelation of Creation's dependency upon its Creator. His appreciation for the domains of discourse made him confident and unafraid of reason's legitimate openness to hypotheses that touch on matters fundamental to our existence.

What, then, is Aquinas committed to in terms of the origin and development of the world? In terms of origin, Creation; in terms of development, intelligibility. These two ultimately acquiesce, for, as Pope Benedict XVI puts it, "To believe in creation means to understand, in faith, the world of becoming revealed by science as a meaningful world that comes from a creative mind."[45] When we read Church fathers on this subject, we must be careful to distinguish their theological from their scientific commitments. What is remarkable is how creatively they engaged scriptural interpretation given the limited vision of the scientific theories available to them.

Our task is not to return to halcyon days, but to restore the confidence Christians once had that the discoveries of science and the revelation of God are two paths to the one Truth knowable by faith and reason. We should rejoice when we reflect on our contemporary knowledge of the mechanisms of creation; understanding has sought Truth, and now faith can seek understanding in turn. As Pope Benedict XVI puts it, "And so today, perhaps, we can understand better what the Christian dogma of creation was always saying but could hardly bring to bear because of the influence of the model from antiquity: creation should be thought of, not according to the model of the craftsman who makes all sorts of objects, but rather in the manner in which thought is creative."[46] The doctrine of Creation is the assertion of both the intelligibility of the physical world, and the need to turn to Him who, as Intelligence itself, is the source of intelligibility. Oddly enough, the Christian is the one committed to science's fundamental faith that the universe can be known, and this can only be because the Christian sees it as a sign pointing toward its Creator.

Saint Vincent College

Notes

1. Pope Benedict XVI, preface to *Evolutionismus und Christentum*, cited in Christoph Cardinal Schönborn's foreword to *Creation and Evolution: A Conference with Pope Benedict XVI in Castel Gandolfo*, ed. Stephan Otto Horn, S.D.S., and Siegfried Wiedenhofer, trans. Michael J. Miller (San Francisco: Ignatius Press, 2007), 10–11.

2. Walter M. Miller, Jr., *A Canticle for Leibowitz* (New York: Bantam Books, 1976), 195.

3. For a summary of the New Atheist "movement" by one of its proponents, see Victor J. Stenger, *The New Atheism: Taking a Stand for Science and Reason* (Amherst, N.Y.: Prometheus Books, 2009), 11–13.

4. Stenger even concedes this point: "All of us [New Atheists] have been criticized for not paying enough attention to modern theology. We are more interested in observing the world and taking our lessons from those observations than debating finer points of scriptures that are *probably* no more than fables to begin with" (ibid., 13; emphasis added). *Reading Genesis after Darwin* (ed. Stephen C. Barton and David Wilkinson [New York: Oxford University Press, 2009]) has numerous articles on the history of Christian interpretation of Creation. In particular, see Andrew Louth, "The Six Days of Creation According to the Greek Fathers."

5. Peter Brown, *Augustine of Hippo: A Biography* (Berkeley and Los Angeles: University of California Press, 2000), 300.

6. As Socrates puts it in *Phaedo*, 62a.

210 SCIENCE, REASON, AND RELIGION

7. See, e.g., St. Augustine, *Letter 137 to Volusianus*.

8. For an introduction to Greek cosmologies more generally, see G. E. R. Lloyd, "Greek Cosmologies," in *Ancient Cosmologies*, ed. Carmen Blacker and Michael Loewe (London: George Allen & Unwin Ltd., 1975), 198–224; the various contributions in *Cosmology and Theology*, ed. David Tracy and Nicholas Lash (New York: The Seabury Press, 1983), provide helpful introductions to the various aspects of the historical relationship between Christian and scientific/philosophical cosmologies.

9. Maria Luisa Gatti offers an interpretation of the Many's origins that, in rejecting the emanationist interpretation, is much more amenable to the Christian view (see "Plotinus: The Platonic Tradition and the Foundation of Neoplatonism," in *The Cambridge Companion to Plotinus*, ed. Lloyd P. Gerson (New York: Cambridge UP, 1999), 29–34. Whatever the merits of her arguments, this was not the view of Medieval commentators and so does not factor into the current discussion.

10. An interesting contrast between Greek philosophical and Christian views on the origin of the universe is found in Galen's *De usu partium* xi, 14; see also Giannis Stamatellos, *Plotinus and the Presocratics: A Philosophical Study of Presocratic Influences in Plotinus' Enneads* (Albany: State University of New York Press, 2007), who notes that this is a rare case in which Plotinus seems to reject a view he attributes to Plato; see ibid., 123–133 for a discussion of the philosophical sources of Plotinus's view that the universe is eternal.

11. It should be mentioned that this view was not universally held. Proclus, for example, argued against Plotinus on this point; see Jan Opsomer, "Proclus vs Plotinus on Matter (*De mal. subs.* 30–7)," *Phronesis: A Journal of Ancient Philosophy* 46.2 (2001): 154–188. For an introduction to the "different versions" of Neoplatonism and the Christian engagement with this tradition, see John Rist, "Plotinus and Christian Philosophy," in Gerson, *The Cambridge Companion to Plotinus*, 386–413.

12. N. Joseph Torchia sees two versions of emanation in Plotinus, one emphasizing necessity, the other the willful turning of lower natures away from the One (see, e.g., N. Joseph Torchia, *Plotinus, Tolma, and the Descent of Being: An Exposition and Analysis* [New York: P. Lang, 1993], 4, 11, 40–42, 88, 120–121); Christianity rejects both alternatives and thus must argue for its alternative account of creation.

13. See, e.g., Book 2, distinction 1, Question 1.

14. I have primarily worked with translations of Aquinas's writings, only checking the Latin when the translations seemed ambiguous. Editions used are noted.

15. See, esp., *Enneads* III.7–8.

16. For a discussion of Aquinas's restriction of creation to God in the context of his intellectual milieu as well as of the difficulties with this claim, see John F. Wippel, "Thomas Aquinas on Creatures as Causes of *Esse*," *International Philosophical Quarterly* 40.2 (2000): 197–213; cf. Paul Pearson, "Creation through Instruments in Thomas' Sentence Commentary," in *Philosophy and the God of Abraham: Essays in Honor of James A. Weisheipl, OP*, ed. R. James Long (Toronto: Pontifical Institute of Mediaeval Studies, 1991), 147–160.

17. See *Commentary on the Book of Causes*, trans. Vincent A. Guagliando, O.P., Charles R. Hess, O.P., and Richard C. Taylor (Washington, D.C.: The Catholic University of America Press, 1996), 40–41: "It is from the first cause, from which a soul [the human soul] has its being, that it is also intellectual and that it is a soul and consequently that it is impressed upon the body[; that being said, with respect to the body,] then the human soul does result in a way

from the impression of an intelligence, insofar as the human body itself is disposed to being susceptive of such a soul through the power of a heavenly body acting on the seed. For this reason is it said that both a man and the sun generate a man"; see also, e.g., *ST* 1aQ45A5, Q65A3.

18. See, e.g., *Commentary on the Book of Causes*, 26.

19. Ibid., 52.

20. Ibid., 17.

21. See *Quaestio disputata de spiritualibus creaturis*, 6.

22. See, e.g., *ST* 1aQ44As1–2,Q45A2.

23. For example, the third way to prove the existence of God in particular rests on the contention that the universe as a whole is contingent, and that contingency itself is impossible without a necessary causal agent.

24. *ST* 1aQ25A5ad3; Benzinger translation.

25. *ST* 1aQ19A3.

26. See *ST* 1aQ19As4, 10.

27. See Cyril Vollert, Lottie Kendzierski, and Paul Byrne, *St. Thomas Aquinas, Siger of Brabant, St. Bonaventure, On the Eternity of the World* (Milwaukee, Wisc.: Marquette University Press, 1964), 2–72, for translations of and discussions on the principal texts.

28. For more information on the polemical context, see John F. Wippel, "Did Thomas Aquinas Defend the Possibility of an Eternally Created World? (The *De aeternitate mundi* Revisited)," *Journal of the History of Philosophy* 19.1 (1981): 21–22.

29. *De aeternitate mundi* 2, 19 (cited in Vollert, Kendzierski, and Byrne, *St. Thomas Aquinas, Siger of Brabant, St. Bonaventure, On the Eternity of the World*).

30. Cited in Aquinas, *ST* 1aQ10A1obj.1.

31. Vollert, Kendzierski, and Byrne, *St. Thomas Aquinas, Siger of Brabant, St. Bonaventure, On the Eternity of the World*, 5.

32. Ibid., 24.

33. For a much more nuanced treatment of the difficulties of interpreting Aquinas's claims given textual variations, see Wippel, "Did Thomas Defend the Possibility of an Eternally Created World?," 32–36. Wippel's conclusion is in agreement with the position outlined here, and he adds that *De aeternitate mundi* is the only text in which Aquinas "clearly defend[s]" it (36).

34. Ibid., 4–5.

35. See, e.g., Sam Harris, *Letter to a Christian Nation* (New York: Alfred A. Knopf, 2006), 68–79; Stenger, *The New Atheism*, 98; Victor J. Stenger, *Quantum Gods: Creation, Chaos, and the Search for Cosmic Consciousness* (Amherst, N.Y.: Prometheus Books, 2009), 102–103; Richard Dawkins seems to be an exception on this point at least (see Richard Dawkins, *The God Delusion* [New York: Houghton Mifflin Co., 2006], 282–286).

36. Sam Harris accurately summarizes the most vocal Christians as being either conservative/fundamentalist or liberal/relativist. The former are creationists and biblical literalists in the narrow sense, the latter demythologizers who see the Gospel as one among many natural paths to moral/spiritual peace (see Sam Harris, *Letter to a Christian Nation*, 3–5).

37. Lk. 13:52.

38. While Aquinas argues that the seventh day should be included as a day unto itself, He also contends that there is a sense in which the seventh day stands outside of the description of Creation (see *ST* 1aQ73A1, esp. ad 2).

39. *ST* 1aQ1A10ad3.

40. See in particular *ST* 1aQ74; see John F. Wippel, *Metaphysical Themes in Thomas Aquinas* (Washington, D.C.: Catholic University of America Press, 1984), 164–173, for a discussion of creatures that, while not actually existing, can be described as "not-yet-existent possible" (163).

41. *Sentences* 2.1.1.4, cited in *Aquinas on Creation: Writings on the "Sentences" of Peter Lombard, Book 2, Distinction 1, Question 1*, trans. Steven E. Baldner and William E. Carroll. (Toronto: Pontifical Institute of Medieval Studies, 1997), 84.

42. See *ST* 1aQ73A1ad3.

43. See Wippel, "Thomas Aquinas on Creatures as Causes of *Esse*," *Metaphysical Themes in Thomas Aquinas II* (Washington, D.C.: Catholic University of America Press, 2007), 188–192.

44. See Hermann Brück's examples of theological and scientific misunderstandings of Big Bang Cosmology ("Astrophysical Cosmology," in Tracy and Lash, *Cosmology and Theology*, 47–48).

45. Pope Benedict XVI, "Schöpfungsglaube und Evolutionstheorie," cited in *Creation and Evolution*, 13.

46. Ibid.; see also Joseph Ratzinger, *In the Beginning . . . : A Catholic Understanding of the Story of Creation and the Fall*, trans. Boniface Ramsey, O.P. (Huntington, Ind.: Our Sunday Visitor, Inc., 1990), esp. 25–29.

A New Way to Reconcile Creation with Current Biological Science

Alexander R. Pruss

Abstract: I shall argue that, appearances to the contrary notwithstanding, current biological science does not rule out the possibility of miraculous intervention in the evolutionary history of human beings. This shows that it is possible to reconcile evolutionary science with the claim that we are designed by God.

1. Introduction

Alexander Pruss has come up with a set of clever arguments for why evolutionary theory is rationally incompatible with the creation doctrine which he took to be the claim that:

God intentionally brought it about, immediately or mediately, that a human species exists, and did so in such a way that the design of that human species can be attributed to that intention, in the way that the design of an artifact can be attributed to the craftsman.[1]

I shall argue for a new way of reconciling evolutionary theory with the creation doctrine which escapes any arguments at all like those of Pruss. I take Pruss's arguments to be a particularly precise way of stating a discomfort with evolutionary theory that many other theists have felt, and hence I will sketch a representative part of his arguments with sufficient detail to show how the present criticism applies. The new approach will be centered around an argument for the counterintuitive claim that miraculous divine intervention in the history of the development of the human species is fully compatible with current evolutionary science.

Pruss considers four options as to how God might create a human species in cooperation with evolutionary processes. (1) God sets up initial conditions that, through deterministic natural processes, lead to the existence of a human species. (2) The processes leading to the existence of a human species are indeterministic, but God has a generalized form of middle knowledge that lets him know how indeterministic processes *would* go, and thus Molinistically sets up the initial conditions

© 2012, *Proceedings of the ACPA*, Vol. 85
DOI: 10.5840/acpaproc20118517

so that the processes *would* end up generating a human species. (3) A Thomistic account on which God controls the outcomes of physically indeterministic events, ensuring that the things that result are what he wants. Or, (4) God sets up inde-terminsitic physical processes that are likely to lead to the existence of a human species, is ready to intervene should they fail to do so, but in fact is lucky enough that he does not need to intervene.[2] Pruss then argues that the first three options are logically incompatible with evolution, while the last is rationally incompatible with it—a rational person couldn't believe both.

To show what is going on here, let me start by quickly sketching Pruss's argu-ments against accounts 1 and 2 (determinism and Molinism), and account 4 (God waiting and ready to intervene). The Thomistic account would take us too far afield. Pruss assumes that evolutionary theory offers an explanation of how a hu-man species arose, or at least how there arose a species with the "notable features" of humanity—Pruss gives intelligence, manual dexterity and vision as examples. This explanation, he insists, is statistical in nature: the conditional probability of the arising of a species with these notable features is "not unlikely" given the relevant description of the initial conditions.

However, Pruss then argues that in a case where the initial conditions of a system have been intentionally set up by an agent in a way that guarantees (either deterministically or Molinistically) a particular result, a statistical claim that does not make mention of the agent's thus having rigged the initial conditions is *not* in fact explanatory of the results. Normally, we can explain statistically why about half of the thousand coins that Fred tossed landed heads in terms of the fact that it is very probable that a thousand tossed coins should do so. But if Fred had the amazing skill of tossing coins at precisely the velocities needed to ensure that they landed as he wished, and if he in fact tossed them so as to guarantee that about half of them would land heads, then the statistical claims about the probabilities of randomly tossed coins having a particular distribution are no longer explanatorily relevant. A genuine explanation would need to involve Fred's skill at tossing coins.[3] Thus according to Pruss, while the statistical and causal facts can be exactly as the evolutionary theorist thinks they are, they fail to explain the notable features of human beings if God has rigged the setup.

On the God-ready-to-intervene account, God watches a stochastic evolutionary process and intervenes as needed. However, while it might not be unlikely that a stochastic evolutionary process would on its own lead to the notable features of the human species, it is highly unlikely that it would lead to the arising of *specifically* a human species. It might just as well result in intelligent reptiles, or the like. The likelihood that we'd get a human species if we rewound the clock and tried again is miniscule. But the creation doctrine says that God specifically decided to create a human species. So on the God-ready-to-intervene account, it is a magnificent stroke of luck on God's part that he got precisely the result he wanted. And it is irrational to believe God was so lucky—assuming God was watching whether to intervene, it seems much more likely that he wasn't lucky, and indeed had to intervene.

Whatever the plausibility of the details of his arguments, Pruss made a mistake emblematic of the debate: he assumed that evolutionary theory gives a statistical explanation of the arising of a human species, or at least a species with the notable features of the human species. But that is a mistake. Pruss confused an idealized future evolutionary theory that *might* make such a claim, but which is a theory that we do not at present have good reason to accept, with current evolutionary biology which, at least insofar as it remains within the boundaries of science, makes no such claim. Once we get clear on this confusion, we will see that there is a surprising way to reconcile current evolutionary biology with the creation doctrine. I do not endorse this reconciliation, but it is one that needs to be considered. Stating the reconciliation will be easy but defending it will be difficult.

2. The Reconciliation

The proposed reconciliation is very simple. God sets up initial conditions that have a not insignificant probability of leading to the arising of a species with our notable features. Then he intervenes at several points in evolutionary history to ensure that indeed a human species arises. This is, of course, the God-ready-to-intervene account but with God not being as improbably lucky as that account postulates.

It might seem as if this suggestion is absurd. After all, surely, current evolutionary science says that a human species arose from one-celled organisms by wholly naturalistic processes. While one might try to deny that this claim of naturalistic descent is true, as intelligent design supporters do, to deny that it *is* a claim of evolutionary science seems absurd. And if it is a claim of current evolutionary science, then divine intervention in the evolutionary process is incompatible with current evolutionary science.

But we shall see that this line of thought is mistaken in two ways. First, I shall argue that, *pace* Pruss's paper, it is false that evolutionary science provides a statistical explanation of the arising of the notable features of a human species. Second, I shall argue that non-numerical attempts to formulate the explanation of the evolution of humans in a way that excludes divine intervention either go beyond what we currently scientifically know or go beyond the bounds of science in general, and in neither case should count as current evolutionary science.

3. Statistical Evolutionary Explanation

Let's start with Pruss's claim that evolutionary science provides a statistical explanation of the notable features of a human species, including especially intelligence.[4] If so, then we should be able to ask: "Given the initial conditions, what probability does evolutionary science assign to the arising of an intelligent organism?" But for multiple reasons we are in no position to answer this question.

First, at this point we simply do not know enough about intelligence in general and its neurological and genetic prerequisites specifically to be able to estimate the probability of an organism arising that exhibits intelligence given the initial conditions at the beginning of evolutionary history. Second, the mathematics is much too hard right now. To estimate mathematically the probability of a billion years of evolutionary history on earth resulting in an organism exhibiting intelligence is far beyond our present day scientific and computational abilities.

There is no scientifically agreed-upon estimate of the probability of intelligent organisms' arising through evolutionary processes. But a statistical explanation involves a probability estimate. So a concrete statistical explanation of the arising of intelligence, and in particular of the human species, is not a part of current biological science.

Maybe although we don't have a specific number for the conditional probability, we do have a lower bound on it, a lower bound sufficiently high for the statistical claim to be explanatory of the arising of intelligence. Let's say we have: P(intelligence | J) > 0.01, where J are the initial conditions. But again we're not at all scientifically in a position to make an estimate like that right now. The two above points are relevant—the mathematics is too hard and we don't know enough about the nature of intelligence.

4. Non-statistical Evolutionary Explanation

Perhaps, though, evolutionary science provides a *non-statistical* explanation of the arising of the notable features of a human species. In the next two subsections, I will consider two ways for it do so. One way is through giving the specific processes by which the human species evolved, processes that are in fact incompatible with divine intervention (at least of the miraculous sort in question). I shall argue that at this point we simply do not know enough about evolutionary processes for that kind of an explanation to be a part of current biological science. The other way is by building naturalism into the account by fiat. And here I shall argue that we have gone beyond science.

4.1. Specific Processes

What would a sketch of an explanation in terms of specific evolutionary processes be like? Consider this naïve attempt:

(1) Intelligent organisms arose from a unicellular organism through the process of random variation and natural selection.

This either means that they arose *solely* by this process, or that they arose *mainly or in part* by this process.

If we mean that intelligent organisms arose *solely* through this process, we contradict current evolutionary science which *denies* that random variation and natural selection are the only processes in play—there are other processes, such as kin and group selection (maybe one can lump these in under "natural selection"—though the worry is that if we put too much there, then the term loses meaning), exaptation, the formation of spandrels, and so on.

But if the claim is that intelligent organisms arose *mainly or in part* by this process, then there is no incompatibility with the proposed reconciliation. It is quite possible for intelligent organisms to arise mainly or in part by random variation and natural selection with *some* divine intervention along the way.

Maybe we can fix the claim by adding in the additional mechanisms:

> (2) Intelligent organisms arose from a unicellular organism solely through the processes of random variation, individual, kin and group selection, exaptation and spandreling.

But this claim is surely not a part of contemporary evolutionary science. Evolutionary biology is not yet a completed science. Confidence that we have managed to enumerate *all* the kinds of selective and non-selective processes active in evolutionary history would be overly hasty.

To be scientifically justified in believing (2), we would have to be scientifically justified in believing that we are not going to discover some new natural process involved in human evolutionary history but not listed in (2), in the way that kin selection was discovered about half a century ago. There were millions of evolutionarily relevant events in the history of the arising of intelligent organisms—only a few of them have been given good explanations at this point, if only because only a few of these events have been expressly identified. Claim (2) is too rash for responsible scientists to make, and I shall charitably assume that it is not a claim of contemporary evolutionary science.

Moreover, the concept of "random variation" itself needs to be examined. Biology is biology and is not, for instance, astronomy. Suppose a mutation is caused by the impact of a cosmic ray. It is not the job of evolutionary science or biology to say where the cosmic ray came from—if anything, that's a question for astronomy. But just as it would be overreaching for biology to deny that the ray came from a star far off in our galaxy—and besides, how would we know this in the case of a cosmic ray that struck millions of year ago?—so too it would be overreaching for biology to deny that the ray was created *ex nihilo* by God for the occasion.

In other words, some of the sources of variation are outside the scope of biological science, and hence no violation of biological theory would follow from a claim that a divinely wrought miracle is the source of those variations. If the term "random" in "random variation" is to be taken as entailing that the variation was not caused by some miracle, then (2) oversteps the bounds of biology.

Maybe, though, by "random" a biologist means "lacking in a causal explanation." But a biologist who insisted on randomness of that sort would be transgressing the boundaries of biology. The biologist as a *biologist* cannot rule out the physical hypothesis that there are deterministic subatomic processes that causally determine the outcomes of the physical processes underlying mutation and recombination—the question whether the subatomic processes are deterministic is a question for physics. Besides, evolutionary theory was originally formulated at a time when physics was deterministic. Granted, since then physics has become indeterministic. But it is quite unclear that this change at the foundational level in physics has affected biological theory. Admittedly, molecular biologists care very much about the underlying physics. But there are deterministic versions of physics, and it seems very unlikely that the debate between, say, Bohmian deterministic quantum mechanics (which has the same empirical consequences as standard quantum mechanics) and standard quantum mechanics can be settled by means of biology.

This was all perhaps a little too quick. Perhaps there is a characterization of randomness that is intrinsic to biology. One biological characterization says that there is no correlation between fitness and variation: variations are not more probable just because they lead to a more or less fit organism. This is an intra-biological statistical assumption that does not involve any overstepping of disciplinary boundaries. But if that is all that "random" in "random variation" means, then this is quite compatible with the claim that some of the variations were produced by God. This is true for two reasons. First of all, variations produced by God need not themselves be correlated with fitness. Since fitness in the evolutionary sense is not to be identified with the good of the organism, we cannot assume that even a perfectly good God would be primarily making variations more likely to result in increased fitness—he might be making fitness-neutral variations to make the organisms fit better with his artistic vision. Secondly, supposing, let us say, that there were a billion variation events in our evolutionary history (in any case, a very big number), and supposing that these were as uncorrelated as any biologist might wish, adding ten variation events that increase fitness would not make for a statistically significant correlation. Hence it is compatible with the uncorrelatedness claim that there are divine interventions.

Besides, no two measurements in biology are *exactly* equal, and just about no actual correlation between event-types is exactly zero. It would be about as great a surprise to find out that the observed correlation between variation and mutation was *exactly* zero on some measure of correlation as it would be to find that writing out the digits in the number measuring the correlation yielded a list of the phone numbers of the researchers, in order from youngest to oldest.[5] So a select number of divine interventions will not affect the assumption of lack of correlation. In fact, the assumption, to be reasonable, must be read as saying that there is *approximately* no correlation. And that does nothing to rule out divine intervention.

One may be worried that more than a few interventions would be needed, indeed that so many interventions would be needed as to make for a correlation between variation and fitness. But that would need to be argued for. Carefully chosen interventions by an omniscient and omnipotent being might be quite effective.

4.2. Building In Naturalism

We can thus see that it is difficult to formulate a biological theory of the origin of human beings in a way that rules out divine intervention. Listing specific processes makes the theory implausible, because it is unlikely that we have discovered all the processes, and building chance in does not help. Here is a different option:

> (3) Intelligent organisms arose from a unicellular organism through naturalistic processes, primarily those of random variation and natural selection.

Naturalism is built-in, so miracles are automatically ruled out. And probably many biologists would agree with (3). But being agreed to by many biologists does not make a claim a pronouncement of biological science—that the sky is blue is not a biological claim, though all biologists agree on it.

The problem with (3) is that to say that something happened through some naturalistic process or other is not to make a claim of science, unless science can actually tell us what the naturalistic process is. But (3) claims that those events in the evolutionary history of intelligent organisms that did not happen through random variation, natural selection or any of the other processes I enumerated earlier or ones like them, happened naturalistically. In other words, (3) tells us that something happened naturalistically, without saying *how* it happened—and that is not a claim of science, and hence it is not a claim of biology.

How could one, after all, gather *scientific* evidence for the claim that something happened through a naturalistic process without actually identifying that process? Indeed, how could one gather *any* evidence for that claim, scientific or not, barring something like divine revelation or a metaphysical argument for naturalism *simpliciter*?

One might claim that there is an inductive argument here: Many things in the evolutionary history of intelligent organisms have been explained naturalistically; none are known not to have a naturalistic explanation; hence, probably, they all have naturalistic explanations. But inductive arguments of the form "Many Fs are Gs; we know of no Fs that are not Gs; hence probably all Fs are Gs" require further statistical analysis to be compelling. Thus, if we randomly chose a statistically significant collection of Fs and found that they are all Gs, we would be justified in concluding that all Fs are Gs. However, this is not what happened in the evolutionary case—we did not choose a random selection of scientific problems and find that naturalistic evolution solved them all.

But now compare this case. We have a test for a type of cancer such that a positive result on the test is close to certain to show that the organism has the cancer, but a negative result is completely inconclusive. The false-positive rate on the test is small but the false-negative rate is high or unknown.[6] We apply the test to a large number of squirrels. We find that the test is positive for many and negative for a number of them. It would be statistically improper to reason: "Many squirrels have the cancer; we know of no squirrels that lack the cancer; hence probably all squirrels have the cancer." It would likewise be improper to reason from the observations, without further statistical analysis of the false negative rate for the test, that probably some squirrels don't have the cancer. Now the evolutionary case is like this. We have a test for whether a feature has a naturalistic explanation. We spend years trying to find such an explanation, and if we find one, we are very confident that there is one. But if we do not find one, this does not give us much confidence that there isn't one. The false-positive rate of the test is, we may suppose, low. In most of the cases in which we find a naturalistic explanation, there really is one there. But there are, of course, a number of open problems—cases where we have not yet found a naturalistic explanation. The false-negative rate of the test is high or unknown—the fact that we have not yet found a naturalistic explanation is little evidence that there is no naturalistic explanation. We are thus not justified in inferring that because many of the features have naturalistic explanations, and we know of none that do not, therefore they probably all have such explanations.

5. Future Science

Suppose we grant that there is nothing in *current* biology that rules out a moderate number of miraculous divine interventions compatible with the claim that intelligent organisms arose primarily through random variation and natural selection. But we might say: surely a *completed* evolutionary theory would give a fully naturalistic story about how intelligent organisms arose. And *that* story would be incompatible with miraculous divine interventions.

However, now the claim that a completed evolutionary theory would give a fully naturalistic story about how intelligent organisms arose either is true by definition—we wouldn't count something a "completed evolutionary theory" unless it gave a fully naturalistic story about this—or is a substantive claim about future scientific development. If it is true by definition, then the claim is useless as an argument against the proposed reconciliation between creation and biology, as we are concerned with reconciling creation with something known empirically.

Suppose now that a substantive claim about future scientific development is being made: future science will find a fully naturalistic story about how intelligent organisms arose. But as a merely futurological claim—perhaps one grounded in the observation that scientists like naturalistic theories and keep on trying until they find one that fits the data—this claim does nothing to make the reconciliation less plausible. Compare the claim that future flat-earthers will have a full story about how GPS satellites manage to work hovering over a flat earth—quite likely they will, human ingenuity being great, but so what?

What would indeed be relevant to the discussion would be a claim that future science will find a *probably-true* fully naturalistic story about how intelligent organisms arose. But any evidence for this claim will, I submit, be parasitic on *present* evidence that it probably *is* true that intelligent organisms arose through a fully naturalistic process—the futurological claims about the course of science drop out of the argument.

Besides, the game of predicting specific future scientific theory is a game at which we are not very likely to succeed. Who in the seventeenth century would have predicted Darwinism, and who in the 19th would have expected quantum mechanics?

6. Proving Too Much?

I have argued that our current biological knowledge is compatible with divine intervention in the history of human evolution. One might think that I have shown more: that *no* possible biological knowledge could justify rejecting divine intervention. There are two attitudes a reader can take to the supposition that I have shown this stronger claim: the reader could applaud, or the reader could think that the stronger claim is a *reductio ad absurdum* of my arguments or their value (I am grateful to a reader for this objection).

However, neither the clapping nor the hissing is in order. Of the arguments in Sections 3 and 4, only the discussion in 4.2 of theories that expressly build naturalism into the biological explanation would apply to every possible biological theory, and biological theories that do not expressly build naturalism into the explanation, but instead list processes or make explanation claims that *entail* that the explanation is naturalistic, would escape those criticisms. Specifically, the squirrel cancer test argument can be avoided as follows if one has a fully spelled-out evolutionary paradigm. Given such a fully spelled-out evolutionary paradigm, one can give a *further* test, beyond just trying to find an explanation that fits the paradigm. The further test is to try to find an explanation incompatible with the specifics of the paradigm.

The argument in Section 3 depended on our present lack of mathematical estimates of the probabilities involved. If future biological theory contains mathematically worked out statistical explanations of the arising of the notable features of the human race, then the arguments of Pruss which I have been criticizing will apply, and the tension between divine design of the human race and statistical evolutionary explanation will return.

The argument in 4.1 depended on the present state of evolutionary biology not giving us scientific reason to think that we have enumerated all the relevant processes. Could we ever have scientific reason to think that? Perhaps. If we find over time that we are no longer adding to the enumerated list of processes, and every evolutionary problem that has been previously identified and that a competent biologist set her sights on has, within ten years, been solved by use of the processes on the list, then science might well make the judgment that the list is complete. Or else a more general theory might be found, of which it is a consequence that the list is complete, a theory whose predictions are borne out.

I have not been arguing that faith and reason cannot conflict in this matter. I have merely argued that they do not in fact conflict.

7. Final Remarks

Is the proposed reconciliation a form of interventionist Intelligent Design? Interventionist Intelligent Design is the conjunction of two claims: first, that a designer intervened at specific points in evolutionary history, and, second, that there is scientific evidence of such intervention. The proposed reconciliation does not make the evidential claim, and hence isn't a form of interventionist Intelligent Design theory. In fact, I think that both opponents and proponents of Intelligent Design are likely to deny that the reconciliation I offer is successful, since both seem to think that there is an incompatibility between current day evolutionary science and divine intervention. And it is this incompatibility that I'm denying.

Nor am I claiming that the divine-intervention story is true. I am only claiming that it is compatible with current biological science. Current biological science is not in a position to make grand claims that there is a naturalistic story about how we arose. All it is in a position to do is to claim is that all organisms on earth are descended from a common ancestor, and that the *primary* processes by which the descent happened were random variation and natural selection, as well as to give a number of very interesting details in the evolutionary story.

Pruss may have successfully shown that a particular kind of theory would be incompatible with the creation of human beings doctrine. But that theory is not yet current biological science. Discussions of the compatibility of creation and evolution tend to mistake futurology for biology, conflating expected completed theories with real science. If we avoid such conflation, we will do better science and better philosophy.[7]

Notes

1. "How Not to Reconcile the Creation of Human Beings with Evolution," *Philosophia Christi* 9 (2007): 145–163. By "a human species," Pruss meant a species which has human-type DNA.

2. For options (2) and (4), see Del Ratsch, "Design, Chance and Theistic Evolution," in *Mere Creation*, ed. William Dembski (Downers Grove: InterVarsity, 1998), 303ff.

3. Pruss, "How Not to Reconcile," 151.

4. Ibid., 146–148.

5. That the correlation is exactly zero would imply that *all* the digits are zero. That the digits encode the phone numbers would only be a statement about a finite number of the digits. Hence the latter claim is less improbable than the former.

6. The false-positive rate of a test for a condition C is the proportion of cases without C which test positive. The false-negative rate is the proportion of cases with C which test negative. For instance, consider this test for being an excellent runner: check if the person received an Olympic gold medal for running. This test has a very low false-positive rate. Very few (in fact, no) people who are not excellent runners have received Olympic gold medals for running. But the test has a very high false-negative rate: many people who are excellent runners have not received Olympic gold medals for running. Knowing that Samantha has received an Olympic gold medal for running is superb evidence that she is an excellent runner; knowing that she has not received such a medal would be very weak evidence against the hypothesis that she is an excellent runner.

7. I would like to thank some anonymous readers for a number of comments that improved this paper.

Intentions, Intentionally Permitting, and the Problem of Evil

T. Ryan Byerly

Abstract: Some of the most persuasive contemporary statements of the problem of evil rely on premises concerning God's intentionally permitting certain things to occur and premises concerning the moral wrongness of intentionally permitting such things. In this paper, I want to pose a dilemma for the defender of such arguments from evil. Either intentionally permitting p implies intending p or it does not. If it does, then the theist may plausibly resist these arguments from evil by insisting that the key claims in them concerning God's intentionally permitting things are false. But, if intentionally permitting p does not imply intending p, then the theist may plausibly resist these arguments by contesting the premises in them which make claims concerning the moral wrongness of intentionally permitting certain things. Either way, the theist will have a response to these versions of the problem of evil.

Introduction

S ome of the most persuasive contemporary statements of the problem of evil rely on premises concerning God's intentionally permitting certain things to occur and premises concerning the moral wrongness of intentionally permitting such things. In this paper, I want to pose a dilemma for the defender of such arguments from evil. Either intentionally permitting p implies intending p or it does not. If it does, then the theist may plausibly resist these arguments from evil by insisting that the key claims in them concerning God's intentionally permitting things are false. But, if intentionally permitting p does not imply intending p, then the theist may plausibly resist these arguments by contesting the premises in them which make claims concerning the moral wrongness of intentionally permitting certain things. Either way, the theist will have a response to these versions of the problem of evil.

In the first section, I set out a clear statement of the argument from evil which makes salient the claims I have in mind concerning God's intentionally permitting certain things and the moral wrongness of intentionally permitting these things. In the second section, I briefly review some contemporary work on intentional action.

© 2012, *Proceedings of the ACPA*, Vol. 85
DOI: 10.5840/acpaproc20118518

224

224

Importantly, we will see that contemporary orthodoxy has it that intentions are not just the same things as intentional actions or permissions. In section three, I present my central argument. Then I conclude in section four by considering just how much this argument accomplishes in offering a response to the arguer from evil.

1. The Problem of Evil and Intentions

Here I will set out a version of the argument from evil which makes salient the reliance of some such arguments on claims concerning God's intentionally permitting certain evils and claims concerning the moral wrongness of intentionally permitting such evils. But three comments are in store before I present the argument. First, the argument I set forth is an evidential argument. It is an evidential argument in that it takes the existence of certain kinds of evils as very good evidence, though not as truth-conducive evidence, against the existence of God. In other words, the argument is not supposed to be such that if its premises are true then the conclusion that God does not exist validly follows. Instead, it is supposed to be such that if the premises are true the conclusion that God does not exist is probabilistically supported. Second, the argument I present focuses on very specific kinds of evils. It is in this way a concrete version of the argument from evil. Third, the argument is a deontological formulation of the argument from evil. It does not appeal to the goodness or badness of states of affairs or talk at all of "greater goods." Instead, the argument focuses on the evaluation of actions by referring to rightmaking and wrongmaking properties of actions.[1]

The argument begins with the following observation:

(1) Our world contains instances of children undergoing lingering suffering and eventual death due to cancer and instances of animals dying agonizing deaths in forest fires.

This claim is uncontroversial between theist and non-theist. But, the theist is also plausibly committed to:

(2) Whatever happens is at least intentionally permitted by God.

In saying that whatever happens is *at least* intentionally permitted by God, I mean to highlight the fact that the theist may want to say that some things are not just intentionally permitted, but intentionally causally brought about by God. God intentionally acts in a more positive way to bring these things about. Some things, perhaps, God only intentionally permits. From (1) and (2) it follows that:

(3) Instances of children undergoing lingering suffering and eventual death due to cancer and instances of animals dying agonizing deaths in forest fires are at least intentionally permitted by God.

However, it is a plausible moral claim that:

(4) Intentionally permitting children to undergo lingering suffering and eventual death due to cancer and intentionally permitting animals to die agonizing deaths in forest fires are actions with very serious wrongmaking properties.

In other words, acting so as to intentionally permit either of these things has at least that much going against it morally speaking. But, it seems to be analytic that:

(5) If an action has a very serious wrongmaking property and no rightmaking properties sufficient to counterbalance that wrongmaking property, then the action is wrong all things considered.

Yet, many have found it plausible that:

(6) Human beings know of no rightmaking properties of God's intentionally permitting children to undergo lingering suffering and eventual death due to cancer and intentionally permitting animals to die agonizing deaths in forest fires which are sufficient to counterbalance the very serious wrongmaking properties of those actions.

But, some have thought that (6) offers very strong inductive support for:

(7) There *are* no rightmaking properties of God's intentionally permitting children to undergo lingering suffering and eventual death due to cancer and intentionally permitting animals to die agonizing deaths in forest fires which are sufficient to counterbalance the very serious wrongmaking properties of those actions.

And from (7) and (5) it follows that:

(8) If God exists, God performs some actions which are wrong all things considered.

But, at least according to classical conceptions of God,

(9) God does not perform any actions which are wrong all things considered.

So,

(10) God does not exist.

It should now be clearer why claims about what God intentionally permits and about the moral wrongness of permitting certain states of affairs to obtain are central to at least some versions of evidential arguments from evil. For, in the above argument, the only substantive premises the theist might go after are (2), (4) and (6), and the only inference which she might target is the inductive inference from (6) to (7). As it turns out, most theists have responded to this kind of argument by targeting the inference from (6) to (7) or targeting premise (6). Typically, those who attack the inference from (6) to (7) are Skeptical Theists, while those who target premise (6) offer some sort of theodicy. But, as is clear, the theist might also respond to the argument by challenging premise (2), premise (4), or both. And that is just what I shall do here. In section three, I shall pose a dilemma for one who would press the above argument from evil, or something much like it, against the theist. Either intentionally permitting p implies intending p or it does not. If it does, then (2) is questionable. If it does not, then (4) is questionable. Before pressing this dilemma, however, I wish to discuss briefly some contemporary work on intentional action in section two.

2. Intentional Action

The contemporary discussion of intentional action gets its start with Elizabeth Anscombe's *Intention* (1963). In this book, Anscombe highlights the fact that we use the "intention" word family in at least three somewhat different ways. We talk of *intending* certain things, we talk of *acting intentionally*, and we talk of *acting with the intention of* doing something or other. Anscombe notes that it would be strange if a theory of intentions did not do anything to unify these uses. And, ever since her observation was made, it has constrained nearly all work on intentions. Anyone offering a theory of intention or intentional action or intentions-with-which has had to answer to the call to unify these uses of the "intention" word family.

Anscombe's own approach was to reduce intending to intentional action and intentions-with-which. Once one had explained intentional action and intention-with-which, there was nothing left to discuss. But this approach did not win the day. Beginning with Donald Davidson,[2] philosophers began to seriously question Anscombe's account due to its lack of attention to cases of what is called "pure intending" as when I intend one day to buy a boat but am not currently doing anything to make it come about. Cases of pure intention, these philosophers insisted, could not simply be reduced to intentional action or intentions-with-which one does some action. Intending need not imply action at all.

Their view has one the day. The contemporary orthodoxy has it that the way to account for the three different uses of the "intention" word family is to begin with intentions and then to explain intentional action and intentions-with-which in terms of them.[3] Most of the discussion has focused on the relationship between intentions and intentional actions. And, I will focus on that work here, too, since it is the most relevant to the current project.

Those who are agreed that intentional action is to be explained in terms of intention disagree concerning exactly how this is to be done. Some say that one intentionally brings about some state of affairs S only if one intends that S obtain.[4] Others deny that one must intend the very state of affairs which one intentionally allows. Sometimes, they insist nonetheless that in order for the subject to intentionally bring about a state of affairs S, the subject must nonetheless have *some* intention which is related to her acting as she does in a specified way.[5]

Another dividing point has to do with exactly what the relationship is which must obtain between an intention and an action in order for the action to have been performed intentionally. Many are attracted to the view that the relation must be some kind of causal relation.[6] The agent's intention must cause the agent's action in the right sort of way. The difficulty here has been to say exactly what is the right sort of way. As Davidson[7] pointed out, we must be very careful to disallow deviant causal chains.[8]

And this is pretty well where the contemporary discussion stands. Some maintain that in order for an agent to intentionally bring about a state of affairs S the agent must intend S. Some add to this requirement the further requirement that the agent's intending S must be causally related to her bringing about S in the right sort of way. Others deny each of these claims. Surely one party or the other is correct.

My own preference is to go with the majority and analyze intentional action, as well as intentional permission, in terms of intentions. I favor the view that intentions are unanalyzable propositional attitudes, much like beliefs. And I favor the view that in order to intentionally act so as to bring about a state of affairs S, or to intentionally permit the obtaining of S, one must intend S. However, I will not presume in what follows that these claims are correct. I presume only that either intentionally permitting a state of affairs S implies intending S or it does not and that intentionally permitting and intending are different things, as contemporary orthodoxy maintains.

3. Intentions, Intentionally Permitting, and the Problem of Evil

It is now time to present my central argument. As previously mentioned, the argument is a dilemma. Either intentionally permitting p implies intending p or it does not. If it does, then either premise (2) in the argument from evil above—the claim that God intentionally permits everything that happens—is tenuous. But, if it does not, then premise (4)—the claim that intentionally permitting certain kinds of evils has a very serious wrongmaking property—is tenuous. So, either way, the theist has something to say in response to the argument from evil.

Let me now support each of the conditional claims central to my argument. First, suppose that intentionally permitting p implies intending p. Presuming that contemporary orthodoxy is correct in taking intentional action and intentions to be different, the theist can very plausibly insist on rejecting (2). For, if intentionally permitting p implies intending p, then (2) implies that God intends everything which happens. But the theist need not maintain this. The central reason for why the theist would have been attracted to (2) in the first place had to do with a concern to uphold God's sovereignty and omnipotence. But, the theist can uphold God's sovereignty and omnipotence without claiming that everything which happens is something he intends. For, although some things may happen which God does not intend, it can nonetheless be true that God permits these things to happen, that he knows that they will happen, that he knows how he could prevent them, and so on. This is plenty enough to preserve God's omnipotence and sovereignty, and none of it implies that God intends all that happens. And, if God does not intend all that happens, then he does not, contra (2), intentionally permit all that happens. It may well be, in particular, that he does not intentionally permit the kinds of evils mentioned in (2). He sovereignly permits them, he knows they will occur, he knows how to prevent them, but he neither intends them nor intentionally permits them.

Of course, one might reply at this stage of the argument by claiming that if God knows that p is about to occur, and he knows how to prevent p, and he permits p nonetheless, that he has thereby both intentionally permitted and intended p.[9] If this claim is correct, then I was wrong to suggest that there is no direct argument from God's sovereignty to his intentionally permitting everything, even given that intentionally permitting p implies intending p.[10] So, my attack on (2) would not stand. Unfortunately, however, this claim is implausible.

In order to show that this claim is implausible, I will discuss two cases where an agent knows that something is about to occur, knows how to prevent it, permits it nonetheless but very plausibly *does not* intend that it occur. Given our supposition that one intentionally permits p only if one intends p, it follows also from these cases that knowing that p is about to occur, knowing how to prevent p, and permitting p is not sufficient for intentionally permitting p.

First, suppose my wife has mono and for that reason often takes an early afternoon nap. She has been doing so every day this week and it is now Friday. Suppose I am busy working on a paper—a paper about intentions and the problem of evil, say—this Friday afternoon in another room. For this reason, I am not at all interested in bothering her from her sleep. I am thoroughly engrossed in my work as usual. Supposing that my wife in fact does continue to sleep, it is plausible under these circumstances to suppose that I know that my wife is going to continue to sleep (suppose, if necessary, that no Gettierizing conditions obtain). Further, it is plausible to suppose that I know how to prevent her from continuing to do so. I could go make a big racket in the bedroom, for instance. Finally, assuming that I do no such thing, it is plausible to affirm that I permit her to continue to sleep. Yet, it is *implausible* that I have thereby intended that she continue to sleep. All I have intended is to continue working. Because of it, I do not go bother her. But, there is no motivation here to suppose that because of this I therefore have intended that she continue to sleep. This can be confirmed by the fact that the conditions for successfully accomplishing all that I intend do not include my wife's continuing to sleep. So, plausibly it is false that if an agent knows that p is about to occur, knows how to prevent p, and nonetheless permits p, then that agent intends p. And given the supposition that intentionally permitting p implies intending p, it is also plausibly false that if an agent knows p is about to occur, knows how to prevent p, and nonetheless permits p, she thereby intentionally permits p.

Consider a second case. Imagine that I am a non-Jew living in Poland at the time of the Third Reich. A Nazi guard has arrived in town and is looking for blood. He wants Jewish blood, but the blood of one who would aid the Jews would be fine too. Suppose there is a houseful of Jews across my street, including many Jewish children. In my house are me, my wife, and my two children. The guard approaches. I suddenly realize that there is a way for me to prevent the massacre of the Jews across the street. If I put a flashy Jewish star on my garment and run away swiftly, hooting and hollering, I will draw away the attention of the guard. He will chase after me with vigor. If he catches me, he will no doubt realize that I was aiding Jews and he will take my blood. Thankfully, though, I am very fast and so it is unlikely that he will catch me. But he might. Meanwhile, while he is chasing me, the Jewish household will be able to catch the train to a faraway village where they will all be safe. Now, suppose that my plan is sufficiently well-enough put together that I know that if I pursue it, the Jewish household will be saved. And, suppose that despite the good that would come of my plan, I decide not to go through with it for fear of leaving my family without a father. This case, too, provides a counter-example to the above claim concerning intentions. For, it is plausible that in this case I know that the massacre of the Jews across the street is about to occur, I know how to prevent it, I nonetheless permit it, but plausibly I do not intend it. Indeed, far from intending it, I hope against hope that it will not occur. I hope I am wrong in thinking that it is going to happen. But alas, I know that it will, and despite my knowing how to prevent it I do not do so. None of this implies that I intend the massacre across the street to occur.

If I am correct concerning our intuitive judgments about what is known, what is permitted, and what is intended in these two examples, then the principle appealed to above is implausible. It is implausible that if an agent knows that p is about to occur, and knows how to prevent p, but permits p, she thereby intends p. And, if this principle is indeed false, it cannot be appealed to in order to respond to my argument for the claim that, if intentionally permitting p implies intending p, the theist need not accept premises (2) and (3) in the argument from evil.[11] Knowing that p will occur, knowing how to prevent p, and permitting p is a combination which is logically distinct from intending p. And, because of this, it is plausible that God may know that the evils of the sort mentioned in (3) will occur, that he may know how to prevent them, and that he may nonetheless permit them without intending them. God sovereignly permits these evils; but, he does not intend their occurrence and so does not intentionally permit them. So, (2) and (3) in the argument from evil are false. At least, the theist may sensibly resist them until offered further argument by the arguer from evil. And this is what I wanted to show. The first key conditional claim in my argument stands: if intentionally permitting p implies intending p, then the theist may plausibly resist (2) and (3).

It now remains to argue for the second key conditional claim in my argument— to show that if intentionally permitting p does *not* entail intending p, then premise (4) is questionable. Suppose, then, that intentionally permitting p does not entail intending p. Thus, (2) and (3) can be true though God does not intend everything and does not intend, in particular, the kinds of evils mentioned in (3). God does intentionally permit everything and he does intentionally permit, in particular, the kinds of evils mentioned in (3). I now want to argue that his doing so, given that intentionally permitting does not entail intending, need not have any wrongmaking property or that his doing so need not have any *very serious* wrongmaking property, i.e., one which cannot be rather easily counterbalanced. If this is so, then the theist can insist that, if intentionally permitting does not entail intending, she need not accept (4).

In order to establish these claims, what I need to argue is that, given the view that intentionally permitting p does not entail intending p, it is possible that someone intentionally permit the sorts of evils mentioned in (3) without her doing so involving any wrongmaking property at all or without her doing so involving a very serious wrongmaking property which cannot be rather easily counterbalanced. In order to do so, I will need to make some assumptions about when someone intentionally permits somethings which are very reasonable in this context. I will assume that if one knows that p is about to obtain, one knows how to prevent p, and one permits p, then one has intentionally permitted p. This assumption is reasonable in this context because it seems to be on the basis of God's knowing that some bad states of affairs like those mentioned in (3) are about to obtain, his knowing how to prevent them, and his nonetheless permitting them, that the arguer from evil concludes that God intentionally permits these evils.[12] With this assumption concerning sufficient conditions for intentionally permitting something in mind, I shall argue that it is possible to intentionally permit evils on the order of those mentioned in (3) without thereby having committed any act with a wrongmaking property or with a very serious wrongmaking property. I will do this by offering two cases where it is plausible that one intentionally permits an evil on the order of those mentioned in (3), but one's doing so involves either no wrongmaking property at all or no very serious wrongmaking property. The conclusion is that if intentionally permitting p does not imply intending p, then (4) is open to question by the theist.

First, consider the case of a California billionaire who watches the national news. The news runs a story about a Florida child who is deathly ill and in need of a very expensive and sophisticated transplant procedure. The family, which cannot afford the operation, is up in arms because the child was severely and repeatedly misdiagnosed, and if the problem had been detected sooner he might not have needed the expensive procedure. The primary aim of the news outlet in running the story is to expose the repeated misdiagnosis and perhaps to influence the hospital to offer the procedure pro bono. But, as they are sad to note, these prospects are dim as the hospital administration is standing its ground extremely firmly (suppose it has just convened a press conference where it announced it would under no circumstances change its decision). Now, suppose that our billionaire is paying close attention. He comes to reasonably believe that the poor child is about to die an agonizing death without receiving the expensive procedure. He also remembers that he has given a great deal to charity recently, specifically to hospitals which are devoted to working with young children. He laments the child's position in the story, but decides that he has given enough lately to help children in a similar situation.

Now suppose that the child does go on to die without receiving the procedure. Plausibly, our billionaire knew that this great evil was about to happen. Plausibly, he also knew how, and was able, to prevent this evil. He is a billionaire, after all. He could have paid for the necessary procedure without hardly feeling a pinch. And, plausibly, he permitted the evil to obtain. So, plausibly, by our assumption above concerning sufficient conditions for intentional permission, the billionaire intentionally permitted the boy to die without the needed operation.

Consider with me our moral intuitions concerning this case. I think most of us will think it a bit much to call the billionaire's action wrong, all-things-considered. It is true that the billionaire failed to do something which would have resulted in a very good state of affairs. But this does not imply that he did anything wrong. Rather, typically, we think that the action he failed to perform—donating the necessary funds to provide for the boy's operation—would have been a *supererogatory* act—an act which had he performed it he would have been going *beyond* his moral duty.[13] This sort of point is often emphasized by those who press what is called the demandingness objection against consequentialist moral theories.[14] But, if it is true that the worst the billionaire has done by his action is that he has failed to do something beyond the call of duty, then he did not perform an action which is all-things-considered wrong. However, it is analytic that if the billionaire's act of permitting the boy to die without the operation was not, all-things-considered wrong, then either it has no wrongmaking properties at all or it has a wrongmaking property which is counterbalanced by some rightmaking property. If the former, then the case demonstrates that it is possible for one to intentionally permit something evil on the order of the evils mentioned in (3) without thereby committing any act with a wrongmaking property. If so, then (4) is false. I think this option—the option according to which the billionaire's act has no wrongmaking property at all—is extremely plausible. But suppose it is the other option which obtains. His act has a wrongmaking property but it is counterbalanced by a sufficient rightmaking property. The question here will be, "What is the rightmaking property which serves to counterbalance the wrongmaking property had by his action?" The answer to the question may be unclear. Plausibly, the rightmaking property will have something to do with exercising his freedom to do what he wants with his own stuff, or some such. But the noteworthy thing here is that whatever the rightmaking property is, it does not seem to be so very serious a rightmaking property. But, if it is not, then the wrongmaking property it counterbalances cannot be so very serious a wrongmaking property either. And, if this is so, then it is possible to intentionally permit evils on the order of those mentioned in (3) without committing an act with a *very serious* wrongmaking property. So, (4) is still false.[15]

Consider a second, very similar example. Imagine I am taking a look at the website of a charitable organization that helps feed the hungry. The website takes donations which will provide for meals for hungry people for forty days. The site maintains an extensive list of millions of starving people with pictures and names of each. When you log on to the website and click "I'd like to donate" the link takes you to a picture and name of someone for whom you can donate to provide meals. If you choose to donate, this very person receives the meals. If you choose not to donate, this person's picture and name go back into the database and go to the end of the rotating list of names and faces. Because there are so many names and so few who log on to the site, it will be a long time before the name and face I draw shows up again when someone else clicks "I'd like to donate." Now, suppose I click "I'd like to donate" and up pops George's name and picture. I notice that it will cost me about as much to support George's meals for forty days as it will cost me to take my wife on two dates. I think hard about the decision. Do I really want to give up these times with my wife? We do care about them. But, George will almost certainly go through intense suffering if I do not donate the money. After a period of deliberation, I decide not to donate.

Now, what do our moral intuitions tell us about my action in choosing not to donate?[16] As in the case of the billionaire, many of us will think it too severe to say I have committed an all-thing-considered wrong action. Rather, I failed to perform a supererogatory action. My giving would have gone beyond the call of duty. However, that being so, my action either had no wrongmaking property at all or it had only a wrongmaking property sufficiently counterbalanced by some rightmaking property. But, again, either option here threatens (4). For, if my action had no wrongmaking property at all, then this case is plausibly one where an agent knows that something evil on the order of those evils discussed in (3) is about to occur, he knows how to prevent it from occurring, and he instead permits it. Thus, it is plausibly a case where an agent intentionally permits an evil on the order of those in (3) but his doing so involves no wrongmaking property. Likewise, if my action in not donating has a wrongmaking property which is sufficiently balanced by a rightmaking property, my action's wrongmaking property was not *so* serious a wrongmaking property. For, there are not any rightmaking properties here which are *so* serious to counterbalance it. Of course there is some value in going on dates with one's spouse. But it is highly questionable that a wrongmaking property which can be sufficiently counterbalanced just by *this* rightmaking property is a *very serious* wrongmaking property. And again, (4) is false.

Each of the foregoing cases then offers a plausible example where an agent intentionally permits an evil on the order of those evils mentioned in (3) to occur and his doing so either does not involve any wrongmaking property at all or it does not involve a very serious wrongmaking property. Plausibly, then, (4) is false. That is, plausibly, if intentionally permitting p does not imply intending p, (4) is false. And this is the second conditional claim necessary for my argument.

I take it, then, that the two conditional claims central to my argument have been offered a plausible defense. First, if intentionally permitting p implies intending p, then premise (2) in the argument from evil above is highly questionable. And, second, if intentionally permitting p does not imply intending p, then premise (4) is highly questionable. But surely intentionally permitting p either implies or does not imply intending p. So, either premise (2) or premise (4) is highly questionable. And thus the theist has a plausible response to the argument from evil.

4. Conclusion

To conclude, I want to briefly consider just how far my argument here goes in defending theism against the argument from evil. First, let me reiterate what my argument *has* accomplished. My argument, if successful, has provided the theist with a plausible response to the formulation of the evidential argument from evil represented above in section one. Further, it has provided the theist with an *atypical* response to that argument. For, typical responses to that argument focus on either premise (6) or on the inference from premise (6) to premise (7). The response I have developed has at least these significant features in its favor.

But the response I have here outlined is limited. We should recall that the response, as stated, will work only for versions of the argument from evil which rely heavily on God's *intentionally* permitting certain things to occur. Many versions of the argument from evil do not do this. For instance, incompatibility (as contrasted with evidential) and axiological formulations of the argument from evil typically do not involve any claims about God's intentionally permitting things.[17] So, the response here developed will not apply to them. Perhaps, though, there are other persuasive responses to those formulations of the argument from evil.[18]

Also, we should note that it is open for the defender of the evidential, deontological argument from evil to modify her argument so that it is not committed to the key claims—premises (2) and (4)—which I targeted in this paper. One fruitful way to do so might be to concentrate not on the relation between moral perfection and morally right actions but on the relation between moral perfection and supererogatory actions. One might argue that, although intentionally permitting evils like those mentioned in (3) of the argument above is not morally wrong, a morally perfect being would nonetheless not do so. For, perhaps, a morally perfect being would perform all compossible supererogatory acts. But, then, it looks as if God has not performed all compossible supererogatory acts. So, God, if he exists, is not morally perfect. I will not discuss this argument in detail here. I only suggest that it is not at all clear that the relationship between moral perfection and supererogatory actions presumed by the argument is correct. There are significant theistic traditions which would in fact resist this claim, for instance on the grounds that performing all such supererogatory actions would detract from God's goal of communicating his special grace to the faithful. Fruitful discussion about the relationship between moral perfection and supererogatory action may be the way to proceed in the discussion of evidential, deontological formulations of the argument from evil. That the argument of this paper has led us to see this is just one more significant feature of that argument.

Another way the defender of the argument from evil might respond to my reply to her argument here might be to point out relevant disanalogies between the cases I discussed in the paper of intentionally permitting evils on the order of those discussed in (3) on the one hand and God's intentionally permitting such evils on the other. Much of the pull to agree that in these examples the actions taken have no very serious wrongmaking properties has to do with the relational distance between the actors and the sufferers.[19] It is in part because the billionaire and the cancer patient do not know one another that we think his action of donating the money would have been supererogatory. Similarly for me when I contemplate donating to provide for George's meals. One might insist that God does not stand at such great relational distance away from his suffering creatures. He is their creator, after all. And perhaps he should even be thought to bear a more intimate relation to them such as being their father. If so, God's intentionally permitting evils like those discussed in (3) may still be all-things-considered wrong. Again, I cannot reply to this objection at length here. All I will say is that it is not at all clear that the relational distance between God and his suffering creatures is not as great as that between the permitters and the sufferers in the examples I mentioned. In many religious traditions, the relational distance is in fact greater, at least when it comes to human sufferers. For, human sinners are said to be God's enemies. But I do not want to push this point here. All I want to highlight is that, if my argument leads us to focus on this interesting and important issue concerning God's relationships with sufferers, then this is just one more significant feature of the argument. Thus, by offering the dilemma above, I have provided the theist with a plausible response to at least some versions of the argument from evil which should advance the discussion of these arguments by leading us to focus on some important and perhaps neglected issues relevant for assessing arguments from evil.

Baylor University

Notes

1. In these ways, this argument follows very closely the presentation of the argument from evil discussed in Michael Tooley, "The Problem of Evil," *Stanford Encyclopedia of Philosophy*, ed. Edward Zalta, available at http://plato.stanford.edu/entries/evil/ (2009).

2. Donald Davidson, "Intending," reprinted in *Essays on Actions and Events* (Oxford: Oxford University Press, 1980).

3. See Kieran Setiya, "Intention," *Stanford Encyclopedia of Philosophy*, ed. Edward Zalta, available at http://plato.stanford.edu/entries/intention/ (2010).

4. E.g., John Searle, *Intentionality: An Essay in the Philosophy of Mind* (Cambridge: Cambridge University Press, 1983).

5. E.g., Gilbert Harman, "Practical Reasoning," reprinted in *The Philosophy of Action*, ed. A. Mele (Oxford: Oxford University Press, 1997), and Michael Bratman, *Intention, Plans, and Practical Reason* (Cambridge, Mass.: Harvard University Press, 1987).

6. I. Thalberg, "Do Our Intentions Cause Our Intentional Actions?" *American Philosophical Quarterly* 21 (1984): 249–260; A. Mele, *Springs of Action* (Oxford: Oxford University Press, 1992); and Kieran Setiya, *Reasons without Rationalism* (Princeton, N.J.: Princeton University Press, 2007).

7. D. Davidson, "Freedon to Act," reprinted in *Essays on Actions and Events* (Oxford: Oxford University Press, 1980).

8. Others, too, have pressed this same concern: e.g., Elizabeth Anscombe, *Intention*, second edition (Oxford: Blackwell, 1963); G. Wilson, *The Intentionality of Human Action* (Stanford, Calif.: Stanford University Press, 1989); and L. O'Brien, *Self-Knowing Agents* (Oxford: Oxford University Press, 2007).

9. Tooley, in "The Problem," presumes without argument that knowing p is about to occur, knowing how to prevent p, and permitting p nonetheless is sufficient for *intentionally* permitting p. But, he is silent concerning whether intentionally permitting p implies intending p.

10. At least, I was wrong if sovereignty requires for every p that one knows whether p will occur, knows how to prevent p, and permits p. Perhaps not this much is required for sovereignty.

11. Of course, it might be maintained that there is something special about God's intentionally permitting these evils which would require that he also intends them. This is not easy to see, however. The best suggestion I know of is that, since God plausibly must make use of these evils as a means to the end of bringing about some greater good, he must intend

them. Or, at least, he must intend that they occur as a necessary means to accomplishing this greater good.

Three points deserve mention in response. First, some theists will reject the idea that God uses evils as *means* to bringing about greater good, since this would have God violating the principle of double effect. Commonly, the principle of double effect, which holds pride of place in Catholic philosophy, implies that it is morally wrong to use evils as a means to a good end. Instead, the evils must be a second—a "double"—effect of what is done to bring about the good. So, at least some theists will resist the idea that God uses evils like those discussed in section one as a means to bringing about some good (see discussion in Alison McIntyre, "The Doctrine of Double Effect," in *Stanford Encyclopedia of Philosophy*, ed. Edward Zalta, available at http://plato.stanford.edu/entries/double-effect [2011]). Second, plausibly, there is quite a difference between intending that these evils occur and intending that they occur as a necessary means to some greater good. It may be that the latter intention is not the sort of intention which is very seriously wrongmaking. Third, there appear to be cases where a person makes use of some event as a means to some end without intending that this event occur or that it occurs as a means to this end. I might, for instance, make use of the event of a cyclist peddling by as a means to the end of watching the cyclist peddle by, but this need not imply that I intend that the cyclist peddle by. For these reasons, it is not clear that God should be treated as a special exception to the general claim that intentional permissions need not imply intentions.

12. Cf. n7.

13. Compare the discussion in Garrett Cullity, "Asking Too Much," *The Monist* 86 (2003).

14. S. Scheffler, *The Rejection of Consequentialism* (Oxford: Clarendon Press, 1982).

15. Note that we can modify the example to include evils like the agonizing deaths of animals in forest fires, if we like, and it will work just as well.

16. Notice, this question may be different from the following question: What are our moral intuitions concerning my action of clicking "I'd like to donate" and then not donating? It might be that our intuitions concerning the latter question are that I have performed an all-things-considered wrong, but that in the case of the question posed in the text I have not performed an all-things-considered wrong.

If one is worried that the actions mentioned in these two questions are not different, then we might modify the case as follows. Suppose that, instead of clicking "I'd like to donate," I sit down on my computer and up pops George's face and name without my request. Along with the face and name comes a description of how the website works. Here I think it is even clearer that we will not say I have performed an all-things-considered wrong by not donating.

17. For a classic incompatibility version, see John L. Mackie, "Evil and Omnipotence," *Mind* 64: 200–212 (1955). For axiological versions see William Rowe, "The Problem of Evil and Some Varieties of Atheism," *American Philosophical Quarterly* 16 (1979): 335–341 and David Conway, "The Philosophical Problem of Evil," *Philosophy of Religion* 24 (1988): 35–66.

18. Many take it, for instance, that Alvin Plantinga, *God, Freedom, and Evil* (New York: Harper and Row, 1974), provides a sufficient refutation of incompatibility formulations, while axiological formulations fail due to their supposal of implausible consequentialist moral theories (see Tooley, "The Problem").

19. The importance of relational distance for moral rightness and wrongness is empha-sized in Thomas Aquinas, *Disputed Questions on the Virtues*, trans. and ed. Margaret Atkins (New York: Cambridge University Press, 2005).

Thomas Aquinas, Perceptual Resemblance, Categories, and the Reality of Secondary Qualities

Paul Symington

Abstract: Arguably one of the most fundamental phase shifts that occurred in the intellectual history of Western culture involved the ontological reduction of secondary qualities to primary qualities. To say the least, this reduction worked to undermine the foundations undergirding Aristotelian thought in support of a scientific view of the world based strictly on an examination of the real—primary—qualities of things. In this essay, I identify the so-called "Causal Argument" for a reductive view of secondary qualities and seek to deflect this challenge by deriving some plausible consequences that support a non-reductive view of secondary qualities from an Aristotelian view (*via* the philosophical commentary of Thomas Aquinas). Specifically, my argument has two facets. First, I show that Aristotle's view both implies recognition of the extramental existence of secondary qualities and is a *prima facia* natural view to take regarding the ontology of secondary qualities. Second, I show that the Causal Argument, which is thought to undermine a natural view of secondary qualities as real things, loses its bite when one examines perception in light the ontological relationship among the categories of quality, quantity and substance.

I.

In *The Metaphysical Foundations of Modern Physical Science*, Edwin Burtt brings out a stark contrast between two world-views: that of the medieval scholastic, which found its philosophical model in Aristotle and Neo-Platonism, and that of the contemporary modern, who envisions the expanse of knowledge as being built on, or at least delimited by, positive science.[1] However, with each distinctive philosophical horizon comes its own host of challenges. Burtt poignantly expresses a dismal consequence of the contemporary modern worldview by reflecting on a passage from Bertrand Russell's *A Free Man's Worship*—a book written by someone who, as a child of the twentieth century, drank deep from the well of thought of Galileo, Kepler, Newton, Darwin, et al. Burtt expresses Russell's view as follows:

© 2012, *Proceedings of the ACPA*, Vol. 85
DOI: 10.5840/acpaproc20118519

To Russell, man is but the chance and temporary product of a blind and purposeless nature, an irrelevant spectator of her doings, almost an alien intruder on her domain. No high place in a cosmic teleology is his; his ideals, his hopes, his mystic raptures, are but the creations of his own errant and enthusiastic imagination, without standing or application to a real world interpreted mechanically in terms of space, time, and unconscious, though eternal, atoms. His mother earth is but a speck in the boundlessness of space, his place even on the earth but insignificant and precarious, in a word, he is at the mercy of brute forces that unknowingly happened to throw him into being, and promise ere long just as unknowingly to snuff out the candle of his little day. Himself and all that is dear to him will in course of time become "buried in a universe of ruins."[2]

This view stands in significant contrast to the world-view of Aristotle and the medieval scholastics. For such scholastics, not only is the natural world immediately present and intelligible to one's mind but a human being as a whole is comprehendible within this natural order.

But when and why did such contrasting views gain purchase? How did the modern viewpoint with its very different notions regarding reality arise? This judgment in favor of a scientific world-view was advocated by Galileo. This makes sense given Galileo's innovations and interests in providing explanations that are expressible in quantificational and mathematical terms. Thus, it is no surprise that he held an eliminativist and projectionist view about those perceived qualities that do not admit of quantification or measurement. He explains his position clearly in the following passage:

But that external bodies, to excite in us these tastes, these odours, and these sounds, demand other than size, figure, number, and slow or rapid motion, I do not believe; and I judge that, if the ears, the tongue, and the nostrils were taken away, the figure, the numbers, and the motions would indeed remain, but not the odours nor the tastes nor the sounds, which, without the living animal, I do not believe are anything else than names, just as tickling is precisely nothing but a name if the armpit and the nasal membrane be removed; . . . and turning to my first proposition in this place having now seen that many affections which are reputed to be qualities residing in the external object, have truly no other existence than in us, and without us are nothing else than names.[3]

The discrepancies between modern scientific and Aristotelian world-views have led philosophers to designate properties that we naively associate with reality as secondary qualities. Secondary qualities—identified by terms such as, 'red,' 'heavy,' 'cold,' 'loud,' 'bitter'—are contrasted with primary qualities, which are those properties of things without which quantificational explanation would not be possible. For this reason, a scientific world-view heretofore has supported a reductive view of secondary qualities. For, we may not have reason to be anti-realist regarding the association between our ideas of primary qualities and the way in which primary qualities exist as properties of objects, yet, we do have reason to wonder if our ideas of secondary qualities express reality regarding the things which we associate with these ideas. As a result, secondary qualities are to be understood as deceptive. They make us think that truly the ideas that we have of things accurately represent the things as they are. However, for Galileo and subsequent philosophers, it is strictly speaking false to say that, for example, Elizabeth Taylor's eyes really are blue.[4] The blueness of her eyes is only how they appear to us, and depends on the particular experience of a given person, which is subjective. Or, Willy Wonka's chocolate is not really sweet. Or, heat is not the warmth we feel on our skin. The only way to understand objects is through their primary qualities by describing them in terms of ideas that are not relative to how they are perceived: for example, we can describe heat through energy absorption and the movement of atoms; or, we can talk about light reflection off surfaces with certain wavelengths, or the constitution of table sugar (which produces a sweet taste) as $C_{12}H_{22}O_{11}$. It is primary qualities that form the basis upon which we obtain scientific knowledge of objects. For example, position, motion and mass form a basis through which one can articulate the scientific concepts of gravity and electromagnetic attraction among ionized particles and protons. The same cannot be said for ideas of secondary qualities.

However, a reductionist view of secondary qualities has its complications. For example, it is one thing to say that secondary qualities are subjective insofar as they are dependent on the particular condition of the perceiver, and it is quite another to say that that they are absolutely subjective. Whereas the former seems true, the latter seems quite false. The latter seems false because we know that colors as perceived by us tell us something about the world around us; they are the way by which primary qualities can be ultimately known. Beyond this, it seems obvious that there is something about the object itself that has the disposition to make us have a given perception of it.[5] Thus, a clearer understanding of what it means for secondary qualities to not be real is required. In his *Problems from Locke* J. L. Mackie hones in on a clear articulation of secondary quality anti-realism through the notion of "resemblance": secondary qualities are properties of things that produce ideas in us that have no resemblance with the things that produce them.[6] On the other hand, primary qualities—referred to by terms such as square, in front of, moving, solid—are such that, "the ideas of primary qualities . . . are resemblances" of the properties of things.[7] Similarly, our ideas of secondary qualities do not resemble things as they exist in things; or, in other words, the world as it is in itself is not like the secondary qualities through which we perceive them. Rather, secondary qualities are dispositions in things to produce certain subjective responses or affections but these dispositions are themselves ultimately caused by primary qualities.[8] So, in this way, one can say that secondary qualities are grounded directly in real things in the world—primary qualities—but on the other hand, we cannot say that secondary qualities are really like the way we perceive them to be.

Since secondary qualities do not resemble our ideas of them, they do not provide an explanation of the world that rivals what can be known through primary qualities. Primary qualities push out the possibility that our ideas of secondary qualities have explanatory power. The connection between primary qualities and science "show that there is no good reason for postulating features of a certain other sort, namely thoroughly objective features which resemble our ideas of secondary qualities."[9] Specifically, they do not provide us with a "case for postulating the existence of qualities with the spatial structure of colours, either in addition to or instead of the hypothesized micro-structures to which physicists would at present refer in explaining colour phenomena."[10] Let us then call this the "Causal Argument" (henceforth, CA) against the objective existence of secondary qualities. Mackie's way of making the primary/secondary quality distinction through the notion of resemblance can be used to articulate the CA in the following way: since, secondary properties can be explained sufficiently in terms of primary qualities and since our ideas of secondary qualities do not resemble the primary qualities through which a sufficient explanation is obtained, we are able to say that secondary qualities do not really exist in things. Our ideas of primary qualities resemble primary qualities and an analysis of objects in terms of primary qualities yield an explanatory view of such objects. Thus, only primary qualities are real. So, although we call an object red, it is not really red in the sense that it resembles our idea of the secondary quality of redness. Things in reality are not as our ideas of secondary qualities would suggest.

Having highlighted the importance of the issue, we shall next offer an Aristotelian-Thomistic response. Our task at this point is try to offer some justification for the belief that so-called secondary qualities exist in things themselves and not specifically in virtue of, or reducible to, primary qualities, even though there is a kind of explanatory priority to those based on primary qualities. We argue that not only can we have knowledge of a specific color property according to its appearance to us, but we can also claim that an object objectively possesses some entity (like an essence or form) that resembles our color experience of that entity. In other words, the property responsible for us having a certain color percept resembles our idea of that property. However, in order to accomplish this task, we need to address CA. In order to do this, we shall do two things: (1) discuss what it means to say (from a Thomistic-Aristotelian analysis) that an idea resembles some extra-mental property. By discussing '(1)', in contrast to a representationalist view of mental content, we shall suggest that there is a special relation of sameness between the percept and the object perceived (viz., the quality inhering in some substance) to provide justification for believing that secondary qualities have objective ontological status. We also need to (2) show that the analysis of an object in terms of its primary qualities does not undermine the positing of existing secondary qualities; in other words one can still claim that secondary qualities are real even though a relevant analysis in terms of primary qualities can be given. We shall take up '(1)' in section II and '(2)' in III.

II.

Our first task is to address some preliminary considerations that offer support to an Aristotelian viewpoint and exposes some ambiguities inherent in Mackie's articulation of the primary/secondary distinction given above.

First, let us examine Mackie's description of secondary qualities as properties (or dispositions) of things that are expressed by ideas that do not resemble the properties of things as they really exist in the things themselves. The term 'resemble' here is ambiguous.[11] What does it mean for an idea to resemble the thing that it represents?[12] In the Cartesian tradition, representation is to be understood precisely as independent from the notion of resemblance. This is so because to say that a concept resembles the thing that is understood through it is to say that there is some sameness existing between the content of the concept and the thing understood. This implication is unacceptable to a modern sensibility.[13] Rather than using resemblance to articulate the relationship between objects and our ideas of them, one is to understand a brute notion called 'representation' in which for idea Y to represent object x is merely to present an accurate notion of x, without there being anything more fundamental to serve as an analysis of this relation. This brings the analysis of the relation to an explanatory end and, many have thought, leads to skepticism. Let us examine an alternative to the Cartesian view. To do so, we shall turn to Aristotle's view of perception found in the *De anima* and its relation to a perceived object. But first we need to briefly discuss what is generally involved with sense perception.

Usually, when one thinks about perception in Thomistic-Aristotelian terms, one thinks of the object perceived and the phantasm that arises in the subject from which an intellectual grasp arises. When discussing sensation, Aquinas comments on the relationship between conscious awareness, which he calls the power of sensation, and the so-called "primary sensitive part," which is that which receives the form of the sensed object:

> Aristotle assigns to sense an organ, observing that the 'primary sensitive part', i.e. organ of sense, is that in which a power of this sort resides, namely a capacity to receive forms without matter. For a sense organ, e.g. the eye, shares the same being with the faculty or power itself, though it differs in essence or definition, the faculty being as it were the form of the organ. . . . So he goes on to say 'an extended magnitude', i.e. a bodily organ, is what receives sensation', i.e. is the subject of the sense-faculty, as matter is subject of form; and yet the magnitude and the sensitivity or sense differ by definition, the sense being a certain ratio, i.e. proportion and form and capacity, of the magnitude.[14]

So, in sensation there is the reception of a form, which is received, Aquinas says, without matter, in the extended magnitude, which is the sense organ. Yet, as receptive it is the material aspect of sensation. This is coupled with the power of sensation proper, which is the formal aspect of sensation, which is presumably the consciousness of the sensible form (also referred to as "seeing one's own seeing," mentioned in the next passage). As mentioned above, there is a resemblance between the form as actualized in sensation and the form received in the sensitive organ. Finally, when discussing the subject and object of sensation, Aquinas gives further support to the idea that there is a likeness between being able to see what one is seeing (the actualized power of sensing), the seeing itself (what is received into the sense organ), and the thing seen (the object). About this, Aquinas says the following:

> [Aristotle] says that while one solution of the difficulty was found by maintaining that the subject seeing colour was not coloured, another might be argued on the assumption that the subject seeing colour is in a certain sense coloured, inasmuch as, in seeing, it takes in a likeness of colour, becoming like the coloured object. This is why the power by which one sees one's own seeing can still be strictly a power of sight. . . . So the one who sees becomes coloured in so far as he retains a likeness of colour and of the coloured thing; and not only sight, but any act of sense is identical in being with the act of the sensible object as such; although the mind can consider them apart.[15]

In this way, it is true to say that in one sense the subject seeing color is colored and in another sense the subject seeing color is not colored. The former sense is true because there is retention of color in the subject from the colored thing and a likeness between them. The latter sense is true because although there is a likeness, the sense organ receives the form from the sensible object without the matter of the object sensed.

With a basic indication of the likeness relationship that holds between what is received in the magnitude of the sense organs, the experience of what is sensed, and the object perceived, we can continue to fill in some details regarding the nature of these forms and the various ways in which they are realized. We can also understand what Aristotle means when he says that a form is received in sensation without matter. Aristotle offers us an analogy in which he explains the resemblance or formal identity between objects, what is received in the sense organ, and what is experienced:

> It must be taken as a general rule that all sensation is the receiving of forms without matter, as wax receives a seal without the iron or gold of the signet-ring. It receives an imprint of the gold or bronze, but not as gold or bronze. Similarly the sense of any sense-object is acted upon by a thing having colour or flavour or sound; not, however, in respect of what each is called as a particular thing, but in so far as each has a certain quality and according to its informing principle.[16]

Here Aristotle is telling us that there is an impression in sensation that has as its source that which comes from the object of the perception. Thus, there is a resemblance between that which is sensed and that which is the ultimate source of the impression; just as there is a resemblance between the gold ring and the impression made in the wax.[17] Due to this relation, the sensation is "able to receive the forms of sense-objects" in different ways.[18] In his *Commentary on Aristotle's De Anima*, Aquinas elaborates further on this passage:

> [W]hile it is true that every recipient receives a form from an agent, there are different ways of receiving form. . . . Sometimes . . . the recipient receives the form into a mode of existence other than that which the form has in the agent; when, that is, the recipient's material disposition to receive form does not resemble the material disposition in the agent. In these cases the form is taken into the recipient 'without matter,' the recipient being assimilated to the agent in respect of form and not in respect of matter. And it is thus that a sense receives form without matter, the form having, in the sense, a different mode of being from that which it has in the object sensed. In the latter it has a material mode of being, [*esse naturale*] but in another sense, a cognitional and spiritual mode.
>
> [T]he sense is affected by the sense-object with a colour or taste or flavour or sound, 'not in respect of what each is called as a particular thing,' it (the sense) is indifferent to what in each case the substance is.'[19]

So, Aquinas is suggesting that forms have a commonality or sameness even among different ways in which they are realized (forms are received and assimilated). There is a connection of resemblance between the perception and that which is perceived. However, he continues to say that the resemblance is not between the perceptive idea in the mind and the thing as it is according to its substance, but according to some accidental reality.[20]

That a form is assimilated between two modes of existence implies that there is something the same or formally identical between that which is the source of an impression and that which is perceived.[21] In the *Metaphysics*, Aristotle discuses this notion of sameness among things in the context of a discussion of differences among categories: some things "are said to be the same essentially, and in the same number of ways in which they are said to be one. For those things whose matter is one in species or in number, and those whose substance is one, are said to be the same. Hence it is evident that sameness is a kind of unity of the being of many things."[22] There are a couple of important features of this passage. The first is that Aristotle is saying that between two things, there can be an essential sameness between them even if they are not numerically identical to each other. For example, there is sameness between Socrates and Plato because they are both men.[23] Plato and Socrates, although distinct beings, are essentially the same. The second point is that this unity among things should be understood in different ways when considering different categories. On this point, Aquinas elaborates: "Now the parts of unity are sameness, which is oneness in substance; likeness, which is oneness in quality; and equality, which is oneness in quantity."[24] This is an important passage because it suggests that unity of accidental forms—such as a color or some other secondary quality—exist in an object and in the mind as a percept of it. The unity that exists between an idea of an object as colored is likeness and not sameness. With likeness there is merely some aspect which is the same while not being sameness according to a substantial designation.

But since unity involves a relation among forms, what is the difference between saying that form x (existing in some object) and form y (existing cognitively in a subject) have sameness in common, whereas form q (existing in some object) and form r (existing cognitively in a subject) have likeness in common? How should these be understood in comparison with the unity that characterizes the unity of equality of quantity? These questions can be answered through an in-depth examination of modes of being. In short, the difference lies in the fact that with substantial forms existing immaterially and intelligently in mind there is nothing occluding identifying the form in the mind with the very form existing outside of the mind because of the immaterial modality of its existence. With the forms of qualities, since they are received in magnitude in the sense organ (the material condition of sensation), although not receiving the matter of the thing outside the mind (such as gold or bronze), nevertheless, since it is received in magnitude the form exists according to a mode of being that does occlude it from full identity or sameness. This relation is called, instead, likeness, which expresses this intermediate situation.

At this point, before we discuss modes of being, and the categories of substance, quantity, and quality we are in fact in a place to understand how realism about secondary qualities follows. This realism follows from our idea about how one could understand the notion of resemblance, which is a condition through which Mackie distinguishes primary and secondary qualities. There is some likeness between a percept and the thing that it is a perception of; not a likeness of the substantial nature of the thing, but only according to an accidental characteristic. In order for there to be resemblance for Aristotle at these different levels, there is required likeness of form expressed between then. In this way, we are able to answer affirmatively the question about whether a ripe apple really is red or not: that an apple really is red is guaranteed by the fact that there is a likeness between the percept and some quality existing in the object.[25] Specifically, the likeness between the percept and the object is *not* to be understood as a disposition in the thing to produce a perception, but rather that the percept itself (and the form as it exists in the magnitude of the sense organ) is like the object which it represents as it is. That is, the fact that our percept is a likeness not of the substance but only of an accidental quality of the substance helps us to avoid the absurd conclusion that a color resembles the material conditions that underlie the color's inherence. In this way, common sense judgments in which we impute color essences to objects need not succumb to a reduction of them to primary qualities.[26]

III.

Based on the notion of resemblance—according to different kind—we were led to conclude that secondary qualities exist in the same kind of way that they are experienced. However, this position seems to be undermined by CA. It is appropriate now to address this problem. In this section I argue that the explanatory primacy based on primary qualities does not ultimately undermine the existence of secondary qualities due to the fact that, based on an understanding of differences and relations among categories, that the mode of being of qualities inhere in quantity. Next, then, we need to expand the notion of modes of being, especially in the context of the different categories of substance, quality and quantity.

We have been discussing three notions that are included under idea of "sameness" or unity (which describes a relation among forms, and specifically for our purposes, forms that exist outside and inside the mind): namely, sameness (proper), equality and likeness. Each of these were associated in a mutually exclusively way with substance, quantity and qualities, respectively. Thus, to do justice to our topic, we need to address the nature of these three ontological categories, and in so doing, we will be able to expand further on the notion of modes of being, since categories are identified by Aquinas and Aristotle as fundamental modes of being.

So, what are categories and what role do they play in an Aristotelian ontology? Aristotle offers the following introduction to the notion of categories:

> Those things are said in their own right to be that are indicated by the figures of predication; for the senses of 'being' are just as many as these figures. Since some predicates indicate what the subject is, others its quality, others quantity, others relation, others activity of passibility, others its place, others its time, 'being' has a meaning answering to each of these.[27]

Categories are fundamental ways in which being is divided; the basic ways in which things are. So, if we were to take all created things that exist and line them up, everything would be able to be sufficiently identified with one of these categories. For this reason, they are called modes of being. For example, the way that a quality exists is different than the way that a substance or relation does.

Two such modes of being are identified in Aristotle's *Categories*. He says, "[s]ome things . . . are present in a subject, but are never predicable of a subject. . . . [Also, t]here is . . . a class of things which are neither present in a subject nor predicable of a subject, such as the individual man or the individual horse."[28] Here Aristotle is distinguishing between two different ways that things exist in the world.

One can connect a mode of being with the notion of a category by reflecting on the relation that predicates have to their subjects. Symington and Gracia explain the relationship between modes of being and the function of the copula and predicate in the following way:

> The copula and the predicate term are both predicated of the subject but with distinct intensions: the copula expresses existence, and the predicate term expresses a formal designation of the subject. Beyond this, a parallel condition is understood to hold between reality and the basic structure of predication: "Socrates is" is to "Socrates is a man" as "to be" is to "to be a man." In this way, "to be a man" is a mode of being ("to be").[29]

Since there are two distinct but integrated meanings that are predicated of an extra-mental subject, we are able to distinguish between a common (or formal) nature and a mode of being that is expressed in the proposition in relation to the subject. For example, "This ripe apple is red," contains a predicate with these two distinct elements: the formal component "red" and the mode of being of the redness in an apple. Let us look at the first three categories to see if we can understand how, for example, the question regarding the existence of redness—which is a quality—fits into an analysis of distinct modes of being.

Substance is the ultimate subject matter of our grasp and knowledge of the world. Aristotle says that, "the term substance is used in two senses. It means the ultimate subject which is not further predicated of something else; and it means anything which is a particular being and capable of existing apart. The form and species of each thing is said to be of this nature."[30] Substance exists on its own and is the ultimate foundation for all other things that exist within it. A mental grasp of substance has a relation of resemblance to substances existing extra-mentally de-scribed as sameness (proper). This sameness can be described as identity of formal content; my grasp of Socrates is identical with Socrates with respect to being a man, and the same thing is true in the relation between Socrates and Plato.

Quality is Aristotle's third category of being. Aristotle says that, "all the modifications of substances which are moved, such as heat and cold, whiteness and blackness, heaviness and lightness, and any other attributes of this sort according to which the bodies of changing things are said to be altered, are called qualities."[31] Examples of qualities are color, heat, shape, etc. Qualities have a mode of being such as to exist in another (inesse). For example, qualities can inhere in the quantity of a substance. Qualities involve incidental changes that exist monadically in substances and quantities. Quality is that which is most directly related through sensation—especially since sensation is activated through alteration or motion (in other words, qualities are the proper object of sensation). They are things existing in things themselves that are related through their likeness in sensation; they are communicated to one's awareness via the translation of form into sensation.

With this preamble in place, we can now address the CA. Secondary quali-ties appear to be suspiciously causally inert. They do not seem to have the kind of impact on the world like primary qualities do: photons traveling through space and impacting the eye seems more tangible than do the transference of a form from an object to a perceiving subject. Does this situation not undermine the very existence of secondary qualities? Along these lines, CA undermines the reality of secondary qualities by pointing out that it is only primary qualities that have explanatory power and not secondary qualities. To counter CA, we need to talk about the category of quantity in relation to quality.

Quantity, is defined by Aristotle as "what is divisible into constituent parts, both or one of which is by nature a one and a particular thing."[32] Aquinas elaborates on this:

> [Aristotle] gives the kinds of quantity; and of these there are two primary
> kinds: plurality or multitude, and magnitude or measure. And each of

these has the character of something quantitative inasmuch as plurality is numerable and magnitude is measurable. For mensuration pertains properly to quantity. However, plurality is defined as what is divisible potentially into parts which are not continuous; and magnitude as what is divisible into parts which are continuous. . . . The same thing holds true of surface and of body.[33]

Quantity has properties that lend itself to numerical comparison, analysis and measurement. Because of this property, quantity makes possible scientific explanation insofar as it can provide explanations for things derived through measurement and mathematical analysis (it allows for the quantification of results).

The ontological reason why quantity lends itself to scientific explanation is because the kind of unity that exists among forms that fall under the category of quantity is equality. When commenting on Aristotle's view of relations, Aquinas expands on this notion of equality:

[W]hen it is said in the case of quantities that this quantity is greater than that one, or is related to that one as what includes is related to what is included in it, not only is this ratio not considered according to any definite species of number, but it is not even considered according to number at all, because every number is commensurable with another. For all numbers have one common measure, which is the unit. But what includes and what is included in it are not spoken of according to any numerical measure; for it is what is so much and something more that is said to have the relation of what includes to what is included in it. And this is indefinite, whether it be commensurable or incommensurable; for whatever quantity may be taken, it is either equal or unequal. If it is not equal, then it follows that it is unequal and includes something else, even though it is not commensurable.[34]

Since magnitudes can be reduced to a unit, there is one common measure. This allows for there to be a more clear understanding of things in terms that can be verified. This clarity allows for a strict comparison among things in terms of equality or inequality. Thus, we see that the sameness or unity between two things regarding quantity is simple mathematical equality, in virtue of the principle of commensurability between units or measurement. Thus, Plato and Socrates are unified by the fact that they are each five feet tall. In this way, we can see that quantity is the ground for so-called primary qualities.

So, why and how is it possible for a causal explanation based on primary qualities (viz., quantity) to be consistent with the existence of qualities (secondary qualities)? Aquinas addresses this by discussing the ways in which quality and quantity are ontologically related:

[The] terms which signify the properties of quantity pure and simple are also transferred to other things besides quantities. For whiteness is said to be large and small, and so also are other accidents of this kind.

> But it must be borne in mind that of all the accidents quantity is closest to substance. Hence some men think that quantities, such as line, number, surface and body are substances. For next to substance only quantity can be divided into distinctive parts. For whiteness cannot be divided, and therefore it cannot be understood to be individuated except by its subject. And it is for this reason that only in the genus of quantity are some things designed as subjects and others as properties.[35]

Thus, Aquinas explains that although a quality like white exists in its own right as its own mode of being with its own distinctive forms (and these forms are translated in perception), nevertheless since they inhere in quantity—they have their being in quantity—they are subject to an accidental quantitative analysis. In this way, "things are said to be accidentally quantitative only because they are accidents of some quantity."[36] The same is true for things like time, sound, and motion, which is also quantifiable in virtue of the fact that quantity is closest to substance.

Thus, we have an answer to our concern about the non-reality of secondary qualities due to the causal efficacy of primary qualities. A given ripe apple really is red insofar as there is a likeness between the perception of the apple's color and that in the apple which had the power to produce it in perception. But this color as it exists in relationship to the object that is colored exists in a way as to inhere in the quantity of the apple. Due to this, since the being of the color is grounded in the being of the quantity of the apple, the notion of color can be understood in a prior way according to the notion of quantification; which, in turn, yields a scientific description of color according to the relation of light wave-lengths, electrons etc. So, 'red' in "This apple is red" can either be understood to have a likeness between the perception of redness and the property of the apple that falls under the category of quality, or it can be understood in relation to that in which it exists: quantity. Quantity is not the ultimate causal account of an object. Rather, substance is that which gives being to quality and quantity.[37]

There are two ways in which secondary qualities are causally efficacious: 1) Since a quantificational analysis does not account for the quality of color as it is experienced, extramentally existing qualities provide an ultimate determination for the content of perception. 2) Due to the relation of likeness between objects and percepts, since quality ultimately inheres in substance, and since we have a grasp of substances through secondary qualities, there must be a resemblance between our percepts and the secondary qualities that inhere in substances.

Thus, it can be fully recognized that a quantificational analysis of secondary qualities is appropriate and even ontologically prior to color as understood according to its ontological designation as a quality without undercutting the reality of secondary qualities in objects and without the stark consequences engendered by scientism.

Franciscan University of Steubenville

Notes

1. Special thanks to Jean Degroot, Tim Connolly, Michael Sirilla, and Steven Striby for their comments on earlier stages of this paper.

2. Edwin Burtt, *The Metaphysical Foundations of Modern Science* (Garden City, N.Y.: Doubleday, 1954), 10.

3. Galileo Galilei, *Il Saggiatore, Opere*, IV (Florence, 1842), 333ff.

4. Of course, one need not hold a falsity view and be an anti-realist about secondary qualities. However, the two have been traditionally connected. For example, Colin McGinn holds that to call something a certain color (meaning what is seen) is not to make a false view based on the fact that the subjective view is ineliminable condition for experience. One could not have experience that consists only of primary qualities. Colin McGinn, *The Subjective View: Secondary Qualities and Indexical Thoughts* (New York: Oxford University Press, 1991), especially chapter 6.

5. Of course this is not an obvious position. One realist view about secondary qualities is called dispositionalism. This view holds that secondary qualities are dispositions to produce a range effects and not something beyond this. For a representation of this view see Christopher Peacocke, "Colour Concepts and Colour Experiences," in *Readings on Color*, ed. Alex Byrne and David R. Hilbert (Cambridge: MIT Press, 1997).

6. J. L. Mackie, *Problems from Locke* (New York: Clarendon Press, 1976).

7. Ibid., 13.

8. For excellent discussions on the primary and quality distinction, mostly in the context of Locke, see Reginald Jackson, "Locke's Primary and Secondary Qualities," in *Locke and Berkeley: A Collection of Critical Essays*, ed. C. B. Martin, D. M. Armstrong (Garden City: Doubleday, 1968), 53–77; and Jonathan Bennett, "Substance, Reality, and Primary Qualities," in the same work. Jackson stresses the objectivity of secondary qualities but as dispositional in virtue of primary qualities. Bennett articulates an argument for the primary/secondary distinction based on the idea that one can be color blind but not shape blind. In this way, primary qualities do not admit of the kind of alteration that secondary qualities do.

9. Mackie, *Problems from Locke*, 18, 19.

10. Ibid., 19.

11. For another approach to understanding the notion of resemblance—specifically in terms of an information-theoretic approach to perceptual cognition and the distinction between primary and secondary qualities based on it—see John Kulviki, "Perceptual Content, Information, and the Primary/Secondary Quality Distinction," *Philosophical Studies* (2005) 122: 103–131. Although an interesting argument, in this paper I am approaching the distinction from a qualitative similarity between felt experience and the object that possesses the quality.

12. Jonathan Bennett, in his *Locke, Berkeley, Hume: Central Themes* (New York: Clarendon Press, 1979), also has difficulty with Locke's notion of 'resemblance' as a way of making the distinction between primary and secondary qualities: "Since ideas cannot resemble either bodies or qualities of bodies, this [notion of resemblance] must be either discarded or transformed. The only plausible transformation is into something like the following: in causally explaining ideas of primary qualities, one uses the same words in describing the causes as in

describing the effects (shape-ideas etc. are cause by shapes etc.); whereas in causally explaining ideas of secondary qualities one must describe the causes in one vocabulary and the effects in another (colour-ideas etc. are caused by shapes etc.). If this is not what Locke's 'resemblance' formulations of the primary/secondary contrast mean, then I can find no meaning in them" (106)

13. For further elaboration for why this view is unacceptable see Reinhardt Grossmann, *The Categorial Structure of the World* (Bloomington: Indiana University Press, 1983), 27, 28.

14. Aquinas, *Commentary on Aristotle's De Anima*, trans. Kenelm Foster, O. P. and Sylvester Humphries, O. P. (New Haven: Yale University Press, 1951), II, Lect. 24, 555.

15. Aquinas, *Commentary on Aristotle's De Anima*, III, Lect. 2, 590.

16. Aristotle, *De anima*, II, 12 (424a16–424b20), found in Aquinas, *Commentary on Aristotle's De Anima*, II, Chapter 12.

17. Although Aquinas holds an identity theory of non-literalism view regarding how he understands Aristotle's view of how the form of an object and the form in sensation are the 'same,' which we are following here, there is controversy in scholarship on Aristotle on what this exactly means. For example, Richard Sorabji in his "Body and Soul in Aristotle," *Philosophy* 49 (1974): 63–89, holds that Aristotle means that to say that the form of red is the same in the eye as that in a red object is to say that the eye is literally red. This view has its detractors. See, Christopher Shields, "Aristotle's Perception" (appendix) in the *Stanford Encyclopedia of Philosophy*, http://plato.stanford.edu/entries/aristotle-psychology/#6, where he mentions Aristotle's view regarding the different senses in which the form is the same under these different existential modalities.

18. Aristotle, *De anima*, II, 12 (424b20) cited from Aquinas, *Commentary on Aristotle's De Anima*, II, Chapter 12.

19. Aquinas, *Commentary on Aristotle's De Anima*, II, Lect. 24, 551, 552.

20. Aquinas mentions elsewhere in his *Commentary on Aristotle's De Anima*, II, Lect. 14, that sight is the most spiritual sensual modality: "by a 'spiritual change' I mean, here, what happens when the likeness of an object is received in the sense-organ, or in the medium between object and organ, as a form, causing knowledge, and not merely as a form in matter. For there is a difference between the mode of being which a sensible form has in the senses and that which it has in the thing sensed. Now in the case of touching and tasting (which is a kind of touching) it is clear that a material change occurs: the organ itself grows hot or cold by contact with a hot or cold object; there is not merely a spiritual change. So too the exercise of smell involves a sort of vaporous exhalation; and that of sound involves movement in space. But seeing involves only a spiritual change-hence its maximum spirituality; with hearing as the next in this order. These two senses are therefore the most spiritual, and are the only ones under our control."

21. In Antony Kenny's "Intentionality: Aquinas and Wittgenstein," in *Thomas Aquinas: Contemporary Perspectives*, ed. Brian Davies, O. P. (New York: Oxford University Press, 2002), 243–256, Kenny argues that Aquinas holds a straight-forward view of identity between that which is sensed and that which is sensing.

22. Aristotle, *Metaphysics*, V, Chapter 9 (1018a5–9), cited from Thomas Aquinas, *Commentary on Aristotle's Metaphysics*, trans. John P. Rowan (Notre Dame: Dumb Ox Books, 1961).

23. In Sandra Edwards, *The Realism of Aquinas*, in *Thomas Aquinas: Contemporary Perspectives*, 97–116, Edwards interprets Aquinas's view of identity as a *qua* view of sameness without abandoning Leibniz's Law.

24. Thomas Aquinas, *Commentary on Aristotle's Metaphysics*, V, Lect. 11, 907.

25. Christopher A. Decaen in "The Viability of Aristotelian-Thomistic Color Realism," suggests that if anything, Aquinas should be considered a Primivist about color properties, although it is not a perfect fit. A Primitivist holds that colors are not reduced "to a surface's quantitative aspects (i.e., to primary qualities)" (201). I agree that Aquinas is most like the Primitivist view (while not being a perfect fit) in that secondary qualities cannot be reduced to primary qualities, but the reason why I argue that this is so is because of the likeness relation between how secondary qualities are experienced and how they exist in things: a quantificational analysis cannot account for this relation but rather expresses a different kind of relation.

26. With an understanding of the notion of sameness of form, especially likeness, which characterizes sensation, we can understand Aquinas's realism about qualities mentioned in the following passage from his *Commentary on De anima*: "For, in the first place, sense-perception is always truthful with respect to its proper objects, or at least it incurs, with respect to these, the minimum of falsehood; for natural powers do not, as a general rule, fail in the activities proper to them; and if they do fail, this is due to some derangement or other. Thus only in a minority of cases do the senses judge inaccurately of their proper objects, and then only through some organic defect; e.g. when people sick with fever taste sweet things as bitter because their tongues are ill-disposed" Aquinas, *Commentary on Aristotle's De anima*, III, Lect. 6, 661.

27. Aristotle, *Metaphysics*, V, trans. W. D. Ross, in *The Complete Works of Aristotle*, Vol. 2 (Princeton: Princeton University Press, 1995), p. 1606 (1017a7–1017a30).

28. Aristotle, *Categories*, in *The Complete Works of Aristotle*, Vol. 1, trans. E. M. Edghill (Princeton: Princeton University Press, 1995), Sect. 2.

29. Paul Symington and Jorge J. E. Gracia, "Grossmann and the Ontological Status of Categories," in *Studies in the Ontology of Reinhardt Grossmann*, ed. Javier Cumpa (Rutgers University: Ontos Verlag, 2010), 133–154.

30. Aristotle, *Metaphysics* V, Chapter 8 (1017b23–26), cited in Aquinas, *Commentary on Aristotle's Metaphysics*, V.

31. Aristotle, *Metaphysics*, V, Chapter 14 (1020b8–12) cited in Aquinas, *Commentary on Aristotle's Metaphysics*, V.

32. Aristotle, *Metaphysics*, V, Chapter 13 (1020a7–8), cited in Aquinas *Commentary on Aristotle's Metaphysics*, V.

33. Aquinas, *Commentary on Aristotle's Metaphysics*, V, Lect. 15, 978.

34. Ibid., V, Lect. 17, 1021.

35. Ibid., V, Lect. 15, 980, 982, 983.

36. Ibid., V, Lect. 15, 980, 982, 984.

37. Decaen, in his excellent paper, "The Viability of Aristotelian-Thomistic Color Realism," *The Thomist* 65 (2001): 179–222, concludes that primary and secondary qualities are not inconsistent. For example, he says that "if the proper subject of color is surface, one would expect the proper subject of a particular species of color to be a particular kind of

surface. Now, surfaces are essentially quantitative and have quantitatively analyzable qualities, such as shape and texture. Thus, it seems that it is in accord with the Aristotelian-Thomistic account to allow for an essentially quantitative proper subject within the definition of color." (205). However, his conclusion is obtained through a different course of thought. I stress the relation of similarity among percepts and objects and then show that based on an understanding of different modes of existence and their relations we can see that they are not inconsistent (and do this through an analysis of three categories of being). Decaen stresses that colors are enlightened by an analysis of the matter through which they are individuated, does not stress the nature of colors at the level of how they are perceived, and does not conduct an analysis of categories and their relations. Instead of an analysis based on modes of existence, Decaen identifies the relationship between colors as perceived and their scientific analysis as that between form and matter: "While the classical account maintains that colors are not to be identified with microphysical properties, as physicalism holds, colors are essentially related to them, as an accident is to its proper subject or a form is to its matter" (207, 208). Finally, Decaen discusses realism of color in the context of discussions among anti-realists and realists, and specifically within the context of the realist views of dispositionalism, primitivism and physicalism. My analysis discusses the problems associated with an anti-realism about secondary qualities, specifically through the definition of primary and secondary qualities not having or having resemblance to the thing to which it refers. In this way, my paper continues the discussion advanced by Decaen in his excellent article.

Cogs, Dogs, and Robot Frogs: Aquinas's Presence by Power and the Unity of Living Things

Michael Hector Storck

Abstract: In this paper, I investigate the nature of complex bodies, especially living things. I argue that a living thing's complexity is fundamentally different from that of a machine, so that living things are substances, while machines are not. I further argue that the best way to understand the unity and complexity of a living thing is to follow Aquinas in holding that the elements and other parts are present in wholes by their powers, rather than as substances. I show that presence by power is not refuted by the discoveries of modern physics, and that it can help us understand the relations between parts and wholes in a more universal way which includes both living and non-living things.

There are two different ways of approaching material things. The first is to begin with our knowledge of the world around us, where things such as weight, sound, and texture are most evident to us. The second is to begin with our knowledge of ourselves, with our awareness of our own consciousness, and of ourselves as knowers. I will approach the nature of complex bodies, and especially of living things, in both these ways, and argue that the complexity of a living thing is fundamentally different, not only from that of a complex machine such as a computer, but also from that of any sort of structure composed of parts which are themselves actual substances, and different in such a way that a living thing is a single substance. I will further argue that the best way to understand the complexity of a living thing is to follow Aquinas in holding its their parts are present by their powers, rather than as substances.

There are two reasons why we need to use both of these approaches when we think about living things. The first reason is that these two approaches complement and presuppose each other. The empirical observations of the scientist in the lab are in fact only possible because of the scientist's consciousness. And even if Descartes, as *res cogitans*, doubts the reality of the things he senses, he could not doubt the truth of his sensations without first having sensations to doubt.[1]

© 2012, *Proceedings of the ACPA*, Vol. 85
DOI: 10.5840/acpaproc20118520

The second reason that we need both approaches is that each of them gives us real and vital knowledge of the material world. We cannot disregard what we know about ourselves from our own self-awareness any more than we can ignore what we learn from our senses, since we are part of the material world (even if, ultimately, our being is more than purely material).

I will begin by talking about a living thing: a dog, for example. At first glance, it seems completely obvious that our dog really is one thing. It moves and acts as one, and vigorously (and loudly) resists any attempt to divide it. But on the other hand, there are some things about the dog that should make us wonder how it can possibly be a single thing. Not only does it have a great complexity and diversity of parts—nose and paws, bones and neurons—it also is always taking in new matter and excreting old (while seeming to remain one and the same dog). The dog is like George Washington's axe, which has had its head replaced three times and its handle replaced twice. We also frequently describe living bodies with words which originally referred to machines: The brain is hard-wired. The heart is a pump. An animal is programmed for this or that. Even the word "organ" originally meant "tool or instrument."

Furthermore, in many ways, a complex machine, a robot, for example, functions much like a dog; it acts on and responds to its surroundings in a very lifelike way. And while no machine has yet been able to reproduce its like, a self-replicating machine which can fashion new parts to repair itself and produce new machines of the same kind does not seem in principle impossible. Yet the machine, so close to a living thing in many ways, is definitely not a single thing. It is constructed out of bolts, wires, and integrated circuits that do not lose their individuality when they are made parts of the machine. So since a machine, which is just a complicated collection of parts, can interact with its environment in lifelike ways, it seems plausible that our dog is only a sophisticated, carbon-based, massively parallel super-computer and not really a single thing, that is, a single substance. Maybe we should name him RX-2307, version 3.2.

And what have the biologists and biochemists been doing when they try to explain living things? Many of them, at least, seem to find the possibility of a living thing being a real unity such that the whole is prior to the parts not worth considering. Sometimes, it seems as if biologists think they can explain and manipulate all beings, both living and non-living, as if they were only collections of atoms, molecules, and other material parts.[2]

And some of these manipulations have been astoundingly successful. Artificial hearts, organ transplants, immunizations, and the whole science of genetics are only a few of the radical and powerful results of focusing on parts of the living thing, seemingly treating it as an ordered aggregate. So, since modern science is so successful at explaining and controlling natural things, perhaps its success can only be accounted for by a real, hard-headed, and unromantic grasp of the truth about the natural world; perhaps the natural world simply *is* nothing other than a system or structure of elements and particles. If this is the case, then the pre-modern tradition of natural philosophy, which treats a living thing as having real unity and the whole as prior to its parts, and which includes such seemingly useless baggage as substantial forms and final causes, is an outmoded absurdity, something refuted and clearly false.

As an example, we should look at a few things that different sorts of biologists have said: In his 2002 book *In Praise of Plants*, Francis Hallé speaks of living things as machines, saying: "all machines, biological or not." In *The Century of the Gene*, which she published in 2000, Evelyn Fox Keller makes a number of comparisons between living things and computer systems before asking how they differ. Her only answer is that "computers . . . are built by human design, while organisms evolved without the benefit of a designer (or so it is generally presumed)." In 1979, F. J. Varela defines a living thing as an "autopoietic machine," while in 1966, John Kendrew states: "Personally I do not think there is . . . any difference in essence between the living and the non-living, and I think most molecular biologists would share this view." And while scientists today might not go so far, in 1937 N. W. Pirie wrote an essay called "The Meaninglessness of the Terms Life and Living."[3]

Furthermore, the view that all things are only arrangements of parts is sometimes thought to have the support of physics, which appears to explain visible macroscopic things in terms of atomic elements and sub-atomic particles, down to the level of quarks, and perhaps even superstrings. Biology is often—though perhaps more often by philosophers than by biologists—presented as nothing more than an extension of physics to very complex carbon-based systems.[4]

This might have been true according to Newtonian physics. Quantum physics, on the other hand, demands that the most fundamental particles depend on some natural unity which contains them. We can illustrate this in the case of the atom.[5]

While an atom is often imagined as a collection of actually existing particles, tiny spheres whizzing around, it must, in fact, be a real whole, and its parts, when they are parts of the atom, must to some extent depend on that whole. Chemical elements have a stability as atoms which cannot be explained if the sub-atomic particles are held to exist as individuals. When quantum physics accounts for the stability of the atom, it can account for this stability only because its equations do not permit the components to be treated as independently existing, that is, as having determinate position and velocity at all times. If the atom is thought of as a positively charged nucleus with negatively charged electrons like little planets, it is an impossibility. If this were the case, then the electron would have to do one of three things: orbit around the atomic nucleus, stand still relative to the atomic nucleus, or move in some way other than orbiting. None of these three is possible. According to Maxwell's theory of electromagnetism, an accelerating charged body will emit energy in the form of electromagnetic radiation. This is why electrons moving through the wire of an antenna generate radio waves. Since the electron is negatively charged, if it orbits the nucleus it will emit radiation and thus lose energy, slow down, and be attracted to the positively charged nucleus. The electron cannot orbit, because if it did, the atom would collapse. If the electron, rather than orbiting, were merely to stay in one place relative to the positively charged nucleus, it would be attracted to the nucleus, and the atom would also collapse. But if the electron moved in some more complex way, it would either continue in a straight line and leave the atom, in which case the atom would not even contain the electron, or else it would eventually have to turn around, and this, again, would produce electromagnetic radiation, so that the electron would lose energy and collapse. There is, then, no way for an atom to contain an electron, if the electron is an actually existing particle which at all times has definite position and velocity in the sense that macroscopic bodies do.[6]

So, because atoms do contain electrons, they can only be explained if their parts do not exist as independent entities; mechanical explanations, which reduce the atom to a mere arrangement of its parts, are simply insufficient. The parts cannot exist in complete actuality, so they must be dependent on the atom, which must therefore be a real whole. This means that, at least in some cases, the whole cannot always be explained by its parts. Yet physics, while not requiring living things to be simply aggregates, also does not prove that living things must be single substances, nor does it give any reasons why the cell should not be treated as a machine.

Why, then, might we think that a living thing is more than an aggregate? Surely, the strongest argument for the unity of a living thing is our own experience. Considered from this point of view, it seems obvious that each of us is one thing, and that we have experiences such as pain or vision which cannot be wholly explained by the physical makeup of our bodies, understood as just a collection of particles, molecules, cells, and organs. How can the motion of ions in neurons ever conceivably explain the sight of a red sunset, or the sensation of pain in a stubbed toe? Not only *do we not have* physical explanations of these things, but, as Thomas Nagel says, "We have at present *no conception* of what an explanation of the physical nature of a mental phenomenon *would be*."[7] Not only have we not been able to explain sight, for example, only in terms of the operation of neurons and chemicals, but we do not even know how one would go about formulating such an explanation.

Furthermore, if we are only a collection of material parts, then it seems impossible for us to have any real knowledge of the world around us. For one thing, it would be unclear what it would mean to say "I." And if I do not exist, then I cannot possibly know anything about biochemistry, nor can I meaningfully say things such as "I know" or "I think." For another thing, if the functioning of our brains can be explained entirely in terms of the laws of physics, and thought is entirely determined by our brains, then it seems that all our beliefs and reasonings would be determined by the operations of the molecules and neurons composing our brains. But if our beliefs can be fully explained by the functioning of our brains, then our beliefs do not seem to be the result of our reasoning, but rather of our brain states. And if our beliefs are not the result of our reasoning, then we have no reason to believe them. So ultimately, a denial of our own unity denies both the possibility of the biochemist as a knower of biochemical truths and biochemistry as a truth-seeking endeavor.[8]

But arguing for substantial oneness from our own experience does seem to ignore something obvious: Our observations, which themselves have a beginning in experience, make it clear that living things are made up of carbon, iodine, calcium, and many other chemical elements. A deficiency of the chemical element iodine can cause headaches, poor memory, and depression. The effects of damaging the brain are even more dramatic. The operation of our senses and even of our minds depends on the condition of our organs and on the chemical elements which they contain. Merely asserting the unity of the living thing seems to ignore and even to disdain the actual bodily nature of living things.

Since this is all true, then if the living thing is a single substance, it is a substance which depends in very important ways on its parts (as does an atom, for that matter). So, how can a living thing be really one, not reducible to its parts, yet still dependent on them? On the one hand, it is problematic for a living thing to be only an aggregate, just a collection of iodine, carbon, and other chemicals which are the real things. But on the other hand, if a living thing is just one substance, all dog, say, then we need to account for the presence of organs and elements in the dog.

In fact, Aristotle and Aquinas addressed this same question, and their answer, referred to as virtual presence or presence by power, is a surprisingly satisfactory solution. Aristotle proposes this solution in *On Generation and Corruption*, where he says, very concisely, that in complex bodies or, as he calls them, mixed bodies, the elements are present *by power*.[9]

To say that an element is present *by power* or *by its powers* seems rather cryptic at first. To make this formula clearer, we need to talk about what an element is, and how an element relates to its powers. Aristotle defines an element as: "The first constituent of which a thing is composed and which is indivisible in kind into other kinds."[10] This definition has two parts. First, an element is something which is not completely destroyed in a complex substance. Rather, it somehow remains in the substance of which it is an element, as is obviously the case. Second, an element is not composed of anything more fundamental. Thus, it cannot be divided into things different in kind.

It is, of course, quite clear that none of the four things Aristotle identified as elements really are elemental. But what is, perhaps, surprising is that, when we come to explain why none of his elements are truly elemental, we are using his very definition of element. It is precisely because earth, air, fire, and water can be broken down into things that are different in kind that they are not really elements. And when the chemical elements were named elements, it was because they were thought to fulfill this definition as the most fundamental components of physical things, and it is for this same reason that the most fundamental particles—which may be the real elements—are called elementary. So the ancient and modern uses of the word "element" are the same, and when we talk about elements today, we are using Aristotle's definition.[11]

Before proceeding with Aristotle and Aquinas, I should stress that, while I will be referring to the four Empedoclean elements, I do not wish to assert that earth, air, fire, and water actually are elements. Rather, since Aristotle and Aquinas spoke in terms of these elements, my referring to them as well will allow me to present their understanding of the elements more accurately.

Aristotle and Aquinas understood that the elements were distinguished by their powers, by means of which they acted on and reacted to the world: Fire was hot and dry, air hot and moist, water cool and moist, and earth cool and dry. Chemical elements and elementary particles are similarly specified by powers such as mass, electronegativity, charge, and spin. It is by means of these active and passive powers that the elements act on and are acted on by each other.[12]

When Aristotle says that the elements are present *by their powers*, he means that the active and passive qualities of the elements are in some way preserved in the mixed body. The elements do not remain in a mixed body as substances, and their substantial forms do not, strictly speaking, continue to exist, but the elements' powers remain in the mixed body. However, the active and passive powers of the elements are contraries. (For example, the heat of fire is contrary to the coldness of water.) Therefore, the qualities of all the elements involved cannot be actually present in the mixed body. (For example, a mixed body composed of fire and water cannot be actually hot and cold at the same time.) But, these qualities, unlike the substantial forms of the elements, can be possessed to a greater or lesser degree. Thus, in a mixed body "a mean quality which partakes [*sapiat*: savors] of the nature of each extreme"[13] can be brought about from the qualities of the elements. For example, grey is in some way like both black and white, and tepid like both hot and cold.[14]

In the mixed body, this intermediate quality is that mixed body's proper quality, just as the unaltered qualities of the elements are their proper qualities. For example, heat and dryness are the proper qualities of fire, and a certain degree of tepidness and humidity would be the proper quality of a mixed body composed of fire and water. The qualities of the elements are found in this middle quality of the mixed body in the same way that extremes "are found in a mean which shares [*participat*] the nature of each of them."[15] So, the proper qualities of the elements cannot be said to be actually preserved—the full heat of fire is not found in a mixed body of which it is an element—but the powers of the elements are in the power of the mixed body partially, because the mean shares in, participates, possesses in part, the extremes.[16]

Of course, in living things there are cells, tissues, and organs, each of which is an additional layer of complexity between the most elemental particles and the living organism. And as I argued before, a living thing's unity is a fundamental fact of our experience, a starting point rather than a conclusion. Because of this, all of the parts, ranging from cells to heart and brain, cannot be present as substances; they must depend on the whole living thing. So, since they cannot be substances, being present as a part can only mean being present as shape, color, texture, etc., in some quantity, dependent on the substantial form of the whole. So that, while Aquinas developed presence by power to explain the presence of the elements, it is also the best explanation for the presence of all the parts of a living thing.

It might seem strange to say that a part such as an eye, that you can see and touch, is present in a way analogous to the way an element is present. That is, to say that an eye just is certain powers in a certain quantity of the body seems rather odd. But we know that iron is localized in hemoglobin just because of the accidents of iron present in that part of the blood, and we know that we have an eye just because we have a sensation of certain sensible qualities in a certain part of the body. And if a thing has either an accidental or a substantial form, and a part of a substance cannot have a substantial form, then a part must be certain specific accidents of the human substance, just as an element is present in a living thing as certain specific powers.[17]

So far, however my argument has been based in great part on our awareness of our own unity. Plants, however, seem—although claims to the contrary have been made—to lack the inside view which we have so clearly in our own case, and which we are fairly certain is had by those animals of which we have the most experience, such as dogs. This internal view is one of our strongest arguments for the unity of animals. In the case of plants, then, what sort of argument can we make that they are really one thing?[18]

When Aquinas discusses living things, he says that the activities of a plant are carried out by means of the powers of corporeal nature. That is, to describe a cell dividing in terms of its organelles does not miss the point in the same way that describing an act of seeing in terms of neurons firing does. So Aquinas adds that a plant's activities differ from those of non-living things because they come from an internal principle. This means that a plant, while lacking awareness, still has an interiority in a way that is not true of non-living things, including machines. While the inside of a rock can be seen by breaking the rock with a hammer, the inside of a plant can only be fully understood by seeing what the plant does (although botanists can learn quite a lot about the organic structure of a plant by dissection).[19]

And as Hans Jonas points out, the very existence of a living thing requires it to have a relationship and connection with the world around it in a way that is deeper and different from anything in the non-living world. A machine can exist indefinitely on a shelf, as long as it is properly rustproofed. A living plant without water, soil, nutrients, and sunlight will die. While the existence of a rock or machine does not essentially depend on its surroundings, even the simplest living thing can no longer exist as living without a certain environment and a relationship with that environment. A living thing has a relation with the world that no non-living thing can have.[20]

So that, even if a living thing is formed by chance, it still must be more than simply a collection of parts that just happens to act in a regular way. It is analogous to hydrogen and oxygen just happening to come together under conditions that cause them to unite and become water. In such a case, the water acts like water not by chance, but because it is a certain kind of thing, because it has the nature of water—although, of course, water is not alive. Similarly, even if the necessary elements just happen to come together in just the right way to form a bacterium or a tree, it is not by chance that the tree acts and lives in a tree-like way.[21]

Further, if an oak tree were only a chance collection of parts that happened to work together to produce certain activities, then it would not be reasonable to expect the same effect to result always or for the most part from such a random collection of parts. But an oak tree does always produce a certain kind of nut, and leaves of a certain size and pattern, because it is a particular kind of thing, even if that thing happens to have been produced by chance. The oak's life follows from its nature as just this kind of thing in the same way that water's properties follow from its nature as this specific kind of thing, so that chance has brought about, not a chance assemblage, but a thing of a certain kind: some particular species of oak.

And, even though I said before that a self-reproducing machine might not be in principle impossible, still, such a machine would not reproduce as does a living thing, because it does not exist in the way a plant does. It does not live. If we imagine such a machine, we see it taking in material from its environment and shaping it into new machines. This is not even similar to what a living thing does. A single-celled living thing, and each of the cells composing a multi-cellular living thing, divides itself into two similar parts. In the living thing, there is not the same distinction between a part that acts and another part that is acted on (as we would imagine there would be in the self replicating machine). Rather, reproduction is something that the living thing as a whole does. Sexual reproduction is even more different from the machine's self-duplication. Here, each parent contributes a cell having half the genetic material for the offspring, and these cells unite to form a new cell which, while resembling the adult organism only genetically, is able to divide and develop into an adult of the species.[22]

Now, the vegetative powers (which are common to plants and animals) include growth and development, nutrition, homeostasis and metabolism, and reproduction. All these powers perform their activities, as Aquinas says, by means of the powers of the elements, but the activities exceed the power of non-living things because they proceed from within, from an intrinsic principle. For example, reproduction is carried out by the powers of carbon, DNA, RNA, etc., but by the powers of these things as parts of the living organism. So, while the unity of an animal, and most especially our own unity, is definitely more certain and more obvious than that of a plant, plants too exhibit a unity not found in a machine or an aggregate. It follows that, just as in the case of an animal, the parts of a plant—not only the most fundamental parts, but also more fundamental yet still not truly elemental parts, including cells and tissues—are best understood as present by their powers.[23]

And, although experimental science does not prove this explanation to be true, it also does not contradict it. After all, we never directly sense or measure the nature of anything, we only sense and measure accidents such as size, color, or temperature. We know that the human body contains carbon, not because we observe the nature of a carbon atom in the human body, but because we observe the accidents, the powers, of a carbon atom. The reason that carbon is essential to living things is that it can form very large molecules, including amino acids (which compose proteins), lipids (which compose many of a living thing's membranes, including cell walls), and DNA molecules. Without this unique property of carbon, life could not exist. Presence by power, as understood by Aquinas, allows the powers of carbon, and of all the material parts which make up our bodies, to remain in the human body, but not their substantial forms.[24]

Therefore, St. Thomas's account of presence by power explains the role of the elements as parts of complex bodies, and at the same time allows a mixed body and a living thing to be really one. This same presence by power is not refuted by the discoveries of modern physics, and even helps us understand what physics is saying about the relation between parts and wholes at an atomic level. Further, because presence by power is more general than the primarily microscopic domain of quantum theory, it allows us to understand the existence of parts in wholes in a more universal way which includes living things.

Ohio Dominican University

Notes

1. René Descartes, *Meditations on First Philosophy*, chaps. 1 and 3: *Ouvres de Descartes*, ed. Charles Adam and Paul Tannery (Paris: Librairie Philosophique J. Vrin, 1983), VII, 17–18, 34; *Discourse on Method*, 4: AT VI, 41–38; See Todd Ganson and Dorit Ganson, "Everyday Thinking about Bodily Sensations," *Australasian Journal of Philosophy* 88.3 (2010): 523–534.

2. While some biologists (and more philosophers) explicitly deny a fundamental distinction between the living and non-living, others adopt a mechanical view of living things simply as a method. For discussions of life from biology textbooks, see William K. Purves et al., *Life: The Science of Biology*, 7th ed. (Sunderland, Mass.: Sinauer Associates, 2004), 15; Cecie Starr and Ralph Taggart, *Biology: The Unity and Diversity of Life*, 7th ed. (Belmont: Wadsworth Publishing Co., 1995), 3. For philosophical discussions of reductionism, see William Bechtel and Robert C. Richardson, *Discovering Complexity: Decomposition and Localization as Strategies in Scientific Research* (Princeton: Princeton University Press, 1993); Todd Jones, "Reductionism and Antireductionism: Rights and Wrongs" *Metaphilosophy* 35.5 (2004): 614–647; Sahotra Sarkar, "Models of Reduction and Categories of Reductionism," *Synthese* 91 (1992): 167–194. See also notes 3 and 4.

3. Francis Hallé, *In Praise of Plants*, trans. David Lee (Portland: Timber Press, 2002), 147; Evelyn Fox Keller, *The Century of the Gene* (Cambridge, Mass.: Harvard University Press, 2000), 130; F. J. Varela, *Principles of Biological Autonomy* (New York: North Holland, 1979), 13; John Kendrew, *The Thread of Life: An Introduction to Molecular Biology* (Cambridge Mass., Harvard University Press, 1966), 91; N. W. Pirie, "The Meaninglessness of the Terms Life and Living," in *Perspectives in Biochemistry*, ed. J. Needham and D. Green (Cambridge: University of Cambridge Press, 1937).

4. J. L. Dowell, "Formulating the Thesis of Physicalism: An Introduction," *Philosophical Studies* 131 (2006): 1–23; J. J. C. Smart, "Materialism," *Journal of Philosophy* 60 (1963): 651–661; Robin Hendry "Models and Approximations in Quantum Chemistry," in *Idealization IX: Idealization in Contemporary Physics*, ed. Niall Shanks, Poznan Studies in the Philosophy of the Sciences and the Humanities (Amsterdam: Rodopi, 1998), 123–142; Peter Machamer, Lindley Darden, and Carl F. Craver, "Thinking About Mechanisms," *Philosophy of Science* 67.1 (2000): 1–25; Alexander Rosenberg, *Darwinian Reductionism: Or, How to Stop Worrying and Love Molecular Biology* (Chicago: University of Chicago Press, 2006); Robert C. Bishop, "Patching Physics and Chemistry Together," *Philosophy of Science* 72. 5 (2005): 710–722.

5. For discussions of the atom in quantum physics, see Andrew Whitaker, *Einstein, Bohr and the Quantum Dilemma* (Cambridge: Cambridge University Press, 1996), 4–13; Enrico Cantore, *Atomic Order: An Introduction to the Philosophy of Microphysics* (Cambridge, Mass.: MIT Press, 1969), 114–115; Werner Heisenberg, *Physics and Beyond*, trans. Arnold J. Pomerans (New York: Harper and Row, 1971), 36, 39–41; George Greenstein and Arthur G.

Zajonc, *The Quantum Challenge: Modern Research on the Foundations of Quantum Mechanics* (Boston: Jones and Bartlett, 1997), 31–56; Richard Feynman, Robert B. Leighton, and Matthew L. Sands, *The Feynman Lectures on Physics*, vol. 3 (Reading, Mass.: Addison-Wesley, 1965), 1–11; Shaughan Lavine, "Is Quantum Mechanics an Atomist Theory?" *Synthese* 89 (1991): 253–268; Peter Mulder, "On the Alleged Non-Existence of Orbitals" *Studies in History and Philosophy of Modern Physics* 41.2 (2010): 178–182. For a Thomistic point of view, see Richard Connell, *Substance and Modern Science* (Houston: Center for Thomistic Studies, 1988), 70–87; Joseph Bobik, *Aquinas on Matter and Form and the Elements: A Translation and Interpretation of the* De Principiis Naturae *and the* De Mixtione Elementorum *of St. Thomas Aquinas* (Notre Dame, Ind.: University of Notre Dame Press, 1998), 243–284; William A. Wallace, "Elementarity and Reality in Particle Physics," in *From a Realist Point of View: Essays on the Philosophy of Science*, 2d. ed. (Lanham: University Press of America, 1983), 185–212; idem, "Is Nature Accessible to the Mathematical Physicist?" unpublished lecture, University of Notre Dame, Summer Thomistic Institute (July 1998), 11–12; Alan B. Wolter, "Chemical Substance," in *Philosophy of Science*, The Philosophy of Science Institute Lectures, St. John's University Studies (Jamaica, N.Y.: St. John's University Press, 1960), 97–98.

6. Whitaker, *Einstein, Bohr and the Quantum Dilemma*, 12; Robert Martin Eisberg, *Fundamentals of Modern Physics*, (New York: Wiley, 1961), 108–109. For a discussion of sub-atomic particles, see Bobik, *Aquinas on Matter and Form and the Elements*, 243–284, 304–305; Wallace, "Is Nature Accessible?" 11–12.

7. Thomas Nagel, "What is it Like to Be a Bat?" in *Modern Philosophy of Mind*, ed. William Lyons (London: J. M. Dent, 1995; reprint, 1999), 159, emphasis added. For discussion of Nagel's arguments, see Peter G. Res, "Who's Talking about Bats? Pitfalls of Subjectivity in Thomas Nagel's, 'What Is It Like to Be a Bat?'" *Dialogue: Journal of Phi Sigma Tau* 50.1 (2007): 22–27; Yujin Nagasawa, "Thomas vs. Thomas: A New Approach to Nagel's Bat Argument," *Inquiry: An Interdisciplinary Journal of Philosophy* 46.3 (2003): 377–394; Michael Gorman, "Nagasawa vs. Nagel: Omnipotence, Pseudo-Tasks, and a Recent Discussion of Nagel's Doubts about Physicalism" *Inquiry: An Interdisciplinary Journal of Philosophy* 48.5 (2005): 436–447.

8. John Searle, "Minds and Brains Without Programs," in *Mindwaves*, ed. Colin Blakemore and Susan Greenfield (Oxford: Basil Blackwell, 1987), 209–233; Colin McGinn, "Could a Machine be Conscious?" in *Mindwaves*, 278–288; Jeffrey Gray, "The Mind-Brain Identity Theory as a Scientific Hypothesis: A Second Look," in *Mindwaves*, 460–483; St. Thomas Aquinas, *Summa Theologiae* (hereafter *ST*), 1, q. 78, a. 1; C. S. Lewis, *Miracles: A Preliminary Study*, revised ed. (1960; reprint, San Francisco: HarperCollins, 2001), chap. 3; E. L. Mascall, *Christian Theology and Natural Science: Some Questions in their Relation* (London: Longmans Green, 1956), 212–219; Daniel C. Dennett, *Freedom Evolves* (New York: Viking, 2003); Jaegwon Kim, *Mind in a Physical World: An Essay on the Mind-Body Problem and Mental Causation* (Cambridge, Mass.: MIT Press, 1998); Augustine Shutte, "The Refutation of Determinism," *Philosophy* 59 (1984): 481–489.

9. Aristotle, *De Generatione et Corruptione*, ed. Harold H. Joachim (Oxford: Clarendon Press, 1922; reprint, Hildesheim: Georg Olms, 1970), 2, 1–4, 7; See also St. Thomas Aquinas, *De Mixtione Elementorum ad Magistrum Philippum de Castro Caeli*, ln. 123–153. For the historical development of Aquinas's understanding of elemental presence, see Mario Enrique Sacchi, "La Presencia virtual de los elementos en la combinación química según Santo Tomás de Aquino," *Aquinas* 37 (1994): 126–141.

10. Aristotle, *Metaphysics*, trans. Hippocrates G. Apostle (Grinnell, Iowa: The Peripatetic Press, 1979), 5, 3, 1014a26–27.

11. Ibid. See also Eric R. Scerri, "Some Aspects of the Metaphysics of Chemistry and the Nature of the Elements" *Hyle: An International Journal for the Philosophy of Chemistry* 11.2 (2005): 127–145; Joseph E. Earley, Sr., "How Chemistry Shifts Horizons: Element, Substance, and the Essential" *Foundations of Chemistry: Philosophical, Historical and Interdisciplinary Studies of Chemistry* 11.2 (2009): 65–77; Timothy J. Crowley, "Aristotle's 'So-Called Elements'" *Phronesis* 53 (2008): 223–242.

12. Aristotle, *De Gen.*, 2, 1–4, 7; Bobik, 167–172.

13. Aquinas, *De Mixt.*, ln. 125–128. The English translation is from Bobik, *Aquinas on Matter and Form and the Elements*, 121.

14. Ibid., ln. 123–132; Christopher A. Decaen, "Elemental Virtual Presence in St. Thomas," *The Thomist* 64 (2000): 287–294.

15. Aquinas, *De Mixt.*, ln. 137–140 (Bobik, 122).

16. Ibid., 123–140; Decaen, "Elemental Virtual Presence," 287–294.

17. It does seem, however, that the idea of the contrary qualities of the elements tempering each other does not apply to all of the layers of complexity—certainly not in the case of an eye.

Furthermore, it is important to note that there are texts where Aquinas states specifically that an integral part, such as an eye or hand, subsists and is in some sense a *hoc aliquid* (*ST*, 1.75.2, ad 1. See also 1.29.1, ad 2, and 1.76.5, ad 3). He also states that quantified parts of the body, such as bones and nerves, are present in act in the body. This does not, however, mean as actual things, as complete substances, but rather as distinguished from parts which are not actually quantified, like the half of a circle, which does not actually have a half until it is actually divided. While there is no substantial form of the heart, its weight and shape are actual, unlike the weight and shape of, e.g., one milliliter of blood, which does not actually have shape or weight until measured and separated from the rest of the blood. On this, see Aquinas, *Commentaria in Octo Libros Physicorum Aristotelis*, 1.9. 8–9; idem, *Quaestiones disputatae de anima*, 9; *ST* 3.90.3. More study of the ontological status of the part of a substance in Aquinas is needed.

18. See Alexandra H. M. Nagel, "Are Plants Conscious?" *Journal of Consciousness Studies* 4.3 (1997): 215–230. Lalit M. Srivastava speaks of a plant's "perception of visible forms of radiation (light) and gravity" (*Plant Growth and Development: Hormones and Environment* [Amsterdam: Elsevier Science/Academic Press, 2002], 663), and Ottoline Leyser and Stephen Day mention "light perception by the seedling" (*Mechanisms in Plant Development* [Oxford: Blackwell Science, 2003], 147). Hallé says a venus flytrap knows how to count "at least to two" (*In Praise of Plants*, 298).

19. Aquinas, *ST*, 1, q. 78, a. 1–2; idem, *In De Anima* 1, 14, ln. 10–21, 2, 7, ln. 47–60; Connell, 110–117; Hallé, *In Praise of Plants*, 298–299; Josef Pieper, "The Philosophical Act," in *Leisure, the Basis of Culture*, trans. Gerald Malsbary (South Bend, Ind.: St. Augustine's Press, 1998), 81–88.

20. Ibid.; Hans Jonas, *The Phenomenon of Life: Toward a Philosophical Biology* (New York: Harper and Row, 1966; reprint, Evanston, Ill.: Northwestern University Press, 2001), 84–86.

21. Aristotle, *Physics*, II, 8; William A. Wallace, "Thomistic Reflections on *The Modeling of Nature*: Science, Philosophy, and Theology" (unpublished lecture: University of Notre Dame, Summer Thomistic Institute, July 1997).

22. Connell, *Substance and Modern Science*, 110–117; Jonas, *The Phenomenon of Life*, 76n, 99–106.

23. Aquinas, *ST*, 1, q. 78, a. 1.

24. James Jeans, *The Mysterious Universe* (New York: Macmillan, 1930), 9–11.

The Indeterminacy Thesis and
the Normativity of Practical Reason

R. Mary Hayden Lemmons

Abstract: This paper argues against the indeterminacy thesis that attempts to defeat traditional natural law by asserting that specific moral norms cannot be based on human nature. As put by Jean Porter (*Nature as Reason* 2005, 338): "the intelligibilities of human nature underdetermine their forms of expression, and that is why this theory does not yield a comprehensive set of determinate moral norms, compelling to all rational persons." However, if this were so, one could adopt any morality with impunity from nature's sanctions. But I argue that nature punishes violators of the natural law in various ways. In addition, I argue that the indeterminacy thesis cannot be supported by appealing to the diversity of moral norms across the globe. Such diversity is required, for instance, both by the reliance of Thomistic natural law on the practical syllogism and by its reliance on practical reason's ability to prescribe for the sake of the person in highly unique situations as required by Wojtyla's Personalistic Norm and Aquinas's norm of neighborly love.

I: The Indeterminacy Thesis:
Nature Cannot Underpin a Universal and Systematic Natural Law

Common objections to the natural moral law include the objection that nature lacks normativity and the objection that, even if human nature were normative, it would be so indeterminate as to suffice only for a pluralistic or relativistic ethic and not for an objective and universal ethic. It is only this latter objection about indeterminacy that sets the parameter of this paper.[1]

The indeterminacy thesis can be radical or moderate. The radical formulation denies the very possibility of natural law by arguing that nature is ambiguous and supports contradictory ethics. Alf Ross puts it like this: "The noble guise of natural law has been used in the course of time to defend or fight for every conceivable kind of demand. . . . Is it nature's bidding that men shall be as brothers, or is it nature's law that the strong shall rule over the weak, and that therefore slavery and class distinctions are part of God's meaning for the world?"[2] Jean Porter puts it like this: "[I]nclinations of the human person are indeterminate . . . they can be expressed

© 2012, *Proceedings of the ACPA*, Vol. 85
DOI: 10.5840/acpaproc20118528

in ways that undermine the agent's attainment of her good, as well as in ways that promote it" (2005, 176). The indeterminacy thesis thereby warrants grounding opposing moralities on human nature:

> [T]here is nothing obvious about the claim that our basic tendencies to care, reciprocity, and non-maleficence should be given moral priority over other standing tendencies, or that our capacities for rationality and responsible freedom are morally the most significant aspects of our nature. Human beings are also naturally inclined to form hierarchically arranged social groups, to compete with one another for material necessities and social status, to vent aggression, and to seek sensual and sexual gratification even at the other's expense. These tendencies may be expressed in ways that are destructive and repugnant, but they can also take forms that are striking, attractive, even praiseworthy, and it is possible to envision a moral system that gives them priority over inclinations toward care and reciprocity. Such a morality would be an authentic natural morality, and yet it would look very different from the scholastic concept of the natural law. (Porter 1999, 142–143)

Nietzsche's ethics is thus also, according to Porter (1999, 144), "a natural morality." It differs from Christian morality in identifying different natural inclinations as having priority.[3] The radical version of the indeterminacy thesis thereby holds that human nature is so indeterminate as to be compatible with ethical relativism.

The more moderate version, on the other hand, argues that human nature can establish some general moral parameters that are almost universally acceptable but not the specific norms characteristic of a single system of natural law and necessary for guidance in specific cases of choice.[4] Jean Porter puts it like this: "Because we are complex creatures, there can be a variety of adequate expressions of our nature. . . . There are many ways of being human, including a plurality of defensible and legitimate expressions of the basic inclinations of human nature" (2005, 333).[5] The resulting natural law pluralism, however, is not also natural law relativism:

> The intelligibilities of human nature inform social norms, and for that reason we can analyze and evaluate particular moralities in terms of their natural origins. . . . Yet, the intelligibilities of human nature underdetermine their forms of expression, and that is why this theory does not yield a comprehensive set of determinate moral norms, compelling to all rational persons. (Porter 2005, 338)

The moderate formulation of the indeterminacy thesis accordingly argues that since human nature is unable to specify "determinate moral norms" that are "compelling to all rational persons,"[6] human nature does not suffice to specify a single, global morality or jurisprudence, e.g., Thomistic natural law.

Thus, given either radical or moderate indeterminism, human nature is not able to underpin an universal and systematic natural law. If so, positing Thomistic natural law as true would be only whimsey.

II: The Moderate Indeterminacy Thesis and Moral Pluralism

On the one hand, the indeterminacy thesis—in both its moderate and radical forms—is correct in holding that human nature cannot underpin versions of natural law characterized by moral and juridical uniformity across the globe in both general and particular obligations—as even Aquinas acknowledges (I-II.94.4). On the other hand, the indeterminacy thesis errs in assuming that universal moral and juridical uniformity is essential to all versions of natural law including Aquinas's. Universal uniformity in both general and particular norms characterizes only axiomatic versions of natural law, such as the one proposed by Grotius.[7] Closed axiomatic ethics may be elegant in having *a closed set* of specific moral norms be applicable in every situation,[8] but they are not realistic.

Non-axiomatic versions of natural law derive their specific norms from basic norms and factual claims about what is *here and now* good and evil through the practical syllogism. But, since what is actually good or evil here and now can vary, the normative obligations derived through the practical syllogism can vary as well. Consider, for instance, the norm obligating the return of borrowed weapons to their owner. This norm is derived through the practical syllogism from the more general norm that harm is to be avoided and the objective fact that refusing to return borrowed weapons harms the owner.[9] But when the return would harm the owner by enabling him to do evil, the practical syllogism does not conclude with the prescription to return the weapon but rather with the prescription to avoid returning the weapon—as noted both by Plato[10] and Aquinas.[11] A more contemporary use of the practical syllogism is given by Andrew Oldenquist (1978, 48); he notes how different parts of the world could judge washing one's car to be moral or immoral depending upon whether water is a cheap commodity or a very precious resource.

The practical syllogism accordingly generates diverse particular judgments from the same universal norm depending on the particularities of a given situation. Consequently, the indeterminacy thesis errs in attributing the variability of moral obligations to the indeterminacy of human nature: variability arises not from the indeterminacy of human nature but rather from variations in the factual conditions used by reason to determine—via the practical syllogism—whether something is a harm to be proscribed or a good to be prescribed.[12]

Porter, however, argues not only that moral norms are not invariable across the globe but also that the indeterminacy of human nature precludes the possibilities of "a comprehensive set of determinate moral norms, compelling to all rational persons" (2005, 338). Tacit within this argument is the mistaken assumption that being rationally compelling is the same as being able to compel the assent of rational persons. But since the considerable effort and specialized learning necessary for being compelled by rational arguments may elude rational agents, assent cannot be the criterion of what is rationally compelling.

For Aquinas, what is rationally compelling is a claim in which the subject-predicate nexus is necessary, either *per se* because self-evident or *per aluid* because the conclusion of a sound argument. Hence, those who lack the learning, or the desire, to grasp the necessary relationship between a claim's subject and predicate are not able to be rationally compelled by that claim—even within the context of ethics or natural law.[13] As a result, a claim or obligation can be rationally compelling without also being able to compel the assent of every rational being. This is especially the case with moral obligations, since passion can interfere with moral insight—as anyone who has ever regretted an immoral act can testify. Hence, since passions can interfere with assenting to rationally compelling norms, moral disagreements do not prove the absence of rationally compelling moral norms.

Consequently, practical reason's reliance on the practical syllogism along with the requirements of recognizing rationally compelling claims and arguments means that neither moral variability nor moral disagreement suffices to prove that human nature is too indeterminate for establishing as universal some set of moral norms—as put forth, for instance, by Thomistic natural law.

Furthermore, if it were the case that the moderate indeterminacy thesis were true, it would be possible for opposing moral judgments about the same particulars here and now to be equally sound manifestations of the natural law. But if this were the case, it would also be the case that particular moral judgments would not pertain, here and now, to what is harmful or beneficial to human beings; or, it would be the case that reason could not discern, here and now, what would be harmful or beneficial. But such is not the case; consider, for instance, the paradigmatic case of returning weapons to their owner. In any particular case, not only will the return be *here and now* beneficial or harmful; but should the return be harmful, making the return would be immoral. Consequently, the criterion of whether an act is beneficial or harmful concerns its relationship to a person: is he, for instance, in a rage or too drunk to handle his weapons safely? Such determinations are made by reason's ability to discern the variables and gauge the impact on the person.

Harms and benefits are, after all, objective realities in which whatever is beneficial enables one to flourish, while harms mitigate that flourishing. This is why reason identifies whatever is naturally commensurate to a person to be objectively good; and whatever is contrary to that naturally commensurate good to be evil. That is also why naturally commensurate goods are identifiable as inalienable rights. These inalienable rights or self-evident goods suffice to establish a uniform and specific natural law—as can be seen by Aquinas's identification of the Decalogue's moral precepts to be the very backbone of morality,[14] and by his identification of these moral precepts as forbidding harm by thought, word, and deed as well as obligating the payment of debts.[15] For instance, the naturally commensurate good of life is protected by the prohibition of murder.[16]

The ability of practical reason to discern, here and now, harms and benefits refutes the moderate indeterminacy thesis and its claim that human nature warrants an objective moral pluralism. This is particularly the case because the commonality of human nature enables each human being to recognize other humans as being other selves, i.e., as having a reason and will capable of knowing and choosing his own ends. To so recognize other humans is to recognize them as persons who should be treated accordingly, i.e., as ends and not as means as put by the Kantian principle of humanity ("Act in such a way that you treat humanity, whether in your own person or in the person of another, always at the same time as an end and never simply as a means").[17] To so treat a person is to will good to a person for that person's own sake; and, this is nothing other than to act in accord with the Golden Rule (treat others as you would be treated and not as you would not be treated).

Human nature, moreover, is such that we naturally feel affectionate goodwill for those we identify as being like ourselves. Those identified as different from ourselves can evoke, on the other hand, the distrust and fear characteristic of xenophobia and the dismissiveness characteristic of racism. All such differences, however, are super-ficial relative to the commonality of human nature. Hence, the natural moral law argues that every human being is to be seen *per se*, or essentially, as another self to whom good is to be affectionately willed.[18] Such caring about another's well-being is identified by Aquinas (*ST* I-II.26.4) as the act of love-of-friendship. Only the affectionate goodwill characteristic of the love-of-friendship accurately reflects the identity of the other as a human being, i.e., as a human person like oneself. Hence, honoring the truth about the other requires loving him. As put by Karol Wojtyla, "A person is an entity of a sort to which the only proper and adequate way to relate is love."[19] Wojtyla's Personalistic Norm re-expresses the obligation to love neighbors as oneself—on the understanding that every person is one's neighbor. Aquinas iden-tifies the precept of neighborly love to be a foundational principle of natural law underpinning the moral precepts of the Decalogue (*ST* I-II.100.3 ad 1).[20] Actions contrary to this love are actions that not only harm, but that also oppose the other's personhood and humanity.

There is no indeterminacy here: not only is human nature instantiated in human persons but it also specifies the objective ways in which persons are benefitted and harmed. This is so, despite the uniqueness of persons, because human nature can only be found as instantiated in unique persons. This means that the objectivity of morality is based on human nature even in unique situations. For instance, human nature identifies breastfeeding as beneficial to infants—except when the mother has AIDS. Thomistic natural law accordingly would argue that it is immoral for a mother with AIDS to breastfeed her infant because that virus would harm her infant and because it is obligatory to avoid harming one's infant. This use of the practical syllogism illustrates not only the specificity of the natural law but also how normative objectivity depends on human nature; after all, it is human biology that renders the AIDS virus so dangerous to persons.

The moderate indeterminacy thesis is thus mistaken: the practical syllogism makes it possible for practical reason to derive specific norms and obligations from general moral norms by taking into account the objective facts about any given situation or states of affairs and determining whether there is a harm to be avoided *here and now* or a benefit to be pursued *here and now*.

III: The Radical Indeterminacy Thesis, Moral Relativism, and Nature's Sanctions

The Radical Indeterminacy Thesis holds that human nature is so under-determined as to be compatible with mutually exclusive ethical systems. If so, human inclinations necessarily form an inconsistent set; and, human flourishing does not require preferring one inclination over others; and, one could flourish by taking any inclination as ethically normative. If so, various types of moral relativism would be just as compatible with human nature as Thomistic natural law.

But if human nature were to warrant both natural law and ethical relativism, there would be inclinations of human nature that ground natural law by inclining one to accord with reason's understanding of good as well as inclinations that ground moral relativism, for instance, by inclining one to act in accord with the feeling of sympathy rather than reason as held by Humeans[21] and Darwinians;[22] or by inclining one to act in accord with whatever feels most pleasurable—whether that be, for instance, the pleasures of Nietzschean megalomania;[23] a self-centered pleasure as in hedonism; or, the pleasure of contributing to the greatest happiness of the greatest numbers as in utilitarianism. The first inclination grounds natural law; the latter grounds various forms of ethical relativism, since feelings vary according to individuals, groups, and cultures. From this perspective of inclinations, the radical indeterminacy thesis can appear to be vindicated, since the inclination to act rationally and the inclination to act as one feels are both part of human nature.[24]

However, if human nature were radically under-determined, acting in accord with feelings would be as satisfactory as acting for objective goods—and none could feel betrayed by feelings. Acting in accord with feelings would then never produce bitter regrets and the lament that "I should have known better." And none, for instance, would become bitter upon realizing that another has manipulated and exploited one's romantic feelings. The human experience of bitterness suffices to show that the human heart is not plagued with radical indeterminacy: it prefers true goods to massaging feelings.[25]

Another reason to prioritize the inclination to live according to reason over the inclination to live by feelings can be found in the reality that only reason enables one to look beyond feelings and determine whether something truly benefits or harms the self. For instance, it is not unusual for reason to command the sacrifice of feeling comfortable and to fast for religious reasons—or for one's annual medical checkup. Likewise, it is possible for a teen girl to decide that indulging in her romantic feelings and having sex with her boyfriend would be harmful. To abstain from satisfying feelings for the sake of what is good for the self is to act in accord with what can be known only through reason. It is then to act in accord with reason. Accordingly, although Aquinas notes that "according to the order of natural inclinations is the order of the natural law" (*ST* I-II.94.2c), he does so to argue that "there is in man an inclination to good, *according to the nature of his reason*, which nature is proper to him . . . and whatever pertains to this inclination belongs to natural law" (Ibid.; emphasis mine). [endnote] And hence "all the inclinations of any parts whatsoever of human nature, e.g., of the concupiscible and irascible parts, in so far as they are ruled by reason, belong to the natural law" (Ibid., ad 2). [endnote] The morality of one's acts is hence not taken from their relationship to the inclinations of human nature but, as put in *ST* I-II.18.1-11, from the end intended by reason and chosen by the will as well as the object of the act, and the circumstances. Aquinas thereby provides us with a personalist criteria of morality as specified by practical reason.

That living by reason is best can also be seen by considering that the human ability to understand universals and make free choices is unparalleled in the animal world. And since few—if any—would choose to live as an animal with only the abilities of a dog, a dolphin, or an ape, human cognitive and volitional abilities are not only what enables one to function as humans but also what enables one to flourish as a human being[26]—as the function arguments of Plato and Aristotle strive to show.[27] That this is also the case for Aquinas can be seen in his argument that human excellence is the virtuous rational life.[28]

From the superiorities bestowed by reason and will, it follows that human nature establishes an objective hierarchy (whereby bodily goods are to be subordinated to the overall well-being of the person as known by reason). And it also follows that only those who love in accord with that hierarchy love themselves—and others—properly (II-II.25.7). For this reason, the intellect—and not feelings—should rule the person; otherwise, the person not only makes mistakes and comes to grief, but also fails to love the inward person most. To love another's inwardness is to love him as another self, i.e., as one with an intellect and will to whom goods are to be willed. To so love is to love what can be known only through reason and loved through the will, while to love another's outwardness is to love something that can be sensed, e.g., his looks, strength, or wealth.[29] But since none of these reveal the self, i.e., the inner person and his character, to love the other on the basis of his outwardness is not to truly love. And to be loved only on the basis of one's own outwardness is never to be truly loved. The loneliness that results from such relationships belies the radical indeterminacy thesis. Thus, the truth about love gives us yet another fact about human nature that justifies preferring the morality based on living by reason over the morality based on living for pleasure. It is living in accord with human nature that makes human excellence possible.[30]

But perhaps while human nature is *not* so indeterminate as to be indifferent to whether one lives by reason or feelings, it *is* indifferent to whether one lives by reason or the will-to-power as proposed by Nietzsche.[31] However, if this were the case, there would be no natural sanctions for refusing to subordinate the will to reason. But philosophers have long argued that the will's efficacy suffers impairments when reason is scorned. Plato, for instance, argued in the first book of his *Republic*, that whenever the will is divorced from reason's rule, self-defeating mistakes occur.[32] As a result, those who act apart from the truths known by reason do nothing that they will. A horse running blind, points out Aquinas (*ST* I-II.58.4. ad 3), cannot but fall, and fall harder the faster it runs.

In addition, those who reject reason also suffer the ultimate penalty: deformity of the soul.[33] For when reason does not rule, discordant desires and vices roil one into misery—as shown by the tears of exhausted toddlers torn between the desire to sleep and the desire to continue playing. The frustration of being unable to adjudicate discordant desires by appealing to objective truths is just one of the penalties of rejecting reason. Another penalty for disdaining reason is the frustration of having one's decisions vitiated by opposing feelings. Consider, for instance, the irritation that one feels when acquiescing to the desire to remain in a cozy bed makes one late for an important appointment. In such cases, the choice to get up on time has been defeated by feelings that have made the will become frustratingly inefficacious. Such loss of efficacy is a key penalty for rejecting reason's rule,[34] since the essence of a sanction is that which displeases the will[35] and since the will is displeased by whatever hinders its motions towards an intentionally chosen end.

Inefficacious willing occurs whenever reason is despised because it is only through reason that one discerns one's options, adjudicates between them, and figures out how to act so that one's chosen intention can be achieved. The intention of rising from bed in the morning, for instance, requires one to decide whether to throw off one's cozy blankets and place one's feet on the icy floor or to wrap the blankets tightly around oneself and hop to the thermostat. Either way, one must "visualize" the options and the action that one chooses; for none can intentionally act without "visualizing" what is intended—as known by every successful athlete and musician. "Visualization" requires not only knowing what act is to be undertaken but also forming the images uniquely tailored to that act (whether that image, or phantasm, be visual, auditory, olfactory, gustatory, kinesthetic, or tactile). (For this reason, the imagination as the storehouse of images plays an indispensable role in action, according to Aquinas in *ST* I.78.4c.) Habit, of course, makes this image formation so effortless as to be subconscious—until changing conditions requires a different action and new images. In such cases, it is difficult to act contrary to habit—as shown by the difficulty Alpine skiers have in learning how to snowboard. Nevertheless, since there is no conscious action without an image, or phantasm, of what that act should be, new skills require acquiring new images either through personal experience or through watching, or otherwise sensing, others perform that skill. Learning a new skill becomes more efficient, when one also deliberates about how to best image its performance and then subordinates one's will to the image that reason has identified as helpful or necessary for performing the act deliberatively chosen by the will. Despising reason is hence not conducive to efficaciously acting in accord with the will's choices.

Inefficacious willing also occurs whenever feelings hinder acting in accord with the will's choices. It is possible for this to occur insofar as the images necessary for intentionally acting engage the emotions.[36] For instance, imagining putting one's warm feet on an icy floor is repugnant, while imagining walking into a room on time feels responsible. So, until the habit of rising from bed in the morning is achieved, repugnant feelings vie with feelings of responsibility as images of icy floors and being on time vie with each other. A good habit of rising will result from consistently choosing to focus on the images that accord with reason and that engage feelings of being responsible; a bad habit will result from consistently choosing to acquiesce to the images that evoke feelings of repugnancy towards getting up. Once the habit is formed, it is difficult to act otherwise because the imagination works according to the laws of association; hence, once certain images, and the resulting feelings, become ingrained, they become preferred and their associations become so strong that it takes real effort to break through the associations and focus on the contrary images that produce contrary feelings that motivate the chosen actions. Hence, the degree to which the imagination is preoccupied with images associated with feelings contrary to reason is the degree to which it becomes difficult to "visualize" what is necessary for acting in accord with one's rational choices, and the degree to which the efficacy of one's will is diminished. Consequently, the will's efficacy depends, in part, on its ability to move reason and the imagination to quickly visualize, or otherwise image, the chosen act, even when it is not to one's liking. So when feelings lock—or tempt one to lock—the imagination on images opposed to the act willed in accord with reason, one must fight to focus the imagination on those images necessary for acting in accord with rational choices. Failure to undertake this effort results in acquiescing to feelings, with the result that one cannot focus on the images that would enable one to act in accord with reason. With the loss of these images, the truth about the particular act is lost, with the result that error is introduced into the practical syllogism—and sins of passion into one's life. If one then repeatedly permits passions to override reason, the will's efficacy can become so impaired that the will can no longer easily move one to act in accord with reason's judgments; and, one becomes ruled by the *fomes*, i.e., by sensuality or feelings including emotional and physiological desires (*ST* I-II.91.6c).

In other words, the will is most efficacious when one typically chooses to follow reason's practical judgments. When one habitually refuses to follow reason in one aspect of life, e.g., eating sweets, reason becomes scorned and less likely to be heeded in all areas of one's life.[37] As a result, inefficacious willing becomes more ingrained and one becomes increasingly frustrated.

Aquinas's identification of this sanction of impeded efficacy reveals his insightfulness into human nature. Human nature is a complex system integrated into a harmonious unit only through the rule of reason—and, not through a will unskilled in moving reason and imagination to form the images that not only facilitate good decisions but also that enable one's chosen intentions to be easily realized; and, not through a will weakened by acquiescing to the feelings ruled by the imagination's laws of association, rather than by reason's understanding of what is objectively true and good; and, not through a will that maliciously overrides reason's identification of what is here and now good, and morally requisite, in order to give preference to some other good, e.g., a selfish pleasure.[38] Without the will's submission to the truths that reason knows, the various subsystems begin functioning abnormally: emotions become unruly and physical desires burdensome. As put by Cicero: "True law is right reason in agreement with nature; it is of universal application, unchanging and everlasting . . . and it is impossible to abolish it entirely. . . . Whoever is disobedient is fleeing from himself and denying his human nature, and . . . he will suffer the worst penalties" (Cicero, *The Republic* III, #XXII 1966, 211). The popular maxim "use it or lose it," thus, also applies to the efficacies of reason and will in so far as it becomes increasingly difficult and uncomfortable—although always still possible—to chose contrary to one's dispositions. Hence, the will's malice as well as slothful acquiescence to feelings renders willing inefficacious and frustrating, while submitting to reason's normative judgments advances the self-integration that makes willing efficacious and joyful, and becomes the state of virtue.

The recognition that efficacious willing requires following reason is not unique to the Thomistic natural law tradition. Even the atheist Ayn Rand argues that the will's refusal to submit to the good as known by reason is self-defeating. As she puts it: the alternative offered by human nature is "rational being or suicidal animal" (Ayn Rand 1964, 23). Not surprising, then, is Nietzsche's confession: "The thought of suicide is a powerful comfort: it helps one through many a dreadful night."[39]

An argument that the will to power over and against subordination to reason's knowledge is ultimately self-defeating or suicidal can be drawn from the work of Rand's protégé, the atheistic psychologist Nathaniel Branden (1969). He points out that the human need to be efficacious is so strong that it is the basis of self-esteem. Self-esteem may be built upon understanding and honoring nature, or upon manipulating others.[40] The self-esteem built upon nature is life-affirming, confident, and joyous, since it is based upon one's own recognition of being able to handle successfully nature and her requirements. The self-esteem built upon the manipulation of others is insecure: it must always be fed by successfully asserting power over others. Such power is enhanced, albeit only temporarily, when others are too afraid to resist. But such fear is alien to the trust that is the basis of love and friendship. Loneliness is thus inescapable—as Nietzsche admits:

> Today the concept of greatness entails being noble, wanting to be by oneself, being able to be different, standing alone and having to live independently. And the philosopher will betray something of his own idea when he posits: "He shall be greatest who can be loneliest, the most concealed, the most deviant, the human being beyond good and evil, the master of his virtues, he that is over-rich in will." (*Beyond Good and Evil* #212, 1966, 139)

But the loneliness that results from a lifetime of willing power breeds depression, and depression eventually idles the will's assertiveness. Therefore, the will to power is actually self-defeating and Nietzsche is mistaken in supposing that the will is invigorated by being beyond good and evil.

Consequently, if the radical indeterminacy thesis were true and human nature were so under-determined as to provide no basis for adjudicating between natural law and Nietzschean megalomania, there would be no natural sanctions for transgressions against natural law.[41] But we have seen that there are such sanctions: alienation from others, depression, and a diminishment of efficacious willing. In addition, there is the bitter remorse of a conscience that realizes not only that one has failed to act according to one's best lights, but also that one has squandered oneself by identifying the pleasures of the flesh or power as one's most important priority. These sanctions ensure that unhappiness arises whenever one consistently fails to live according to reason and its truths—as psychologists attest.[42] Such unhappiness is not a Divine "lightning bolt," although—as an inbuilt reaction of human nature—it reflects the design of its Creator. As the old adage states, "nature never forgives." And, as Nathaniel Branden points out, "Man is free to act against the requirements of his nature, . . . but he is not free to escape the consequence: misery, anxiety, destruction" (1969, 234–235). Consequently, the sanctions resulting from Nietzschean lawlessness suffice to show that nature is not indifferent to the morality that one adopts. Efficacy of one's choices requires one to chose in accord with the truths known by reason. Failure to do so is ultimately self-defeating; because, since the necessity of the natural moral law is the necessity of *eudaimonia*, the sanctions of natural law are increasing degrees of unhappiness for the immoral. Happiness, after all, is a greater good than any achieved by breaking the law, while the loss of happiness is a penalty greater than any incurred by obeying the law.[43]

Conclusion

The failures of the moderate indeterminacy thesis arise from reason's ability to use the practical syllogism to derive a variety of particular norms from the common universal norms, to discern whether or not something is objectively beneficial or harmful, here and now, and to recognize that other human beings are to be treated as persons, i.e., with respect, goodwill, and love. The radical indeterminacy thesis fails because it is possible for human beings to adopt ethical systems that impede the efficacy of their choices, that cause intense regret for not acting according to their best lights, and that breed loneliness. In brief: the indeterminacy theses fail because it is neither the case that practical reason is too obtuse to command the *here and now* objective requirements of human flourishing nor the case that one's human nature is so amorphous as to be unaffected by one's moral values.[44]

University of St. Thomas (Minnesota)

Notes

1. I have dealt with these objections before. David Hume's Is-Ought Fallacy both in "Rediscovering Eudaimonistic Teleology," *The Monist* 75.1 (January 1992): 71–83; and in *Ultimate Normative Foundations: The Case for Aquinas's Personalist Natural Law* (Lanham: Lexington Books, 2011), 203–205. The Indeterminacy Thesis in *Ultimate Normative Foundations*, 219–224. In this paper, my discussion of the Indeterminacy Thesis reprises and revises the discussion in *Ultimate Normative Foundations*.

2. Alf Ross, "A Critique of the Philosophy of Natural Law," in *On Law and Justice* (London: Stevens and Sons, Ltd.,1958), 258–259. The gist of this argument can also be found in the works of Plato; see *Republic*, Book One, 340d–341a; 343b–344d; and especially see the *Gorgias*, 482d–486d.

3. Jean Porter, *Natural and Divine Law: Reclaiming the Tradition for Christian Ethics* (Grand Rapids, Michigan: William B. Eerdmans Pub. Co., 1999), 144–145.

4. Jean Porter, *Nature as Reason: A Thomistic Theory of the Natural Law* (Grand Rapids: William. B. Eerdmans Publ. Co., 2005), 335.

5. Also see Porter, *Nature*, 339: "[There is a] plurality of possible expressions of human nature at the level of social morality. For this reason, we cannot speak of the natural law at the level of determinate norms, but must speak of natural moralities in the plural."

6. Ibid., 338.

7. A. P. D'Entrèves, *Natural Law: An Introduction to Legal Philosophy*, 2nd Edition (London: Hutchinson & Co, Ltd., 1970), 55; Also, see Steven J. Pope, "Natural Law in Catholic Social Teachings," in *Modern Catholic Social Teaching: Commentaries and Interpretations*, ed. Kenneth R. Himes, O.F.M. (Washington, D.C.: Georgetown University Press, 2005), 46. Grotius is also famous for declaring that even if there were no God, natural law would persist. By so doing, he was not interested in secularizing natural law, according to Charles Edwards, "The Law of Nature in the Thought of Hugo Grotius," *Journal of Politics* 32.4 (1970): 784–807. Nor was Grotius the first to suggest the possibility of a secular natural law; it was also suggested by Gabriel Biel, according to Paul E. Sigmund, *Natural Law in Political Thought* (Cambridge: Winthrop Publishers Incorporated, 1971), 59; and, by Gregory of Rimini in his *On the Sentences* Bk. 11, d. 34, d. 1 a.2, according to E. B. F. Midgley, *The Natural Law Tradition and the Theory of International Relations* (New York: Harper and Row, 1975) 477n26. For more discussion see Brian Tierney, "The Idea of Natural Rights: Studies on Natural Rights, Natural Law and Church Law, 1150–1625," in *Emory University Studies in Law and Religion* (Atlanta: Scholars Press, 1997; Reprinted 2001, Grand Rapids, Michigan: William B. Eerdmans Publishing Company, 2001).

8. Closed axiomatic systems mistakenly presuppose that deduction from basic norms eliminate the need for insight, argues William Sweet, "The Foundations of Ethics and Moral Practices," in *The Bases of Ethics*, ed. William Sweet, 220–242. *Marquette Studies in Philosophy*, No. 23, ed. Andrew Tallon (Milwaukee: Marquette University Press, 2000), 224: "We cannot, as the Enlightenment approach suggests we can, take account of all values and find a set of rules that can help us to prioritize these values while at the same time recognizing them for what they are and giving them their moral weight. Moreover, a 'rationalistic' procedure based on the mere following of certain rules falls short; what we need instead is the development of skill in judgment—something suggested by Aristotle's model of the practically wise person, the *phronimos*. Here, reason leaves room for the notion of 'insight.'"

9. Cf. *ST* I-II.100.1 and 3 as well as I-II.100.11.

10. *Republic* I.331c: "[A]s everyone I presume would admit, if one took over weapons from a friend who was in his right mind and then the lender should go mad and demand them back, that we ought not to return them in that case and that he who did so return them would not be acting justly."

11. This example enters the natural law tradition through Plato's first book of the *Republic* and stays there through its citation by Aquinas in *ST* I-II.94.4c.

12. Moral variability, moreover, is to be expected when practical reason is responsible for moral judgments: "The practical reason . . . is busied with contingent matters, about which human actions are concerned: and consequently although there is necessity in the general principles, the more we descend to matters of detail, the more frequently we encounter defects. Accordingly, then . . . in matters of action, truth or practical rectitude is not the same for all, as to matters of detail, but only as to the general principles: and where there is the same rectitude in matters of detail, it is not equally known to all" (*ST* I-II.94.4c).

13. For Aquinas's discussion of the role of argument in establishing moral norms see *ST* I-II.94.2, 4; I-II.100.1, 3.

14. *ST* I-II.100.3c: "[T]wo kinds of precepts are not reckoned among the precepts of the decalogue: viz., first general principles, for they need no further promulgation after being once imprinted on the natural reason to which they are self-evident; as, for instance, that one should do evil to no man . . . and again those which the careful reflection of wise men shows to be in accord with reason."

15. *ST* I-II.100.5c.

16. *ST* I-II.95.2c: "[T]hat one must not kill may be derived as a conclusion from the principle that one should do harm to no man."

17. Immanuel Kant, *Grounding for the Metaphysics of Morals*, trans. James W. Ellington, (Indianapolis, Cambridge: Hackett Publishing Company, 1981), #429, p. 36.

18. Aquinas explains that the fact that some human beings are our enemies insofar as they seek to harm us does not override the obligations of love; hence, their attempts to harm should be stopped with the minimum degree of force necessary and their successful attempts should be punished to the degree necessary to restore justice. For a Thomistic exegesis of these points see Lemmons, *Ultimate Normative Foundations*, 160, 175n11, 304n22, 339–348.

19. Karol Wojtyla, *Love and Responsibility*, trans. H. T. Willetts, rev. ed. (New York: Farrar-Straus-Giroux, 1981), 41.

20. For exegeses of neighborly love as basic in Thomistic natural law see John Finnis, *Aquinas: Moral, Political, and Legal Theory* (Oxford: Oxford University Press, 1998). R. Mary Hayden, "Love and the First Principles of St. Thomas's Natural Law," (Ann Arbor: University Microfilms International, 1988); Lemmons, "Are the Love Precepts Really Natural Law's Primary Precepts?" *Proceedings of the American Catholic Philosophical Association* 66 (1992): 45–71; and Lemmons, *Ultimate Normative Foundations*.

21. David Hume, *Treatise of Human Nature* Bk 3, part 3, section 1 (1992, 589): "Moral good and evil are certainly distinguish'd by our sentiments, not by reason."

22. Lemmons *Ultimate Normative Foundations*, 7: "Charles Darwin, for instance, attempted to explain obligations by reducing them to expressions of the moral sense, identifiable as conscience's feelings of right or wrong caused by replaying one's actions in the light of the ever present social instincts rooted in the emotion of sympathy." See Darwin's *The Descent of Man and Selection in Relation to Sex* (New York: D. Appleton and Company: 1897), 97–115.

23. Egotism, and especially megalomania, can be very pleasurable as shown by this passage from *Beyond Good and Evil* #260 (1966, 205): "The noble type of man experiences *itself* as determining values; it does not need approval; it judges, 'what is harmful to me is harmful in itself'; it knows itself to be that which first accords honor to things; it is *value-creating*. Everything it knows as part of itself it honors: such a morality is self-glorification. In the foreground there is the feeling of fullness, of power that seeks to overflow, the happiness

of high tension, the consciousness of wealth that would give and bestow: the noble human being, too, helps the unfortunate, but not, or almost not, from pity, but prompted more by an urge begotten by excess of power. The noble human being honors himself as the one who is powerful, also as one who has power over himself, who knows how to speak and be silent, who delights in being severe and hard with himself and respects all severity and hardness. . . . Noble and courageous human beings who think that way are furthest removed from that morality which finds the distinction of morality precisely in pity, or in acting for others, . . . faith in oneself, pride in oneself, a fundamental hostility and irony against 'selflessness' belong just as definitely to noble morality as does a slight disdain and caution regarding compassionate feelings and a 'warm heart.'"

24. There are other ways to support the radical indeterminacy thesis. One could argue, for instance, that human nature inclines equally to selfishness and to altruism. This argument, however, usually reduces to one about the pleasures of selfishness and the pleasures of helping others and whether such pleasures are mutually exclusive and whether one is superior to the other. It thus presupposes that human nature is determined by pleasure. It thereby fails to presuppose an indeterminacy in human nature.

25. See Plato, *Republic*, Book One, 336b–338d.

26. Cf. Aristotle *Nicomachean Ethics* X.3 (11741a1–2).

27. For Plato's function argument see the *Republic*, Bk I, 352b–354a; for Aristotle's see the *Nicomachean Ethics*, I.7 (1097b25–1098a20); for Aquinas's see *ST* I.75.3,6–7; I.76.1,3; I.83.1; *De Veritate* 24.1–2.

28. *ST* I-II.94.3c: "For it has been stated that to the natural law belongs everything to which a man is inclined according to his nature. Now each thing is inclined naturally to an operation that is suitable to it according to its form . . . [w]herefore, since the rational soul is the proper form of man, there is in every man a natural inclination to act according to reason: and this is to act according to virtue. Consequently, considered thus, all acts of virtue are prescribed by the natural law: since each one's reason naturally dictates to him to act virtuously."

29. The intelligible good is the object of the human will, "while sensitive or imaginary good is proportionate not to the will but to the sensitive appetite" (*ST* I-II.19.3c).

30. *Republic* I, 351b–c, 353e, and Bk. X, 619a–b.

31. For an in-depth analysis and critique of Nietzsche's morality see Lemmons, *Ultimate Normative Foundations*, 256–262.

32. See *Republic* Bk. I, 336c, 340e, 343b–c. Also see *Gorgias* 466e.

33. *Republic* Bk. 1, 351a: "justice is wisdom and virtue . . . injustice is ignorance." Ibid., 352a: "Then in the individual too . . . [injustice] will in the first place make him incapable of accomplishing anything because of inner faction and lack of self-agreement." *Theaetetus* 176b–177a: "[W]e should make all speed to take flight from this world to the other, and that means becoming like the divine so far as we can, and that again is to become righteous with the help of wisdom. . . . There are two patterns . . . in the unchangeable nature of things, one of divine happiness, the other of godless misery . . . in doing injustice they are growing less like one of these patterns and more like the other. The penalty they pay is the life they lead . . . that other region which is free from all evil will not receive them after death."

34. *ST* I-II.69.2ad 1: "Although sometimes the wicked do not undergo temporal punishment in this life, yet they suffer spiritual punishment. Hence Augustine says (*Conf. I*):

Thou hast decreed, and it is so, Lord,—that the disordered mind should be its own punishment. The Philosopher, too, says of the wicked (*Ethics ix.4*) that *their soul is divided against itself,* . . . *one part pulls this way, another that*; and afterwards he concludes, saying: *If wickedness makes a man so miserable, he should strain every nerve to avoid vice."*

35. *ST* I-II.46.6 ad 2: "[P]unishment consists in being contrary to the will, painful, and inflicted for some fault."

36. The relationship between reason and feelings is somewhat more complex than I have indicated here since emotional self-control requires controlling the sense images that cause emotions and since exercising that control requires the cogitative sense to perceive the universal in images. See, for instance, *ST* I.81.3 and especially ad 2. Also see the excellent explication given by George P. Klubertanz S.J., *The Discursive Power: Sources and Doctrine of the Vis Cogitativa According to St. Thomas Aquinas* (St. Louis: The Modern Schoolman, 1952).

37. The denigration of reason causes all volitional acts to be inefficacious; hence, Aristotle and Aquinas were correct in holding the well-known "unity of the virtues thesis." For a fuller and more traditional discussion see, for instance, Shane Drefcinski, "A Very Short Primer on St. Thomas Aquinas's Account of the Various Virtues" available at http://www.uwplatt.edu/~drefcins/233AquinasVirtues.html (Last accessed 1/8/12).

38. Cf. *ST* I.78.1c: "[S]in occurs in human acts, sometimes through a defect of the intellect, as when anyone sins through ignorance, and sometimes through a defect in the sensitive appetite, as when anyone sins through passion, so too does it occur through a defect . . . of the will [due to loving] . . . more the lesser good." Also *ST* I.78.3c: "A sin committed through malice is more grievous than a sin committed through passion for three reasons. First, because, as sin consists chiefly in an act of the will, . . . a sin is all the more grievous, according as . . . the sin belongs more to the will . . . Secondly, because the passion, . . . soon passes away, so that man repents of his sin, and soon returns to his good intentions; whereas the habit [of malice] . . . is a permanent quality . . . Thirdly, because he who sins through certain malice is ill-disposed in respect of the end itself, which is the principle in matters of action; and so the defect is more dangerous than in the case of the man who sins through passion."

39. *Beyond Good and Evil* #157 (1966), 91.

40. Branden's arguments can be found within his chapter 10, "Social Metaphysics," of *The Psychology of Self-Esteem: A New Concept of Man's Psychological Nature* (Toronto: Bantam Book, 1969).

41. My treatment of natural law sanctions closely follows that of Aquinas. He, however, approaches these sanctions somewhat differently. In *ST* I-II.87.1c Aquinas argues that violations of the moral law subject man to three realms of punishment: one of which is inflicted by himself, namely a remorse of conscience; the others are inflicted by his fellow humans and by God. Of the first, not much needs to be said other than remorse is a horrible feeling of shame. Humans punish moral violators either by the withdrawal of their friendship or by legal prosecutions. In this regard, it is important to note that the criminal codes of many countries primarily center upon those immoral acts that harm others, e.g., murder, theft, perjury, etc. Of the punishment inflicted by God for moral violations, the critical question is whether God's punishment is only extrinsic or also intrinsic to natural law. If only extrinsic, then immoral acts—invoking neither remorse of conscience nor interpersonal sanctions—do not incur a sanction until God acts; just as the perjurer does not incur jail time until the trial

judge acts. Aquinas, however, while not disputing God's role as Ultimate Judge, also identifies an intrinsic sanction, namely, the usurpation of reason by sensuality (*ST* I-II.91.6c). Of interest are also *ST* I-II.90.3 ad 2, which states that the law has coercive power so that it is efficacious for inducing to virtue, and *ST* I-II.96.5c, which states that it is the contrary wills of the wicked that subjects them to the law.

42. For a sampling see M. Scott Peck's *The Road Less Traveled* (New York: Simon and Schuster, 1978), and Nathaniel Branden's *Honoring the Self* (Toronto: Bantam Books, 1983). Hugo Meynell also documents some of these psychologists—and notes their relevance for morality—in his intriguing book, *Freud, Marx, and Morals* (Totowa, N.J.: Barnes & Noble, 1981).

43. This argument about the sufficiency of natural law's sanction is adapted from an argument about eternal happiness by Thomas Higgins, S.J. *Man as Man: The Science and Art of Ethics*, rev. ed. (Milwaukee: Bruce Publishing Co, 1958), 106–107. The adaption is fair since Aristotle's function argument, which Higgins presupposes, establishes that natural human happiness is functioning rationally.

44. For a fuller treatment of nature's normativity see my book, *Ultimate Normative Foundations: The Case for Aquinas's Personalist Natural Law* (Lanham: Lexington Books, 2011).

Bibliography

Aquinas, Thomas. 1947. *Summa Theologica*. Translated by English Dominicans. 3 vols. New York: Benziger Brothers, Inc.

Branden, Nathaniel. 1969. *Psychology of Self-Esteem: A New Concept of Man's Psychological Nature*. Toronto: Bantam Books.

————. 1983. *Honoring the Self*. Toronto: Bantam Books.

Cicero. 2006. *De Re Publica, De Legibus*. Translated by Clinton Walker Keyes. The Loeb Classical Library, ed. T. E. Page, et al. Cambridge: Harvard University Press.

D`Entrèves, Alexander Passerin. 1970. *Natural Law: An Introduction to Legal Philosophy*. 2nd Edition. London: Hutchinson & Co, Ltd.

Drefcinski, Shane. "A Very Short Primer on St. Thomas's Aquinas's Account of the Various Virtues." Available at http://www.uwplatt.edu/~drefcins/233AquinasVirtues.html (last accessed 1/8/12).

Edwards, Charles. 1970. "The Law of Nature in the Thought of Hugo Grotius," *Journal of Politics* 32.4: 784–807.

Finnis, John. 1998. *Aquinas: Moral, Political, and Legal Theory*. Oxford: Oxford University Press.

Hayden, R. Mary. 1988. "Love and the First Principles of St. Thomas's Natural Law." Ann Arbor: University Microfilms International.

Higgins, Thomas, S.J. 1958. *Man as Man: The Science and Art of Ethics*. Rev. Ed. Milwaukee: Bruce Publishing Co.

Hume, David. 1992. *Treatise of Human Nature*. Reprinted. Buffalo, New York: Prometheus Books.

Kant, Immanuel. 1981. *Grounding for the Metaphysics of Morals*. Translated by James W. Ellington. Indianapolis, Cambridge: Hackett Publishing Company.

Klubertanz, George, P., S.J. 1952. *The Discursive Power: Sources and Doctrine of the Vis Cogitativa According to St. Thomas Aquinas*. St. Louis: The Modern Schoolman.

Lemmons, R. Mary Hayden. 1992a. "Are the Love Precepts Really Natural Law's Primary Precepts?" *Proceedings of the American Catholic Philosophical Association* 66: 45–71.

———. 1992b. "Rediscovering Eudaimonistic Teleology." *The Monist* 75.1 (January): 71–83.

———. 2011. *Ultimate Normative Foundations: The Case for Aquinas's Personalist Natural Law*. Lanham: Lexington Books.

Meynell, Hugo. 1981. *Freud, Marx and Morals*. Totowa: Barnes & Noble.

Midgley, E. B. F. 1975. *The Natural Law Tradition and the Theory of International Relations*. New York: Harper and Row.

Nietzsche, Friedrich. 1966. *Beyond Good and Evil: Prelude to a Philosophy of the Future*. Translated with Commentary by Walter Kaufmann. New York: Vintage Books (Random House).

Oldenquist, Andrew G. 1978. Second Edition. *Moral Philosophy: Text and Readings*. Boston: Houghton Mifflin Company. Reprint by Waveland Press, Inc. (Prospect Heights) 1984.

Peck, M. Scott. 1978. *The Road Less Traveled*. New York: Simon and Schuster.

Plato. 1930. *Republic*. Translated by Paul Shorey. Cambridge and London. Loeb Classical Library. Reprinted *The Collected Dialogues of Plato*, ed. Edith Hamilton and Huntington Cairns. Bollingen Series 71. Princeton: Princeton University Press, 1961.

———. 1935. *Theaetetus*. Translated by F. M. Cornford. Cambridge and London. Loeb Classical Library. Reprinted *The Collected Dialogues of Plato*, ed. Edith Hamilton and Huntington Cairns. Bollingen Series 71. Princeton: Princeton University Press, 1961.

———. 1955. *Gorgias*. Translated by W. D. Woodhead. Cambridge and London. Loeb Classical Library. Reprinted *The Collected Dialogues of Plato*, ed. Edith Hamilton and Huntington Cairns. Bollingen Series 71. Princeton: Princeton University Press, 1961.

Pope, Steven J. 2005. "Natural Law in Catholic Social Teachings." In *Modern Catholic Social Teaching: Commentaries and Interpretations*, ed. Kenneth R. Himes, O.F.M., 41–71 Washington, D.C.: Georgetown University Press.

Porter, Jean. 1999. *Natural and Divine Law: Reclaiming the Tradition for Christian Ethics*. Grand Rapids, Michigan: William B. Eerdmans Pub. Co.

———. 2005. *Nature as Reason: A Thomistic Theory of the Natural Law*. Grand Rapids: William. B. Eerdmans Publ. Co.

Rand, Ayn. 1964. "The Objectivist Ethics." In *The Virtue of Selfishness: A New Concept of Egoism*, 13–35. New York: New American Library. Originally published 1961.

Ross, Alf. 1958. "A Critique of the Philosophy of Natural Law." In *On Law and Justice*, 258–259. London: Stevens and Sons, Ltd.

Sigmund, Paul E. 1971. *Natural Law in Political Thought*. Cambridge: Winthrop Publishers Incorporated.

Sweet, William. 2000. "The Foundations of Ethics and Moral Practices." In *The Bases of Ethics*, edited by William Sweet, 220–242. Marquette Studies in Philosophy, No. 23, edited by Andrew Tallon. Milwaukee: Marquette University Press.

Tierney, Brian. 1997. *The Idea of Natural Rights: Studies on Natural Rights, Natural Law and Church Law, 1150–1625*. Emory University Studies in Law and Religion. Atlanta: Scholars Press. Reprinted 2001; Grand Rapids, Michigan: William B. Eerdmans Publishing Company.

Wojtyla, Karol. 1981. *Love and Responsibility*. Translated by H. T. Willetts. Rev. Ed. New York: Farrar-Straus-Giroux.

A Science With No Scientists?
Faith and the First Principles of *Sacra Doctrina* in Aquinas

Vincent J. DeVendra

Abstract: The first question of Thomas Aquinas's *Summa Theologiae* makes the argument that sacred doctrine is an Aristotelian science and, furthermore, the most certain of the sciences. According to Aristotle, this means that the first principles of sacred science must be certain. The normal modes of grasping the certainty of principles are either by demonstrating them by a higher science or by a direct grasp of them by the natural light of the agent intellect. Both of these avenues, however, are closed to sacred science. It would seem, then, that if sacred doctrine is a science, it can have no scientists in the wayfaring state. Aquinas unties this knot by proposing a third way of grasping the certainty of the first principles, namely, by faith. Only by the supernatural and graced assent of faith can the articles of faith be known as certain and allow sacred doctrine to fit into the mold of an Aristotelian science.

A t first glance, Thomas Aquinas's claim that *sacra doctrina* qualifies as a science in the Aristotelian sense of the term, in the same way as metaphysics or mathematics, may seem like an odd claim. Aristotle lays down such strict qualifications for demonstration and science in the *Posterior Analytics* that it seems highly unlikely that any body of propositions that proceeds from divine revelation could fulfill them. But Thomas takes his claim seriously— *sacra doctrina* proceeds from certain and necessary first principles, which are the articles of faith,[1] and so yields *scientia* of the conclusions, if the demonstrations are reasoned correctly. Perhaps the most tenuous part of his argument is that revealed truths can be known with just as much, or sometimes even more certainty than any truth known naturally, say for instance, the principle of non-contradiction.[2] It makes sense that *if* one can know that the principles of sacred doctrine really are revealed by God, the principles of sacred doctrine can be known with the greatest certainty. But, that's a big "if," and one which, I contend, needs to disappear in order for a science to have anybody who knows it.

To put it in another way, for someone to actually possess some part of sacred doctrine as a science, it is necessary but not sufficient that the articles of faith, which

© 2012, *Proceedings of the ACPA*, Vol. 85
DOI: 10.5840/acpaproc20118529

are the principles of sacred doctrine, are necessarily true and self-evident *per se*. For a science merely to *exist*, without any reference to some human intellect, it is sufficient that its principles be necessarily true. But, if there are to be practitioners of that science, that is, if a science is to have any scientists, then its first principles must be necessarily true *as well as* certain *to* the scientist. While Aquinas makes the distinction between what is known *per se*, i.e., without reference to any knower, and what is known *quoad nos*, i.e., to an actual knower, his treatment seems at first glance to be insufficient. Aquinas closes off to sacred science the normal path to grasping first principles with certainty, the natural light of the agent intellect. He must, then, open up another. This path is the supernatural light of faith. In this paper, I will examine Aquinas's arguments concerning the first principles of sacred doctrine found in the first question of his *Summa Theologiae*. I will argue that Aquinas attempts to provide both *per se* and *quoad nos* certainty of the first principles of sacred doctrine. In order to do this, he appeals to faith as a cognitive process, the *cognitio fidei*,[3] which must play a role parallel to the agent intellect, providing the certainty, which already belongs to the articles of faith in themselves, to the knower, thus offering an entrance point for an otherwise epistemologically impenetrable science.

I. Intelligbility and Certainty

Before examining Aquinas's account of *sacra doctrina*, it will be helpful to look to Aristotle to understand a crucial distinction that Aquinas employs in service of his claim that it is a true Aristotelian science. Aristotle says the following in the *Posterior Analytics*: "Now 'prior' (*proteron*) and 'better known' (*gnōrimōteron*) are ambiguous terms, for there is a difference between what is prior and better known by nature (*phusei*) and what is prior and better known to us."[4] Aristotle uses this distinction many places in his writings to distinguish what is most accessible to us, viz., the particular, from what is most intelligible, viz., the universal. The more universal the object of knowledge is, the more difficult it is to grasp, but also the higher the level of intelligibility—that is, there is a lot more there to be grasped. In any demonstration, the principles must be "better known" in the sense of being more intelligible. Thus, even though a particular proposition may be clearer and more evident *to me*, this does not imply that objectively, that proposition is "better known." The sort of intelligibility that a proposition has *per se*, without reference to any knower but simply because of its own internal intelligibility, makes it self-evident. That is to say that any intelligible truth cannot be otherwise, since its terms bear a necessary relation to one another. However, the distinction points out that a truth's intelligibility and necessity need not be considered in relation to any knower. It is an independent consideration. And, since a self-evident proposition does not imply any knower who actually experiences with certainty the truth of some proposition, there is also another kind of certainty which we may call subjective; that is, once I grasp a self-evident proposition with my intellect, thereby recognizing its necessity myself, that principle is for me subjectively certain.[5]

Evidently, then, if a science is going to have any scientists,[6] any necessarily true first principle of that science must be potentially subjectively certain. If a principle is necessarily true, it follows that if a knower has an appropriate and adequate power of intellect, she can understand and grasp that internal necessity and know that principle with certainty. Let's take a look at an example: Suppose Sally opens a box of pizza and takes notice of its contents. She wants to know something about the shape of the pizza, and through further experience and observation as well as some thought, she concludes the following: "This pizza is a circle. A circle is a shape which has some central point which is equidistant from every point on its circumference." Wonderful! Sally has unlocked a principle of geometry.

Now, suppose Billy is a bit slower than Sally. He opens up the pizza box with Sally, and he too notices the shape. Billy, however, is too dull to understand anything scientific about it. He is unable to do the intellectual work that would eventually result in him understanding the definition of a circle. Now the definition of a circle is still a necessary and self-evident truth, and yet, Billy's intellect is not capable of understanding it. Only Sally can go on to have scientific knowledge about circles; she is on her way to being a geometer while Billy is not. But what if we push the example one step further? Suppose now that neither Billy nor Sally nor any other human has the intellectual capability to understand the definition of a circle. Even in this case, the principle remains as it always has been—self-evident and intelligible. And yet, there is no state of subjective certainty. There may still be a science, insofar as there is a body of truths, arranged so that some can be known from others *if* the intellect were capable of grasping the principles, but there are no scientists, since the intellect, in fact, is not so capable. There is no subjective certainty for any human being. Now, it could be that sacred science is like this, a science formed of necessary highly intelligible truths with no scientists, and since this science concerns God, who is beyond the grasp of the intellect, this would not be terribly surprising. For Aquinas, God's essence is incomprehensible and impenetrable, and though there is in fact a science which treats God's essence, it is certainly not available to anyone in this life, at least not in the way geometry is; our intellects simply are not up to it.[7]

Turning now to the first question of the *Summa*, Aquinas argues not only that sacred doctrine is a science, but it is nobler than the other sciences, and one respect in which he claims it is nobler is its certainty. To the objection that while the articles of faith can be doubted, the principles of other sciences cannot be, and that therefore other sciences are more certain, Aquinas responds,

> It may well happen that what is in itself the more certain may seem to us the less certain on account of the weakness of our intelligence, 'which is dazzled by the clearest objects of nature; as the owl is dazzled by the light of the sun.' Hence the fact that some happen to doubt about articles of faith is due not to the uncertain nature of the truths, but to the weakness of human intelligence; yet the slenderest knowledge (*cognitone*) that may be obtained of the highest things is more desirable than the most certain knowledge (*cognitio*) obtained of lesser things.[8]

Let us notice that Aquinas is employing Aristotle's distinction about what is better known by nature and what is better known to us. Although the principles of other sciences may be much easier to arrive at, it is not due to some lack of intelligibility on the part of the articles of faith that this is true. However, weak though the human intellect may be, Aquinas still allows that the "slenderest knowledge may be obtained," and this knowledge is, importantly, certain to the one who has it.[9] Notice, however, that the word Aquinas uses for knowledge here is *cognitio*, not *scientia*. Using this more generic term is not unusual for Aquinas, but in this circumstance it does allows him to say that there is indeed a kind of knowledge of the articles of faith, but not with the self-evidence with which the principles of other sciences are known. We will speak more on this later, but right now, it is sufficient to show that Aquinas does think that there are sacred scientists—their *cognitio* is a sufficient entry point into the science of sacred doctrine.

Given this claim, we must go on to determine in what way the principles of sacred doctrine must be grasped in order for them to be certain. Says Aquinas, in the body of article 1 of the *Summa Theologiae*'s opening question.

> We must bear in mind that there are two kinds of sciences. There are some which proceed from a principle known by the natural light of the intellect, such as arithmetic and geometry and the like. There are some which proceed from the light of a higher science: thus the science of perspective proceeds from the principles established by geometry, and music from principles established by arithmetic. So it is that sacred doctrine is a science, because it proceeds from principles established by the light of a higher science, namely, the science of God and the blessed. Hence, as music believes the principles delivered to it by arithmetic, so sacred doctrine believes the principles revealed to it by God.[10]

The principles of any science are not demonstrable from within that science. Thus, according to this passage, the indemonstrable first principles of any science must be arrived at in one of two ways: 1) By having already been demonstrated by a higher science to which the lower science is subalternated, or 2) by the natural light of the intellect. Let's look at them in turn.

Let us consider the first way of knowing a principle, viz, by being demonstrated by a higher science. To take an example, the definitions of geometrical objects are principles of geometry that are independent of any higher science; they are primary absolutely speaking. The principles of optics, however, while they must be assumed from within optics, are capable of demonstration from within geometry. These principles are primary in a qualified way—primary within the given science, but not absolutely speaking.

For Thomas, sacred doctrine is counted among the subalternated sciences.[11] According to Aquinas, there is an inaccessible science which God and the blessed have of God's essence—let us call it the heavenly science—and this heavenly science is capable of producing demonstrations (of a sort) for the revealed first principles of the sacred doctrine. These demonstrations, however, are unknown by any of us humans who aren't in heaven.[12] By saying that sacred doctrine is subalternate, it seems that Aquinas is able to sidestep the question of grasping evidently its first principles. Aquinas does in fact argue this very point in *De Veritate* q.14, a.9, ad.3:

> One who has a subalternate science does not perfectly possess the character of knowing unless his knowledge is united in some way with the knowledge of one who has the subalternating science. Nevertheless, the one who knows on the lower level is not said to have scientific knowledge about those things which he presupposes, but about the necessary conclusions which are drawn from the presupposed principles. In this sense, also, one who believes can be said to have scientific knowledge about hose things which he concludes from the articles of faith.[13]

Certainly, every subalternated science is unable to prove its principles; it must assume them. Thus, the optician, *qua* optician, cannot know the first principles of optics, but receives them from geometry; they are the conclusions of a higher science. It seems, then, that as a subalternated science, sacred doctrine's first principles need not be grasped evidently, but can merely be assumed, being received as conclusions of the heavenly science.[14] The question remains, however, whether the principles of a subalternated science can be certain if knowledge of the demonstrations of those principles from its higher science cannot be produced. Surely, within any subalternated science, the principles are assumed and not known. But *sacra doctrina* stands alone, insofar as a sacred scientist not only must assume the principles, but is unable to demonstrate them using the subalternating science. If the optician wishes complete certainty about some demonstration that concerns angles of reflection, he must know why his principles are certain. In order to do this, he takes off his optician's hat and puts on the geometer's one. But this path is impassable for the sacred scientist. While every scientist of a normal subalternated science is capable of jumping to the higher science to prove the principles of the lower, the sacred scientist cannot in any way become a heavenly scientist. Mere assumption of the articles of faith is ultimately unsatisfying. We still are missing our entrance point, being able to say that only if the principles are true are our conclusions. To have *scientia* of conclusions that do not necessarily follow from true premises is a cold comfort.

What about the second way of knowing first principles Aquinas mentions, viz., by the light of the natural intelligence? Aquinas explicitly denies that this is the case. While "other sciences derive their certitude from the natural light of human reason . . . , [sacred doctrine] derives its certitude from the light of the divine knowledge," says Aquinas in a.5 of the *Summa*.[15] Thus, while the principles of metaphysics are self-evident—known to be certain as soon as the terms are grasped—the principles of sacred doctrine cannot be. Furthermore, Aquinas repeatedly calls it to our attention that if the first principles of sacred doctrine, the articles of faith, are known self-evidently, they cease to be believed, and therefore, cease to belong to the realm of faith.[16] That which is known self-evidently cannot be simultaneously believed. If it were the case that the truth of the articles of faith is grasped with certainty as soon as the terms were known, there would be no need for these principles to be revealed by God. However, notice that Aquinas opens up a third option beyond presupposition through subalternation and the natural light, to explain how the principles of a science can be grasped, viz., "the light of divine knowledge." I will discuss faith and this divine light in the next section, but let us note now that the articles of faith cannot be self-evident in the way that, say, the principle of non-contradiction is self-evident; they exceed the natural ability of the intellect and so are not known by the natural light.

We can now fully articulate the problem, which Aquinas must solve if he is to claim that sacred doctrine is in fact an accessible science. While all the other sciences have principles that can either be 1) demonstrated by a higher science or 2) known by the natural light, the principles of sacred doctrine cannot be known in either of these ways. Having seemingly ruled out both possibilities, we find ourselves at an impasse. If there are going to be sacred scientists, the principles must not only be knowable in themselves, but these truths must be subjectively certain as well. Those who are aware that the principles are not certain to them can in no way know that those same principles are certain in themselves. Thus, without some sort of epistemic access to the certainty of the first principles of sacred doctrine, the whole of it remains unknowable. But as we have seen, Aquinas amends his original classification, and admits a third possibility: the light of divine knowledge, or faith. While this might mean that sacred doctrine is *sui generis*, being the only science whose principles are grasped in this way, it will at least allow a point of entrance, providing the same or even a higher level of certainty than the natural powers of the intellect are capable of providing.

II. *Cognitio Fidei*

In article 8 of the first question of the *Summa*, Aquinas's elaborates on this third method of grasping first principles, which he calls in other places the *cognitio fidei*. This article is concerned with the question of whether sacred doctrine is a matter for argumentation. By this, Aquinas means two things. First, if the first principles are assumed by two people, then the conclusions of the purported demonstrations that follow from them can be the subject of argumentation for them. Thus, if we say that both Sally and Billy suppose that Sacred Scripture is infallible and certain, they still may arrive at opposite conclusions due to a flaw in reasoning by one or the other. Perhaps Sally believes that Scripture supports transubstantiation while Billy believes it supports consubstantiation. Since they share their belief in the principles from which their respective arguments are drawn, they have grounds for an argument about their contrary conclusions. But what if they do not share the same principles? It can be either that they share some of them, in which case Sally can argue from the ones Billy the heretic does hold to the others he does not, or it could be the case that Billy the heathen holds none of the articles of faith, in which case they can have no argumentation from within sacred doctrine. However,

Sally can help Billy to believe the articles of faith in another way. Let's have it in Aquinas's own words:

> If our opponent believes nothing of divine revelation, there is no longer any means of proving the articles of faith by reasoning, but only of answering his objections—if he has any—against *faith*. Since faith rests upon infallible truth, and since the contrary of a truth can never be demonstrated, it is clear that the arguments brought against faith cannot be demonstrations, but are difficulties which can be answered.[17]

Given the fact that what is revealed by God must be true, Billy can never demonstrate the contrary of any of the articles of faith, since something false can never be demonstrated. He can only have reasons why he does not believe, or why he considers it irrational to believe. Reason cannot lead to belief in the articles of faith, but it can get in the way of believing them. Consider the following passage from *De rationibus fidei*: "First of all I wish to warn you that in disputations with unbelievers about the articles of Faith, you should not try to prove the Faith by necessary reasons . . . we believe them *only* because they are revealed by God."[18] Aquinas suggests here that it is unwise or even impossible to argue for faith. Rather, the best reason can do is, to quote the same work, "show that the Catholic Faith holds is not false."[19] Since the articles of faith transcend the ability of the intellect to grasp them, arguments in their favor are hubristic, damaging the "sublimity of Faith." Sally may disabuse Billy of his notion that it is absurd for a thing to be both three and one, but she cannot argue him into believing in the Trinity, and for her to try would be at least a severe miscalculation of the incomprehensible nature of God's essence. So, faith is beyond the ability of natural reason but still must be able to produce certainty in the believer.[20]

If the normal way of being certain about something is through natural cognitive abilities, there is also another way. In *De veritate* q.14, a.1, ad.7, Aquinas considers two kinds of certainty: "The first is firmness of adherence, and with reference to this, faith is more certain than any understanding and scientific knowledge, for the first truth which causes the assent of faith, is a more powerful cause than the light of reason, which causes the assent of understanding or scientific knowledge. The second is the evidence to which assent is given. Here, faith does not have certainty, but scientific knowledge and understanding do." Firm adherence to some proposed truth must have a cause. That cause can be the natural intellect, which is capable of recognizing the self-evidence of any naturally knowable principles, or that cause can be God Himself, the first truth. While the natural intellectual powers are capable of error, the testimony of God can never be in error. The certainty of faith comes through a recognition that the articles of faith are proposed by God to the believer.

We constantly accept what we are told from those who we have good reason to believe know something without knowing it ourselves.[21] The degree of certainty may change with the reliability of the authority or the likelihood of the claim and

how consistent it is with other things we do know. Thus, when my friend in Pittsburgh tells me that it's raining there, I have a relatively high degree of certainty that
he's telling me the truth—I believe him. When the meteorologist on the morning
news tells me that it's going to rain tomorrow, I still believe her—she is right most
of the time, but I wouldn't bet the bank on it, so to speak. However, even when
the authority is reliable and the claim is relatively non-controversial, there is still
a possibility for doubt that comes with any belief. There is always the chance that
my friend in Pittsburgh has lost his mind, or is lying to me. But if there were an
authority that were utterly infallible, such that whatever that authority tells me
cannot but be true, then even though I would not be able to see the truth of the
testimony of that authority for myself, I would still hold it with the same level, or
even a higher level, of certainty. This infallible authority could not belong to any
human, since we are always able to err, but God is unchangeable and infallible—
whatever he tells us we can be utterly sure of. A perfect authority provides perfect
certainty. In Aquinas's words, "a man of little science is more certain about what he
hears on the authority of an expert in science, than about what is apparent to him
according to his own reason: and much more is a man certain about what he hears
from God, Who cannot be deceived, than about what he sees with his own reason,
which can be mistaken."[22]

III. Argument from Authority

What is this process of believing something from God, though? It is not as
if God speaks directly to every believer. Not all are so blessed to have the kind of
extraordinary experience of transformative grace that St. Paul had, for instance. Few
are knocked of their horses, and yet many believe. The ordinary way of coming
to believe the articles of faith is something more like the way Augustine believed
after hearing the preaching of St. Ambrose. It seems like quite a leap from having
a few conversations with or hearing the preaching of a believer to assenting to the
articles of faith with an even firmer adherence than the articles of some naturally
known science like geometry. According to Aquinas, the real moment of the "leap
of faith" is to believe that God is speaking through some earthly messenger. "The
testimony of a man or an angel would lead infallibly to the truth only insofar as we
considered the testimony of God speaking in them," he says in De Veritate.[23] A human, or even an angel, can lie and deceive, but if God is speaking through that man
than his testimony is infallible. Given his account of faith, we can see clearly why
Aquinas defines sacred doctrine as the science which treats things under the *ratio*
of divine revelation. Belief in revelation, the fact that God speaks infallibly through
messengers in the course of history, is the foundational belief of all the other articles
of faith.

Let me just briefly mention that this belief in the revelation is still obviously
beyond the natural cognitive abilities of any human being. There is no process of
reasoning that could come to the sure conclusion that God is speaking infallibly
through someone. Only God's grace can account for assent to the articles of faith.

Thus, Aquinas says, "Since man, by assenting to matters of faith, is raised above his nature, this must accrue to him inwardly; and this is God. Therefore faith, as regards the assent which is the chief act of faith, is from God moving man inwardly by grace."[24]

We can now return to our original question: can sacred science have any scientists? The answer we must arrive at is peculiar. Only the believer can answer this question, since only the believer has experienced the certainty of the articles of faith. To one who has not made the graced assent and so has not experienced the certainty that comes through that grace, the sacred scientist stands merely as a pseudo-science, internally integral, but with no entrance points, certain only *if* the principles are certain, and having no way for the "if" to disappear. The non-believer must remain ambivalent about this question. Maybe there are sacred scientists, and maybe there are not. It all depends on that "if."

But, for the believer, the matter stands differently. Although the articles of faith are not self-evident and therefore can even be doubted, the true believer holds them even more firmly than any other beliefs. This allows Aquinas to make the claim that "faith is in some way science and vision."[25] Although the articles of faith are not seen in the natural light, they are seen in the supernatural light of faith. They are not certain because of their evidence to the one who believes them, but they are firmly adhered to nonetheless. For this reason, Aquinas can claim that *sacra doctrina* is a science. It may be a science in an analogous sense, surely one that Aristotle never would have dreamed of. Still, the graced assent of faith to the otherwise unknowable first principles of sacred doctrine is an originative source of understanding which proceeds not from the natural light of the agent intellect, but from the supernatural light of God.

I think Aquinas has some things to show us about the cognitive processes of coming to believe the teachings of traditional Christianity. I'll wrap up with just a few: First, while reason surely has its part to play in Christian belief-formation, we ought not to over-intellectualize the affair. No one can be argued into believing. The role of reason ought to be concentrated on showing the reasons why believing the doctrines of Christianity is not absurd, and not on providing such overwhelming evidence for the truths of faith that it would be irrational *not* to believe them. To put in differently, we the role of reason outside the confines of sacred doctrine ought not to be to prove that strong claim that the articles of faith are rational, but simply to prove the weak claim, that they are *not irrational*. Secondly, Aquinas gives us a good account of the sureness (*certitudo*) of faith. The believing Christian may want to say that she believes the articles of faith even more deeply than anything she else she knows. A believing physicist should sooner doubt quantum theory and a believing logician should sooner doubt the principle of non-contradiction (an illustrative example, I hope) than any part of the Nicene Creed. But *why* is this the case? What good reason should anyone have for holding so firmly what is beyond one's ability to grasp? Simply this: One should realize one's own intellectual insufficiency and trust that God's truth is far more infallible than any truth naturally known. However slight the chance that one is wrong about the truth of what she understood as a self-evident proposition, there is simply no chance that articles of faith, revealed by God Himself, are not true.

Boston College

Notes

1. Thomas Aquinas, *Summa Theologiae* [*ST*], I, q.1, a.5, ad.1; a.7, corp. All translations are from Fathers of the English Dominican Province (New York: Benzinger, 1948), with modifications.

2. Cf. *ST* I, a.5, corp.

3. For an in-depth treatment of *fides* as *cognitio*, see M. V. Dougherty, "Aquinas on the Self-Evidence of the Articles of Faith," *Heythrop Journal* (2005): 168–169.

4. Aristotle, *Posterior Analytics* [*PA*], 1.2, 70b34–a1. Translation from *The Basic Works of Aristotle*, ed. R. McKeon (New York: Random House, 1941).

5. Cf. *ST* II-II, q.4, a.8, corp. Aquinas distinguishes between a principle *per se nota simpliciter* and *quoad nos*. Cf. Kenneth Konyndyk, "Aquinas on Faith and Science," *Faith and Philosophy* 12 (1995): n9.

6. The word "scientist" should be understood in the context of this paper as one who has acquired *scientia*. The word should not carry any connotations of lack or searching, as it might have in a modern context. The Aristotelian scientist is not one who seeks knowledge, but who has it firmly.

7. Cf. *ST* I, q.1, a.7, ad. 1. Sacred doctrine has God for its object, but *not* his essence. This science will be discussed in the next section, but it is important to note here that it looks quite a bit different than any human science. Demonstrations are not necessary within it, since God's essence is seen directly and wholly, instead of piecemeal and discursively, the way that, say, principles of natural theology are known. See John Jenkins, *Knowledge and Faith in Thomas Aquinas* (New York: Cambridge University Press, 1997), 56–66. Nevertheless, the fact remains that for Aquinas, there is knowledge that can properly be called *scientia* that is inaccessible to human knowers—objectively certain *par excellence*, but failing to provide *scientia* for any human knower.

8. *ST* I, q.1, a.5, ad. 1.

9. Cf. *ST* I, q.1, a.8, ad. 2, II-II, q.5, a.4, corp. This claim needs to be qualified. The degree to which one has faith is the same as the degree to which one holds the articles of faith as certain. Thus, Augustine can say that he would sooner doubt any of the other sciences than Scripture, but for those with less faith, there is always the temptation to doubt. Furthermore, the certainty that can be had of the articles of faith does not determine the intellect to assent to their truth, so that even the most fervent believer must *will* to assent to them. This is not the case with, say, the principle of non-contradiction, which once grasped, cannot be doubted.

10. *ST* I, q.1, a.1, corp.

11. Subalternation has its roots in *PA* 1.8. For Aquinas's definition of the term, see *In Boethium de Trinitate*, q.5, a. 1, ad. 5: "[Subalternation] occurs when in a higher science there

is given the reason for what a lower science knows only as a fact." Translation from Armand Maurer, *The Division and Methods of the Sciences* (Toronto, Pontifical Institute of Mediaeval Studies, 1986). In "On the Alleged Subalternate Character of *Sacra Doctrina* in Aquinas," *Proceedings of the ACPA* (2004), M. V. Dougherty contests the claim that there are two distinct sciences, viz., heavenly science and sacred doctrine. Rather, he thinks, the two form a unity, but are known in different ways by those in heaven and those on earth. But, in *ST* I, a.2, corp, one of the passages Dougherty cites, the structure Aquinas employs clearly shows the subaltern character of *sacra doctrina*. As we have seen, he divides sciences into those whose principles proceed from intelligence and those whose principles are received from a higher science. Sacred science is the latter kind. I do not dispute that the principles must somehow be known to us as proceeding from that higher science—there must be something analogous to self-evidence, and we shall see in the course of this paper. But, the subalternated character of sacred doctrine is secure.

12. As previously noted (n.6), these "demonstrations" look a lot different than human demonstrations. It may perhaps be more pertinent to say that the heavenly science can make completely evident the first principles of sacred doctrine, since "demonstration" carries with it connotations of discursive reason. I maintain the language in order to emphasis the relationship of subalternation which obtains between the heavenly and sacred sciences.

13. Thomas Aquinas, *De Veritate* q.14, a.9, ad.3. Translations of *De Veritate* from James V. McGlynn, S.J., trans. (Chicago: Henry Regnery Company, 1953), with modifications.

14. See Jenkins, *Knowledge*, 54ff. Jenkins critiques Marie Dominique Chenu's view that sacred doctrine is not properly a subaltern science, since it has the same subject matter as the heavenly science to which it is subalternated: "The need for a subaltern *scientia* is not due to the fact that the subaltern discipline has a different though related subject matter, as optics treats visual lines while geometry treats lines abstracted from any matter, but to the fact that humans have limited cognitive abilities to discover and understand the divine truths on which their salvation depends, and that they, unlike God, understand in complex propositions and reason discursively" (77). While the heavenly science is non-discursive and treats God's essence in itself, sacred doctrine receives particular propositions about God in propositional and discursive form, and in effect, non-essentially. While the object of sacred doctrine is God, it is *not* God's essence. Cf. *In Boethium*, q.3, a.4, corp. For our purposes, the key point is that the heavenly science, which provide the evidence for the principles of sacred doctrine, is not accessible to us, and therefore, another way of obtaining *scientia* must be found.

15. *ST* I, q.1, a.5, corp.

16. See, for instance, *ST* II-II q.1, a.5, corp.; II-II q.8, a.2, corp. These and others are noted in M. V. Dougherty, "Self-Evidence," n2, p. 177.

17. *ST* I, q.1, a.8, corp, my emphasis.

18. Thomas Aquinas, *De rationibus fidei*, chap. 2. Translations by Joseph Kenny, http://dhspriory.org/thomas/Rationes.htm.

19. *De rationibus fidei*, chap. 2.

20. Cf. Alvin Plantinga, "Warranted Christian Belief: The Aquinas/Calvin Model," from *The Rationality of Theism*, ed. Godehard Bruntrup and Ronald K. Tacelli (Boston: Kluwer, 1999), 141: "By faith—the whole process—something becomes *evident*—i.e., acquires warrant, has what it takes to be knowledge. And what becomes evident or warranted

294SCIENCE, REASON, AND RELIGION

is indeed not seen. This doesn't mean that it is indistinct, blurred, uncertain, or a matter of guesswork; what it means is that the belief in question isn't made evident by the workings of the ordinary cognitive faculties, with which we were originally created." Note that Plantinga may have chosen a better word than "evident," considering that in Aquinas's usage of the term, the articles of faith are precisely *not* evident. John Jenkins reads Plantinga to be arguing that this evidence does appeal to the natural intellect, and that we have rational arguments that are able, without the help of grace, to convince of us the truth of the articles of faith (173–175). I agree with Jenkins that this "naturalist interpretation" of faith fails, especially given the evidence cited in this paragraph.

21. Cf. Konyndyk, "Aquinas," 8.

22. *ST* II-II, q.4, a.8, ad.2.

23. *De veritate* q.14, a.8, corp.

24. *ST* II-II q.6, a.1, corp.

25. *De veritate* q.14, a.4, corp: "Fides etiam scientia et visio quodammodo dicitur."

American Catholic Philosophical Association
Eighty-Fifth Annual Meeting

Minutes of the 2011 Executive Council Meeting

Westminster Room, Chase Park Plaza Hotel, St. Louis
28 October 2011

The meeting was called to order at 10:00 am, and began with a prayer by Pres. Balestra. In attendance were: Dominic Balestra (President), Richard C. Taylor (Vice President), Steve Jensen (Treasurer), Matthew Cuddeback, Fr. Christopher Cullen, Tobias Hoffman, Michael Tkacz, Michael Dougherty, Atherton Lowery, Christopher Lutz, Bernard Prusak, Jack Carlson, David Foster, J.L.A. Garcia, Bonnie Kent, Liz Murray, Therese-Anne Druart (Past President) and Ed Houser (Secretary). Attending as non-voting members were David Clemenson (*ACPQ* Editor), Fr. Arthur Madigan, and Mary C. Sommers (incoming Executive Council Members). The Executive Committee (Tobias Hoffman, Christopher Cullen, Dominic J. Balestra, Richard C. Taylor, Edward Houser) convened earlier at 9:45.

The Secretary presented his Report, after which there was discussion about the number of members, which has increased slightly from 2009, but is still short of the numbers from 2006–2008. The Secretary's Report was then accepted by the Council.

The Treasurer presented the Financial Statement and Treasurer's Report. Dr. Jensen reported that, based on the rules for awarding support to younger scholars in order for them to attend the national meeting, which are based on a three year average of the Association's financial condition, while the Association could not offer assistance to younger scholars in 2011, it likely will be able to offer assistance in 2012. These two reports were accepted by the Council.

The Treasurer said that the Financial Affairs Committee had no report. Christopher Lutz was elected as a member of this Committee.

ACPQ Editor David Clemenson gave his report, which included a number of proposals on which the Council voted.

© 2012, *Proceedings of the ACPA*, Vol. 85
DOI: 10.5840/acpaproc20118521

1. In response to the *ACPQ*'s proposal for a "Rising Scholar Award," the proposal was accepted, including an award of a $ 500 prize and a one year membership in the ACPA.
2. The *ACPQ* Editor listed a number of nominees who could be added to the *ACPQ* Board of Editorial Consultants. With the addition of a charge to the Editor to strike a pluralistic balance in his appointments, the list from which the Editor can pick new members of the *ACPQ* Board of Editorial Consultants was approved.
3. Two suggested topics and guest editors for special issues were approved: "Alasdair MacIntyre," Guest Editor, Christopher Lutz, Fall 2014; and "Double effect reasoning," Guest Editor, John Zeis, Summer 2015.

New Members of the ACPA were accepted unanimously.

Robert Spaemann was elected Aquinas Medalist for the 2012 Meeting.

The 2012 Meeting will be held in Los Angeles and hosted by Loyola Marymount University. Suggestions for 2013 and 2014 were discussed, but no decision was made.

Two new members of the Executive Committee for 2011-2012 were elected from current second year Council members. They are: Christopher Lutz (St. Meinrad Seminary) and Bernard Prusak (Villanova). The other members of the Executive Committee for 2011-2012 are: Richard C. Taylor (President), John O'Callaghan (Vice President), and Ed Houser (Secretary).

The VP/President for 2012, Dr. Taylor, raised the issue of the ACPA paying honoraria to Plenary Speakers, in the event the President's institution is not able to contribute to their honoraria. There was some discussion early in the meeting, but the issue was put off to 'new business.' At the end of the meeting, before adjourning the Council voted that $500 per plenary speaker could be provided by the Association, if funds were not forthcoming for this purpose from some other source.

New business not considered: The Treasurer, Dr. Jensen, had a proposal to reduce annual dues, but it was not considered, owing to time constraints. The Secretary agreed to put this proposal on the Agenda of the 2012 Executive Council Meeting.

The lengthy meeting was adjourned slightly before 2:00pm, just in time to let the "International Society for MacIntyrean Equiry" have the room for their meeting, part of which the Secretary was happy to attend.

Respectfully submitted,

R. E. Houser
Secretary, ACPA

American Catholic Philosophical Association

Secretary's Report (2010–2011)

I. News from the National Office

A. Future Annual Meetings of the ACPA

The ACPA continues to encourage inquiries and offers from individuals who think that their institutions may be willing and able to sponsor a future Annual Meeting of the ACPA. In response to a generous offer from Loyola Marymount University, the Executive Committee of the ACPA determined that the Association's 2012 Annual Meeting will take place in Los Angeles, California, and will be hosted by Loyola Marymount University. We are looking for volunteers for 2013 and 2014.

B. Details Regarding the 2012 Annual Meeting in Los Angeles, California

President-Elect Richard C. Taylor announced (and the Executive Committee of the Association approved) the following theme for the Association's Annual Meeting, to be held in October or November 2012, in Los Angeles: "Philosophy in the Abrahamic Traditions"; An announcement of this theme, along with the submission guidelines, was emailed to all members in the May 2011 mailing. The call for papers for the 2012 Annual Meeting is also posted on the ACPA's website: http://www.acpaweb.org. Papers should be received as email attachments at the ACPA Office, University of St. Thomas, acpa@stthom.edu or houser@stthom.edu, no later than 2 April 2, 2012.

II. ACPA Membership

In 2010, the ACPA roster included **1084** *active* members. The *active* members in 2001 through 2010 (all segregated according to membership category) is as follows:

Membership Category	2010	2009	2008	2007	2006	2005	2004	2003	2002	2001
Professor	153	159	176	176	183	201	209	198	185	198
Associate Professor	126	120	134	118	126	122	131	137	124	153
Assistant Professor	201	222	167	170	155	155	142	147	125	152
Instructor	0	0	41	59	67	74	73	68	53	64

© 2012, *Proceedings of the ACPA*, Vol. 85
DOI: 10.5840/acpaproc20118522

pp. 297–300

Membership Category	2010	2009	2008	2007	2006	2005	2004	2003	2002	2001
Lecturer	0	0	36	31	33	38	39	41	37	43
Student	250	235	238	236	216	208	181	152	132	173
Emeritus/Emerita	106	110	125	126	132	131	132	129	122	139
Associate	80	78	81	92	98	97	97	91	80	100
Institutional	78	76	14	13	16	15	21	13	11	14
Library	0	0	60	61	60	60	66	60	58	63
Life	68	77	79	79	80	81	83	88	86	96
Exchanges	22				49	49	34	35	36	35
Totals	**1084**	**1077**	**1151**	**1161**	**1215**	**1231**	**1208**	**1159**	**1049**	**1230**

New Membership

2010	2009	2008	2007	2006	2005
54	92	101	98	113	108

III. ACPA Publications

A. ACPQ

In 2010, four issues of the *American Catholic Philosophical Quarterly* (volume 84) were published. The journal is edited by Dr. David Clemenson, assisted by Dr. W. Matthews Grant, Dr. Christopher Toner, and Ms. Ann M. Hale.

The 2001–2010 distribution to *active* members, etc., are as follows:

Distribution Type	2010	2009	2008	2007	2006	2005	2004	2003	2002	2001
ACPA Members	1062	1077	1151	1161	1166	1182	1174	1124	1013	1195
Subscribers	452	485	487	453	488	531	469	516	501	508
Exchanges	36	36	37	34	49	49	34	35	36	35
Totals	**1550**	**1598**	**1675**	**1648**	**1703**	**1762**	**1677**	**1675**	**1550**	**1738**

B. Proceedings

Dr. Edward Houser and Dr. Thomas Osborne edited volume 84 of the *Proceedings of the ACPA*, entitled *Philosophy and Language*.

The 2001–2010 distribution to *active* members, etc. are as follows:

Distribution Type	2010	2009	2008	2007	2006	2005	2004	2003	2002	2001
ACPA Members	1062	1077	1151	1161	1166	1182	1174	1124	1013	1195
Subscribers	131	88	133	148	129	120	129	132	147	143
Exchanges	32	27	27	27	42	43	47	66	75	39
Totals	**1225**	**1192**	**1311**	**1336**	**1337**	**1345**	**1350**	**1322**	**1235**	**1377**

C. Acknowledgments

On behalf of the ACPA, I would like to thank Dr. David Clemenson and all at the University of St. Thomas (MN) for their work in producing the *American Catholic*

Philosophical Quarterly. I would also like to thank the University of St. Thomas (MN) for its ongoing institutional support of the *American Catholic Philosophical Quarterly.*

IV. ACPA Annual Meetings

A. Eighty-Fourth Annual Meeting (2010)

The Eighty-Fourth Annual Meeting of the ACPA was held November 5–7 in Baltimore, MD, and was sponsored by Loyola University Maryland. The conference theme, selected by ACPA President Thérèse-Anne Druart, was: "Philosophy and Language." On behalf of the Association, I would like to thank the 2010 Program Committee: Nadja Germann, John Greco, Christopher Kaczor, and Christopher Martin. The 2010 Aquinas Medalist was Alasdair MacIntyre. The winner of the 2010 Young Scholar's Award was Daniel De Haan, of University of St. Thomas (TX), for his paper, "Linguistic Apprehension as Incidental Sensation in Thomas Aquinas." Loyola University Maryland gave financial support, for which I would like to thank them.

B. Eighty-Fifth Annual Meeting (2011)

The Eighty-Fifth Annual Meeting of the ACPA will be held 28–30 October in St. Louis, MO, and will be sponsored by St. Louis University. The conference theme, selected by ACPA President Dominic J. Balestra, will be: "Science, Reason, and Revelation." On behalf of the Association, I would like to thank the 2011 Program Committee: Catherine Deavel, Alex Eodice, and Glen Statile. The winner of the 2011 Aquinas Medal will be Jorge J. E. Gracia. The Young Scholar's Award will be given to Travis Dumsday, Livingstone College, for his paper "Why Thomistic Philosophy of Nature Implies (Something Like) Big-Bang Cosmology."

V. ACPA Elections

The complete results of this year's ACPA election (concluded April 2, 2011) are as follows:

Vice-President/President-Elect:
   John O'Callaghan (Notre Dame University)

Executive Council Members:
   Arthur Madigan, SJ (Boston College)
   Janet Smith (Sacred Heart Major Seminary)
   Mary C. Sommers (University of St. Thomas, Houston)
   Alice Ramos (St. John's University)
   Joshua Hochschild (Mt. St. Mary's University)

On behalf of the Association, I would like to thank these newly-elected individuals, and to thank all who were willing to stand for election.

VI. Thanks and Acknowledgments

On behalf of the ACPA, I would first like to thank John Boyer, John Macias, Jessi Jacobs, and Jim Capehart for their work as graduate students who are sponsored by the University of St. Thomas. Finally, I would like to thank the University of St. Thomas (Houston, TX) for its very generous financial and institutional support.

R. E. Houser
ACPA Secretary

Bishop Wendelin J. Nold, Professor of Graduate Philosophy
Center for Thomistic Studies
University of St. Thomas, Houston

American Catholic Philosophical Association

Treasurer's Report (2010)

I. Financial Statement

The Financial Statement shows that 2010 was a positive year for the ACPA. In 2010, the ACPA's total net gain of revenues over losses was $68,373 (compared to $70,707 in 2009). The Financial Statement shows that at the end of 2010, the Association's total liabilities and net assets were $513,397 (compared to $432,802 in 2009). Of this amount, $494,782 represents net (unrestricted) assets (compared to $426,409 in unrestricted assets in 2009). In 2010, therefore, the ACPA's net assets increased by $68,373.

	2010	2009
Total Assets	$513,397.00	$432,802.00
Liabilities	-$18,615.00	−$6,393.00
Net Assets	$494,782.00	$426,409.00
Gain or Loss from Previous Year	$68,373.00	$70,707.00

II. Annual Revenues and Expenses

Between 2009 and 2010, total annual revenues decreased by $12,845 (total revenues in 2010 were $112,758, while in 2009 they were $125,603), and total annual expenses decreased by $10,511 (total expenses in 2010 were $44,385, while in 2009 they were $54,896).

	2010	2009
Annual Revenues	$112,758.00	$125,603.00
Change in Revenues	-$12,845.00	$149,318.00
Annual Expenses	$44,385.00	$54,896.00
Change in Expenses	-$10,511.00	$12,204.00

© 2012, *Proceedings of the ACPA*, Vol. 85
DOI: 10.5840/acpaproc20118523

III. Annual Meeting

A summary of revenues and expenses in connection with the 2010 Annual Meeting is attached. The Association is very grateful to the local host institution – Loyola University of both more – for its direct donation of $6000 (including a $3000 grant from the ACPA) in connection with the meeting. The attached financial statements show that the 2010 Annual Meeting resulted in a $7348 deficit of expenses over revenues (compared to a deficit of $5,660 in 2009).

	2010	2009
Annual Meeting Earnings or Losses	–$7,348.00	–$5,660.00

IV. Assets and Investments—Total: $513,397

The Statement of Financial Position lists our assets on December 31, 2010, as follows:

A. Cash and Cash Equivalents: $150,080

A. Cash and Cash Equivalents: $150,080

On December 31, 2010, the Association held $150,080 in Chase Manhattan checking and savings account, a TIAA-CREF money market, and the University of St. Thomas accounts.

	2010
Chase accounts	$134,197.16
TIAA-CREF	$11,473.46
UST accounts	$4,409.20
Total Cash	$150,080.00

B. Inventory and Supplies: $685

C. Non-cash Investments: $353,943

On December 31, 2010, the Association's non-cash investment holdings with TIAACREF were valued at $353,943.

V. Liabilities—Total: $18,615

Account Payable: $18,615

The amount of $18,615 represents expenses incurred by the ACPA in 2010 (such as fees attributable to work performed in 2010), but not yet paid for until after December 31, 2010, i.e., after the closing date for 2010 statements from the ACPA's bank and investment manager. Accordingly, the ACPA carried these not-yet-paid expenses as a liability.

VI. Reminder

The Association depends heavily for revenue on membership dues and subscription payments. Therefore, the National Office reminds members to be prompt in paying their dues and/or subscription charges.

VII. Donations

As always, the Association welcomes donations. Since the ACPA is a tax-exempt organization under section 501(c)(3) of the Internal Revenue Code, all donations to Association are tax-deductible to the full extent allowed by law.

VIII. Acknowledgements

On the behalf of the Association, the Treasurer would like to thank the University of St. Thomas in Houston for its generous financial support of the Association throughout 2010. In 2010, the Association received $9,000 in cash donations and $12,900 in in-kind donations from the University of St. Thomas, for a total of $21,900.

American Catholic Philosophical Association
Financial Statements

Years Ended December 31, 2010 and 2009

© 2012, *Proceedings of the ACPA*, Vol. 85
DOI: 10.5840/acpaproc20118524

pp. 305–314

American Catholic Philosophical Association
Accountants' Compilation Report

Years Ended December 31, 2010 and 2009

TABLE OF CONTENTS

American Catholic Philosophical Association
Accountants' Compilation Report

Years Ended December 31, 2010 and 2009

To the Board of Directors
American Catholic Philosophical Association
Houston, Texas

We have compiled the accompanying statements of financial position of American Catholic Philosophical Association (the Association) as of December 31, 2010 and 2009, and the related statements of activities and changes in net assets and cash flows for the years then ended, and the accompanying supplementary information contained in Schedule I. We have not audited or reviewed the accompanying financial statements and supplementary information and, accordingly, do not express an opinion or provide any assurance about whether the financial statements and supplementary information are in accordance with accounting principles generally accepted in the United States of America.

Management is responsible for the preparation and fair presentation of the financial statements and supplementary information in accordance with accounting principles generally accepted in the United States of America and for designing, implementing and maintaining internal control relevant to the preparation and fair presentation of the financial statements and supplementary information.

Our responsibility is to conduct the compilation in accordance with Statements on Standards for Accounting and Review Services issued by the American Institute of Certified Public Accountants. The objective of a compilation is to assist management in presenting financial information in the form of financial statements and supplementary information without undertaking to obtain or provide any assurance that there are no material modifications that should be made to the financial statements and supplementary information.

Management has elected to omit substantially all of the disclosures required by accounting principles generally accepted in the United States of America. If the omitted disclosures were included in the financial statements and supplementary information, they might influence the user's conclusions about the Company's financial position, results of operations and cash flows. Accordingly, the financial statements and supplementary information are not designed for those
who are not informed about such matters.

Hutchinson and Bloodgood LLP

May 13, 2011

American Catholic Philosophical Association
Statements of Financial Position

Years Ended December 31, 2010 and 2009

ASSETS	2010	2009
Current assets		
Cash—checking and savings	$ 150,080	$ 105,505
Accounts receivable	6,189	23,416
Inventory and supplies	685	724
Prepaid expense	2,500	—
Investments, at market value	353,943	303,157
Total assets	$ 513,397	$ 432,802

LIABILITIES AND NET ASSETS	2010	2009
Current liabilities		
Accounts payable and accrued expenses	$ 18,615	$ 6,393
Unrestricted net assets	494,782	426,409
Total liabilities and net assets	$ 513,397	$ 432,802

See independent accountants' compilation report.

American Catholic Philosophical Association
Statements of Activities and Changes in Net Assets

Years Ended December 31, 2010 and 2009

SUPPORT AND REVENUES	2010	2009
Annual meeting	$ 19,707	$ 27,378
Royalties	20,315	20,812
Donations from University of St. Thomas	21,900	24,500
Miscellaneous income	10	—
Interest and dividends	5,023	3,970
Net realized and unrealized gains in investments	45,803	48,943
Total support and revenues	112,758	125,603
EXPENSES		
Annual meeting	27,055	33,038
Subscription expense	—	1,120
Salaries and wages	12,900	15,500
Postage	30	441
Insurance	447	936
Accounting services	3,400	2,900
Web service charges	406	72
Miscellaneous	147	889
Total expenses	44,385	54,896
Increase in unrestricted net assets	68,373	70,707
NET ASSETS, BEGINNING OF YEAR	426,409	355,702
NET ASSETS, END OF YEAR	$ 494,782	$ $ 426,409

See independent accountants' compilation report.

American Catholic Philosophical Association
Statements of Cash Flow

Years Ended December 31, 2010 and 2009

CASH FLOWS FROM OPERATING ACTIVITIES	2010	2009
Increase in unrestricted net assets	$ 68,373	$ 70,707
Adjustments to reconcile increase in unrestricted to net assets to net cash provided by operating activities		
Net realized and unrealized gains in investments	(45,803)	(48,943)
Net change in:		
Accounts receivable	17,227	(12,126)
Inventory and supplies	38	38
Prepaid expense	(2500)	—
Accounts payable and accrued expenses	12,222	(5,420)
Net cash provided by operating activities	49,557	4,256
CASH FLOWS FROM INVESTING ACTIVITIES		
Net change in investments	(4,982)	(51,905)
Net cash used in investing activities	(4,982)	(51,905)
Net increase in cash and cash equivalents	44,575	(47,649)
CASH AND CASH EQUIVALENTS AT BEGINNING OF YEAR	105,505	153,154
CASH AND CASH EQUIVALENTS AT END OF YEAR	150,080	$ 105,505

See independent accountants' compilation report.

American Catholic Philosophical Association
Supplementary Information

Years Ended December 31, 2010 and 2009

American Catholic Philosophical Association
Schedule I: Revenues and Expenses of Annual Meeting

Years Ended December 31, 2010 and 2009

REVENUES	2010	2009
Registration and banquet	$ 16,707	$ 14,378
Donations:		
Loyola University	3,000	10,000
Loyola Marymount University	—	3,000
		27,378
EXPENSES		
Banquet expenses	18,066	22,104
Invited speakers costs	—	1,500
Young scholar award	250	450
Aquinas medal and engraving	67	198
Meeting registration services	3,210	3,349
Printing and duplicating expenses	1,960	—
Postage expenses	1,122	2,178
Travel	2,380	3,259
	27,055	33,038
Excess (shortage) of revenues over expenses	$ (7,348)	$ (5,660)

See independent accountants' compilation report.

American Catholic Philosophical Association

ACPQ Editor's Report

Contents of Report

Appendices

I. Summary of *ACPQ*-Related Activity 2010–2011

a. New guidelines on PDC website for authors and guest editors

In its 2010 meeting the Executive Council (EC) approved the posting to relevant websites of the following set of documents:

© 2012, *Proceedings of the ACPA*, Vol. 85
DOI: 10.5840/acpaproc20118525

- "Article Submission Guidelines"
- "Style and Formatting Guidelines for Accepted Articles"
- "Book Review Guidelines"
- "Guidelines for Referees"
- "Guidelines for Special Issue Editors"

These documents were successfully posted to the *ACPQ* website maintained by the journal's publisher, the Philosophy Documentation Center (PDC), and now serve as a convenient resource for authors, referees, and guest editors.

b. State of the ACPQ: general remarks

Submissions. The journal is barely receiving enough publishable submissions to fill out issues of a respectable length (this is not true of the special issues, where, typically, many of the articles are solicited by the guest editor). We have at present virtually no backlog of articles awaiting publication. The proposed Rising Scholars Award may attract more submissions from scholars in the early stages of their career, but the journal needs submissions from established scholars as well. The editorial staff welcome suggestions from the Council for solving this problem.

Publication schedule. One of the special issues was received late from the guest editor; this caused a delay in the publication of subsequent issues. The editorial staff are working to bring the *ACPQ*'s schedule of publication into conformity with the PDC's (Philosophy Document Center) timeline.

Statistics on submissions, turn-around times, etc. These are given in appendix (i). Please note the following:

- The double asterisks after "Published Articles" in the "Approximate Turn-Around Times" section indicate that two of these articles were in the revise-and-resubmit category; the amount of time between receipt of these articles and their final acceptance was significantly greater than that for the other articles.

- Special-issue articles are taken into account in the calculations for all categories *except* "Turn-Around Times".

- The "date of final acceptance" is the date on which notice of acceptance is sent to the author, not the date when the final version of the article is received. For conditionally accepted articles, in particular, the "date of final acceptance" is the date on which notice is sent to the author that the revised version has been accepted.

II. Background of Proposals Submitted for
the Executive Council's Consideration (Appendices (a)–(d))

In its November 2010 meeting the ACPA's Executive Council (EC) requested from the *ACPQ* editor proposals concerning policy for and composition of the *ACPQ*'s board of editorial consultants. No written policy regarding editorial consultants was received from the previous editorial office.

Policy on editorial consultants

In drafting the proposal for this policy the editorial staff's first step was to send to all current editorial consultants a letter (May 2011) requesting that they complete a short questionnaire (see Appendices (e) and (h)). In some cases the response was very prompt; in others, the consultant was sent a reminder (in some cases more than one). As of this writing, responses have been received from nineteen of the twenty-two present members of the board of editorial consultants. Responses to the questionnaire were taken into account in developing our proposed policy, contained in Appendix (a). A final letter was sent (see Appendix (f)) in early October to all editorial consultants (see Appendix (b)) who had not responded to previous communications, asking them whether they wished to continue their association with the journal.

Nominees for membership in the board of editorial consultants

Taking into account the resignation of four editorial consultants, the passing of James Ross, and the responses (or failures to respond) of the present editorial consultants (these responses helped shape our notions of what qualities to seek in an editorial consultant), the editorial staff have developed a list of nominees for a new board of editorial consultants. The master list, given in Appendix (b), includes all current consultants who expressed a desire to continue their service to the *ACPQ*, as well as a number of philosophers who seem to the staff to be in a position to advance the work of the journal. The editorial staff recognize (of course) that there are philosophers whose names don't appear on this list but who would make excellent editorial consultants for the *ACPQ*. Additional nominations from the Council are welcome.[1]

Topics and guest editors for special issues

The current list of approved special issues is

Topic: "Wittgenstein" Guest editor: Mario von der Ruhr, vol. 85 no. 4 (Fall 2011; now in preparation)

Topic: "Ockham" Guest editor: Takashi Shogimen, vol. 86 no. 3 (Summer 2012)

Topic: "John Dewey" Guest editors: John McDermott and Larry Hickman, vol. 87 no. 2 (Spring 2013)

Topic: "Aquinas and the Arabic Philosophical Tradition" Guest editor: Richard Taylor, vol. 88 no. 1 (Winter 2014)

Topics and guest editors for two more special issues, to appear in Fall 2014 and Summer 2015, are proposed in Appendix (c).

Rising Scholars' Award

The *ACPQ* report to the EC's November 2010 meeting contained the suggestion that an annual award be presented to the best paper by a recent philosophy Ph.D. The EC invited a formal proposal; the editorial staff's proposal is contained in Appendix (d).

Appendix (a): Policy Regarding
ACPQ Editorial Consultants (Proposed October 2011)

I. Expectations for service by members of the board of editorial consultants of the ACPQ

    a. Members of the board of editorial consultants of the *American Catholic Philosophical Quarterly* (*ACPQ*) are typically expected to serve the journal in (some substantial portion of) the following ways:

        i.   serving as referees for articles within their areas of expertise,

        ii. reviewing books within their areas of expertise,

        iii. recommending potential referees for articles or reviewers for books,

        iv. considering the *ACPQ* as a favored venue for publishing their own work,

        v. encouraging colleagues to submit suitable work to the journal,

        vi. being disposed to accept invitations to serve as a guest editor for a special issue in their area of expertise, or advising the editorial staff concerning themes, editors, or contributors for special issues,

        vii. offering advice (solicited or not) on the journal's policies, practices, and standards,

        vii. associating their professional reputation with the journal.

    b. Service in "some substantial portion" of the ways just listed need not entail service in more than one of these areas, provided that substantial service is rendered in that area.

    c. Editorial consultants serve at the pleasure of the American Catholic Philosophical Association (ACPA), represented (for this purpose) jointly by the Executive Committee and the editor of the *ACPQ*.

    d. In the unlikely event that an editorial consultant becomes unwilling or unable to serve in (a substantial portion of) the ways listed above that member may, by decision of the Executive Committee of the ACPA (a simple majority of the Committee concurring), and upon recommendation of the *ACPQ*'s editor, be released from further service on the board (notice to this effect will be sent by the editor to the individual immediately upon the Executive Committee's decision).

II. Policy governing invitations to serve as editorial consultants

    a. All those invite to serve as editorial consultants of the *ACPQ* will have first been approved by simple majority vote of the Executive Council of the ACPA.

    b. Those invited to serve as editorial consultants are, at the time of their invitation, to be sent a copy of the "Policy governing serving members of the board of editorial consultants of the *ACPQ*" (part I of this document).

    c. Membership on the board is effective immediately upon receipt by the *ACPQ*'s editor of the individual's acceptance of the invitation.

Appendix (b): Nominees for Membership on the *ACPQ*'s Board of Editorial Consultants

The individuals in category (i) are nominated by the *ACPQ* editorial staff for continue membership on the board of editorial consultants of the *ACPQ*.

The editorial staff request permission from the Executive Council to invite any of the individuals in category (ii)—on the understanding that the total number of editorial consultants is not to exceed twenty-five. Membership on the board will become effective immediately upon receipt by the editor of the individual's acceptance of the invitation (invitations may well be declined by some of those listed). Guidance from the Executive Council regarding whom on this list to invite first, or regarding additions to or deletions from this list, are welcome.

Categories (iii) and (iv) comprise all members of the current board who have either resigned or have not (as of this writing) expressed a desire to continue their association with the journal. Individuals in category (iv) received three separate letters (two of which were delivered both by surface mail and by e-mail) asking whether they wished to remain as editorial consultants.

(i) Continuing members
Dominic Balestra, Fordham
Joseph Boyle, St. Michael's
Patrick Byrne, B.C.
John Crosby, Franciscan U.
Daniel Dahlstrom, B.U.
Thomas Flynn, Emory
Lloyd Gerson, Toronto
Arthur Madigan, B.C.
Timothy B. Noone, C.U.A.
Janet Smith, Sacred Heart Major Seminary
Roland J. Teske, Marquette
Linda Zagzebski, Oklahoma
John Zeis, Canisius

(ii) Pool of nominees
Deborah Black, Toronto
  http://philosophy.utoronto.ca/people/faculty/deborah-black

Michael Baur, Fordham
  http://www.michaelbaur.com/research.html

Stephen Brock, Pontificia Università della Santa Croce
  http://www.pusc.it/fil/p_brock/

John Cottingham, emeritus, Reading
  http://web.mac.com/jgcottingham/JGC/John_Cottingham.html

Kevin Flannery, Gregorian
   http://www.vatican.va/roman_curia/pontifical_academies/san-tommaso/
publications/pastyearbook64-86.pdf

Alfred Freddoso, Notre Dame
   http://www.nd.edu/~afreddos/books.html

Jorge Gracia, SUNY Buffalo
   http://www.acsu.buffalo.edu/~gracia/

John Greco, St. Louis
   https://sites.google.com/a/slu.edu/john-greco/

John Haldane, St. Andrews
   http://www.st-andrews.ac.uk/~jjh1/

Russell Hittinger, Tulsa
   http://www.thomasinternational.org/about/adboard/russellhittinger.htm

Mary Beth Ingham, Loyola Marymount
   http://bellarmine2.lmu.edu/philosophy/faculty/ingham.html

Gyula Klima, Fordham
   http://faculty.fordham.edu/klima/

John F.X. Knasas, St. Thomas, Houston
   http://www.stthom.edu/Public/index.asp?page_ID=4621

Robert Koons, Texas
   http://www.robkoons.net/

Michael Loux, Notre Dame
   http://philosophy.nd.edu/people/all/profiles/loux-michael/

Mark Murphy, Georgetown
   http://www9.georgetown.edu/faculty/murphym/

David Oderberg, Reading
   http://www.reading.ac.uk/dsoderberg/dso.htm

Thomas Osborne, St. Thomas, Houston
   http://www.stthom.edu/Faculty_Bios/M_thru_O/Osborne_Jr_Thomas_M.aqf

Alex Pruss, Baylor
   https://bearspace.baylor.edu/Alexander_Pruss/www/

Nicholas Rescher, Pittsburgh
   http://www.pitt.edu/~rescher/

John Rist, emeritus, Toronto; visiting professor at the Institutum Patristicum
Augustinianum, Rome
   http://president.cua.edu/inauguration/john-rist.cfm

Katherin Rogers, Delaware
   http://www.udel.edu/rogers/CV.htm

Robert Sokolowski, C.U.A.
  http://philosophy.cua.edu/faculty/rss/

Eleonor Stump, St. Louis
  http://sites.google.com/site/stumpep/

Charles Taylor, emeritus, McGill
  http://www.mcgill.ca/philosophy/people/faculty/taylor

Chris Tollefsen, South Carolina
  http://www.twotlj.org/CTollefsen.html

Robert Wood, Dallas[2]

(iii) Resignations
  Jan Aertsen, emeritus, Köln
  John Caputo, emeritus, Villanova
  Louis Dupré, emeritus, Yale
  Alfonso Gomez-Lobo, Georgetown
  Adiraan Peperzak, Loyola U. Chicago
  Lance Simmons, Dallas

(iv) Members of the present board of editorial consultants from whom the editorial office has (as of Oct. 18th) received no reply
  Thomas Hibbs, Baylor
  Kenneth Schmitz, Trinity College, Toronto
  Dennis Sepper, Dallas

Appendix (c): Suggested
Topics and Guest Editors for Upcoming Special Issues

Topic: "Alasdair MacIntyre." *Guest editor:* Christopher Lutz. Vol. 88 n. 4 (Fall 2014)

Topic: "Double-effect Reasoning." *Guest editor:* John Zeis. Vol. 89 n. 3 (Summer 2015)

Appendix (d): Proposal for *ACPQ* Rising Scholars Essay Contest

1. The contest is to be held annually.

2. For purposes of this contest, a "rising scholar" is any academically trained philosopher beneath the rank of associate professor (e.g., assistant professors, lecturers, and "A.B.D." graduate students).

3. Publicity for the contest will take the form of editorial notes in the *ACPQ* and notices on the ACPA web site.

4. Deadline for submissions will be August 1st.

5. Papers are to be of the length, format, and style characteristic of articles published by the *ACPQ*.

6. Papers are to be related in some substantial and easily recognizable way to the Catholic intellectual tradition.

7. A "screening panel" designated by the editor will cull all papers clearly not of publishable quality and will select finalists (not to exceed three) from the remainder; this panel's work is to be completed in early September.

8. Authors of finalist papers will be notified in by September 15th that their papers are still under review for the contest and for publication in the journal.

9. A "finalists' panel" designated by the editor (different from the screening panel) will select the winner from among the finalists.

10. The journal reserves the right not to select any paper as winner of the contest, should the editor, advised by the screening and finalists' panels (and by anyone else the editor may choose to consult), judge that none of the submissions merits this honor.

11. The author or authors of the winning paper will be notified by October 15th.

12. The author or authors of the winning paper will be recognized in the following ways:

    a. the winning paper will be published in the *ACPQ*, and will be identified in that issue as the winning entry in the contest;

    b. the author of a single-authored winning paper will receive (i) a monetary award from the ACPA, in the amount of $500, and (ii) a one-year membership to the ACPA;

    c. each co-author of a co-authored winning paper will receive (i) a share, equal to that of the other co-authors, of the $500 monetary prize and (ii) a one-year membership to the ACPA.

Appendix (e): Template of Letter Sent to Present
ACPQ Editorial Consultants

May 13, 2011

Professor *NNN*
Address

Via U.S. Mail and E-mail

Dear Professor *NNN*,

At the request of the Executive Council of the American Catholic Philosophical Association, I am in the process of reviewing policies and procedures for the *American Catholic Philosophical Quarterly*'s board of editorial consultants.

A number of our consultants have served the journal in a variety of ways, e.g., submitting articles, or by refereeing submissions, or by recommending others as referees (and, of course, by permitting their names to be publicly associated with the journal). Let me take this occasion to thank you for your own service over the past several years.

The *ACPQ* does not have in place a well-defined "job description" for editorial consultants. My immediate aim is to clarify, for the journal and those associated with it, just what an editorial consultant is and does. Although decisions about such matters rest, ultimately, with the ACPA's Executive Council (which is vested with the authority that editorial boards exercise at many other journals), it is my responsibility to advise the Executive Council in this area.

To that end, I am seeking information from you on just the few points contained in the enclosed (brief!) questionnaire. Would you please fill it out and return it to me by July 15th?

Thanks, again, for all your service to the journal, and thanks for your attention, at such a busy time of year, to this matter.

Yours truly,

David Clemenson
Editor

Appendix (f): Template of Final Letter Sent to Non-responding *ACPQ* Editorial Consultants

Date

Professor *NNN*
Address

Via U.S. Mail and E-mail

Dear Professor *NNN*:

Earlier this year I sent a letter *via* e-mail and surface mail to all present editorial consultants of the *ACPQ*, asking them to indicate whether they wished to continue as an editorial consultant for the journal, and, if the answer to that question was "yes," to fill out a brief questionnaire. In mid-July my associate editor, Christopher Toner, sent a follow-up letter to those who had not replied to the first mailing. According to our records you did not reply to either of these letters.

There's no need now to complete the questionnaire; responses have already been tallied. But I would still like to know whether you are interested in continuing as an editorial consultant. Later this month I will be submitting to the Executive Council of the American Catholic Philosophical Association a list of names of those nominated for the *ACPQ*'s new board of editorial consultants. If by **Tuesday, October 25th** I receive word from you that you wish to continue as a member of the board, I'll include your name on that list. Otherwise, I'll assume that you wish to resign from the board.

I very much hope that you will choose to continue your association with the *ACPQ*. Whatever you decide, allow me to take this opportunity to thank you for your years of service to the journal.

If you have any questions, I may be reached at dclemenson@stthomas.edu or at 651.962.5356. I hope to hear from you soon.

Best wishes,

David Clemenson
Editor

Appendix (g): Draft of Advertisement for
ACPQ Rising Scholars Essay Contest

ACPQ Rising Scholars Essay Contest

The *American Catholic Philosophical Quarterly* (*ACPQ*) is pleased to announce its first annual Rising Scholars Essay Contest. Any scholar who will not have attained the rank of associate professor by August 1st, 2012 is invited to submit a paper that contributes to the development or elucidation of the Catholic philosophical tradition. The winning essay will be published in the *ACPQ* and specially designated in the journal as winner of the contest.

The author of a single-authored winning paper will receive a $500 award and free membership for one year in the American Catholic Philosophical Association (ACPA).

Each co-author of a co-authored winning paper will receive a share, equal to that of the other co-author(s), of a $500 award, together with a free membership for one year in the ACPA. All co-authors of the winning paper must be below the rank of associate professor at the time of the submission deadline, August 1st, 2012.

Participants should keep in mind the following contest rules:

- Papers must be submitted by e-mail to acpq@stthomas.edu no later than August 1, 2012. The accompanying e-mail should have as its subject line "For essay contest" and should include the author's name, academic rank (as of August 1st, 2012), institutional affiliation, and an abstract of up to 150 words.

- Papers should be prepared for blind review and should be of the length, format, and style characteristic of *ACPQ* articles. Participants may consult a recent edition of the journal or a copy of the submissions guidelines, posted at http://secure.pdcnet.org/acpq/Submission-Guidelines.

- No author may enter more than one paper in the contest.

- Entering a paper in the contest constitutes agreement by all the paper's authors to its publication in the *ACPQ* should it be accepted for that purpose; such agreement is not contingent on the paper's winning the contest. Papers entered in the contest must therefore not be under consideration for publication elsewhere.

  - The winning paper will be published in the *ACPQ* and will be specially designated in the *ACPQ* as winner of the contest.

  - Notification will be sent by September 15th, 2012 to those authors whose papers have reached the finalists' stage.

  - Authors not receiving such notification by September 15th, 2012 may assume that their paper has not been accepted for publication by the *ACPQ* and should consider themselves free at that time to submit their paper to another journal.

  – The author(s) of the winning paper will be notified by October 15th, 2012.

• Inquiries may be directed to acpq@stthomas.edu.

Endnotes

1. The editorial staff have decided (reluctantly) not to risk the awkwardness that might have attended the singling out of certain members of the Executive Council for nomination as new members of the *ACPQ*'s board of editorial consultants. There seemed, however, no compelling reason to refrain from nominating current officers of the ACPA for *continuation* of their service as editorial consultants, since the board's current members are already "singled out" by the fact of their membership. The editorial staff's decision not to nominate new editorial consultants from the ranks of the Executive Council does not, of course, preclude the Council's doing so.

2. Due to technical difficulties at the University of Dallas' website at the time of this writing, the URL for Bob Wood's webpage is not included. Bob was of course *ACPQ* editor until 2008.

Necrology (2011–2012)

Rev. Joseph Flannagan, Boston College, Boston, Massachusetts

Rev. Donald Kraus, Pittsburgh, Pennsylvania

Dr. James T.H. Martin, St. John's University, New York

Dr. Frank Strelchun, New Canaan, Connecticut

Alfonso Gomez-Lobo, Georgetown University

Requiescant in pace

© 2012, *Proceedings of the ACPA*, Vol. 85
DOI: 10.5840/acpaproc20118526

Available Back Issues of the Proceedings

Volumes

© 2012, *Proceedings of the ACPA*, Vol. 85
DOI: 10.5840/acpaproc20118527

71	1997	*Virtues and Virtue Theories*
72	1998	*Texts and Their Interpretation*
73	1999	*Insight and Inference*
74	2000	*Philosophical Theology*
75	2001	*Person, Soul, and Immortality*
76	2002	*Philosophy at the Boundary of Reason*
77	2003	*Philosophy and Intercultural Understanding*
78	2004	*Reckoning with the Tradition*
79	2005	*Social Justice: Its Theory and Practice*
80	2006	*Intelligence and the Philosophy of Mind*
81	2007	*Freedom, Will, and Nature*
82	2008	*Forgiveness*
83	2009	*Reason in Context*
84	2010	*Philosophy and Language*

Please send orders to:

Philosophy Documentation Center
P.O. Box 7147
Charlottesville, VA 22906-7147
800-444-2419 (U.S. & Canada), or 434-220-3300
Fax: 434-220-3301
E-mail: order@pdcnet.org
Web: www.pdcnet.org

All back issues of the *Proceedings* are $30 each, plus shipping (see rates below). Make checks payable to the Philosophy Documentation Center. Please send checks in U.S. dollars only. Visa, MasterCard, and Discover are accepted for your convenience.

Shipping and handling charges for book orders are as follows:

Total Price	Delivery within U.S.	Delivery outside U.S.
$ .01–$ 50.00	$ 5.00	$ 8.00
$ 50.01–$ 100.00	$ 7.50	$ 12.00
$ 100.01–$ 200.00	$ 10.00	$ 16.00
$ 200.01–$ 300.00	$ 13.00	$ 19.00
$ 301.00–$ 400.00	$ 16.00	$ 22.00
$ 400.01–$ 500.00	$ 19.00	$ 25.00
$ 500.01–$ 1000.00	$ 22.00	$ 28.00
Over $ 1000.00	$ 25.00	$ 31.00

For international airmail rates, please contact the PDC.